D0545245

IMPLICIT RACIAL BIAS ACROSS THE LAW

Despite cultural progress in reducing ... of ... ... rities continue to define American life. This book is for anyone who wonders why race still matters and is interested in what emerging social science can contribute to the discussion. The book explores how scientific evidence on the human mind might help explain why racial equality is so elusive. This new evidence reveals how human mental machinery can be skewed by lurking stereotypes, often bending to accommodate hidden biases reinforced by years of social learning. Through the lens of these powerful and pervasive implicit racial attitudes and stereotypes, *Implicit Racial Bias Across the Law* examines both the continued subordination of historically disadvantaged groups and the legal system's complicity in this subordination.

Justin D. Levinson is Associate Professor of Law and founding Director of the Culture and Jury Project at the University of Hawai'i at Mānoa William S. Richardson School of Law. Levinson's research explores the challenges to efficient decision-making, particularly in the context of implicit racial and gender stereotypes. He has written numerous articles and conducted empirical studies on implicit bias, including on implicit gender bias in the legal profession, skin tone bias in the evaluation of criminal evidence, and the implicit presumption of guilt for black males. He has also written about issues of cultural psychology and economic decision-making. Levinson previously practiced corporate and securities law at Wilson, Sonsini, Goodrich, & Rosati in Palo Alto, California, where he counseled technology companies at various stages of development.

Robert J. Smith is Assistant Professor of Law at the University of North Carolina, Chapel Hill, where he teaches Criminal Law, Criminal Procedure, and Evidence. He previously served as the legal and policy advisor to Harvard Law School's Charles Hamilton Houston Institute and represented death-sentenced inmates as a staff attorney at the Louisiana Capital Appeals Project. He has authored or coauthored articles in the *Boston University Law Review*, *Washington Law Review*, *Case Western Reserve Law Review*, *Louisiana Law Review*, *Southern University Law Review*, *Harvard Law and Policy Review Online*, *Northwestern University Law Review Colloquy*, and *Michigan Law Review–First Impressions*.

Tonbridge School Library

A86667

Implicit Racial Bias Across the Law

Edited by

JUSTIN D. LEVINSON

University of Hawai'i at Mānoa
William S. Richardson School of Law

ROBERT J. SMITH

University of North Carolina, Chapel Hill

CAMBRIDGE UNIVERSITY PRESS

CAMBRIDGE UNIVERSITY PRESS
Cambridge, New York, Melbourne, Madrid, Cape Town,
Singapore, São Paulo, Delhi, Mexico City

Cambridge University Press
32 Avenue of the Americas, New York, NY 10013-2473, USA

www.cambridge.org
Information on this title: www.cambridge.org/9781107648180

© Cambridge University Press 2012

This publication is in copyright. Subject to statutory exception
and to the provisions of relevant collective licensing agreements,
no reproduction of any part may take place without the written
permission of Cambridge University Press.

First published 2012

Printed in the United States of America

A catalog record for this publication is available from the British Library.

Library of Congress Cataloging in Publication Data

Implicit racial bias across the law / [edited by] Justin D. Levinson, Roger J. Smith.
    p.   cm.
Includes bibliographical references.
ISBN 978-1-107-01095-6 (hardback) – ISBN 978-1-107-64818-0 (pbk.)
1. Discrimination in justice administration – United States.   2. Race discrimination – Law and
legislation – United States.   3. Bias (Law) – United States.   I. Levinson, Justin D. (Justin David),
1974–   II. Smith, Roger J. (Roger John), 1948–
KF384.I47   2012
342.7308'73–dc23   2011048919

ISBN 978-1-107-01095-6 Hardback
ISBN 978-1-107-64818-0 Paperback

Cambridge University Press has no responsibility for the persistence or accuracy of URLs for external or
third-party Internet websites referred to in this publication and does not guarantee that any content on
such websites is, or will remain, accurate or appropriate.

A86661   342.730873 LEV

To our parents

Contents

Contributors

Michelle Wilde Anderson is Assistant Professor of Law at the University of California, Berkeley, School of Law.

Dorothy A. Brown is Professor of Law at Emory University.

G. Ben Cohen is *Of Counsel* to the Justice Center's Capital Appeals Project in New Orleans, Louisiana.

Danielle M. Conway is the Michael J. Marks Distinguished Professor of Business Law at the University of Hawai'i at Mānoa William S. Richardson School of Law and Director of the University of Hawai'i Procurement Institute.

Naomi Duke, MD, is the Medical Director of the West Suburban Teen Clinic in the greater Twin Cities area of Minnesota and a PhD candidate at the University of Minnesota.

The Honorable Nancy Gertner is U.S. District Court Judge (retired) for the District of Massachusetts and Professor of Practice at Harvard Law School.

Rachel D. Godsil is the Eleanor Bontecou Professor of Law at Seton Hall University School of Law.

Michele Goodwin is the Everett Fraser Professor in Law at the University of Minnesota and holds joint appointments at the University of Minnesota Medical School and the University of Minnesota School of Public Health.

Melissa Hart is Associate Professor of Law at the University of Colorado Law School.

Jerry Kang is Professor of Law at UCLA School of Law and Korea Times–Hankook Ilbo Chair in Korean American Studies at UCLA's Asian American Studies Center.

Charles R. Lawrence III is Professor of Law at the Georgetown Law Center and Centennial Professor at the University of Hawai'i at Mānoa.

Justin D. Levinson is Associate Professor of Law and Director of the Culture and Jury Project at the University of Hawai'i at Mānoa William S. Richardson School of Law.

Breann Swann Nu'uhiwa is a Post–Juris Doctor Research Fellow at the Ka Huli Ao Center for Excellence in Native Hawaiian Law, which is housed at the University of Hawai'i at Mānoa William S. Richardson School of Law.

Charles Ogletree is the Jesse Climenko Professor of Law at Harvard Law School and the Founder and Executive Director of the Charles Hamilton Houston Institute for Race and Justice at Harvard Law School.

Victoria C. Plaut is Assistant Professor of Law and Social Science and Affiliate Faculty in Psychology at the University of California, Berkeley, School of Law.

Laurie A. Rudman is Professor of Psychology at Rutgers University.

Deana Pollard Sacks is Professor of Law at Texas Southern University Thurgood Marshall School of Law.

Susan K. Serrano is Director of Educational Development at the Ka Huli Ao Center for Excellence in Native Hawaiian Law, which is housed at the University of Hawai'i at Mānoa William S. Richardson School of Law.

Robert J. Smith is Assistant Professor of Law at the University of North Carolina, Chapel Hll.

Michele Park Sonen is Law Clerk for the Honorable Susan Oki Mollway, Chief Judge, District of Hawai'i.

Johanna Wald is Director of Strategic Planning and Development at the Charles Hamilton Houston Institute for Race and Justice at Harvard Law School.

Eric K. Yamamoto is Professor of Law at the University of Hawai'i at Mānoa William S. Richardson School of Law.

Danielle M. Young is a postdoctoral researcher in Rutgers University's Department of Psychology.

Acknowledgments

We would like to thank the terrific scholars whose work is collected in this book. We also wish to express our gratitude to Aviam Soifer, Dean of the William S. Richardson School of Law at the University of Hawai'i, for his generous financial support. Nicholas Costa provided outstanding research assistance.

IMPLICIT RACIAL BIAS ACROSS THE LAW

Introduction

Racial Disparities, Social Science, and the Legal System

Justin D. Levinson

Discussions of race in the United States have taken on an optimistic tone, led by confident commentators who tout America's successful retreat from its racist past. This new, hopeful dialogue comes complete with factual support. For example, racial minorities have reached the pinnacle in government and leadership roles, which positions them atop traditionally Caucasian hierarchies; instances of overt racism have been declining for decades; and America's diverse and multicultural society keeps growing, affording new educational and job opportunities to traditionally disadvantaged peoples. Without a closer look, one could embrace this new vision of race in the United States without seeing or considering an ominous subterranean context.

Yet a deeper examination reveals the complexity of America's racial challenges and the legal system's unwitting complicity in the persistence of racial disparities. America's racial progress does offer comfort if viewed in isolation (after all, declining overt racism is something to embrace), but it also obscures systematic racial bias that forges ahead, undeterred. Massive racial disparities in America persist – in the criminal justice system, in economic advancement, in property ownership, and beyond. Consider the incarceration statistics: despite comprising only about 13 percent of the population, today African Americans make up almost 50 percent of the incarcerated. Economic figures similarly do little to comfort those who hope that equality has been achieved: African American and Latino families are disproportionately likely to be in the bottom fifth of Americans based on earnings per family. The story of property ownership is not much better: fewer than half of African American and Latino families are homeowners compared to 75 percent of Caucasian families.

When measured in the context of the legal system and beyond, these continuing disparities should no longer be understood by referencing dated and racist notions of nature or biology, nor should they be examined simply by invoking the vision of the standouts, those leaders who have emerged against the odds from underrepresented communities into the public eye. Instead, continuing systematic racial disparities must be understood by engaging in a deeper, social science–based inquiry that considers how a multitude of forces, particularly implicit biases, converge on society and the legal system.

In deconstructing the ways that racial disparities continue to plague the United States, emerging scientific evidence on the human mind helps demonstrate why equality may be so elusive. This new evidence reveals how human mental machinery can be skewed by lurking stereotypes, often bending to accommodate hidden biases reinforced by years of social learning. Although implicit bias may be harder to conceptualize than traditional symbols of racial discrimination (for example, the skinhead), its truth is revealed to us through rigorous scientific method used by scores of social scientists to consistently reveal a disquieting but potent truth: despite cultural progress in reducing overt acts of racism, the effects of implicit racial attitudes and stereotypes are powerful and pervasive. This book argues that these effects are so powerful and pervasive that they help explain not only the continued subordination of historically subordinated groups but also the legal system's complicity in that subordination.

The science underlying this hidden and biased context, known to social scientists as implicit social cognition, explains how the vast majority of Americans still perceive the world in race-tinged constructs, and it demonstrates how people have the potential to rely on racial and gender stereotypes in almost any law-relevant situation, even without awareness that they are doing so. In the legal context, implicit racial biases can be easy to perceive, or they can be more deeply hidden. Here are a few examples:

- *Corporate decision-making*: A corporate manager, without knowing it, relies on stereotypes when evaluating an employee. The manager, influenced by racial stereotypes related to laziness, notices more easily that an employee seeking promotion has been late to work or occasionally takes breaks in excess of corporate time limits. The manager notes these instances in corporate human resources records.
- *Governmental action*: Congress and the IRS, attempting to formulate an auditing scheme to maximize auditing efficiency and deter tax fraud, decide to audit people who claim the earned income tax credit, a credit that IRS policymakers and auditors perceive to be a minority-benefiting tax measure. Although their audit is supported by evidence that the EITC is erroneously claimed at a high rate, it is also based on unfounded racial stereotypes about the morality and trustworthiness of the perceived targets of the audits.
- *Health care*: A patient complains of chest tightness and a feeling of heavy pressure. He is afraid, in pain, and surrounded by his loving family. A doctor checks his vitals, tests his blood for cardiac enzymes, and performs an EKG. The

doctor consults the test results and makes a treatment decision. She believes that her decision is entirely evidence based, but in fact it has been influenced by her perception of the patient's diet, his willingness to change life habits, and his cooperativeness. In turn these perceptions have been driven by the patient's race.

Each of these examples raises questions about implicit bias and racial justice in the American legal system. To pursue these questions further, one might ask in turn: Does either corporate law or employment discrimination law deal with the corporate manager's (unconscious) selective documentation of racially stereotypic facts about an employee? Can members of a minority community successfully challenge an IRS audit scheme that was initiated because of implicit racial stereotypes? And when stereotype-driven assumptions lead to decisions to treat patients differently, does health care law allow for objection or reform?

This edited volume tackles these issues and many more. Each chapter confronts the dangerous role of implicit racial bias in a different area of law,[1] discusses its challenges, and proposes future directions. Most of these discussions are cutting edge; implicit bias is typically discussed in limited legal contexts. Outside of criminal law and employment discrimination law, scholars are still only beginning to consider the deep and troublesome role of how implicit bias manifests itself in law and society. This volume introduces new discussions of implicit bias across fundamental areas of the law, including the legal areas of property, tort, corporate, health, education, communications, taxation, intellectual property, and environmental, while also building on discourse in the traditional areas of employment discrimination and of criminal law and procedure.

I. THE SCIENTIFIC BASICS

A social scientific understanding of implicit bias may be helpful here. The concept of implicit bias has two key components. First, as the name implies, it is implicit, which means that it is generally outside the awareness and control of a person. Second, also as the name implies, it is biased, which means that it disproportionately affects people in meaningful ways.[2] A few brief examples of studies on implicit bias and their implications help demonstrate the dangerousness of the implicit biases that often lurk below our consciousness. Chapter 1 picks up where this brief introduction

---

[1] Robert J. Smith and I have selected fourteen important areas of law for this volume. Our list is by no means exclusive, and we hope that future projects tackle implicit bias in these and other contexts.

[2] Anthony Greenwald and Linda Krieger give a more formal scientific definition. They explain a bias as "a displacement of people's responses along a continuum of possible judgments" and implicit biases as "discriminatory biases based upon implicit attitudes or implicit stereotypes." Anthony G. Greenwald & Linda Hamilton Krieger, *Implicit Bias: Scientific Foundations*, 94 CAL. L. REV. 945, 950–51 (2006).

leaves off, presenting a detailed summary of the science underlying implicit racial bias.

Eliciting stereotypes: Imagine listening to a hip-hop song on an iPod. Do you like the beat? Perhaps. Do the lyrics rhyme and are they catchy? Likely. Do they trigger racial biases within you? Probably. As social psychologists have found, listening to rap songs for just a few minutes has the power to transform the way you think about the world.[3] Imagine that after listening to the music, you made a hiring decision, or you taught a class, or you witnessed a crime. Research shows that you are likely to use a vast network of racial stereotypes triggered by the music (even those entirely unrelated to the themes of the music) to guide you as you make decisions.

Pulling the trigger: Pretend you are a police officer on beat patrol. You receive a report of an armed robbery that has just occurred a few blocks away. Your senses are heightened as you look for suspicious activity. You turn the corner and see a man who looks at you with trepidation. "Don't move," you demand, and approach the man with your weapon drawn. The man reaches into his pocket and quickly removes an object. Do you shoot? Social scientists have found that people presented with a lifelike simulation of this situation are quicker to shoot armed black men than armed white men and to make more shooting errors by firing on unarmed black men than unarmed white men.[4]

Allocating resources: Envision you are on the board of directors of a successful company. Today, the company is deciding how to support local charities. Many charities are in contention. Will you support a program for the Girl Scouts? The NAACP? Or the opera? Might your resource allocation decisions, unbeknownst to you, track your implicit biases, thereby steering money toward charities that cater to the already privileged? That is quite possible, based on research findings showing that implicit stereotypes predict how people allocate resources to certain groups.[5]

II. EARLY LEGAL DISCOURSE

Scholars are beginning to consider the massive impact of implicit bias across the law, especially in a couple of well-developed areas. Here, I briefly highlight the early work on implicit bias in the law and set the stage for the chapters in this volume.

The consistent results of implicit social cognition research are startling, and for some who experience these studies firsthand (for example, through easy-to-access web-based demonstrations[6]), the results lead to deep reflection. It is surprising,

---

[3] Laurie A. Rudman & Matthew R. Lee, *Implicit and Explicit Consequences of Exposure to Violent and Misogynous Rap Music*, 4 GROUP PROCESSES & INTERGROUP REL. 133 (2002).

[4] Joshua Correll et al., *The Police Officer's Dilemma: Using Ethnicity to Disambiguate Potentially Threatening Individuals*, 83 J. PERSONALITY & SOC. PSYCHOL. 1314 (2002).

[5] Laurie A. Rudman & Richard D. Ashmore, *Discrimination and the Implicit Association Test*, 10 GROUP PROCESSES & INTERGROUP REL. 359, 368 (2007).

[6] *See, e.g.* https://implicit.harvard.edu/implicit/demo/takeatest.html (last visited Oct. 3, 2011).

then, that legal scholarship has yet to consider systematically the implications of implicit social cognition research. Although the social scientific methods for detecting implicit bias have filled the pages of academic journals for over a decade, legal scholars have struggled to contextualize this new science into more than a few important areas of discourse. Perhaps this struggle might be best explained because other than in areas where it is more noticeable, such as in employment discrimination and criminal law, it is initially difficult to consider intuitively how implicit bias might function – for example, in legal areas that deal with tax, property, and corporations. A brief discussion of what discourse on implicit bias has revealed about law will help contextualize what has yet to be considered.

The most salient issues demonstrating the power of implicit bias emerge in the employment context. Linda Hamilton Krieger, who introduced social cognition research to the employment discrimination community, argued that Title VII's "intent to discriminate" requirement should be replaced by a causation standard.[7] This work, informed by a then cutting-edge understanding of social science research, followed in the footsteps of Charles Lawrence's groundbreaking article, "The Id, the Ego, and Equal Protection: Reckoning with Unconscious Racism," which focused primarily on constitutional law and called on society to take responsibility for all of its biases, both conscious and unconscious.[8] These articles stoked a scholarly interest in considering hidden biases. In the context of employment discrimination law, for example, well over a dozen scholars have followed Krieger's lead, debating and critiquing how evidence of implicit bias may fit within legal tests in the employment context. Implicit bias, then, has become a popular and controversial topic in the employment discrimination context.

Less popular and comprehensive, yet still partially uncovered, is the role of implicit bias in criminal law and policy. In this area, just a few scholars have delved deeply into implicit social cognition.[9] In separate projects, my colleagues and I have relied on implicit bias research to argue, for example, that judges and juries misremember case facts in racially biased ways,[10] that skin tone affects the way jurors evaluate

---

7   Linda Hamilton Krieger, *The Content of Our Categories: A Cognitive Bias Approach to Discrimination and Equal Employment Opportunity*, 47 STAN. L. REV. 1161 (1995).

8   Charles R. Lawrence III, *The Id, the Ego, and Equal Protection: Reckoning with Unconscious Racism*, 39 STAN. L. REV. 317 (1987). Although Lawrence's article drew primarily on Freudian psychology, his powerful and well-reasoned arguments set the stage for discussions of implicit social cognition. In fact, this article was so successful in deconstructing bias in light of constitutional principles that we chose not to include a chapter on constitutional law in this volume. Instead, we invited Lawrence to address his other area of expertise, education law, in light of implicit bias findings.

9   Many more have speculated about its potential for explaining injustice in the criminal justice system.

10 Justin D. Levinson, *Forgotten Racial Equality: Implicit Bias, Decisionmaking, and Misremembering*, 57 DUKE L.J. 345 (2007). Although the empirical study in this article did not test judges' implicit memory biases, there is reason to believe that judges display similar implicit biases compared to the rest of the population. *See* Jeffrey J. Rachlinski et al., *Does Unconscious Bias Affect Trial Judges?*, 84 NOTRE DAME L. REV. 1195 (2009).

evidence,[11] that the process of "death-qualifying" jurors during capital jury selection automatically triggers implicit racial stereotypes,[12] and that people implicitly associate black with guilty.[13] Thus far, three of these four arguments have direct empirical support.[14]

Beyond employment discrimination law and criminal law, however, scholars have been slower to consider deeply the way implicit biases propagate inequality throughout the legal system.[15] Although many scholars have become intrigued by the concept of implicit bias and frequently mention it as something to be investigated further, implicit bias–focused scholarship in most areas of law is still quite thin. This volume provides a comprehensive and critical analysis of implicit bias across fourteen areas of law, each written by experts in the field.

III. THIS VOLUME

The volume begins by engaging the scientific underpinnings of implicit bias. In Chapter 1, I join with psychologists Danielle Young and Laurie Rudman to detail the science behind implicit racial bias, setting the stage for each of the remaining chapters. Readers unfamiliar with implicit social cognition methods and findings will find this chapter to be a helpful starting point. The remainder of the volume examines a wide range of legal areas in light of implicit bias.

Each contribution offers a new approach to discourse in its individual field, yet the authors' treatment of implicit racial bias throughout the volume can be synthesized. First, the chapters paint a broad picture of the way implicit racial bias may function

---

[11] Justin D. Levinson & Danielle Young, *Different Shades of Bias: Skin Tone, Implicit Racial Bias, and Judgments of Ambiguous Evidence*, 112 W. Va. L. Rev. 307 (2010).

[12] Justin D. Levinson, *Race, Death and the Complicitous Mind*, 58 DePaul L. Rev. 599 (2009).

[13] Justin D. Levinson, Huajian Cai, & Danielle Young, *Guilty by Implicit Bias: The Guilty Not Guilty Implicit Association Test*, 8 Ohio St. J. Crim. L. 187 (2010). For another important article on implicit racial bias and criminal law, see L. Song Richardson, *Arrest Efficiency and the Fourth Amendment*, 95 Minn. L. Rev. 2035 (2011).

[14] We have yet to test whether "death qualifying" jurors during capital jury selection automatically triggers racial stereotypes.

[15] Some scholars have succeeded in considering implicit racial bias in areas of law other than employment and criminal law, but these articles tend to stand alone in their fields. For example, Jerry Kang has considered implicit bias in the context of communications law and policy and was the first legal scholar to engage comprehensively with the updated methods of implicit social cognition. Jerry Kang, *Trojan Horses of Race*, 118 Harv. L. Rev. 1489, 1497–1539 (2005). For other interesting discussions of implicit bias outside of employment and criminal law, see Dale Larson, *Unconsciously Regarded as Disabled: Implicit Bias and the Regarded – As Prong of the Americans with Disabilities Act*, 56 UCLA L. Rev. 451 (2008); Antony Page, *Unconscious Bias and the Limits of Director Independence*, 2009 Ill. L. Rev. 237 (focusing on a range of cognitive biases, including automatic ingroup preference); Antony Page & Michael J. Pitts, *Poll Workers, Election Administration, and the Problem of Implicit Bias*, 15 Mich. J. Race & L. 1 (2010) (arguing that poll workers rely on implicit bias in interacting with voters); Robert G. Schwemm, *Why Do Landlords Still Discriminate (And What Can Be Done About It)?*, 40 J. Marshall L. Rev. 455 (2007).

as an interconnected and often impenetrable barrier across law and society. In this lens, consider how the story lines of several chapters might intersect for members of a stereotyped family or community:

> A young girl walks to school, eager for the opportunity to engage and learn, despite the so-called achievement gap. Later that morning, her mother reports to the courthouse, jury summons in hand, excited to participate in a civic responsibility. On the same day, her grandfather goes to the local Emergency Room, afraid that his chest pains might mean that he has suffered a heart attack. Nearby, a nonprofit organization serving underprivileged youth prepares to make its "pitch" to a local corporation, seeking a charitable donation that will allow it to survive and fulfill its mission.

Each of these story lines, which by themselves illustrate separate challenges within the educational, civic, health, and economic spheres, becomes connected by implicit bias. For example, Charles Lawrence, in Chapter 7 on education law, considers how implicit bias may affect the way that racial disparities in education are explained and addressed, resulting in powerful harms to black children. Robert Smith and Ben Cohen, in considering capital punishment in Chapter 14, argue that implicit bias may lead to the disproportionate exclusion of African American jurors. Michele Goodwin and Dr. Naomi Duke, in Chapter 6 on health care law, argue that quality medical treatment may be reserved, due to implicit racial stereotypes, for members of privileged groups. And in my chapter on corporations (Chapter 9), I suggest that implicit bias may lead companies to donate money to elite (white) charities instead of to nonprofits that benefit minorities. In reading the chapters, it is crucial not only to grapple with their topic-focused claims but also to note that each potentially biased domain does not stand alone; rather, it is part of a network of interconnected forces that can impede justice.

Another way to synthesize the chapters in this volume is to consider the similarities and differences in the authors' specific claims of biased decision-making. By reflecting on the contributors' claims in this way, one can gain new perspective on each subject area, as well as understand how implicit bias may actually manifest in additional domains beyond those considered by the authors. Taking this decision-focused perspective highlights the breadth of the authors' claims: they explore decisions made by individual actors (e.g., neighbors, judges, or doctors), those made by groups (e.g., juries or corporate boards), and those made by government or administrative entities (e.g., Congress or the IRS).

In Chapter 3, Charles Ogletree and his colleagues, for example, suggest that a wide range of individual decision-makers, including prosecutors, defense counsel, police, and judges, may be biased in the criminal law context, perhaps even all related to a single trial. Jerry Kang takes a different approach in Chapter 8 on communications law. He focuses on a unique relationship between law and bias: the biases triggered and heightened in large groups of citizens by a complicit system of law and policy.

Other contributors blend their claims of bias. For example, in Chapter 2, Michelle Wilde Anderson and Victoria Plaut claim that a range of biased decisions, including those made by groups (city councils) and individuals (tax assessors and neighbors), affect property law and development. When considering the authors' various claims of bias, it becomes apparent that some of these claims may inform even other chapters. For example, borrowing from Kang, criminal law commentators could explore whether certain crime policies might actually become delivery mechanisms of bias, rather than reflections of bias. Or, borrowing from Ogletree and colleagues, communication law scholars could argue that administrative decisions serve not just as a trigger for bias but also are a result of bias.

Focusing on the specific claims of bias additionally informs discussions of how to respond to implicit bias. For example, should implicit bias be countered by training decision-makers, advocating for more neutral laws, or encouraging more diversity in organizations? In the context of employment discrimination law, Judge Nancy Gertner and Melissa Hart claim in Chapter 5 that current case law amplifies the opportunity for an individual judge's implicit biases to affect a summary judgment decision. To address this problem, one might attempt to reduce the influence of implicit bias on individual trial judges, perhaps through bias reduction or diversity training. Another solution might include a push for legislatively initiated change to reshape the bias supporting laws. Arguments made by other authors perhaps necessitate broader solutions. For example, in Chapter 10 Dorothy Brown argues that Congress and the IRS made stereotype-driven decisions in choosing to audit citizens who claimed the earned income tax credit. Resolving potential bias by Congress may be harder to address through training, and reforming federal law generally requires congressional approval. Thus, additional solutions may be required. Yet, if implicit bias is so powerful that Congress is susceptible to it, solutions short of cultural change may well be fleeting. As the chapters discuss, the potential for implicit bias to affect nearly all decision-makers means that creative and comprehensive remedies will likely be needed.

These chapters, rooted in the major subjects of law, provide a comprehensive look at the dangers of implicit racial bias in the legal system. Individually, they offer a compelling look at the potential harms that implicit bias can play in a particular legal domain. Taken together, they amplify the depth and interconnectedness of implicit racial bias in all areas of the law. By doing so, they highlight the major challenges that lie ahead for policymakers, practitioners, scholars, and citizens as they participate in the continuing struggle for fairness and equality.

1

Implicit Racial Bias

A Social Science Overview

Justin D. Levinson, Danielle M. Young, and Laurie A. Rudman

A little after 2:00 a.m. on the first day of 2009, San Francisco Bay Area Rapid Transit (BART) Officer Johannes Mehserle arrived at the Fruitvale BART station after receiving reports of a fight on a train.[1] On arrival, he was directed by another officer to arrest Oscar Grant, who, along with other fight suspects, was sitting on the ground next to the wall of the station. As Mehserle, who was joined by other officers, prepared to arrest Grant, Grant began to stand up, and Mehserle forced him to the ground face first. Another officer stood over Grant and uttered, "Bitch-ass n-."[2] As Mehserle attempted to handcuff Grant, some eyewitnesses testified that Grant resisted by keeping his hands under his torso. Although Grant was lying face down and was physically restrained by another police officer at the time of his alleged resistance, Mehserle removed his department-issued handgun from its holster and shot Grant in the back from point-blank range. Grant died later that morning.

At trial, the jury convicted Mehserle of involuntary manslaughter, but acquitted him of more serious homicide charges that would have treated the killing as intentional. The involuntary manslaughter conviction indicates that the jury likely believed two key pieces of Mehserle's testimony: first, that he thought Grant was reaching for a gun, and second, that he mistook his own gun (which was on the right side of his body and weighed twice as much) for a Tazer (on the left side of his body). How could an officer possibly perceive a mostly compliant, restrained man as a gun-toting threat?

Research on implicit racial bias suggests that, when implicit racial stereotypes are activated, the human mind is capable of major feats, such as turning an

---

[1] The facts we present are largely based on bail hearing documents and video recordings of the event. For one video recording, *see* thecaliforniabeat, *New Footage of Oscar Grant Shooting*, YouTube (Feb. 24, 2010), http://www.youtube.com/watch?v=KxnFQ_IvOt4.

[2] Philip Matier & Andrew Ross, *BART 'N-word' bombshell waiting to go off*, S.F. Chronicle, June 29, 2009, *available at* http://www.sfgate.com/cgi-bin/article.cgi?f=/c/a/2009/06/28/BA4E18EMPH.DTL&tsp=1.

innocent hand into one reaching for a gun. For more than a decade, researchers have explored how implicit racial bias (as contrasted with self-reported, or explicit, racial bias) contributes to systematic racial discrimination. Implicit racial bias explains the process whereby the human mind automatically and unintentionally reacts to different groups in divergent ways, a process that can have unfortunate consequences. One fundamental aspect of the implicit racial attitudes uncovered by implicit social cognition research is that they frequently differ from people's self-reported (often egalitarian) racial attitudes. Because of the automatic nature of these biases, people are often unaware of them or how they affect their judgments.

In this chapter, we lay the foundation for studying implicit racial bias across the law by examining examples from more than a decade of research on the unconscious and automatic activation of racial stereotypes. This examination includes a discussion of the ease with which racial stereotypes are activated (particularly through the phenomenon known as "priming"), a consideration of how social scientists measure implicit bias (including through the Implicit Association Test and the shooter bias "videogame"), and an exploration of the relationship between implicit bias and real-world behaviors and decision-making. The chapter concludes by describing empirical studies of implicit racial bias in the legal system.

RACIAL PRIMING: THE UNCONSCIOUS ACTIVATION OF STEREOTYPES

Priming is a term imported from cognitive psychology that describes a stimulus that has an effect on an unrelated task. Psychologists have defined it as "the incidental activation of knowledge structures, such as trait concepts and stereotypes, by the current situational context."[3] Simply put, priming studies show how causing someone to think about a particular domain can trigger associative networks related to that domain.[4] Activating these associative networks, which can include stereotypes, can affect people's decision-making and behavior, often without their conscious awareness.

A study conducted by John Bargh and his colleagues provides a simple example of priming outside of the racial context.[5] In the study, which was designed to examine the behavioral effects of activating stereotypes related to the elderly, the researchers primed participants by exposing them to one of two lists of words. Half of the participants unscrambled sentences that contained words designed to subtly prime participants with the category of elderly; thus, the sentences included

---

[3] John A. Bargh et al., *Automaticity of Social Behavior: Direct Effects of Trait Construct and Stereotype Activation on Action*, 71 J. PERSONALITY & SOC. PSYCHOL. 230, 230 (1996).

[4] Several of the descriptions we provide of priming and the Implicit Association Test are based, sometimes verbatim, on the descriptions given in Justin Levinson, *Forgotten Racial Equality: Implicit Bias, Decisionmaking, and Misremembering*, 57 DUKE L. J. 345 (2007), and Justin D. Levinson, *Race, Death and the Complicitous Mind*, 58 DEPAUL L. REV. 599 (2009).

[5] Bargh, *supra* note 3.

words such as "wise," "helpless," "wrinkle," and "bingo." The other half of the participants unscrambled sentences using words that contained no particular theme (e.g., "thirsty," "private," and "clean"). The researchers hypothesized that participants who unscrambled sentences containing the elderly stereotyped words would become primed by them. That is, those participants would have activated their usually dormant knowledge of traits and stereotypes of the elderly. Bargh and his colleagues further suggested that simply activating these traits and stereotypes would cause behavioral changes. Specifically, they predicted that participants who were primed for the concept of elderly would walk more slowly down the hallway after believing they had completed the experiment compared to participants who were not primed. This hypothesis was confirmed: primed participants indeed walked down the hallway more slowly than nonprimed participants. Furthermore, participants who were primed with the elderly words were unaware that they had even been exposed to an elderly prime. This example sets the stage for a discussion of the ease with which racial stereotypes may be primed, as well as the important behavioral implications of priming.

Ease of Activation

Racial and ethnic stereotypes can be primed with ease. In one simple and elegant study, participants watched a video in which a research assistant held cue cards containing word fragments.[6] All participants watched identical videos, except for the identity of the research assistant. Half of the participants saw a video in which the research assistant was Asian, and the other half saw a video in which the research assistant was Caucasian. In the video, the assistant held cue cards containing incomplete words, including words that were potentially stereotypic of Asians, such as "RI_E", "POLI_E," "S_ORT," and "S_Y." Participants were asked to generate as many word completions as possible for each card during a fifteen-second period. Results of the study showed that simply seeing an Asian research assistant was enough to activate ethnic stereotypes of Asians. Participants who watched the video with the Asian assistant completed more stereotype words (RICE, POLITE, SHORT, and SHY) than participants who watched the video with the Caucasian assistant.

The cue card study demonstrated that even simple visual cues (seeing an Asian person) can prime a person's racial and ethnic stereotypes. Laurie Rudman and Matthew Lee tested whether auditory, rather than visual, cues could similarly prime participants' racial stereotypes.[7] Participants in their study listened to either rap or pop music for thirteen minutes.[8] As they hypothesized, Rudman and Lee found

---

[6] Daniel T. Gilbert & J. Gregory Hixon, *The Trouble of Thinking: Activation and Application of Stereotypic Beliefs*, 60 J. PERSONALITY & SOC. PSYCHOL. 509 (1991).

[7] Laurie A. Rudman & Matthew R. Lee, *Implicit and Explicit Consequences of Exposure to Violent and Misogynous Rap Music*, 5 GROUP PROCESSES & INTERGROUP REL. 133, 138–39 (2002).

[8] Participants were led to believe that they were participating in a marketing study.

that rap music indeed activated participants' racial stereotypes, including stereotypes associating African Americans with attributes such as hostile, violent, and dangerous. Furthermore, participants whose racial stereotypes were activated subsequently rated a black (but not a white) person's behavior as less intelligent and more hostile. Finally, participants' self-reported (explicit) prejudice levels did not predict their judgments of a black person, indicating that automatic biases can leak into people's decision-making without their endorsement or awareness. This study demonstrates that even simple auditory primes (such as hearing music) can automatically activate a network of associated implicit racial stereotypes.

Research has also shown that racial stereotypes can be activated by crime-related primes. Jennifer Eberhardt and her colleagues primed some participants with crime-related images,[9] such as a police badge, a fingerprint, and guns, as part of a "dot-probe" task that measures attention by seeing how quickly participants can find a dot on a screen. This dot was presented on a computer screen near the face of either a white male or a black male. Participants who were primed with crime-related images found the dot faster near black faces compared to participants who were not primed, suggesting a high degree of cognitive association between the concepts "crime" and "black male." The researchers found similar results by priming participants with basketball-related words. Participants who had been primed with basketball-related words found the dot faster near black faces than participants who were not primed.

Decision-making and Behavioral Consequences of Priming

Racial stereotypes are not only primed easily in a variety of situations but their activation can also wreak havoc on decision-making and behavior. Keith Payne examined how merely showing participants a photograph of a white or black face for 200 milliseconds could affect the speed at which they could subsequently identify weapons.[10] In the study, participants saw photos of black or white faces followed immediately by photos of objects. The participants' only task, Payne told them, was to quickly identify the objects when they appeared on the screen.[11] Payne also told them that the flashing photographs of faces served only to signal the participant that a photograph of an object was about to appear. The study found that when participants saw photos of black faces immediately before photos of guns, they were significantly faster at identifying the guns. Similarly, when participants saw photos of white faces immediately before photos of tools, they were significantly faster at identifying the tools. Payne's study shows that racial stereotypes can be elicited automatically in a

---

[9] Jennifer L. Eberhardt et al., *Seeing Black: Race, Crime, and Visual Processing*, 87 J. PERSONALITY & SOC. PSYCHOL. 876 (2004).

[10] B. Keith Payne, *Prejudice and Perception: The Role of Automatic and Controlled Processes in Misperceiving a Weapon*, 81 J. PERSONALITY & SOC. PSYCHOL. 181, 185–86 (2001).

[11] *Id.* The objects consisted of guns and non-gun objects (the non-gun objects were hand tools, such as a socket wrench and an electric drill).

number of milliseconds and that these stereotypes can affect the speed and accuracy of meaningful object classification tasks.

In addition to affecting task performance, priming can affect people's judgments of others' behavior. Patricia Devine had participants watch flashing category words that were associated with African Americans, such as "blacks" and "Negroes," and flashing stereotype words that were associated with African Americans, such as "poor" and "athletic."[12] After the priming was accomplished, participants read a story about a person engaging in ambiguously hostile behaviors – such as demanding money back from a store clerk – and were asked to make judgments about the person engaging in these behaviors. Participants who were primed with more stereotyped words judged the actor's ambiguous behavior as more hostile than participants who were primed with fewer stereotyped words. As Devine summarized, "The automatic activation of the racial stereotype affects the encoding and interpretation of ambiguously hostile behaviors for both high- and low-prejudice subjects."[13] Although traits such as "poor" and "athletic" are unrelated to the trait of "hostile," the stereotype congruence between the primed stereotypes and the trait of hostility made participants more likely to judge a behavior as hostile.

Another study of priming's effects on decision-making was conducted by James Johnson and Sophie Trawalter, who primed participants by playing segments of either a violent or nonviolent rap song.[14] Participants later read supposedly unrelated stories of ambiguous behavior and were asked to make judgments about people in the stories. Those who heard the violent rap music, compared to other participants, judged a black male's aggressive behavior as caused by dispositional factors (for example, a violent personality) rather than situational factors (for example, stress related to a relationship break-up). In addition, participants who heard the violent rap music were more likely to judge a black job applicant as less qualified for a job requiring intelligence. This study shows that racial stereotype primes (here, rap music) can influence seemingly unrelated judgments (here, job qualification) so long as they are broadly related (both are stereotypes of African Americans).

Priming and the Self: Stereotype Threat

Thus far, the priming research we have reviewed shows that in legal contexts, scholars should be on the lookout for racial stereotype priming. Yet, commentators should be concerned with more than the activation of biased decision-making by primed observers. As Bargh's study of priming elderly stereotypes and walking speed shows,

[12] Patricia G. Devine, *Stereotypes and Prejudice: Their Automatic and Controlled Components*, 56 J. Personality & Soc. Psychol. 5, 9 (1989) (citing J. C. Brigham, *Ethnic Stereotypes*, 76 Psychol. Bull. 15 (1971)).

[13] *Id.* at 11.

[14] James D. Johnson & Sophie Trawalter, *Converging Interracial Consequences of Exposure to Violent Rap Music on Stereotypical Attributions of Blacks*, 36 J. Experimental Soc. Psychol. 233, 239 (2000).

they must also be concerned with the way priming can unconsciously affect the self. Some of the most famous priming experiments have studied the effect of racial, ethnic, and gender stereotypes on students' test-taking performance. In contrast to the foregoing priming studies, the primes in these studies affect a person's performance based on his or her own stereotyped identity. Claude Steele and Joshua Aronson first identified the concept of "stereotype threat" by priming college students in test-taking situations.[15] They primed Caucasian and African American college students by asking them to identify their race just before they took a test. The researchers found that such a simple priming task had profound effects on African American test performance: African American participants took longer to answer questions and achieved lower overall scores than Caucasian participants, but only when they were primed. Thus, Steele and Aronson found that priming a participant's racial identity likely implicated a complex relationship between African American identity and negative stereotypes relating to ability. They called this phenomenon "stereotype threat."

Steele and Aronson also found that stereotype threat could be elicited even by indirectly priming the racial stereotype. In this study, when they told half of the participants that the test results would be used to evaluate performance but did not ask them to identify their race, they found results similar to those obtained when they primed race directly: African American students in the indirect prime condition performed worse than Caucasian students in the same condition, whereas African American and Caucasian students performed similarly in the nonprime condition. This study demonstrates the ease and influence of indirect racial priming. Simply priming a nonexplicit but related stereotype, even without mentioning race, can cause profound results. Although it would not be intuitive to many that using race-neutral concepts can elicit powerful racial stereotypes, social cognition research shows that priming can occur as long as historical, cultural, or popular associations connect the concept with a racial stereotype. In the case of stereotype threat, African American student participants associated the evaluation instruction as implicating negative stereotypes relating to African Americans and intellectual ability.

Follow-up studies of stereotype threat have shown that it can be elicited by using even more indirect primes. Margaret Shih and colleagues used an indirect method of priming student-participants' ethnic identity, but found similarly powerful results.[16] In that study, the researchers asked Asian American female participants to fill out questionnaires before taking a math test. Some questionnaires asked the participants about their roommate and dormitory living situations (this condition was designed to prime gender identity), whereas others asked them about their family, including

---

[15] Claude M. Steele & Joshua Aronson, *Stereotype Threat and the Intellectual Test Performance of African-Americans*, 69 J. PERSONALITY & SOC. PSYCHOL. 797 (1995).

[16] Margaret Shih et al., *Stereotype Susceptibility: Identity Salience and Shifts in Quantitative Performance*, 10 PSYCHOL. SCI. 80 (1999).

what languages were spoken at home and how many generations of their family had lived in the United States (this condition was designed to prime ethnic identity). This method of indirect priming significantly affected the participants' test performance. Participants who had their Asian identity primed performed best on the test, whereas participants who had their female identity primed performed worst on the test. Considered together, these studies on stereotype threat show the dangers of subtly priming people's negative stereotypes about the groups to which they belong.

DEFINING THE IMPLICIT – REACTION TIMES, SHOOTER BIAS, AND THE IMPLICIT ASSOCIATION TEST

This chapter has explained how easily racial stereotypes can be primed and how priming can affect decision-making and behavior in troubling ways: for example, in object recognition tasks, when making judgments about others' ambiguous behaviors, and in academic test performance. Each of the reviewed studies shows the dynamic nature of implicit cognitive processes – processes that are important components of human decision-making. This chapter now turns to ways that social scientists measure implicit bias, examining two types of studies that use reaction times to measure implicit bias: shooter bias studies and the Implicit Association Test (IAT).

Quick Trigger Finger: The Shooter Bias

In the aftermath of the killing of Oscar Grant, as had happened with the killing of unarmed black men before him, observers wondered whether Officer Mehserle would have grabbed his gun and pulled the trigger if Grant had been white. Faced with this question after each instance in which police shot unarmed black men, social scientists developed a measure of "shooter bias." Shooter bias studies use custom-made videogames to examine race-based differences in reactions to potentially threatening individuals.[17] The bias can be tested when participants play a videogame that instructs them to shoot perpetrators (who are holding guns) as fast as they can but not to shoot innocent bystanders (who are unarmed but holding a non-gun object, such as a cell phone). The "shooter bias" refers to the consistent results of these studies: participants tend to shoot black perpetrators more quickly and more frequently than white perpetrators and conversely decide not to shoot white bystanders more quickly and frequently than black bystanders.

Once shooter bias became an established phenomenon in study participants who were not police officers, researchers wondered whether police officers would also display the bias. After all, unlike civilians, police officers receive extensive handgun

---

[17] Joshua Correll et al., *The Police Officer's Dilemma: Using Ethnicity to Disambiguate Potentially Threatening Individuals*, 83 J. PERSONALITY & SOC. PSYCHOL. 1314 (2002).

training and exercise visual discrimination tasks (such as detecting a gun) as a regular part of their job. Perhaps, then, police officers could resist or overcome the bias shown by other citizens. Joshua Correll and his colleagues tested this question by using both a community sample and a sample of police officers.[18] They found that, although police officers were generally faster and more accurate than the community sample, their reaction times followed the same pattern as that of community members: police officers were faster to "shoot" armed black perpetrators than armed white perpetrators and took longer to make "don't shoot" decisions for unarmed black targets than for unarmed white targets.

Researchers have investigated the cognitive roots of shooter bias, hypothesizing that it may manifest in brain processes that moderate responses to fear. To that end, Correll and his colleagues looked at fluctuations in participants' electrical brain activity (known as "event-related brain potentials") while the participants played the shooter bias videogame.[19] Measuring event-related brain potentials can identify when people detect threats and when they have a desire to control a behavioral response. The results of the study showed that, as participants played the videogame, racial discrepancies manifested in the electrical activity of their brains. That is, participants' brain activity showed more threat-related brain activity when presented with black actors than white actors (even for black actors without guns) and more control response activity for white actors than black actors. These brain responses correlated with the participants' performance – the more biased brain activity they displayed, the more shooter bias they exhibited.

The Implicit Association Test

Shooter bias studies are not the only social science measure that uses reaction times and accuracy rates to measure potential racial bias. Within legal discourse, the most frequently discussed measure of implicit social cognition is the Implicit Association Test (IAT). The IAT pairs an attitude object (such as a racial group) with an evaluative dimension (good or bad) and tests how response accuracy and speed indicate implicit and automatic attitudes and stereotypes. Participants sit at a computer and are asked to pair an attitude object (for example, black or white, man or woman, fat or thin) with either an evaluative dimension (for example, good or bad) or an attribute dimension (for example, home or career, science or arts) by pressing a response key as quickly as they can. For instance, in one task,

---

[18] Joshua Correll et al., *Across the Thin Blue Line: Police Officers and Racial Bias in the Decision to Shoot*, 92 J. PERSONALITY & SOC. PSYCHOL. 1006 (2007). The study looked at two measures of shooter bias: response times and accuracy. This chapter reports the results for the reaction time study in the text. The study of accuracy demonstrated that police officers were generally more accurate in their decisions to shoot than the community sample.

[19] Joshua Correll et al., *Event-Related Potentials and the Decision to Shoot: The Role of Threat Perception and Cognitive Control*, 42 J. EXPERIMENTAL SOC. PSYCHOL. 120, 122 (2006).

participants are told to quickly pair pictures of African American faces with positive words from the evaluative dimension. In a second task, participants are obliged to pair African American faces with negative words. The difference in the speed at which the participants can perform the two tasks is interpreted as the strength of the attitude (or, in the case of attributes, the strength of the stereotype). For example, if participants perform the first task faster than the second task, they are showing implicitly positive attitudes toward blacks. Similarly, if they are faster to perform tasks that oblige categorizing women with home than tasks that oblige categorizing women with career, they are showing implicit sex stereotyping.

Nilanjana Dasgupta and Anthony Greenwald succinctly summarize the science underlying the IAT: "When highly associated targets and attributes share the same response key, participants tend to classify them quickly and easily, whereas when weakly associated targets and attributes share the same response key, participants tend to classify them more slowly and with greater difficulty."[20] Laurie Rudman and Richard Ashmore add, "The ingeniously simple concept underlying the IAT is that tasks are performed well when they rely on well-practiced associations between objects and attributes."[21]

Scores of studies have found that people harbor implicit associations that are biased against stereotyped group members.[22] According to Brian Nosek and his colleagues, who reviewed hundreds of thousands of IATs taken on the web and elsewhere, the IAT has consistently shown that a majority of test takers exhibit implicit racial bias – and other nonracial biases – on a variety of measures.[23] For example, 68 percent of participants demonstrated an implicit preference for "white people" versus "black people" (or "light skin" versus "dark skin"), 75 percent of participants showed an implicit preference for "abled people" versus "disabled people," and 69 percent of participants showed an implicit preference for "thin people" versus "fat people." Similar to other community members, law students have also been shown to harbor implicit biases, such as showing an implicit association between men and judges (and women and paralegals).[24]

One particularly interesting characteristic of IAT results, as well as the results of other implicit measures, is that they frequently diverge from self-reported (explicit) racial attitudes. That is, people who display strong implicit biases are often not

[20] Nilanjana Dasgupta & Anthony G. Greenwald, *On the Malleability of Automatic Attitudes: Combating Automatic Prejudice with Images of Admired and Disliked Individuals*, 81 J. PERSONALITY & SOC. PSYCHOL. 800 (2001).

[21] Laurie A. Rudman & Richard D. Ashmore, *Discrimination and the Implicit Association Test*, 10 GROUP PROCESSES & INTERGROUP REL. 359 (2007).

[22] *See* Anthony Greenwald et al., *Understanding and Using the Implicit Association Test: III. Meta Analysis of Predictive Validity*, J. PERSONALITY & SOC. PSYCHOL. (2009).

[23] Brian Nosek et al., *Pervasiveness and Correlates of Implicit Attitudes and Stereotypes*, 18 EUR. REV. SOC. PSYCHOL. 36 (2008).

[24] Justin D. Levinson & Danielle Young, *Implicit Gender Bias in the Legal Profession: An Empirical Study*, 18 DUKE J. GENDER L. & POL'Y 1 (2010).

the same people who claim to have strong explicit biases.[25] According to Devine, "[e]ven those who consciously renounce prejudice have been shown to have implicit or automatic biases that conflict with their nonprejudiced values."[26] For example, in the context of shooter bias, explicit measures of racial preferences do not correlate with results for the videogame. That is, people who exhibit greater amounts of shooter bias are not necessarily the same ones who endorsed more racially unequal preferences.[27] A related and somewhat surprising finding in IAT research has been that members of bias-affected groups, who at least self-report favoring their own group, sometimes harbor implicit biases against their own group. For example, both male and female law students have been shown to display implicit gender stereotypes that are sometimes negative toward women.[28] Similarly, Nosek and his colleagues reported that older people show an implicit preference for young over old.[29]

Despite its consistent results, the IAT has not been without critique.[30] One question regarding the IAT is whether it measures something entirely unconscious or only partially unconscious. Russell Fazio and Michael Olson explored this question and argued that it is difficult, if not impossible, to know if these associations are in fact completely unknown to the participant. In fact, in many nonsensitive domains, the IAT has been shown to correlate well with explicit measures (such as voter intention).[31] It is important to acknowledge that, although the entirely unconscious nature of the attitudes tested by the IAT may be legitimately questioned, support for the automaticity of the association is unquestioned because results are based on swift reaction times. This automaticity assertion is bolstered by research demonstrating

---

[25] See Patricia G. Devine, *Implicit Prejudice and Stereotyping: How Automatic Are They? Introduction to the Special Section*, 81 J. PERSONALITY & SOC. PSYCHOL. 757, 757 (2001).

[26] *Id.*

[27] *Id.* Not all studies show no relationship between implicit and explicit attitudes. Some studies reveal at least a weak correlation between the two. *See, e.g.*, Russell H. Fazio & Michael A. Olson, *Implicit Measures in Social Cognition Research: Their Meanings and Use*, 54 ANN. REV. PSYCHOL. 297, 304 (2003) (observing that there is "no simple answer" to the issue of whether and how implicit and explicit attitudes are related, but nonetheless suggesting that both are predictive of behavior in different ways); Wilhelm Hofmann et al., *A Meta-Analysis on the Correlation Between the Implicit Association Test and Explicit Self-Report Measures*, 31 PERSONALITY & SOC. PSYCHOL. BULL. 1369, 1382 (2005) (finding a relationship between implicit and explicit attitudes).

[28] Levinson & Young, *Implicit Gender Bias, supra* note 24.

[29] Nosek et al., *supra* note 23.

[30] Within legal scholarship, a few scholars have cautioned against embracing the results of the IAT as a measure of bias to be considered in lawmaking. *See, e.g.* Gregory Mitchell & Philip E. Tetlock, *Antidiscrimination Law and the Perils of Mindreading*, 67 OHIO ST. L.J. 1023 (2006). Most psychologists and legal scholars, however, have argued that the IAT has been sufficiently validated as a measure. *See, e.g.*, Samuel R. Bagenstos, *Implicit Bias, "Science," and Antidiscrimination Law*, 1 HARV. L. & POL'Y REV. 477 (2007); John T. Jost et al., *The Existence of Implicit Bias Is Beyond Reasonable Doubt: A Refutation of Ideological and Methodological Objections and Executive Summary of Ten Studies that No Manager Should Ignore*, 29 RES. IN ORGANIZATIONAL BEHAV. 39 (2009).

[31] *See* Greenwald et al., *supra* note 22.

that as people age, their decreased ability to inhibit biased responses manifests in IAT scores.[32]

The IAT Predicts Real-World Behaviors

Social scientists have also been captivated by the question of whether the IAT has predictive validity, that is, the ability to predict real-life behaviors. One of the most pressing questions surrounding measurement in psychology is whether a measurement means anything in the real world. If a person possesses an implicit dislike of snakes, but shows no signs of bias against snakes in the real world, what is that person's implicit bias actually measuring? And is that measure useful? Predictive validity research helps answer such questions. It establishes the validity of an implicit measure (such as the IAT) by determining its relationship with a reasonable real-world measure. The IAT has been shown to predict discriminatory decision-making and behavior in a broad range of ways. Here, we review three particularly compelling studies of the IAT's predictive validity and then discuss a meta-analysis that was conducted on more than one hundred IAT studies.

Rudman and Ashmore tested whether the IAT predicted economic discrimination.[33] Student-participants first took a series of IATs, including those testing negative stereotypes related to Jews and Asians. On a separate occasion, the same participants completed a survey designed to test economic discrimination. Participants were told that their input was needed in determining how to administer a mandatory 20 percent budget cut to university student organizations. They were then provided a list of current student organizations along with funding levels and were asked to allocate the new, reduced budget across the various groups. The researchers then compared the student-participants' IAT scores with their recommended budget cuts and found that scores on the stereotype IAT predicted economic discrimination. Specifically, "people who associated minority group members with negative attributes and majority group members with positive attributes were also likely to recommend budget cuts for the target minority group's student organization."[34] Rudman and Ashmore's study demonstrates a meaningful connection between implicit racial bias and economic inequality.

In a study that linked implicit racial bias to inequality in the provision of health care services, Alexander Green and his colleagues tested whether physicians held implicit racial bias against African Americans and whether this bias predicted their decisions to treat patients.[35] Nearly 300 emergency room and internal medicine

---

[32] Karen Gonsalkorale et al., *Aging and Prejudice: Diminished Regulation of Automatic Race Bias Among Older Adults*, 45 J. Experimental Soc. Psychol. 410 (2009).

[33] Rudman & Ashmore, *supra* note 21.

[34] *Id.* at 367.

[35] Alexander R. Green et al., *Implicit Bias Among Physicians and its Prediction of Thrombolysis Decisions for Black and White Patients*, 22 J. Gen. Internal Med. 1231 (2007).

physicians in Boston and Atlanta participated in the study. They were presented with a vignette in which a patient, who was described as either black or white, arrives at an emergency room suffering from acute coronary syndrome. The doctors were asked to recommend a course of treatment for the patient and were then asked to complete three IATs testing their implicit racial biases. The study showed that these physicians not only implicitly preferred white patients to black patients but also that their implicit racial biases predicted whether or not they would recommend thrombolysis (clot-busting) treatment to a white or black patient suffering from myocardial infarction. The more the doctors implicitly preferred the white patients, the more likely they were to recommend thrombolysis treatment to white but not black patients. No similar predictive validity was found by asking doctors about their explicit racial preferences. On average, the physicians self-reported no racial preferences at all.

Implicit racial bias has also been shown to predict employment discrimination. Dan-Olof Rooth examined whether human resources officers at corporations harbored implicit bias that affected their choices of which candidates to interview for vacant positions.[36] In the first stage of his study, Rooth responded to more than 1,500 job postings in Sweden for a variety of jobs, ranging from computer professionals to motor vehicle operators. For each job posting, Rooth sent two equal resumes, with the only difference being whether the applicant's name appeared to be Swedish or Arabic/Muslim. He then measured whether the fictitious candidates were summoned for interviews. After this first interview stage was complete, Rooth tracked down the human resources officers responsible for the hiring decisions and invited them to participate in his study (these participants were unaware of the bias-related purpose of the study). Rooth provided an IAT testing implicit racial stereotypes of Swedes and Arab/Muslims and evaluated whether it predicted the human resources officers' previous decision of whether to interview the applicants. The study found that the human resource officers' implicit racial stereotypes of Arabs predicted whether they would call Arab job candidates for interviews. Human resources officers who held implicit stereotypes relating to Arabs were less likely to interview candidates with Arab-sounding names.

Taken individually, these studies on the IAT as a predictor are cause for concern. Yet a recent meta-analysis confirms the predictive validity of the IAT generally, particularly when it is employed in socially sensitive domains such as race. Greenwald and colleagues analyzed 122 studies that mapped IAT scores onto various predictors, such as behaviors, judgments, or physiological measures.[37] They included in their analyses a comprehensive list of IAT studies (going beyond those on race) that

---

[36] Dan-Olof Rooth, *Automatic Associations and Discrimination in Hiring: Real World Evidence*, 17 LABOUR ECON. 523 (2010).

[37] Greenwald et al., *supra* note 22.

tested a range of implicit attitudes, stereotypes, self-concepts, and self-esteem.[38] The researchers coded each study on a number of items including social sensitivity (a study of implicit racial bias, for example, was coded as being highly socially sensitive). Results showed that the IAT's relationship to predictive validity measures varied, ranging from low to high. Overall, explicit measures had a larger relationship with the response criterion. However, when dealing with socially sensitive issues such as race, the relationship between explicit measures and the response criterion was diminished, whereas the relationship between the IAT and response criterion was not. In fact, when looking specifically at interracial (or other intergroup) topics, IATs were more accurate than explicit measures in predicting behaviors, judgments, and physiological responses. This result confirms that implicit biases, particularly in the context of race, are meaningful. It would be advisable, then, if scholars concerned with racial bias in the legal system systematically examined implicit racial bias across the law.

IMPLICIT BIAS RESEARCH IN THE LEGAL SETTING

Although the vast majority of empirical studies on implicit bias have been conducted outside of the legal setting, a limited number of studies have used priming procedures, IATs, or both to measure bias in the law. As the following review demonstrates, significant progress has been made in empirically examining implicit racial bias in a few narrow domains, but most legal areas have generally been overlooked.

The first empirical use of the IAT in the legal setting occurred when Theodore Eisenberg and Sheri Lynn Johnson tested whether capital defense attorneys harbor implicit racial bias.[39] The researchers found that the defense attorney participants, a group one might expect to resist bias, in fact harbored strong implicit bias against African Americans. Eisenberg and Johnson, however, did not test whether the defense attorneys' implicit bias predicted anything about their behavior or decisions. Nonetheless, this study documented implicit bias among a particularly noteworthy participant population, and it opened the door for future research.

An early empirical examination of priming in the legal setting was conducted by Justin Levinson in 2005.[40] Levinson hypothesized that simply placing citizens on juries activates implicit and explicit knowledge structures that change the way people make decisions. He provided study participants with the facts of a crime and asked half of them to imagine that they were jurors in the criminal trial. The other half of the

---

[38] The resulting studies included a range of areas of research that dealt with topics from smoking to racial inequality.

[39] *See* Theodore Eisenberg & Sheri Lynn Johnson, *Implicit Racial Attitudes of Death Penalty Lawyers*, 53 DePaul L. Rev. 1539, 1542 (2004).

[40] Justin D. Levinson, *Suppressing the Expression of Community Values in Jurors: How "Legal Priming" Systematically Alters the Way People Think*, 73 U. Cin. L. Rev. 1059 (2005).

participants were informed that they were simply reading newspaper accounts of the crime. The results of the study showed that mock juror participants were significantly harsher in making judgments of criminal intentionality than participants making lay judgments about the same facts. In addition, when the defendant was portrayed as an outgroup member, participants in the legal prime condition appeared to become even harsher in their decisions.

In a law-focused study that employed both the IAT and priming, Jeffrey Rachlinski, Sheri Lynn Johnson, and their colleagues examined whether judges harbored implicit bias, and tested whether the IAT could predict race-based judicial decision-making.[41] Judges completed a black/white IAT and subsequently decided hypothetical court scenarios in which the race of the legal actor was subliminally primed. The researchers found first that judges displayed an implicit preference for white over black, and second, that the IAT predicted responses in the judgment tasks in which the race of the legal actor had been primed subliminally. For example, when the defendant was subliminally primed to be black, judges who scored in a pro-white direction on the IAT handed down harsher sentences.

Levinson and Danielle Young tested how priming mock jurors with the image of a dark-skinned perpetrator might alter judgments about the probative value of evidence.[42] Levinson and Young provided all jurors with the story of an armed robbery. After reading the story, participants were shown five crime scene photos for four seconds each. All participants saw the same five photos, except that in the third photo, half of the participants saw a dark-skinned perpetrator and the other half saw a lighter skinned perpetrator.[43] The researchers then presented participants with various pieces of evidence that were described as trial testimony and instructed them to rate each piece of evidence based on its probative value. As hypothesized, Levinson and Young found that participants who had seen a photo of a darker skinned perpetrator were more likely to evaluate the evidence as tending to indicate guilt.

Levinson, Huajian Cai, and Young also created an IAT specifically for the criminal law context.[44] Similar to Rachlinski and colleagues' study of judges, Levinson and his colleagues examined the predictive validity of the IAT. In this project, however, the researchers designed a Guilty/ Not Guilty IAT that they expected might be a more meaningful measure in the legal context. Levinson, Cai, and Young, as predicted, found that participants held a strong implicit association between black and guilty

---

[41] *See* Jeffrey J. Rachlinski et al., *Does Unconscious Bias Affect Trial Judges?*, 84 Notre Dame L. Rev. 1195 (2009).

[42] Justin D. Levinson & Danielle Young, *Different Shades of Bias: Skin Tone, Implicit Racial Bias, and Judgments of Ambiguous Evidence*, 112 W. Va. L. Rev. 307 (2010).

[43] None of the other photos showed the perpetrator.

[44] Justin D. Levinson, Huajian Cai, & Danielle Young, *Guilty by Implicit Bias: The Guilty-Not Guilty Implicit Association Test*, 8 Ohio St. J. Crim. L. 187 (2010).

compared to white and guilty. In addition, they found that the IAT scores predicted participants' evidence judgments.[45]

In another project that employed an IAT tailored specifically for the legal setting, Jerry Kang and his colleagues created an IAT designed to test whether people rely on implicit ethnic biases when evaluating the performance of litigators.[46] Specifically, the researchers tested implicit bias and related evaluations for Asian male litigators compared to white male litigators. The researchers predicted that participants would implicitly associate white males with characteristics frequently associated with successful litigators relative to Asian males, who would be more likely to be associated with characteristics frequently associated with successful scientists. As the results of the study showed, participants did in fact implicitly associate white males with successful litigators compared to Asian males. In addition, these implicit associations showed predictive validity. The IAT scores predicted participants' judgments of white and Asian litigators' performance in a mock trial.

A study by Young, Levinson, and Scott Sinnett used priming to follow up Levinson and colleagues' Guilty/ Not Guilty IAT, which raised the issue that the presumption of innocence may have a different implicit meaning for white and black defendants.[47] The researchers hypothesized that the presumption of innocence itself would actually prime participants to think about guilty African Americans, a counterintuitive result that might call into question the racial fairness of the presumption of innocence. Participants watched a video recording of a U.S. District Court judge reading a series of jury instructions. Half of the participants received instructions that included a presumption of innocence instruction, and the other half received an alternative matched-length instruction. After receiving the jury instruction, which the researchers hypothesized would act as a racial prime, participants completed a computer-based dot-probe task to assess if participants' attention was primed for black faces. Participants who were given the presumption of innocence instruction were faster to find a dot when it appeared on the same side of the screen as black faces than when it appeared on the same side of the screen as white faces. Participants who did not receive the presumption of innocence instructions displayed a similar response time for both white and black faces. These results demonstrate that presumption of innocence instructions prime attention for black faces.

[45] *Id.* at 206. The Guilty-Not Guilty IAT scores predicted overall judgments of evidence, but did not predict these judgments based on the skin tone of the perpetrator. Later analysis showed that Pleasant-Unpleasant IAT scores predicted judgments based on the skin tone of the perpetrator.

[46] Jerry Kang et al., *Are Ideal Litigators White? Measuring the Myth of Colorblindness*, 7 J. Empirical Leg. Stud. 886 (2010). Although we do not describe it in the text, another 2010 study employed the IAT to test whether law students possess implicit gender biases related to women in the legal profession. *See* Levinson & Young, *supra* note 24 (finding, for example, that law students associate men with judges and women with paralegals).

[47] Danielle Young, Justin D. Levinson, & Scott Sinnett, Presumption of Innocence: Biasing Racial Cues (2011) (unpublished manuscript) (on file with authors).

The foregoing studies show the progress made in empirically testing implicit bias in the legal domain. Yet, the summaries also underscore the limited nature of these studies. Future research should continue to empirically investigate implicit racial bias in the legal setting.

CONCLUSION

In light of the evidence linking implicit racial bias to a variety of discriminatory outcomes, legal scholars and empiricists must consider deeply the various ways in which implicit bias may affect all areas of the law in which disparities appear. The killing of Oscar Grant, which reopened old wounds for many Americans clinging to the prospect of a future with equal justice, serves as a stark reminder of the powerful role that racial stereotypes can play, even in a society that espouses racial equality. Although significant research has begun to pave the way for progress in the legal system, researchers must continue paving a path to justice.

2

Property Law

Implicit Bias and the Resilience of Spatial Colorlines

Michelle Wilde Anderson and Victoria C. Plaut

How much is a home worth? Who wants to live in it? Who can live in it? What kind of land uses are nearby? What kind of services does the home receive? Underlying the answers to those questions for any given piece of real property lie hundreds of private decisions by individuals. These individuals occupy many roles: buyer, seller, lender, tax assessor, landlord, tenant, real estate professional, land use planner, investor, landowner, and more.[1]

In the era of de jure segregation, the relationships of these individuals' decisions to spatial colorlines were obvious: American homes and neighborhoods were ordered according to express racial rules. Blacks can live here, whites there. Amenities, services, and other land privileges flowed to white neighborhoods. Between the 1940s and 1970s, however, fair housing advocates worked to dismantle de jure segregation in American housing. Express references to race in maintaining spatial colorlines were widely erased from law and public discourse. Indeed, scholars have noted a "positive shift in 'fundamental norms with regard to race.'"[2] Yet colorlines continue to exist in access to housing, land values, exposure to subprime lending, the siting of amenities and disamenities, and private investment. What explains this persistence?

We are grateful to Ian Haney López for invaluable substantive comments on this chapter; to Alem Tecle, Tony LoPresti, Jerett Yan, and the Culture, Diversity, and Intergroup Relations Lab for research assistance and helpful comments; and to Leslie Stone for assistance with manuscript preparation.

[1] To be clear, individual decisions are situated within and informed by sociocultural and historical contexts. *See* Victoria C. Plaut, *Diversity Science: Why and How Difference Makes a Difference*, 21 PSYCHOL. INQUIRY 77 (2010). In addition, such decisions are intertwined (in often indistinguishable ways) with decisions of the state. *See* Ian Haney López, *Institutional Racism: Judicial Conduct and a New Theory of Racial Discrimination*, 109 YALE L.J. 1717 (2000).

[2] Camille Zubrinsky Charles, *Can We Live Together? Racial Preferences and Neighborhood Outcomes*, in THE GEOGRAPHY OF OPPORTUNITY: RACE AND HOUSING CHOICE IN METROPOLITAN AMERICA 45, 48 (Xavier de Souza Briggs, ed., 2005) (quoting Lawrence Bobo, *Racial Attitudes and Relations at the Close of the Twentieth Century*, in AMERICA BECOMING: RACIAL TRENDS AND THEIR CONSEQUENCES 273 (N. Smelser, W. J. Wilson, and F. Mitchell, eds., 2001).

What explains the contradiction between a world of laws that make no mention of race and a world of segregation and neighborhood disadvantage on the ground? Lawyers and scholars of many disciplines have searched for answers to these questions for years.[3]

Implicit racial bias offers additional insight into the question of how and why racially ordered housing and neighborhoods have survived so long after the demise of de jure segregation and the gradual decline in explicitly racist social norms. Such bias describes the way our minds work even when we lack racial animus. This chapter discusses what the research on implicit bias, and social psychology more broadly, teaches us about questions relating to property, housing, and land use. Adding to the significant body of evidence from social psychology regarding implicit bias in general (evidence that is described elsewhere in this book), this chapter presents implicit bias research specifically testing how people judge neighbors and neighborhoods.

To investigate the implications of implicit bias in this setting, Part I surveys evidence of persistent colorlines in housing, neighborhoods, and mortgage markets. In Part II, we describe our conceptualization of implicit bias and assess current research about the way it operates in spatial contexts. We pose the question of legal application in Part III: Does law recognize implicit bias in the housing and land use contexts? The answer being largely no, we imagine in Part IV how the law of antidiscrimination in housing and land use might change if it did.

I. EVIDENCE OF SPATIAL COLORLINES AND RACIAL PREFERENCES IN HOUSING AND LAND USE

We first turn to the reality of housing and land use on the ground. Research on the presence of spatial colorlines is usefully sorted into three categories – raced space, raced preferences, and raced transactions – each of which is explained in this part. Although important gains along all three dimensions have been made in recent decades, progress remains both slow and substantially incomplete.[4]

Our first category, raced space, captures evidence of racial segregation and the neighborhood conditions that racial groups experience on the ground. It is the

---

[3] *See, e.g.*, Michelle Adams, *Intergroup Rivalry, Anti-Competitive Conduct and Affirmative Action*, 82 B.U. L. Rev. 1089, 1109–10, 1149–52 (2002) (hypothesizing that competitive dynamics among racial groups for a scarce resource such as access to prosperous neighborhoods operate to preserve inequalities established during a previous era); Richard Thompson Ford, *The Boundaries of Race: Political Geography in Legal Analysis*, 107 Harv. L. Rev. 1843, 1847–56 (1994) (arguing that an originally segregated landscape characterized by unequal services and conditions triggers a "circle of causation," in which inferior neighborhood conditions generate a self-fulfilling, race-neutral justification for racial exclusion).

[4] For valuable overviews of the nature and extent of ongoing residential racial discrimination and segregation, *see, e.g.*, Fragile Rights Within Cities: Government, Housing, and Fairness (John Goering, ed., 2007); The Geography of Opportunity: Race and Housing Choice in Metropolitan America (Xavier de Souza Briggs, ed., 2005).

street-level metric: Who lives where and what do their homes and neighborhoods look like? Initial reports of data from the 2010 census (as well as analysis of data from the 2000 census) indicate reduced but ongoing segregation in which racial groups continue to experience high rates of racial isolation. For instance, the average white resident lives in a census tract that is 79% white (although whites represent 64% of the general population); the average black person resides in a tract that is 46% black (compared to their 13% share of the general population); and the average Hispanic lives in a tract that is 45% Hispanic (compared to Hispanics' 16% share of the general population).[5] Segregation levels remain high in absolute terms, but change over time differs among groups: for instance, rates have fallen for blacks but not for Hispanics.[6] If patterns from Census 2000 hold as 2010 data analysis emerges, there will be considerable variation in segregation across the country, predicted by factors such as regional location, size of the urban population, proximity to a university, or size of the local minority population (i.e., minorities who represent a small share of the local population tend to be more integrated).[7] Minority preferences account for some degree of segregation, but research indicates that this factor is driven by fear of white hostility and is a weaker cause of segregation than commonly assumed.[8]

Concentrated poverty tracks these rates of segregation: blacks and Hispanics are much more likely to live in neighborhoods with high rates of poverty. According to the most recent analysis available (using Census 2000 data), 69% of the eight million people living in census tracts with the highest poverty rates (above 40%) are black or Hispanic, even though such groups represent only about a quarter of the population.[9] By contrast, more than 72% of whites live in higher income communities where the poverty rate is below the national average; blacks and Hispanics live in such tracts at less than half that rate.[10]

Evidence of raced space also captures material conditions in people's neighborhoods, including housing standards; access to basic services like water, wastewater disposal, sidewalks, and streetlights; access to amenities like parks, open space, and

---

[5] Figures describing the racial composition of census tracts come from William H. Frey, *Census Data: Blacks and Hispanics Take Different Segregation Paths*, BROOKINGS INSTITUTE: STATE OF METROPOLITAN AMERICA No. 21 (Dec. 16, 2010), *available at* http://www.brookings.edu/opinions/2010/1216_census_frey.aspx. Figures describing the race of the general U.S. population come from U.S. CENSUS, OVERVIEW OF RACE AND HISPANIC ORIGIN 2010: US CENSUS BRIEFS, Table 1 (2011), www.census.gov/prod/cen2010/briefs/c2010br-02.pdf.

[6] Frey, *supra* note 5.

[7] *See, e.g.*, Camille Zubrinsky Charles, *The Dynamics of Racial Residential Segregation*, 29 ANN. REV. OF SOC. 167, 170–76 (2003); John Iceland, *Racial and Ethnic Residential Segregation and the Role of Socioeconomic Status, 1980–2000*, in GOERING ed., *supra* note 4.

[8] *See* Maria Krysan & Reynolds Farley, *The Residential Preferences of Blacks: Do They Explain Persistent Segregation?* 80(3) SOC. FORCES 937 (2002).

[9] U.S. CENSUS BUREAU, AREAS WITH CONCENTRATED POVERTY: 1999, CENSUS 2000 SPECIAL REPORT 5, 8 (July 2005), www.census.gov/prod/2005pubs/censr-16.pdf.

[10] *Id.* at 8.

transportation; and proximity to locally undesirable land uses (LULUs) like freeways and industrial facilities. Systematic national evidence on the last of these criteria has indicated an overconcentration of LULUs in communities of color, resulting in cumulative health impacts that create dramatic public health disparities between white and minority neighborhoods.[11] We also know that minorities living in rural areas, particularly rural counties that are majority minority, face severe housing habitability problems (particularly the absence of adequate plumbing); black, Hispanic, and Native American rural households live in substandard housing at three times the rate of rural non-Hispanic whites.[12] For the other criteria, we lack comprehensive national research; however, case studies of specific locales indicate a concentration of amenities like parks in whiter communities,[13] deteriorated housing conditions in minority neighborhoods,[14] and a severe lack of basic infrastructure in populous minority communities at the fringes of many smaller American cities.[15]

The second category of colorlines evidence is raced preferences, defined here as consumer choices in considering neighborhoods and housing. For several decades, researchers in sociology and other fields have investigated housing preferences in the context of race. The biggest national study on the subject, the Multicity Study of Urban Inequality 1992–94, is now out of date, but its dramatic findings of discrimination nearly three decades after the passage of the Fair Housing Act nonetheless indicated the slow pace of change in consumer housing choices. The study consisted of an extensive, multifaceted research survey with 8,916 respondents that covered four cities (Atlanta, Boston, Detroit, and Los Angeles) and four racial groups (white, black, Hispanic, and Asian).[16] Respondents were asked about feeling comfortable and willing to move into neighborhoods with varying levels of integration between their own racial group and one other group. White responses indicated comfort with

---

[11]　*See, e.g.*, Robert D. Bullard et al., *Toxic Wastes and Race at Twenty: 1987–2007* (2007), *available at* www.ejnet.org/ej/twart.pdf; Rachel Morello Frosch & Russ Lopez, *The Riskscape and the Color Line: Examining the Role of Segregation in Environmental Health Disparities*, 102 ENVTL. RES. 181 (2006). For an example of many of the regional studies that have been performed, *see* MANUEL PASTOR ET AL., STILL TOXIC AFTER ALL THESE YEARS: AIR QUALITY AND ENVIRONMENTAL JUSTICE IN THE SAN FRANCISCO BAY AREA (Center for Justice, Tolerance & Community, University of California, Santa Cruz, 2007).

[12]　HOUSING ASSISTANCE COUNCIL, RACE, PLACE, AND HOUSING: HOUSING CONDITIONS IN RURAL MINORITY COUNTIES 12, 18, 25, 30 (2004), *available at* http://216.92.48.246/pubs/RacePlaceandHousing/index.htm.

[13]　*See, e.g.*, Pascale Joassart-Marcelli, *Leveling the Playing Field? Urban Disparities in Funding for Local Parks and Recreation in the Los Angeles Region*, 42 ENV.T & PLANNING 1174 (2009); Emily Talen, *The Social Equity of Urban Service Distribution: An Exploration of Park Access in Pueblo, Colorado and Macon, Georgia*, 18 URB. GEOGRAPHY 521 (1997).

[14]　*See, e.g.*, Emily Rosenbaum, *Racial/Ethnic Differences in Asthma Prevalence: The Role of Housing and Neighborhood Environments*, 49 J. HEALTH & SOC. BEHAV. 131 (2008) (finding that "deteriorated housing conditions" contributed to high rates of asthma among minorities living in New York City).

[15]　*See* Michelle Wilde Anderson, *Cities Inside Out: Race, Poverty, and Exclusion at the Urban Fringe*, 55 UCLA L. REV. 1095, 1106–12 (2008).

[16]　Charles, *supra* note 2, at 53.

some level of integration (up to one-third nonwhite), but such comfort fell sharply when nonwhites reached a bare majority. The lowest levels of comfort emerged for integration with blacks: less than 40% of white respondents reported feeling comfortable if 8 of 15 homes were black and less than 30% of white respondents expressed a willingness to move into such a neighborhood. Measures of willingness to move into an integrated neighborhood are particularly salient given other research indicating that "white avoidance" (in which whites are reluctant to move into areas of heavy black concentration) is a more influential contemporary dynamic than more familiar "white flight" dynamics (in which whites exit neighborhoods into which African Americans are moving).[17]

Spatial colorlines are also expressed in raced transactions, our third category of evidence, which include discrimination in housing rental, sale, assessment, and lending practices. The major national indicator for discrimination in the search for housing, both sale and rental, is the U.S. Department of Housing and Urban Development's Housing Discrimination Study of 2000, which applied paired-testing methodology to a representative sample of twenty-two metropolitan housing markets nationwide.[18] In approximately one in five visits to a real estate or rental office, black and Hispanic home seekers did not receive assistance and information that were provided to equally qualified whites; Native Americans faced even higher rates of discrimination. Discrimination against minority home seekers included denial of information about available units, denial of the chance to inspect units, steering toward units in minority neighborhoods, offers of inferior financial terms, and inferior assistance and follow-up with housing transactions.

One of the most important symbols of fair housing progress, the increase in minority homeownership in the 1990s and 2000s,[19] suffered a devastating blow with the foreclosure crisis – a blow that revealed deep colorlines in the housing credit markets. The nature and extent of the crisis drew national attention to a pattern of raced credit transactions identified by researchers more than ten years ago: minority housing loan consumers have less access to prime loans and much greater exposure to high-cost loans with less favorable terms.[20] Such patterns disadvantage both rich and poor minorities, and they persist even when controlling for class and credit risk.

---

[17] INGRID GOULD ELLEN, SHARING AMERICA'S NEIGHBORHOODS: THE PROSPECTS FOR STABLE RACIAL INTEGRATION 104–30 (2000).

[18] See Margery Austin Turner & Stephen L. Ross, How Racial Discrimination Affects the Search for Housing, in DE SOUZA BRIGGS, ed., supra note 4; Margery Austin Turner et al., Housing Discrimination in Metropolitan America: Unequal Treatment of African Americas, Hispanics, Asian Americans, and Native Americans, in GOERING, ed., supra note 4. In paired testing, white and minority home seekers separately presented equal qualifications to rental or real estate offices to inquire about advertised housing.

[19] See, e.g., john a. powell, Reflections on the Past, Looking to the Future: The Fair Housing Act at 40, 41 IND. L. REV. 605, 608 & nn. 23–24 (2008) (citing statistics).

[20] See William C. Apgar & Allegra Calder, The Dual Mortgage Market: The Persistence of Discrimination in Mortgage Lending, in DE SOUZA BRIGGS, ed., supra note 4.

Illustrating that access to good loans varied by race, African American borrowers earning 120% of area median income living in high-income black communities had 12% fewer prime loans than equivalent white borrowers in 2001.[21] As evidence that sales of subprime loans to low-income borrowers also varied by race, 27% of refinance loans to low-income borrowers in low-income neighborhoods were subprime, as compared to a rate of 42% for low-income African American borrowers living in low-income African American neighborhoods.[22] Racial segregation of those groups "racialized" the effects of the foreclosure crisis: by enabling subprime brokers to target minority neighborhoods for house-to-house marketing and sales, segregation spatially concentrated foreclosures from bad loans within minority neighborhoods.[23]

Racial identification and colorlines thus persist in neighborhood demographics, housing preferences, and housing transactions.

II. LESSONS ON RACE, HOUSING, AND SPACE FROM SOCIAL PSYCHOLOGY

How can we explain the stubbornness of these spatial colorlines? Any number of decisions organize housing, neighborhoods, and land use. Each of these decisions presents an opportunity for discretion and the exercise of independent judgment, and each such act of judgment permits implicit bias to operate in ways that protect or promote racial discrimination and segregation. For instance, consider the following:

- Buyers and tenants decide where they want to live and how much they are willing to pay for housing in a given neighborhood, establishing a level of competition that affects sale price and rental value.
- Appraisers estimate property values that affect access to credit and taxes.
- Lenders and mortgage brokers evaluate credit worthiness, determining who has access to loans and the interest rates, fees, and other conditions of such credit.
- Sellers and landlords select among prospective buyers and tenants, and real estate professionals facilitate and broker these relationships.

---

[21] *Id.* at 102–03.

[22] *Id.* at 108; *see also* Lei Ding et al., *Neighborhood Patterns of High-Cost Lending: The Case of Atlanta*, 17 J. Affordable Housing & Com'ty Dev. L. 193, 212 (2008) (finding that in Atlanta, "African American and Hispanic borrowers have a higher likelihood of obtaining a higher-priced loan, no matter which neighborhoods they live in and no matter what their income levels are."); Debbie Gruenstein et al., Unfair Lending: The Effect of Race and Ethnicity on the Price of Subprime Mortgages 3 (May 31, 2006), www.responsiblelending.org/mortgage-lending/.../rr011-Unfair_Lending-0506.pdf (finding "large and statistically significant" racial disparities in lending, even after controlling for legitimate credit risk indicators); P.S. Calem et al., *The Neighborhood Distribution of Subprime Mortgage Lending*, 29 J. Real Estate Financ. Econ. 393, 401 (2004) (finding that for "refinance loans, a Census tract that is entirely African-American homeowners has about a 19 percent higher subprime share in Philadelphia and a 17 percent higher share in Chicago compared with a tract where homeowners are all white, all else equal").

[23] Jacob S. Rugh & Douglas S. Massey, *Racial Segregation and the American Foreclosure Crisis*, 75 Am. Soc. Rev. 629, 629, 630–31, 645–46 (2010).

- Local governments decide where to locate amenities and services – everything from parks to landscaping, water systems to sewage lines, streetlights to sidewalks.
- Private actors propose, and public agencies permit, land uses that are considered neighborhood disamenities, such as polluters, freeways, and high-density housing.
- Private actors control and invest in properties, deciding what use to make of a property (a liquor store or a bakery, a car mechanic or a shop?) and how much money to put into improvements.
- And on and on.

Current research from social psychology, sociology, and social neuroscience investigates or implicates these decisions. After providing a working definition of implicit bias in the first section, this part presents this research.

A. *Conceptualization of Implicit Bias (Beyond Prejudice)*

Explicit prejudice has shown a steady decline in the last few decades. However, as this book suggests, more implicit forms of bias persist, with significant consequences for behavior toward outgroup members.[24] Much of the psychological research on implicit bias has focused on implicit prejudice, or preference for one racial group over another. As Chapter 1 discusses in detail, the tasks typically used in this research (e.g., the Implicit Association Test)[25] assess automatically activated associations (e.g., white with good vs. black with bad) that operate largely without intention or outside of awareness. The reliance of these tasks on automatic preferences render them minimally susceptible to efforts by individuals to present themselves in a positive light.[26]

Importantly, the conceptualization of implicit bias that we use in our analysis reaches beyond implicit prejudice to consider cognitive associations that may exist and exert their influence above and beyond unconscious antipathy toward people of a particular group. While much work on implicit bias research has focused on a general preference for a certain group over another, we focus here on associations of racial groups with specific concepts such as disorder, criminality, undesirable neighborhood conditions, industrial wastelands, and less-than-human status. Our purpose is not to discredit the more traditional conceptualization of implicit bias as

[24] John T. Jost et al., *The Existence of Implicit Bias Is Beyond Reasonable Doubt: A Refutation of Ideological and Methodological Objections and Executive Summary of Ten Studies that No Manager Should Ignore*, 29 RES. ORG. BEH. 39–69 (2009); *see also* John F. Dovidio et al., *Why Can't We Just Get Along? Interpersonal Biases and Interracial Distrust*, 8(2) CULT. DIVERS. & ETHNIC MINORITY PSYCHOL. 88 (2002) (describing nonverbal manifestations of implicit bias).

[25] *See e.g.*, Anthony G. Greenwald et al., *Measuring Individual Differences in Implicit Cognition: The Implicit Association Test*, 74 J. PERSONALITY & SOC. PSYCHOL. 1464 (1998).

[26] Brian A. Nosek, *Moderators of the Relationship Between Implicit and Explicit Evaluation*, 134 J. EXPERIMENTAL PSYCHOL. GEN. 565 (2005).

implicit prejudice, but rather to provide a more complete picture of implicit bias in housing and land use. As we describe in the remainder of this part, these implicit, raced associations matter – whether they operate in the absence of unconscious prejudice or in addition to it.

Our conceptualization of implicit bias can be understood as a spectrum running from explicit prejudice to implicit prejudice to implicit, raced associations. Three transitions occur along this spectrum: the expression of racial views moves from explicit to implicit, the source of these views changes from the conscious to the unconscious, and the source of these views transforms from not just individual, atomized actors but also to socially shared meanings that develop from and reinforce group relations.

B. *Perceptions of Disorder and Crime*

Raced associations of disorder and crime provide a powerful implicit mechanism for the maintenance of spatial colorlines. One study by Sampson and Raudenbusch tested the association of race with neighborhood disorder in approximately 500 census block groups in Chicago.[27] Survey respondents were asked how much of a problem they considered physical disorder (i.e., graffiti, litter, vacant housing/storefronts) and social disorder (drinking in public, selling or using drugs, and disturbance caused by teens) to be in their neighborhood.[28] The researchers then linked these perceptions to the demographic composition of the neighborhood, as indicated by Census data, while accounting for actual conditions, as indicated by police records on rates of violent crime and by systematic social observation coded for the presence of physical and social disorder (e.g., graffiti, garbage, beer bottles; drinking in public, adults fighting, selling drugs). Results showed that neighborhoods' ethnic, racial, and class composition informed both whites' and blacks' perceptions of disorder beyond the actual, systematic observation of disorder. The researchers replicated this finding with data from community leaders who lived outside the community. Just as for residents, leaders' perceptions of disorder were predicted by neighborhood racial composition, while controlling for observed disorder and the evaluations of residents.

Neighborhood racial composition also informs people's perceptions of crime – a key influence on housing choices.[29] For example, using data from Chicago, Baltimore, and Seattle, Quillian and Pager found a positive relationship between the percentage of young black men in a neighborhood and perceptions of crime, even

---

[27] Robert J. Sampson & Stephen W. Raudenbusch, *Seeing Disorder: Neighborhood Stigma and the Social Construction of "Broken Windows,"* 67(4) Soc. Psychol. Q. 319 (2004).

[28] *Id.* at 324 n.4 (concluding from other data that "residents perceive aspects of disorder 'to be a problem' primarily to the extent that they 'see' those aspects of disorder.").

[29] *See, e.g.,* Julie Berry Cullen & Steven D. Levitt, *Crime, Urban Flight, and the Consequences for Cities,* 81(2) Rev. Econ. & Stat. 159 (1999); Min Xie & David McDowall, *The Reproduction of Racial Inequality: How Crime Affects Housing Turnover,* 48(3) Criminology 865 (August 2010).

after accounting for actual crime rates.[30] The two foregoing studies bring a sobering message: people perceive neighborhood disorder and crime on the basis of the racial composition of residents, independent of signs of actual disorder and crime.

Recent research has also revealed a strong, cognitive association of race with crime. In one study by Payne, participants discriminated between weapons and harmless objects (i.e., hand tools) after being exposed to pictures of black or white faces.[31] When participants only had a half-second to respond, they more readily made a false claim of seeing a weapon if primed with black faces than if primed with white faces. Further underscoring the robustness of this implicit race–crime link, Eberhardt and colleagues demonstrated its bidirectionality: not only did participants identify a weapon faster when primed with black faces, but they also attended to black faces faster when primed with weapons.[32] These effects were not limited to undergraduate participants; notably, the researchers found the same patterns when they tested police officers.

Not only has this research unveiled a robust cognitive association between race and crime, but it also suggests that these effects operate outside of conscious awareness – and absent conscious racial intent. For example, as discussed in Chapter 1, the "shooter bias" studies used a videogame to find that race affects people's decision to shoot or not shoot an armed or unarmed target (i.e., a man holding, for example, a revolver or a cell phone).[33] Participants made the decision to shoot an armed target more quickly if he was black and made the decision not to shoot an unarmed target more quickly if he was white. Moreover, participants were more likely to mistakenly shoot an unarmed black target than an unarmed white target.[34] Notably, this shooter bias was related to perceptions of white Americans' cultural stereotypes of African Americans as aggressive, violent, and dangerous but not to personal endorsement of these stereotypes or to personal prejudice.[35]

---

[30] Lincoln Quillian & Devah Pager, *Black Neighbors, Higher Crime? The Role of Racial Stereotypes in Evaluations of Neighborhood Crime*, 107 AM. J. SOC. 717 (2001).

[31] B. Keith Payne, *Prejudice and Perception: The Role of Automatic and Controlled Processes in Misperceiving a Weapon*, 81 J. PERSONALITY & SOC. PSYCHOL. 181 (2001).

[32] Jennifer L. Eberhardt et al., *Seeing Black: Race, Crime, and Visual Processing*, 87 J. PERSONALITY & SOC. PSYCHOL. 876 (2004).

[33] Joshua Correll et al., *The Police Officer's Dilemma: Using Ethnicity to Disambiguate Potentially Threatening Individuals*, 83 J. PERSONALITY & SOC. PSYCHOL. 1314 (2002).

[34] For similar findings, *see also* Anthony G. Greenwald et al., *Targets of Discrimination: Effects of Race on Responses to Weapons Holders*, 39 J. EXPERIMENTAL SOC. PSYCHOL. 399 (2003).

[35] The cognitive link between race and crime – and aggression more generally – has deep historical roots; empirical demonstrations date back to at least 1947. *See* GORDON WILLARD ALLPORT & LEO JOSEPH POSTMAN, THE PSYCHOLOGY OF RUMOR (1947); *see also* Patricia G. Devine, *Stereotypes and Prejudice: Their Automatic and Controlled Components*, 56 J. PERSONALITY & SOC. PSYCHOL. 5 (1989); Birt L. Duncan, *Differential Social Perception and Attribution of Intergroup Violence: Testing the Lower Limits of Stereotyping of Blacks*, 34 J. PERSONALITY & SOC. PSYCHOL. 590 (1976); H. Andrew Sagar & Janet W. Schofield, *Racial and Behavioral Cues in Black and White Children's Perceptions of Ambiguously Aggressive Acts*, 39 J. PERSONALITY & SOC. PSYCHOL. 590 (1980).

Together these studies shed light on an important component of implicit bias in property-related decision-making: the widespread – often implicit – perception of predominantly black neighborhoods as suffering from disorder and crime. They also help explain why land use decisions geared at "disorder suppression" (like exclusionary zoning, public nuisance laws, and public housing demolition) so often lead to displacement of communities of color.[36]

C. Race–Space Associations

Several studies suggest that race–space associations (e.g., stereotypes of undesirable neighborhood conditions) affect important decisions about land values, neighborhood desirability, and amenities and disamenities. For example, Krysan and colleagues conducted an experiment in which participants in Chicago and Detroit viewed a video of a neighborhood designed to portray a certain social class and then gave their impressions of and predictions about the neighborhood's condition in terms of property upkeep, housing cost, safety, future property values, and quality of schools.[37] The researchers varied the composition of residents depicted in each type of neighborhood to include three racial variations (black, white, or mixed) within each social class. The results showed that, for white participants, simply seeing black residents in a neighborhood elicited more negative evaluations of the neighborhood conditions – even though in all other aspects but race the neighborhoods were identical.

A 2011 study by Bonam and colleagues further illuminates the connection between racial stereotyping of spaces and property values.[38] In this study, the researchers asked adult residents of the San Francisco Bay area (primarily of white and Asian background) to evaluate a house for sale. The house evaluation included the degree to which they liked the house, predictions of the house's appeal to others, and estimations of its market value. To assess stereotyping, the researchers then asked participants to imagine the neighborhood around the house and to report their expectation of residents' satisfaction with city services (e.g., street cleaning and garbage collection), housing and property upkeep, public schools, neighborhood safety, shopping, and access to banks. Finally, researchers also measured participants' predictions about neighborhood desirability. All participants received a buyer profile (e.g., desired square footage) and viewed pictures and a profile of a home meeting all of the criteria listed in the buyer profile. The researchers pretested pictures of the

---

[36] *See* NICOLE STELLE GARNETT, ORDERING THE CITY: LAND USE, POLICING, AND THE RESTORATION OF URBAN AMERICA 3, 20, 77–81, 101–25, 151–66 (2010).

[37] Maria Krysan et al., *In the Eye of the Beholder*, 5(1) DU BOIS REV.: SOC. SCI. RES. ON RACE 5 (2008); *see also* Maria Krysan et al., *Does Race Matter in Neighborhood Preferences? Results from a Video Experiment*, 115(2) AM. J. SOC. 527 (2009).

[38] Courtney M. Bonam et al., Devaluing Black Space: Black Locations as Targets of Housing and Environmental Discrimination (2011) (unpublished manuscript) (on file with authors).

home to make sure it was associated with a middle class homeowner and that it did not invoke an assumption that a black or white family would likely live there. While all information about the home and buyer remained constant across participants, the researchers varied the race of the family selling the home by inserting a black or white family into a picture of the living room. Importantly, the photos – each of a heteronormative family of four – did not vary along dimensions of perceived social class, racial prototypicality, friendliness, or attractiveness.

The findings of this study are highly suggestive of implicit bias. Although they evaluated exactly the same house according to the same buyer needs, participants who evaluated the house when for sale by a black family rated it more negatively than those who evaluated the house when for sale by a white family. On the stereotyping questions predicting neighbors' satisfaction with neighborhood characteristics – none of which was explicitly linked to race – participants who viewed the house for sale by the black family associated it with less resident satisfaction than those who viewed the house for sale by the white family. Statistically, this implicit stereotyping explained the racial disparity in house evaluations. Moreover, the researchers found that implicit stereotyping affected participants' sense of neighborhood desirability, which in turn affected their evaluations of the home's market value and the degree to which they liked the home.

In another study, Bonam and colleagues asked a nationally representative sample of whites to respond to a scenario involving the placement of a chemical plant. Playing the role of a chemical production company employee responsible for recommending the location of the plant near a neighborhood, participants indicated their level of opposition to the proposed placement. Half the participants were led to believe that the neighborhood was predominantly white and half that the neighborhood was predominantly black. Additionally, to manipulate perceptions of house values, participants were either given local and national housing cost information or were not given this information. In addition to assessing opposition, the researchers gauged participants' space stereotypes (e.g., how likely it is that chemical plants and other industrial facilities such as power plants and incinerators already exist nearby), sense of connection to the neighborhood, environmental concern, perceived neighborhood house values, perceived socioeconomic status of residents, and racial bias.

Results showed that participants were less likely to oppose the plant when the neighborhood was black than when it was white – regardless of housing cost information – even when controlling for participants' perceptions of house values and socioeconomic status, their concern for the environment, and their explicit feelings toward blacks. Race therefore played a role above and beyond these other factors. What about race made a difference? Participants making a decision about a predominantly black neighborhood held stronger industrial stereotypes of the neighborhood and felt less connected to the neighborhood than those evaluating the suitability of the white neighborhood. Both industrial stereotypes and the lower sense of connection resulted in lower opposition to the chemical plant. Taken together, these studies suggest the operation of implicit associations of raced spaces with lower value and desirability, with more "black" spaces (homes and neighborhoods) stereotyped as having fewer amenities and greater disamenities.[39]

These implicit, raced associations cast negative perceptions in excess of material reality (i.e., minority neighborhoods are perceived to be more disordered and deteriorated than they really are), but they also reinforce material inequality. As illustrated by Bonam and colleagues' results, these associations justify ongoing harms to minority neighborhoods (like the siting of disamenities) and reify the market advantage of living in white neighborhoods through judgments about housing value. Race–space associations therefore not only distort material reality; they undergird the material advantaging of white neighborhoods relative to minority ones.

D. *Dehumanization*

Implicit bias in important property-relevant decisions (such as placement of a chemical plant, application of building standards, and approval of affordable housing) is also informed by research on dehumanization. Research in social psychology has revealed significant and persistent implicit dehumanization linked to race. The majority of this research has focused on blacks, whose less-than-human status was once codified in law by the three-fifths clause[40] and other provisions. As the following studies suggest, this status has been preserved in the public's mind and in material reality. Research by Goff and colleagues has demonstrated, for example, that an implicit black–ape association alters visual perception and attention and implicates treatment of blacks.[41] Goff and colleagues subliminally primed participants with black or white faces or with no prime and found that those exposed to black faces more readily identified images of apes. Notably, the black–ape facilitation was not related to explicit racial attitudes or to people's motivation to control their prejudice. The researchers found the link to be bidirectional: participants primed with apes also visually attended much faster to black than white faces. Participants were also faster to categorize stereotypically black names with apes (e.g., ape, monkey, chimp) than with big cats (e.g., tiger, lion, cheetah). Importantly, as suggested by the foregoing race–crime research, this implicit association of black with ape was not mediated (or accounted for) by scores on a white-good, black-bad Implicit Association Test. Moreover, only 9% of participants indicated being aware of the cultural stereotype of blacks as apelike, underscoring the implicit nature of the association.

---

[39] Although much of the empirical work on raced associations covered here focuses on blacks (particularly crime and race–space associations), some research in social psychology suggests that these and other associations (e.g., Asians as perpetual foreigners, Latinos as perpetual foreign invaders, Native Americans as historical – to the extent they are represented at all) have important implications for the spatial exclusion of other racial minority groups as well. See Plaut, *supra* note 1, at 92.

[40] *See* US. Const. art. I, § 2, cl. 3.

[41] Phillip A. Goff et al., *Not Yet Human: Implicit Knowledge, Historical Dehumanization, and Contemporary Consequences*, 94(2) J. Personality & Soc. Psychol. 292 (2008).

Suggesting important real-world consequences of this implicit dehumanization, the researchers found that people justified police violence against blacks more when subliminally primed with ape words – but found no such effect for whites. Moreover, suggesting the powerful influence of stereotypic portrayals in the media, the researchers also found that in news coverage of capital cases black defendants were more likely to be portrayed as apelike than white defendants and that these portrayals were associated with a higher probability of being sentenced to death.

Cognitive associations of an outgroup (e.g., blacks) with animals is one of multiple modes of dehumanization.[42] For example, research on "infrahumanization," or denying human essence to outgroups suggests that people are reluctant to attribute uniquely human emotions (as opposed to those emotions shared with animals) to outgroups as opposed to ingroups.[43] People also discriminate against outgroup members on the basis of these emotions. For instance, they show less prosocial reactions and more avoidant rather than approach reactions to outgroup members who express uniquely human emotions.[44] Similar studies have focused on perceptions of personality traits of outgroup versus ingroup members (i.e., traits deemed to be uniquely human versus those deemed to be expressed by both humans and animals). Research in Canada has found, for example, that dehumanizing representations of outgroups (in this case immigrants) play an important role in the connection between disgust sensitivity and prejudice against outgroups.[45] However, echoing the implicit nature of the black–ape association, the dehumanization processes observed in these studies operate largely outside of conscious awareness and are not synonymous with outgroup hostility.

That certain outgroups are dehumanized automatically is further underscored by research in social neuroscience suggesting that the brain treats some social groups as less than human. Previous research has shown that some groups (e.g., poor blacks, poor whites, welfare recipients, Hispanics, and homeless people) typically receive low ratings on competence and warmth and elicit contemptuous prejudice (i.e., anger, contempt, disgust, hate, and resentment).[46] Using functional magnetic

---

42 *See* Nick Haslam, *Dehumanization: An Integrative Review*, 10(3) Personality & Soc. Psychol. Rev. 252 (2006).

43 Ruth Gaunt et al., *Intergroup Relations and the Attribution of Emotions: Control over Memory for Secondary Emotions Associated with Ingroup Versus Outgroup*, 38 J. Experimental Soc. Psychol. 508 (2002); Jacques-Philippe Leyens et al., *Psychological Essentialism and the Differential Attribution of Uniquely Human Emotions to Ingroups and Outgroups*, 31(4) Eur. J. Soc. Psychol. 395 (2001).

44 Jeroen Vaes et al., *On the Behavioral Consequences of Infra-Humanization: The Implicit Role of Uniquely Human Emotions on Intergroup Relations*, 85(6) J. Personality & Soc. Psychol. 1016 (2003).

45 Gordon Hodson & Kimberly Costello, *Interpersonal Disgust, Ideological Orientations, and Dehumanization as Predictors of Intergroup Attitudes*, 18(8) Psychol. Sci. 691 (2007).

46 Susan T. Fiske et al., *A Model of (Often Mixed) Stereotype Content: Competence and Warmth Respectively Follow from Perceived Status and Competition*, 82 J. Personality & Soc. Psychol. 878 (2002).

resonance imaging (fMRI),[47] Harris and Fiske examined participants' neural activity while they viewed pictures of individuals from two such socially devalued groups: homeless people and drug addicts.[48] The pictures of these individuals not only evoked disgust in study participants but also did not result in activation of participants' medial prefrontal cortex – the part of the brain that is usually involved in social cognition (i.e., the region typically activated when individuals think about people as opposed to objects). Although the study did not test responses to racially stigmatized groups, the previous research showing classification of poor racial minorities consistent with homeless people and drug addicts suggests that such "less-than-human" neural responses could reasonably be expected for these groups as well.

What does dehumanization mean for the treatment of socially devalued groups? Not only can it lead to and be used to justify genocide and aggression,[49] but it can also facilitate moral exclusion, in which rules and fair treatment need not apply to a morally excluded group.[50] Although none of this work directly links dehumanization to property decision-making, it strongly suggests a robust association between many socially devalued groups and a less-than-human status that can be expressed through property relations. It lends support to the link suspected by some legal scholars between race and lower infrastructure standards and weaker building codes in minority communities.[51] These conditions, which are associated with filth, disease, and disgust, serve both to reproduce dehumanized associations and to justify and perpetuate dehumanizing conditions.

III. THE PLACE OF IMPLICIT BIAS IN HOUSING/LAND USE ANTIDISCRIMINATION LAW

Across the better part of the twentieth century, fair housing advocates worked to dismantle the express racial ordering of American housing.[52] If we apply their gains to

---

[47] Functional MRI is a standard technique used in neuroscience that detects changes in blood oxygen levels and blood flow related to neural activity in the brain. *See, e.g.,* SCOTT A. HUETTEL ET AL., FUNCTIONAL MAGNETIC RESONANCE IMAGING (2d ed. 2004).

[48] Lasana T. Harris & Susan T. Fiske, *Dehumanizing the Lowest of the Low: Neuroimaging Responses to Extreme Out-Groups,* 17(10) PSYCHOL. SCI. 847 (2006).

[49] Daniel Bar-Tal, *Delegitimization: The Extreme Case of Stereotyping and Prejudice, in* STEREOTYPING AND PREJUDICE: CHANGING CONCEPTIONS, 169 (Daniel Bar-Tal et al. eds., 1989); Goff et al., *supra* note 41; ERVIN STAUB, THE ROOTS OF EVIL: THE ORIGINS OF GENOCIDE AND OTHER GROUP VIOLENCE (1989); Naomi Struch & Shalom H. Schwartz, *Intergroup Aggression: Its Predictors and Distinctness from In-Group Bias,* 56 J. PERSONALITY & SOC. PSYCHOL. 364 (1989).

[50] Susan Opotow, *Moral Exclusion and Injustice: An Introduction,* 46 J. SOC. ISSUES 1 (1990); Victoria M. Esses et al., *Justice, Morality, and the Dehumanization of Refugees,* 21 SOC. JUST. RES. 4 (2008).

[51] *See, e.g.,* Anderson, *Cities Inside Out, supra* note 15, at 1101, 1104–05; Jane E. Larson, *Free Markets Deep in the Heart of Texas,* 84 GEO. L.J. 179, 222–28, 229 (1995) ("Since the earliest days of Anglo presence in the Texas border region, images of personal filth and poverty and crude and disorderly housing have been offered as evidence of the innate inferiority of Mexicans."); Richard Delgado, *Rodrigo's Twelfth Chronicle: The Problem of the Shanty,* 85 GEO. L. J. 667, 672–73 (1997).

[52] For a history of legal advocacy for fair housing, *see, e.g.,* Wendell E. Pritchett, *Where Shall We Live? Class and the Limitations of Fair Housing Law,* 35 URB. LAW. 399 (2003).

our conceptualization of bias as a spectrum from explicit prejudice to implicit prejudice to implicit, raced associations, we observe both the extent of progress and the distance untraveled. Fair housing advocacy yielded constitutional and statutory protections against discrimination in housing, land use decisions, and the spending of public funds on the built environment. These reforms limited explicit prejudice (i.e., prejudice codified in law or expressed by state actors). They also made inconsistent progress against implicit prejudice. Implicit, raced associations, however, remain invisible to and unconstrained by law. This section reads spatial antidiscrimination law in terms of this spectrum of bias.

Law is most active at the express end of the bias spectrum, clearly prohibiting purposeful, intentional, racial discrimination. Fair housing advocates and courts outlawed zoning laws that explicitly divided cities by race, court enforcement of racially restrictive covenants on property, public housing assignment policies that segregated tenants, and other segregation measures.[53] The laws operative at this end of the spectrum include the equal protection clause of the Fourteenth Amendment of the U.S. Constitution, the Fair Housing Act (FHA), sections 1981 and 1982 of the Civil Rights Act of 1866, private rights of action under Title VI of the Civil Rights Act of 1964, and many analogous state laws.[54]

Such prohibitions against intentional discrimination bar two general categories of conduct: (1) laws that are discriminatory on their face (e.g., a zoning ordinance enforcing housing segregation), and (2) laws or practices that are neutral on their face but are applied in a discriminatory manner (e.g., a public housing assignment policy does not mention race, but officials assign households to developments according to race). To prove intentional discrimination successfully, plaintiffs must usually produce "direct evidence" (like overly racist statements) that discriminatory animus "actually motivated" the challenged action – a standard that requires a plaintiff to prove that a defendant expressed prejudice against a protected group.[55] As race relations have progressed, evidence of this type has become increasingly scarce.

From the point of view of social psychology and the spectrum of bias described here, an actor who conceals discriminatory intent still harbors explicit prejudice. The prohibition against intentional discrimination, however, reaches such conduct

---

[53] *See* Shelley v. Kraemer, 334 U.S. 1 (1948); Buchanan v. Warley, 245 U.S. 60 (1917); Hills v. Gautreaux, 425 U.S. 284 (1976).

[54] *See* U.S. CONST. Amend. V, XIV; 42 U.S.C. § 3604 *et seq.* (2006); 42 U.S.C. §§ 1981–82 (2006); 42 U.S.C. § 2000d *et seq.* (2006). For analogous state laws, *see, e.g.,* Cal. Gov't. Code § 11135 (West 2005). A few additional antidiscrimination protections in housing and land use also exist, including the due process clause of the Fifth and Fourteenth Amendments and the Thirteenth Amendment. These laws have been construed to apply in very narrowly defined factual circumstances. Because this narrowing has been unrelated to issues of defendant motivation, evidence of implicit bias is unlikely to affect interpretation of these laws.

[55] *See, e.g.,* Gallagher v. Magner, 619 F.3d 823, 831 (8th Cir. 2010) (defining direct evidence and specifying that such evidence excludes "stray remarks . . . , statements by nondecisionmakers, or statements by decisionmakers unrelated to the decisional process itself" [internal citations and quotation marks removed]).

only if the plaintiff can produce indirect or circumstantial evidence that creates "an inference of discriminatory intent."[56] Successful allegations of this kind are very unusual.[57] Some courts also seek to uncover veiled, explicit prejudice by carefully scrutinizing a defendant's subjective or arbitrary justifications for a challenged housing decision.[58] These courts have held that canny people may hide or lie about explicit bias by relying on subjective explanations.[59] That skepticism does not, however, translate into an assumption that subjective reasons for a housing decision are necessarily pretextual.[60]

As far as these forays into a defendant's motives may venture, they are constrained by the central limitation of all intentional discrimination cases: the discrimination must be knowing (intentional, explicit racism), and a plaintiff must prove the defendant's "actual" (not "hypothetical") reasons for an adverse housing decision.[61] This means that prohibitions on intentional discrimination theoretically can reach a defendant who masks his or her prejudice, but they can push no further to address implicit bias or associations that operate below the surface of a defendant's conscious control.

Beyond this coverage at the explicit end of the bias spectrum, only the federal Fair Housing Act and some state analogs offer limited additional coverage reaching toward implicit prejudice.[62] Thus far at least, courts have interpreted the Fair

---

[56] *See* Robert G. Schwemm, Housing Discrimination Law and Litigation 10–8–10–9 (2010) (analyzing the inference of intent for purposes of the FHA); *id.* at 28–10–28–11 (analyzing proof of intent under the equal protection clause of the Fourteenth Amendment).

[57] Comm. Concerning Comty. Improvement v. City of Modesto, 583 F.3d 690, 703 (9th Cir. 2009).

[58] *See* Schwemm, *supra* note 56, at 10–10–10–21 (analyzing proof of intent under the Fair Housing Act, including a defendant's burden of production to articulate a legitimate nondiscriminatory reason for his or her action).

[59] *See, e.g.*, Frazier v. Rominger, 27 F.3d 828, 832 (2d Cir. 1994) ("In some cases, it may be expected that these subjective justifications will be a sham, camouflaging nothing more than an animus towards minority applicants." [internal citations omitted]); Pughsley v. 3750 Lake Shore Drive Co-op. Bldg., 463 F.2d 1055, 1056 (7th Cir. 1972) ("when the asserted justification is itself somewhat arbitrary, it is particularly important that the trier of fact consider all admissible evidence that may illuminate the real motivation of the defendants").

[60] *See* Frazier v. Rominger, 27 F.3d 828, 832 (2d Cir. 1994) (finding that sometimes, a "proffered justification will accurately reflect the defendant's real motivation"); Soules v. U.S. Dep't of Hous. & Urban Dev., 967 F.2d 817, 82–23 (2d Cir. 1992) (finding that "[t]here is less reason to be wary of subjective explanations, though, where a defendant provides objective evidence indicating that truth lies behind his assertions of nondiscriminatory conduct" [internal citations omitted]).

[61] *See* Robinson v. 12 Lofts Realty, Inc., 610 F.2d 1032, 1039–1040 (2d. Cir 1979); Frazier v. Rominger, 27 F.3d 828, 832 (2d Cir. 1994).

[62] The equal protection clause, the Civil Rights Act of 1866, and Title VI only reach intentional discrimination. *See* Village of Arlington Heights v. Metro. Hous. Dev. Corp., 429 U.S. 252 (1977) (first applying the intent requirement of the equal protection clause in a housing case); Gen. Bldg. Contractors Ass'n v. Pennsylvania, 458 U.S. 375, 382–91 (1981) (applying the intent requirement to Section 1981 of the Civil Rights Act of 1866); Phiffer v. Proud Parrot Motor Hotel, Inc., 648 F.2d 548, 551 (9th Cir. 1980) (applying the intent requirement to Section 1982 of the Civil Rights Act of 1866); Guardian Ass'n v. Civil Service Comm'n of City of New York, 463 U.S. 582, 591–96 (1983) (interpreting Section 601 of Title VI to require proof of intentional discrimination); Alexander v. Sandoval, 532 U.S.

Housing Act to prohibit some discriminatory effects of a housing-related decision,[63] which are defined to include two types of claims: disparate impact (for instance, a zoning policy with significantly greater adverse impact on members of a protected class) or perpetuation of segregation (such as municipal actions to block the development of housing expected to be occupied by minorities in predominantly white neighborhoods).[64] Plaintiffs in such cases can challenge neutrally worded policies and/or neutrally applied practices (not a single act by the defendant) that nevertheless cause more harm to some racial groups.

Discriminatory effect liability arose from two important insights about the nature of bias. The first is that motive is a slippery, private thing. In the face of legal liability for express discrimination, people (whether public or private actors) have every reason not to disclose it, and the plaintiff's burden to prove it may be insurmountable.[65] Second, this doctrine sought to move the legal system toward harm reduction and integration, regardless of perpetrator motive.[66]

Yet such cases are increasingly difficult to prove for a number of reasons. For one, evidence of discriminatory intent provides the surest course for relief, even in discriminatory effect cases – a rule that keeps such cases closely tethered to the explicit end of the bias spectrum. Several circuits make some evidence of intent one of the factors for proving discriminatory effect in perpetuation of segregation claims.[67] Other rules similarly hamper discriminatory effect claims. For instance, a plaintiff must prove that members of a protected class are significantly more adversely affected by the challenged policy or practice than nonclass members; complex statistical proof of impact (usually prepared by experts) is required, and over time, courts have narrowed the band of cognizable significance and adequate

---

275, 293 (2001) (holding that within Title VI, only Section 601 gives a private right of action in federal court).

[63] Every circuit to have considered the issue recognized discriminatory effect liability. *See* Schwemm, *supra* note 56, at 10–33–10–38 (citing cases). However, the Supreme Court recently took certiorari on the issue (though the case was ultimately withdrawn), indicating that the Court may intend to upend this settled law. *See* Gallagher v. Magner, 619 F.3d 823 (8th Cir. 2010) *certiorari granted by* 132 S. Ct. 548 (Nov. 7, 2011).

[64] Schwemm, *supra* note 56, at 10–42–10–43, 10–52.

[65] *See, e.g.*, United States v. City of Black Jack, Mo., 508 F.2d 1179, 1185 (8th Cir. 1974) ("Effect, and not motivation, is the touchstone [of the FHA], in part because clever men may easily conceal their motivations, but more importantly, because whatever our law was once, we now firmly recognize that the arbitrary quality of thoughtlessness can be as disastrous and unfair to private rights and the public interest as the perversity of a willful scheme" [internal quotation marks and alternations removed]).

[66] *See id.*; *see also* Charles R. Lawrence III, *The Id, the Ego, and Equal Protection: Reckoning with Unconscious Racism*, 39 STAN. L. REV. 317 (1987) (theorizing how a motive-centered jurisprudence undermines the reduction of harms caused by discrimination).

[67] *See* Metro. Hous. Dev. Corp. v. Village of Arlington Heights, 558 F. 2d 1283, 1290 (7th Cir. 1977) (establishing intent as a factor in perpetuation of segregation cases); Schwemm, *supra* note 56, at 10–55 n.18 (citing circuits that make intent a factor); *see also* R.J. Investments, L.L.C. v. Bd. of County Comm'rs for Queen Anne's County, 414 Fed.Appx. 551, 554 (4th Cir. 2011) (holding that a plaintiff failed to show discriminatory impact because there was "not a scintilla of evidence" of discriminatory intent).

proof.[68] Finally, analysis of these claims (as with intentional discrimination claims) gives defendants an opportunity to show a "business necessity sufficiently compelling to justify the challenged practice"[69] or "bona fide and legitimate justifications for its action,"[70] and such evidence is drawing increased deference by courts.[71] These constraints mean that a case without some evidence of explicit, intentional discrimination is difficult to win even under the Fair Housing Act.

The mandate to prove racially discriminatory intent thus pervades all antidiscrimination laws in the housing and land context. The law sees only explicit prejudice and those cases of implicit prejudice that are most suggestive of a biased defendant. According to our legal system, racial discrimination in housing is a phase of history now behind us. Any last cases are merely the stragglers, slow to catch on to a more moral modernity. Implicit prejudice is largely unconstrained by law. Implicit racial associations are unseen and unremedied, whatever their harms.

IV. THE IMPLICATIONS OF RECOGNIZING IMPLICIT BIAS

Research on implicit bias indicates the dramatic ways that racial minorities, particularly African Americans, are dehumanized, discounted, and disparaged in property contexts. As described in the previous part, housing and land use antidiscrimination laws fall far short of reaching these harms. At least two implications follow.

First, in civil rights cases, implicit bias research should educate judges and other lawmakers about the ways that race operates even where it is not on the surface of statements in evidence, thus drawing courts back from the harsh skepticism they now apply to disparate treatment and discriminatory effect claims.[72] Implicit bias research supports a higher probability that bias – and the long, painful history of racial hierarchy that underlies it – is operative in a wider range of circumstances than

---

[68] *See, e.g.,* Artisan/Am. Corp. v. City of Alvin, 588 F.3d 291, 298–99 (5th Cir. 2009) (rejecting the plaintiff's expert statistical evidence where it concerned a probable but not actual applicant pool for housing, regardless of the practical availability of an actual pool); Reinhart v. Lincoln County, 482 F.3d 1225, 1230–31 (10th Cir. 2007) (rejecting the plaintiff's expert evidence of disparate impact and specifying a complex method of proof).

[69] Betsey v. Turtle Creek Assoc., 736 F.2d 983, 988 (4th Cir. 1984).

[70] Huntington Branch, NAACP v. Town of Huntington, 844 F.2d 926, 939 (2d Cir. 1988), *aff'd in part,* 488 U.S. 15 (1988).

[71] *See, e.g.,* Oti Kaga, Inc. v. S.D. Hous. Dev. Auth., 342 F.3d 871, 883–84 (8th Cir. 2003).

[72] As one example of a case highlighting the implications of implicit bias research, see Hallmark Developers v. Fulton County, Georgia, 466 F.3d 1276 (11th Cir. 2006). The evidence produced in the case included few explicit references to race as a motivating factor in defendants' decisions (though there were some). Yet defendants' actions to exclude affordable housing expected for occupancy by blacks were not otherwise justified by any specific concerns with the project. Defendants' vague and unspecific objections to the "quality" of the project, despite pressure to articulate more precise and remediable criticisms, were consistent with what may have been a shared but unspoken view among defendants that the occupying population would cause harm to the community, such as crime, disorder, and deterioration.

recognized by courts today. This research suggests that racial dynamics articulated verbally are only one dimension of deeper, implicit prejudice and race–space associations that continue to animate decisions related to property and to harm racial minorities. Implicit bias research undermines the notion that ongoing exclusion and adverse housing impacts on minorities are the result of market forces or other race-neutral dynamics alone. This research should inform the Supreme Court's consideration of disparate impact liability under the Fair Housing Act.[73]

This does not mean, of course, that all adverse housing decisions are appropriate for a litigation-based remedy. Undoubtedly, there is a point beyond which implicit bias research alone should not carry a finding against a specific defendant subject to individualized sanctions. The shared harms of implicit bias should result in shared solutions and integration-based remedies. Indeed, research showing the strength of implicit bias against racial minorities lends support to theories that view racial dynamics as structural, institutional, and social processes rather than a system of atomistic, individualized decisions.[74] Race–space associations and other indicators of implicit bias undermine confidence in the ability of adversarial dispute resolution (a test of an individual defendant's culpability) to go any further in disturbing deeply rooted colorlines.

The second key implication of evidence of implicit bias is to signal the importance of investment in fair housing policies and programs, such as state or local inclusionary zoning laws; federal, state, and local grantmaking to improve housing quality and infrastructure in rural and urban areas; fair lending laws; investment in community economic development programs; regional equity programs; and federal enforcement of local governments' statutory obligation to "affirmatively further" fair housing through land use planning.[75] Such measures go to the heart of both a cause and consequence of implicit bias: to preserve the existing distribution of material advantage. In addition, they escape the fiction underlying antidiscrimination law and litigation that we can disentangle the actions of private individuals from the public domain and identify a market that exists free of state influence. Freed of both individualized blame-seeking and the state action muddle, fair housing policies seek to provide shared remedies for shared harms.

---

[73] *See* Gallagher, 132 S.Ct. 548, *supra* note 63.

[74] *See, e.g.,* Haney López, *supra* note 1; john a. powell, *Structural Racism: Building upon the Insights of John Calmore*, 86 N.C. L. Rev. 791 (2008); *see also* Ian Haney López, *Post-Racial Racism: Racial Stratification and Mass Incarceration in the Age of Obama*, 98 Cal. L. Rev. 1023, 1027 (2010) (emphasizing a "structural racism" approach that focuses on "larger social processes rather than interpersonal dynamics").

[75] *See e.g.,* Cecily T. Talbert et al., *Recent Developments in Inclusionary Zoning*, 33 Urb. Law. 701 (2006) (providing an overview of state and local inclusionary zoning programs); Elizabeth K. Julian, *Inclusive Communities Financial Institutions: Investing in a More Ambitious Vision for the Future*, in Public Housing and the Legacy of Segregation 61–65 (Margery Austin Turner et al., eds. 2009) (describing current community development and financial institution programs and proposing changes).

V. CONCLUSION

Spatial colorlines in property and land use persist despite significant shifts in explicit norms concerning race. Current research on implicit bias in the context of housing, neighborhoods, and land use helps explain the resilience of these patterns. Experiments testing automatic biases and associations beneath the conscious surface indicate that the American mind is marked by colorlines that associate minorities with criminality, assign lower comfort and value to homes occupied by or near minorities, and depict minorities as less than human. Antidiscrimination law in the context of property fails to account for the presence of these associations.

Implicit bias affects the conditions of the material world by legitimizing social structure and by influencing access to good housing in neighborhoods with good schools, public and private investment, and other factors. Of course, the mind – perhaps in ways intended to preserve group advantage – also maps existing material reality: deteriorated material conditions, lower housing values, and elevated crime rates reinforce implicit bias. Spatial colorlines thus reinforce implicit bias as much as they are produced by it. We leave further exploration of this cycle of bias to materiality to bias for another day, but we offer this concluding observation: whatever the underlying causes of implicit bias may prove to be, its existence provides an additional layer of insight into why housing inequality and segregation persist despite the dismantling of an express racial order in American property law.

3

Criminal Law

Coloring Punishment: Implicit Social Cognition and Criminal Justice

Charles Ogletree, Robert J. Smith, and Johanna Wald

The United States has become the world's leader in incarceration. The size and pervasiveness of the criminal justice regime have no parallel in history. One in 100 citizens are locked away in prisons and jails[1] – a figure that reflects a tenfold expansion in the corrections population in less than four decades.[2] If we count those individuals who are currently on probation or parole, more than 7 million men and women are under legal supervision – a number equal to the population of Israel.[3] This system of mass incarceration – which includes policing, corrections, and the courts – employs 2.2 million Americans[4] – which exceeds the 1.7 million Americans employed in higher education and the 650,000 employed by the system of public welfare.[5] At the turn of the millennium, approximately 1.5 million children had at least one parent in jail or prison, and 10 million have had a parent in jail at some time during their lives.[6]

---

[1] The Pew Center on the States, One in a Hundred: Behind Bars in America in 2008 (2008), *available at* http://www.pewcenteronthestates.org/uploadedFiles/One%20in%20100.pdf.

[2] The Sentencing Project, Facts About Prisons and Prisoners (2007), *available at* http://www.ala.org/ala/aboutala/offices/olos/prison_facts.pdf.

[3] Amanda Petteruti & Nastassia Walsh, Moving Target: A Decade of Resistance to the Prison Industrial Complex 6 (2008), *available at* http://www.justicepolicy.org/uploads/justicepolicy/documents/moving_target.pdf.

[4] *Id.*

[5] Jason Ziedenberg, Deep Impact, Quantifying the Impact of Prison Expansion in the South (2003), *available at* http://www.justicepolicy.org/uploads/justicepolicy/documents/03-04-rep-deepimpact_ac.pdf. Annual expenditures for this revolving prison system reached $57 billion in 2001 ($167 billion for police, prisons, and courts combined), and these figures do not begin to account for productivity losses or other social costs. *See* Fox Butterfield, *With Longer Sentences, Cost of Fighting Crime Is Higher*, N.Y. Times, May 3, 2004, *available at* http://www.nytimes.com/2004/05/03/national/03STUD.html.

[6] Council on Crime and Justice, Children of Incarcerated Parents (2006) *available at* www.racialdisparity.org/files/CCJ%20CIP%20FINAL%20REPORT.pdf.

Racial disparities are a defining feature of this regime. One in eight black males between the ages of 20–29 are in prison or jail on any given day, as compared with 1 in 59 white males of the same age.[7] At the beginning of the new millennium black males had almost a 1 in 3 chance of serving time in prison, as compared with 3 in 50 for white males.[8] The Leadership Conference on Civil Rights has suggested that current criminal justice policies and practices "threaten to render irrelevant fifty years of hard-fought civil rights progress."[9]

There are varied explanations for these disparities. Most analyses point to a constellation of complex and interrelated structural and institutional factors that include poverty, high rates of joblessness, low levels of education, and the clustering of blacks and Latinos in concentrated urban areas that are more heavily policed than predominantly white suburban and rural areas. In this chapter, we put forth a complementary analysis, one intended to fill in gaps that we consider to be missing from these structural analyses. The ongoing racial disparities evidenced in every phase of the criminal justice system can be at least partly explained by the levels of implicit racial bias held by key actors in the system. Although we cannot yet offer "the smoking gun" that indisputably links the presence of implicit bias among decision-makers to harsher criminal sanctions for black Americans, our hypothesis is backed by a robust and fast-growing literature that has developed over the past decade. This scholarship demonstrates conclusively that Americans (whites and people of color alike) possess negative implicit biases against black citizens. These implicit race biases are held by liberals and conservatives; by young people and old; and by residents on the East Coast, the West Coast, the South, and the Midwest. They often coexist, unknowingly by the holder, alongside more overtly egalitarian views. What makes them so important in any discussion about race and the law is that these implicit biases frequently determine our actions and sway our decisions.[10] In the criminal justice context, these biases lead, for example, to more arrests and harsher sentences for blacks than for whites who commit similar offenses.

It is vital to understand and document more fully how and where implicit biases operate within the criminal justice system. Doing so will enable us to develop

---

[7] United States Census Bureau, Profile of General Population and Housing Characteristics: 2010 (2010), *available at* http://factfinder2.census.gov/faces/tableservices/jsf/pages/productview.xhtml?pid=DEC_10_DP_DPDP1&prodType=table.

[8] Thomas P. Bonczar, Prevalence of Imprisonment in the US Population, 1974–2001, at 8 (2003), *available at* http://bjs.ojp.usdoj.gov/content/pub/pdf/piuspo1.pdf.

[9] Ronald H. Weich & Carlos T. Angulo, *Justice on Trial: Racial Disparities in the American Criminal Justice System*, Leadership Conf. on C.R. (2000), *available at* http://www.protectcivilrights.org/pdf/reports/justice.pdf.

[10] *See* Jerry Kang & Mahzarin Banaji, *Fair Measures: A Behavioral Realist Revision of "Affirmative Action,"* 94 Cal. L. Rev. 1063 (2006); Anthony Greenwald & Linda Krieger, *Implicit Bias: Scientific Foundations*, 94 Cal. L. Rev. 945 (2006).

policies, practices, and strategies aimed at identifying and reducing their effects. In this chapter, we offer specific illustrations of how implicit racial bias influences the actions of key decision-makers at various phases of our criminal justice system. This chapter is not intended to be a comprehensive examination of the role of implicit bias within the criminal justice system; rather its objective is to match the literature on implicit bias with actual examples of its "real-world" effects. From the formulation of criminal justice policy, to the decision to target citizens of a particular race, to the selection of criminal petit juries, the impact of implicit race bias on decisions about arrests, sentences, and severity of punishment is broad and deep.

This chapter proceeds in five parts. Part I sets the stage for this analysis, introducing key implicit racial bias studies that demonstrate that the face of crime in America is black. More specifically, it documents that black citizens are considered to be more dangerous, hostile, and prone to criminality and also less fully human than white citizens. Building on this foundation, Part II examines the role that implicit racial bias plays in the formulation of crime policy. Part III examines why implicit racial bias might drive disparate outcomes in the enforcement of criminal laws. This part examines the phenomenon in two distinct contexts: (1) the decision to punish a student in the school discipline context and (2) the use of unnecessary force in police–citizen encounters. Part IV uses the example of discriminatory jury selection to explore how implicit racial bias might contribute to the exclusion of black citizens from the criminal justice decision-making process. Part V concludes the chapter.

I. THE FACE OF CRIME IN AMERICA IS BLACK

Who commits crime? Are criminals dangerous by nature, or are they driven to crime by the circumstances and conditions in which they live? Are criminals incorrigible, or could they become productive, law-abiding members of society? Many Americans reflexively answer those questions in the following manner: blacks commit crime, blacks are prone to violence and are dangerous by disposition, and blacks possess largely fixed personality traits and thus are incapable of change. Our argument is that because crime and law enforcement are inseparable from our conception of the criminal, these automatic, negative assumptions about blacks trigger a host of assumptions about how society should act to prevent crime or to rehabilitate and release those who commit crimes. The results are laws and policies that have the effect of targeting black citizens, particularly young black men, and of creating disparate criminal sentencing regimes. Before we articulate some possible mechanisms through which implicit race biases translate into disparate outcomes in criminal law policy, law enforcement, and community participation, we explore the literature that demonstrates a series of commonly held core implicit biases that operate against black citizens.

A. *Black People Are Hostile, Dangerous, and Prone to Criminality*

Black citizens are often associated with violence, dangerousness, and crime. The process might go something like this. A person sees a black face. The brain categorizes the person as being black, which in turn triggers a storehouse of beliefs about black people: they are dangerous, criminal, violent. Without consciously comparing the automatically activated stereotype-driven knowledge to consciously held ethical beliefs or to careful fact checking, the brain uses this stereotypic knowledge as a filter through which other incoming information is processed. A person whose brain has activated the concept of crime, dangerousness, and violence is likely to interpret incoming stimuli in a manner consistent with crime, dangerousness, and violence.

Take, for example, a study by Professor Jennifer Eberhardt and her colleagues where participants were shown a series of images of either crime-relevant (gun, knife) or crime-irrelevant (camera, book) objects.[11] All of the objects were displayed in the context of a neighborhood calculated to appear to the participants as socioeconomically disadvantaged. The images first appeared in extremely degraded fashion, but gradually came into sharper focus over forty-one frames. The goal was to chart how quickly the participants recognized the objects to be crime-relevant. Before the first images appeared on the screen, however, each participant was shown a consciously imperceptible image of a white face, a black face, or no face. The results showed that participants recognized a "knife" or "gun" in far fewer frames when primed with a black face than when primed with either a white face or no face. Indeed, when primed with a white face, participants took significantly more frames to accurately identify a "knife" or a "gun" than when they were not primed with a face. This study suggests that, literally, the "face" of crime in America is black and, more, that being white is actively disassociated with (at least street) crime.

The process of seeing a black face and thinking hostility, dangerousness, or criminality is likely driven by fear. Consider a study conducted by Professor Matthew Lieberman and his colleagues that used functional magnetic resonance imaging (fMRI) technology to measure the level of amygdala activity of participants after seeing a black versus a white face.[12] The amygdala is a region of the brain that mediates emotional responses, including fear from perceived threats. Lieberman found that amygdala activity in both white and black participants increased when shown a black face versus a white face. The authors concluded that the most plausible explanation for this universal increase in amygdala activity is activation of the stereotype of blacks as threatening.

---

[11] Jennifer L. Eberhardt et al., *Seeing Black: Race, Crime, and Visual Processing*. 87 J. PERSONALITY & SOC. PSYCHOL. 6 (2004).

[12] Matthew D. Lieberman et al., *An fMRI Investigation of Race-related Amygdala Activity in African-American and Caucasian-American Individuals*, 8 NATURE NEUROSCIENCE 720 (2005), *available at* http://www.scn.ucla.edu/pdf/nature%20neuroscience%20press/nn1465.pdf.

The general concept that seeing a black face triggers a host of negative stereotypes that then act like tinted lenses through which situational stimuli are interpreted is troubling enough. That this chain reaction activates a fear response is worse. Yet it is the clustering of black people into disproportionately poor and crime-ridden urban neighborhoods that dramatically aggravates these elements. There is more opportunity for activation of the black-dangerousness, black-criminal, and black-violence-prone stereotypes, which means more situational stimuli are interpreted through the filter of these stereotypes, which translates into more pedestrians, police officers, and politicians who mistake handshakes for the exchange of drugs, wallets for weapons, and youths gathered to play basketball for gangs. We see black, think danger, and find crime without the mental due process that is afforded to other citizens in other locales. The implications for the criminal justice are endless.

B. *Black People Are Less Human than White People*

It is easy to imagine how the association between black people and dangerousness, violence, and crime drives criminal justice outcomes: crimes seen as disproportionately committed by black people might be punished more harshly. Police officers interacting with black citizens might be more inclined to stop and frisk a black youth than a white youth even if both are engaging in the same behavior. Judges might assign a higher bond to a black suspect charged with the same offense as a white suspect. There is a different side of the criminal justice coin, however.

At the same time that our criminal justice system over-targets poor black people, it under-serves many of the communities where (the same) people of color live in concentrated poverty and are exposed to violence on a daily basis. Implicit racial bias may help explain this cycle, which might be perpetuated through the implicit dehumanization of black citizens. In a study by Philip Goff and colleagues, participants viewed a degraded image of an ape that came into focus over a number of frames.[13] The study found that, when primed with a consciously undetectable image of a black face, participants were able to identify the ape in fewer frames. When primed with a consciously undetectable white face, however, participants required more frames to recognize the ape than when they received no prime at all. This study indicates that citizens implicitly associate blacks with apes and also have negative associations between whites and apes, a finding that the authors suggest might stem from the conception of blacks as "less evolved" (and thus closer in evolutionary terms to apes) than white people.

It appears that the black–ape association has frightening real-world consequences. Professor Goff asked a different set of participants to watch a video of a black suspect

---

[13] *See* Philip A. Goff et al., *Not Yet Human: Implicit Knowledge, Historical Dehumanization, and Contemporary Consequences*, 94 J. PERSONALITY & SOC. PSYCHOL. 292, 306 (2008).

being beaten by police officers.[14] Before viewing the video, participants were primed either with a consciously undetectable image of an ape or a consciously undetectable image of a big cat. Participants primed with the ape image were more likely to report that the police beating was "deserved" and "justified" than those participants primed with the big cat image. This finding is consistent with the broader literature on dehumanization, which suggests that as a person becomes dehumanized it is both increasingly more difficult for people to express empathy toward and attribute a range of positive emotions to the dehumanized subject.

This dehumanization of black citizens is relevant in the criminal justice context. Politicians and police departments alike must decide how to allocate scarce public safety resources. The conception of black citizens as beings who are generally inferior to white citizens is relevant as police officers with limited resources determine which areas to patrol. Such stereotypes could be responsible for the under-allocation of resources to black communities that occurs when police ignore or neglect neighborhoods with a high concentration of minority group members. If police officers see black citizens as being inferior to white citizens, and believe that blacks are criminal by nature and less capable of change, then the conclusion might be that it will not make much difference to police a minority-group-dominated neighborhood with high concentrations of poverty and crime. This lack of consideration for the humanity of blacks, and especially blacks who live in areas of concentrated violence and poverty, has an impact not only on whether officers police their neighborhoods but also on how severe officers perceive a reported crime to be and how vigorously the officers are willing to investigate a case or track down a suspect. Similarly, after offenders have served their time, the determination of who to release early or how restrictive parole conditions should be might be influenced by the conception that black citizens have less dynamic personality traits and are thus less capable of rehabilitation and redemption than white citizens.

Now that we have explored how black citizens are associated with crime, violence, and dangerousness and also that they are considered to be less human than white citizens, the remainder of this chapter views the ramifications of these implicit race biases for the formulation of crime policy, the enforcement of criminal laws, and the participation of community members on criminal petit juries.

II. IMPLICIT RACIAL BIAS AND THE FORMULATION OF CRIME POLICY

Consider how crime policy is formulated. If politicians think of a black male when they think of what the punishment for a particular crime should be, then the idea that black citizens are violent, dangerous, and prone to criminality might lead to the conclusion that the punishment should be swift and harsh in order to incapacitate and to deter. Again, fear is often present in these decisions. Think of the arguments

[14] *Id.*

that unchecked violence or drug use would radiate out from poor urban areas into the suburbs (i.e., into the areas where many politicians and their most influential constituents and donors live).

Len Bias and the crack–powdered cocaine sentencing disparity, as discussed in this section, offer a vivid example of these dynamics at work. This disparity – which Congress recently reduced from 100:1 to 18:1 – is a significant factor driving the huge racial disparities that now exist in our jails and prisons. Data on federal convictions reflect a black–crack cocaine/white–powdered cocaine dichotomy: 82% of federal defendants convicted in 2006 for distributing crack cocaine were African American, whereas only 9% were white.[15]

A dose of history speaks volumes. In the early 1980s crack cocaine use began to increase throughout urban communities, quickly gaining media attention as an example of illicit drug use on the rise. The use of crack cocaine came to be associated with increasing violence in cities. Then, in June 1986, one day after being drafted by the Boston Celtics as the number two overall pick in the National Basketball Association draft, 22-year-old standout college basketball star Len Bias died suddenly after ingesting cocaine. Although Bias, an African American, actually died after using cocaine in its powder form, the widespread perception was – and still is – that Bias died from using crack.

The political response to Bias's death was swift and ferocious. Within months, the Senate passed the Anti-Drug Abuse Act, which included the 100:1 crack–powdered sentencing disparity. Len Bias's name was mentioned eleven times during the Senate hearings on the Bill.[16] The persistence of the inaccurate description that crack cocaine caused Len Bias's death, and the 100:1 disparity that its narrative appears to have helped dictate might well have been driven by implicit race bias. Our legislators saw a young black male dead from a cocaine overdose and assumed that the dead man must have died from crack cocaine. Once the debate became racialized, fear of black people ratcheted up the perceived dangerousness of crack cocaine use versus the use of powdered cocaine, and the stereotype that blacks are violent and prone to criminality further justified the huge disparity between sentences for the use of crack and powdered cocaine.

The far-reaching effects of implicit bias on policymaking might also be found beyond the specific example of the crack–powdered disparity to the genesis of America's "drug war" more generally. Instead of attempting to cure addiction or targeting the underlying causes of rampant drug abuse, our nation's lawmakers chose to invest huge resources in enforcement of lengthy mandatory prison sentences for drug use.

---

[15] HUMAN RIGHTS WATCH, TARGETING BLACKS: DRUG LAW ENFORCEMENT AND RACE IN THE UNITED STATES (2008), *available at* http://www.hrw.org/sites/default/files/reports/us0508_1.pdf.

[16] United States Sentencing Commission, *The National Legislative and Law Enforcement Response to Cocaine*, in REPORT TO CONGRESS ON COCAINE AND FEDERAL SENTENCING POLICY, Ch. 6 (1995), *available at* http://www.ussc.gov/Legislative_and_Public_Affairs/Congressional_Testimony_and_Reports/Drug_Topics/199502_RtC_Cocaine_Sentencing_Policy/CHAP6.HTM.

Almost one-fifth of persons being held in state prisons and jails in 2008 were impris-
oned for nonviolent drug offenses.[17] Black citizens bear the brunt of the broken
system. Although blacks and whites use and distribute drugs at comparable rates,[18]
African Americans were arrested for drug offenses in every year between 1980 and
2007 at rates between 2.8 and 5.5 times higher than whites.[19] The common mis-
perception that blacks use drugs more prevalently than whites might be driving a
type of self-fulfilling prophecy. Research from the field of cognitive science demonstrates that, although people tend to make unconscious associations between African
Americans and crime generally, the strongest racial association is between blacks
and drug offenders.[20]

Despite equal rates of drug use, Americans mistakenly assume that blacks use
drugs more than whites.[21] It is reasonable to assume that because the face of drug
crime is black, when policymakers (and their constituents) consider crime policy
options, the stereotype of the violent black criminal has a substantial impact on drug
policy.

III. IMPLICIT RACIAL BIAS AND DISPARITIES IN THE ENFORCEMENT OF CRIMINAL LAWS

Even when crime policies are free from racial taint, implicit and otherwise, racial
disparities in the criminal justice system are visible in the enforcement of criminal
laws. America arrests and incarcerates a highly disproportionate number of black
individuals. This part of the chapter explores how the association between black
citizens and crime, dangerousness, and violence could drive racial disparities in
the enforcement of our criminal laws. We first explore a troubling and escalating
"school-to-prison pipeline," with a focus on how discretionary disciplinary decisions
made by school administrators, teachers and school resource officers, and juvenile
court personnel (including judges, clerk magistrates, and probation officers) can

---

[17] Heather West et al., Prisoners in 2009 (2010), *available at* http://bjs.ojp.usdoj.gov/content/pub/
pdf/p09.pdf.

[18] Office of Applied Studies, Substance Abuse and Mental Health Services Administration,
The NSDUH Report: Illicit Drug Use, by Race/Ethnicity, in Metropolitan and Non-
Metropolitan Counties: 2004 and 2005 (2009), *available at* http://oas.samhsa.gov/2k7/popDensity/
popDensity.htm (finding that 9.6% of black respondents who live in a large metropolitan area reported
using an illicit substance within the past 30 days as compared to 8.5% of white respondents). Similar
trends exist in small metropolitan (8.5% versus 8.4%) and nonmetropolitan (8.5% versus 7.4%) areas.
Id.

[19] Human Rights Watch, Decades of Disparity: Drug Arrests and Race in the United States
(2009), *available at* http://www.hrw.org/reports/2009/03/02/decades-disparity.

[20] Stephanie Bontrager et al., *Race, Ethnicity, Treatment and the Labeling of Convicted Felons*, 43
Criminology 589 (2005).

[21] Katherine Beckett, *Drug Use, Drug Possession Arrests and the Perception of Race: Lessons from Seattle*,
52 Soc. Problems 419 (2005).

be tainted by implicit racial bias. We then discuss the discriminatory allocation of excessive force in police–citizen encounters.

A. *Implicit Racial Bias and the Enforcement of School Discipline*

School disciplinary procedures are important for a discussion on implicit racial bias in criminal law because of what has become known as the school-to-prison pipeline. The pipeline starts with the growing numbers of children and teens in the United States who are being suspended and expelled from public schools. Such suspensions and expulsions help push students onto the prison track. Thus, unjustifiable racial disparities in school disciplinary procedure are an early entry point for unjustifiable racial disparities in juvenile justice outcomes.

For more than three decades, numerous studies and investigations have revealed that harsh school discipline policies are imposed on children of color at highly disproportionate rates.[22] Children of color, and particularly black boys, are disproportionately suspended, expelled, and arrested for behaviors committed in school. The most obvious explanation for the disproportionately harsh treatment of children of color is that these children commit infractions at greater rates than their white counterparts. This view, however, is not supported by available data. A meta-study conducted by Professor Russell Skiba and colleagues concluded that no "published research studying differential discipline and rates of behavior by race ... has found any evidence that the higher rates of discipline received by African-American students are due to more serious or more disruptive behavior."[23] What Skiba did find, however, is that African American students are referred to the principal's office for more subjective behaviors, such as "disrespect" or "disorderly conduct," than white students. These disproportionate referrals result in disproportionate punishment. For instance, a massive study of one million Texas seventh-grade students tracked over six years – the largest such study of its kind – found that African American and Latino students were punished more harshly for discretionary first offenses than their white peers.[24]

The decision to suspend or expel a student begins with the decision to isolate that student for discipline in the first place. When a teacher (or, increasingly, a school resource officer) views a situation (for example, where a student is involved in a loud verbal altercation), the teacher's background experiences and automatic associations shape his or her interpretation of the scene. Recall that black males, and particularly young black males, are often viewed implicitly as dangerous, hostile, and even less

---

[22] *See, e.g.*, Russell J. Skiba et al., *The Color of Discipline: Sources of Racial and Gender Disproportionality in School Punishment*, 34 Urb. Rev. 4 (2002).

[23] *Id.* at 335.

[24] Michael Thompson, Breaking School Rules: A Statewide Study of How School Discipline Relates to Students' Success and Juvenile Justice Involvement (2011), *available at* http://justicecenter.csg.org/files/school_discipline_report_PR_final.pdf.

than fully human. Certain students – often black males – are punished by school administrators and school resource officers for their perceived "dangerousness," or potential to be dangerous, rather than for their actual behavior.[25] Professors Sandra Graham and Brian Lowery examined whether these racial stereotypes also affect decisions made by police officers and probation officers.[26] When primed with words calculated to invoke the category "black," stereotypes affected the judgments of (actual) police officers and juvenile probation officers regarding the juvenile offenders' character, culpability, negative traits, and "deserved punishment." These subjective impressions can (and often do) mean the difference between one student being sent back to the classroom and another student being sent to the principal's office, or between one student getting a warning for a fistfight and another getting arrested and referred to juvenile court on assault and battery charges.

Once the student reaches the principal's office (or in more serious scenarios, the juvenile judge or probation officer), evaluation of the evidence depends on the statements provided by eyewitness or secondhand reports that teachers or resource officers provide about the incident. There is reason for concern that implicit race bias infects this process. Ethnographic studies of both classroom interactions and disciplinary hearings reveal that teachers and school officials target black students for the harshest punishments in ambiguous situations that require the officials to exercise the greatest judgment and discretion.[27] This research suggests that (often white middle-class) teachers single out students of color for suspensions because they do not recognize cultural cues as well as their white peers do.

In a study that casts doubt on the ability of teachers and principals to administer race-neutral school discipline, Professor Justin Levinson conducted an experiment to test whether implicit race bias affected jurors' memories of case facts.[28] Levinson provided jury-eligible participants with a fictional story about a confrontation between two men. Some jurors read about "William" the white defendant, whereas others read about "Tyronne" the black defendant. The rest of the story remained constant. When Levinson asked jurors to remember pertinent facts about "the confrontation," he found that the race of the defendant affected how they recalled the story's details. Participants more frequently remembered aggressive details when Tyronne rather than William was the defendant. Levinson concluded "that the race of a civil plaintiff or a criminal defendant can act implicitly to cause people to misremember a case's facts." The participants even remembered "facts" that did not

---

[25] *See, e.g.,* Ronnie Casella, *Punishing Dangerousness Through Preventative Detention,* 99 NEW DIRECTIONS YOUTH DEV. 55 (2003).

[26] Sandra Graham & Brian Lowery, *Priming Unconscious Racial Stereotypes About Adolescent Offenders,* 28 LAW & HUM. BEHAV. 499 (2004).

[27] Frances Vavrus & Kim M. Cole, *I Didn't Do Nothin': The Discursive Construction of School Suspension,* 34 URB. REV. 87 (2002).

[28] Justin D. Levinson, *Forgotten Racial Equality: Implicit Bias, Decision Making, and Misremembering,* 57 DUKE L.J. 345 (2007).

appear in the story more often when those facts were stereotype-consistent, such as facts that portrayed black males as aggressive. Thus, racially charged stereotypes of being prone to violence and dangerous that apply to young black males might cause other students and teachers to evaluate and report ambiguous evidence of school disciplinary code violations in racially biased ways and also may have a negative impact on the ability of school administrators to weigh such evidence in a racially neutral manner.

In addition to in-school discipline, school-based arrests have risen dramatically over the past decade and, in some jurisdictions, make up the majority of juvenile court referrals. For many youths of color, schools have become the point of entry into the criminal justice system, which is why reducing school-based arrests and court referrals has become the focal point of so much reform advocacy. The same implicitly biased analysis that seems to drive teachers and principals to be more likely to impute wrongdoing to black students under ambiguous circumstances could also influence the decision-making of corrections officers or juvenile court judges who must set the punishment for these students once they enter the juvenile justice system. Indeed, research suggests that decision-makers possess the perception that misbehavior by blacks is more dispositional than misbehavior by white students. For example, Professors George Bridges and Sara Steen analyzed official court assessments of juvenile offenders and found that "[p]robation officers consistently portray black youths differently than white youths in their written court reports, more frequently attributing blacks' delinquency to negative attitudinal and personality traits."[29] When evaluating the risk of recidivism, even the severity of the crime at issue or the seriousness of the juvenile's previous record did not receive the same weight as the perceived "negative internal attributes" that the black children possessed.[30] In sum, the operation of implicit race bias increases the risk that school disciplinary measures – and the juvenile delinquency proceedings that often follow exclusionary school discipline – are not administered in a race-neutral fashion.

B. *Implicit Racial Bias and Excessive Force in Police–Citizen Encounters*

We began this section on disparities in criminal law enforcement with the school-to-prison pipeline example to demonstrate the significant impact of implicit bias even in a context where the primary goal is to educate not incarcerate. Most enforcement disparities, however, occur outside the schoolhouse doors. Racial misunderstandings and bias plague interactions between police officers and civilians. We use the example of officer-involved shootings to demonstrate that the stereotype that blacks are violent and dangerous can affect the way that police officers treat black suspects.

---

[29] George S. Bridges & Sara Steen, *Racial Disparities in Official Assessments of Juvenile Offenders: Attributional Stereotypes as Mediating Mechanisms.* 63 Am. Soc. Rev. 554, 557 (1998).

[30] *Id.* at 554–57.

On March 16, 2011, the U.S. Department of Justice (DOJ) released its findings from an extensive civil investigation of the New Orleans Police Department (NOPD).[31] The report, which emphasized the "troubling disparities in [the New Orleans Police Department's] treatment of the City's African-American community" and the failure of the NOPD to take "sufficient steps to detect, prevent, or address bias-based profiling and other forms of discriminatory policing on the basis of race,"[32] is worth exploring in some depth here because it offers a vivid illustration of where and how implicit bias can take root. A particular dismaying finding involves the NOPD's use of lethal force.

In 2010, a federal grand jury had indicted five New Orleans police officers for needlessly shooting black New Orleans residents near the Danziger Bridge one week after Hurricane Katrina in 2005.[33] The DOJ report confirms that this type of unnecessary lethal force is not isolated, but rather is reflective of "many instances . . . in which NOPD officers used deadly force contrary to NOPD policy or law." The use of lethal force has a clear racial component: each of the twenty-seven individuals fatally shot by New Orleans police officers between January 2009 and May 2011 was black.

Several studies suggest that the use of force (whether lethal or not) might be tied to implicit race bias, and as discussed earlier, blacks, especially young black males, are stereotyped as being hostile (e.g., "violent," "aggressive," "angry," or "menacing.").[34] A police officer deciding how to approach a suspect – to question him or her, to approach the vehicle, to conduct a stop and frisk, or to decide whether to shoot – necessarily engages in a rough risk calculation: How is this person going to react? Will this person respect my authority as a police officer? Is this person likely to have a gun? Is this person likely to react to being confronted with anger? Is this person going to shoot me? Such calculations are not made in a vacuum, but involve these questions: Is this a "high-crime" neighborhood? Is this a neighborhood where I believe there is a high level of respect for police authority? Does this neighborhood look and feel like my neighborhood – or is it different (richer, poorer, whiter, blacker, more or less populated)?

These types of variables interact with stereotypes about the suspect in milliseconds to shape the actions taken by police officers. The potential impact of implicit race bias in those split-second decisions is best captured by a videogame created by Professor Joshua Correll. The game depicts a picture of either a white or a black suspect and

---

[31] United States Department of Justice, Civil Rights Division, Investigation of the New Orleans Police Department, (2011), *available at* http://www.justice.gov/crt/about/spl/nopd_letter.pdf.

[32] *Id.*

[33] *See* Laura Maggi & Brendan McCarthy, *Judge in Danziger Case Sickened by "Raw Brutality of the Shooting and the Craven Lawlessness of the Cover-Up,"* New Orleans Times Picayune, Apr. 7, 2010, *available at* http://www.nola.com/crime/index.ssf/2010/04/judge_sickened_by_raw_brutalit.html.

[34] Scott A. Akalis et al., *Crime Alert! How Thinking About a Single Suspect Automatically Shifts Stereotypes Toward an Entire Group*, 5 Du Bois Rev.: Soc. Sci. on Race 217 (2008) (finding that "participants showed implicit stereotypes reflecting a far greater association of Blacks than Whites with hostility").

then couples that suspect with either a gun or an innocuous object (i.e., a wallet).[35] Study participants were asked to play the videogame by looking at the suspects as they appeared on the screen and then to determine whether or not to shoot. The results displayed a bias among all participants – but especially white participants – to *shoot* unarmed black defendants and to *not shoot* armed white suspects.

The authors of the study subsequently tested whether police officers would out-perform community members in the decision to shoot (or not shoot) unarmed suspected. The results were mixed. Police officers showed strong signs of implicit race bias in how quickly they recognized a target as being a potential threat. In other words, law enforcement professionals are not immune to stereotypes about blacks, and especially young black men, as "hostile" and "dangerous." However, police officers did not demonstrate implicit bias in the ultimate decision to shoot.[36] This finding suggests that extensive training *might* reduce levels of implicitly biased decision-making. Yet not every police force provides adequate training. Indeed, the DOJ report found that the "basic elements of effective policing – [including] train-ing – have been absent for years [in New Orleans] . . . rais[ing] the risk that NOPD officers . . . rely on inappropriate factors such as racial stereotypes and bias in their decision-making." Officers choose to shoot (or not), often while in a crime-ridden neighborhood, and always in a fraction of a second. In the absence of adequate training and in the face of startling racial disparities in officer-involved shootings, the operation of implicit race bias can result in unjustifiable racial disparities in officer-involved shootings. Moreover, in the context of less lethal decision-making, such as the decision to employ excessive physical force to control a suspect in police custody – or even to get the suspect in custody in the first place – the decreased gravity of the decision might lead to less reflection and thus an increased likelihood that implicitly biased perceptions of danger or hostility drive the racially biased use of force.

IV. IMPLICIT RACIAL BIAS AND COMMUNITY PARTICIPATION IN CRIMINAL JUSTICE

The use of lethal force by police officers against the citizens they are sworn to pro-tect erodes community trust. So does community under-policing. When the same community residents (and their friends and family members) who are singled out for police mistreatment later appear in court for jury duty, the state often dispropor-tionately excludes them from jury service in significant part because of their lack of esteem for law enforcement. In most cases, litigants do not ask the questions that

---

35 *See* Joshua Correll, *Event-Related Potentials and the Decision to Shoot: The Role of Threat Perception and Cognitive Control*, 42 J. EXPERIMENTAL SOC. PSYCHOL. 120, 128 (2006).
36 Joshua Correll et al., *Across the Thin Blue Line: Police Officers and Racial Bias in the Decision to Shoot*, 92 J. PERSONALITY & SOC. PSYCHOL. 1006 (2007).

would allow the parties to determine the views of a prospective juror – *would you sympathize with the defendant due to race or class solidarity, would you understand the crime charged as a cultural phenomenon and thus be less included to vote to enforce the law?* Even questions that are frequently posed – *do you favor the defense, are you skeptical of law enforcement?* – are often answered in a generic manner that does not eliminate the need for the litigants to use gut feelings about prospective jurors rather than rely on the substance of their answers alone.[37]

In the absence of sufficient information, prosecutors rely on implicit knowledge to choose whom to select for a jury. Some of that stereotypical knowledge – *"the juror looked hostile to the prosecution," "he did not make eye contact," "she did not sound educated"* – likely has no basis in reality. Other stereotypical knowledge, however, is accurate. We recently represented a Louisiana man named Corey Miller who was convicted of second-degree murder (over the dissent of two black jurors). Although the pool of eligible jurors began with a sizable number of black citizens, the prosecution wielded its cause and peremptory challenges to systematically eliminate all but three black prospective jurors. One of the most effective questions employed by the assistant district was, *On a scale of 1–10, how do you feel about the Jefferson Parish Police Department?* (Jefferson Parish is the county located next to Orleans Parish. Its [now-deceased] sheriff, Harry Lee, famously told his deputies to stop "young blacks in rinky-dink cars" driving in white neighborhoods.[38]) Not surprisingly, black citizens of Jefferson Parish, on average, rated local law enforcement less favorably than their white counterparts did. The prosecutors used this relative gap between esteem for law enforcement as a "race-neutral" reason for striking black jurors.

However, the prosecutors in Corey Miller's case did not need to rely on race as proxy to determine that black jurors have less esteem for local law enforcement than white jurors do: they had valid, race-neutral proof that the average black prospective juror held a lower opinion of local law enforcement than the average white prospective juror (i.e., the individual juror ratings of police officers that were lower for black jurors than similarly situated white jurors on the panel). The interesting point here is that filling in the assumption that black jurors would rate police less favorable than white jurors does not change the outcome because black prospective jurors in Corey Miller's case did rate the police less favorably. Thus, eliminating implicit racial bias is not always a solution to underrepresentation of black citizens on juries, because, in many neighborhoods, the stereotype that black citizens possess lower opinions of law enforcement is accurate. Providing the missing information about how jurors feel about law enforcement would still result in that juror being dismissed (because

[37] The point is that the process doesn't provide all of the information that litigants would hope to know about jurors. Use of pre-trial juror questionnaires is one possibility for providing litigants with more complete information about jurors. But we simply mean to point out here that there is room for implicit racial bias to operate in this process.

[38] Alan Sayre, *Sheriff Harry Lee Dead at 75*, USA Today, Oct. 1, 2007, *available at* http://www.usatoday.com/news/nation/2007-10-01-2580256326_x.htm.

black citizens tend to rate police performance less favorably and would indicate as much on juror questionnaires).

Thus implicit bias has infected the jury selection process. Distrust of the police is more prominent among black citizens than white citizens.[39] Part of the discrepancy stems from firsthand encounters with law enforcement that blacks interpret as racist, either explicitly (e.g., the police's use of terms with racial meaning, such as "nigger" or "boy") or vicariously (e.g., being stopped for "driving while black"). Secondhand stories also account for some of the attitude gap. Negative attitudes toward the police tend to be cumulative, with the initial impression providing a durable frame with which future interactions are viewed. Thus, the antecedent implicit bias that drives the disparate treatment of black students in school disciplinary situations and of black suspects shot by the police also significantly influences juror attitudes toward the police. In turn, these attitudes lead prosecutors to strike black jurors more frequently than white jurors. Implicit bias also is important because it is an explanatory device for how and why the friends and neighbors whom we respect and trust (i.e., prosecutors and police officers) exercise discretion to disadvantage people of color. It is also important as a measurement device that bridges the gap between subjective explanations for a strike and empirical data about the number of jurors struck, meaning that the Implicit Association Test (and similar tools) allow us to demonstrate the risk that race bias will infect decision-making in the average case.

V. CONCLUSION

Although not comprehensive, this overview aims to illustrate the broad range of scenarios in which the pernicious impact of implicit race bias can surface in the criminal justice system. A reasonable interpretation of the mounting implicit bias literature, read in light of the profound racial disparities that define our criminal justice system, should put to rest any claims that we have arrived at a "post-racial" or "color-blind" justice system.

Steps to reduce the effects of implicit bias can be viewed as a vital, heretofore missing, piece of a larger strategy aimed at rooting out unequal treatment by our courts and our law enforcement professionals. However, we want to emphasize that narrowly tailored solutions to eliminate implicit bias must be only part of the solution. Detection of implicit bias matters in different ways depending on the context. In some circumstances, rooting out implicit bias itself might reduce an existing disparity. For example, in the school discipline context, it is reasonable to believe that training aimed specifically at increasing awareness among teachers,

---

[39] For instance, the Project on Human Development in Chicago Neighborhoods (PHDCN), which examined racial and ethnic differences in attitudes toward social deviance, the police, and the law in 343 urban neighborhoods in Chicago. *See* Jeremy Travis, Director, Summary of Presentation by Felton Earls at Harvard University School of Public Health: Linking Community Factors and Individual Development (September 1998), *available at* http://www.ncjrs.gov/pdffiles/fs000230.pdf.

school administrators, and school resource officers of the implicit biases they hold may well reduce overall numbers of suspensions, expulsions, and arrests in school, as well as the racial disparities among those most harshly punished.

However, in other instances, eliminating or reducing implicit bias may simply clear the underbrush; thus allowing us to see the underlying structural problem more clearly. Laws banning convicted felons from voting, or mandatory minimums for certain drug offenses may well have been enacted because of the implicit bias held by lawmakers. Nonetheless, the ultimate prescriptive remedies in those situations are substantive: ending felony disenfranchisement, eliminating the crack–powder disparity, and repealing mandatory minimum sentences. In other words, identifying and rooting out implicit bias are akin to diagnosing a vision problem and providing corrective lenses. Once we put them on, our enhanced vision brings into sharper focus the obstacles in our path. The need to recognize, assess, and (to the extent possible) eliminate implicit bias in both types of scenarios is urgently needed, but strategies to do so should be considered a complement to, not a substitute for, structural reforms needed to provide a more fair and humane criminal justice system for all.

4

Torts

Implicit Bias–Inspired Torts

Deana Pollard Sacks

Bias based on race, religion, gender, color, national origin, ancestry, disability, sexual orientation, physical appearance, and a myriad of other largely immutable characteristics is still ubiquitous today. These biases are not as easy to detect as old-fashioned, explicit racism (even for the beholder). Yet twenty-first century bias has the same old consequences: employment discrimination; discriminatory charges, arrests, prosecutions, convictions, and sentences; defamation and invasion of privacy; and harassment and other interpersonal antisocial conduct, such as ostracism. The loss of employment opportunities, liberty infringement, emotional pain, and other harm caused by the constant manifestations of implicit bias are unquantifiable. Because most of us are oblivious to this social problem, proactive measures to combat the injustices that flow from implicit bias have yet to be initiated on a meaningful scale.

Implicit bias is a social issue, not an individual problem. Accordingly, it is socially desirable to expose implicit bias and instigate public discourse concerning its pervasiveness and harmful social effects. The benefit to victims is self-evident, but perpetrators and all members of society stand to gain self-awareness through enlightenment about the inner workings of their minds, which may be contrary to the dictates of their consciences. Publicizing the existence and injurious effects of implicit bias could further self-actualization and individual liberty and would create social awareness, which could benefit society in many ways. However, it seems doubtful that a public education campaign about the perverse consequences of implicit bias would be sufficient to eradicate its operation. Could the law of torts be of service in this regard?

This chapter considers how tort remedies for implicit bias could publicize this serious social problem, awaken individuals to their own implicit biases, stimulate robust public and private discussion about the problem, and deter its antisocial and often grossly unfair social consequences. The first issue to explore is the propriety of engaging tort liability as a means of combating implicit bias. Next, assuming tort law can and should respond to this social problem, a few examples of tortious behavior caused by implicit bias are provided, and tort remedies are proposed. Anticipated challenges to the proposed tort remedies are identified and addressed in the last portion of this chapter.

I. IS TORT LAW A PROPER VEHICLE TO REDRESS THE SOCIAL PROBLEM OF IMPLICIT BIAS?

The rationale for tort law has undergone conceptual changes since its inception, and a brief review of the dominant phases of existential justification helps show that tort liability could offer some relief for the social problem of implicit bias. Tort liability originated in criminal proceedings and is regarded as the civil counterpart to criminal sanctions, serving both retributive and deterrent purposes.[1] American tort liability has centered primarily on a principle of fault, certainly since the mid-nineteenth century.[2] Although punishment for blameworthy conduct remains a primary function of tort law, the mid-twentieth century ushered in a new conception of tort liability based on public policy, as opposed to fault. The "social engineering" function of tort law includes shifting the costs of accidents based on pragmatic principles to minimize overall costs and to assure compensation for injuries, thereby influencing social norms and shaping civil relationships, sometimes entirely without regard to fault.[3] As illustrated by the advent of strict products liability, which allows consumers to recover for fault-free and unpredictable injuries caused by mass-produced products that create at-large risks to society (such as exploding Coca-Cola bottles), a shift from the fault principle to enterprise liability theory changed the social meaning of tort liability.[4] Originating in workers' compensation schemes developed in England and the United States at the turn of the twentieth century, strict liability based on agency per se, as opposed to *wrongful* agency, currently rivals the fault principle as a theory of tort liability.[5] Modern tort liability can be divorced entirely from moral culpability, serving a social function independent of fault.

The turn of the twenty-first century witnessed significant changes to legal theory based on human psychology and law as "expression."[6] Originating in part to explain

---

[1] DAN B. DOBBS, THE LAW OF TORTS 4 (2000).

[2] Brown v. Kendall, 60 Mass. (6 Cush.) 292 (1850) (fault requirement adopted to replace strict liability for personal harms caused directly).

[3] W. PAGE KEETON ET AL., PROSSER & KEETON ON TORTS 536 (5th ed. 1984) [hereinafter PROSSER & KEETON ON TORTS]; DOBBS, *supra* note 1 at 977.

[4] *See* Guido Calabresi, *Some Thoughts on Risk Distribution and the Law of Torts*, 90 YALE L.J. 499, 500 (1961). Common law strict liability, such as cattle owner liability for harms caused by trespassing cattle, existed for centuries.

[5] *See* Gregory C. Keating, *The Theory of Enterprise Liability and Common Law Strict Liability*, 54 VAND. L. REV. 1285, 1286 (2001).

[6] *See, e.g.,* Cass R. Sunstein, *On the Expressive Function of Law*, 144 U. PA. L. REV. 2021, 2026–29 (1996); Richard McAdams, *The Origin, Development, and Regulation of Norms*, 96 MICH. L. REV. 338, 358 (1997).

subjects' inefficient responses to incentives that contradicted "rational actor" expectations derived from a neoclassical economic analysis, "behavioral economics"[7] recognized that human rationality is bounded by feelings, intangible values, and social norms.[8] Social norms became understood as influencing human behavior possibly more than formal sanctions and as being particularly efficient because, once constructed, their influence is costless.[9]

A. *Law as Expression of Social Norms*

Law as expression formulates rules that create, expose, or modify social norms and can be effective with or without formal penalties.[10] People are foremost social creatures who generally make behavioral choices based on their perception of what others are doing. Most humans' fear of social disapproval is greater than their fear of legal sanctions.[11] Although there is some debate about the relationship between law and social norms,[12] it seems clear that there is some relationship and that it is probably bidirectional, symbiotic, and often synergistic. Norms influence social behavior by their very existence, reducing the need for regulation through legal processes. To the extent that the law can create positive social norms, it should be used for this purpose.

There is evidence that expressive law can significantly affect norms and behavioral choices. For example, when Sweden outlawed all forms of child corporal punishment in 1979 *without* threat of prosecution or civil penalties for violations, a well-documented change to parenting norms followed, from violent to nonviolent forms of child discipline. The government's purpose was to change the public's attitude toward child corporal punishment, and the law's success is attributed to its unparalleled publicity – the government went all out, and 99 percent of Swedes were familiar with the law within two years of its promulgation.[13] It is recognized that the Swedish law's efficacy as behavior-modifying normative expression relates to the public's level of awareness about the law.

---

[7] *See, e.g.,* Richard A. Posner, *Rational Choice, Behavioral Economics, and the Law,* 50 STAN. L. REV. 1551 (1998); Russell B. Korobkin & Thomas S. Ulen, *Law and Behavioral Science: Removing the Rationality Assumption from Law and Economics,* 88 CAL. L. REV. 1051, 1055 (2000).

[8] The "economic" value of social norms was recognized as "one who violates a consensus incurs a cost." *See* McAdams, *supra* note 6, at 369.

[9] *See* Deana A. Pollard, *Sex Torts,* 91 MINN. L. REV. 769, 819–22 (2007).

[10] *See, e.g.,* Sunstein, *supra* note 6, at 2026–29; Dan M. Kahan, *Social Influence, Social Meaning, and Deterrence,* 83 VA. L. REV. 349, 377–78 (1997); Pollard, *supra* note 9, at 819–24 (applying behavioral law theories to regulation of sexual disease transmission via tort liability).

[11] Pollard, *supra* note 9, at 819–22.

[12] *Id.* at 810–12, 819–24 (citations omitted).

[13] The Swedish government disseminated 16-page color pamphlets to all parents with small children, *inter alia,* and published the law on milk cartons "to assure that it was present at family mealtimes when parents and children could discuss the issue together." *See* Joan E. Durrant, *The Swedish Ban on Corporal Punishment: Its History and Effects,* in FAMILY VIOLENCE AGAINST CHILDREN: A CHALLENGE FOR SOCIETY 19–25 (1996), *available at* http://www.nospank.net/durrant.htm.

Tort law is particularly well suited to create norms in response to contemporary social problems, because it is constantly evolving: "Perhaps more than any other branch of the law, the law of torts is a battleground of social theory."[14] As stated by the Supreme Court, tort law's "flexibility and capacity for growth and adaptation is [its] peculiar boast and excellence."[15] When society decides that an interest is entitled to legal protection, tort law can respond with a novel remedy if necessary. A contemporary tort may be defined as conduct that causes injury for which courts and society are willing to impose civil sanctions, and the rules can change quickly as needed to tweak our social order toward greater justice.

B. *Tort Law's Evolutionary Character*

The shift from a fault-based theory of products liability to strict products liability exemplifies tort law's capacity to evolve to meet contemporary concepts of social justice and accountability for injury. To actualize the shift, formerly required elements of negligence were set aside where necessary to shift the costs of harm caused by products onto the product manufacturers. This move can be illustrated by some of the diethylstilbestrol cases, in which strict liability was imposed in favor of teenage cancer victims based on novel "market share" cause-in-fact analysis; this liability was imposed despite the fact that the manufacturers could not have foreseen the injury – a traditional requirement under proximate cause analysis – because the girls faced expensive lifesaving medical treatment through no fault of their own and a civilized society simply must provide them with access to such treatment. Enterprise liability has no doubt produced safer products over the past half-century, sparing much human suffering.

Tort law's evolutionary character is further exemplified by the current state of transition relative to the bystander "no duty" rule. Frightening examples of psychopathic disregard for the plight of strangers underscore the obsolescence and potentially destructive social effect of the no duty rule, causing some courts to reject the rule swiftly in appropriate circumstances by capitalizing on tort law's flexibility. In 1983, a California court of appeal rejected longstanding limits to the first element of negligence – a duty of care – where the court simply could not tolerate a bartender's outrageous disregard for human life, in the form of his refusal to allow a nonpatron to use the telephone to make a free emergency phone call to save another nonpatron's life.[16] Realistically, no recognized duty of care arose from the facts, and the bartender's conduct appeared to fall squarely within the bystander no duty rule. Therefore the court relied on a variety of legal rules creating duties

---

[14] PROSSER & KEETON ON TORTS, *supra* note 3, at 15.
[15] Hurtado v. California, 110 U.S. 516, 530 (1884).
[16] *See* Soldano v. O'Daniels, 141 Cal. App.3d 443, 190 Cal. Rptr. 310 (1983).

of care in similar factual settings by analogy. It found that the defendant's conduct was "morally outrageous and indefensible"[17] and that the "attitude of extreme individualism so typical of Anglo-Saxon legal thought may need reexamination in light of current societal conditions."[18] The court upheld the negligence claim, noting numerous examples of tort law's evolution to advance social justice in the latter half of the twentieth century, including recognition of "wrongful life" claims, adoption of comparative fault to replace common law contributory negligence rules, and, of course, the introduction of strict products liability.[19]

Similarly, a New Jersey court demonstrated less concern about finding an established duty of care than about the gross indifference to human life that two teenage boys exhibited. The boys were in their friend's car when it struck a motorcyclist, saw the motorcyclist unconscious on the highway in dire need of assistance, and then chose to make dozens of phone calls to friends from two cell phones without bothering to call for assistance to the motorcyclist, who ultimately died.[20] The court found that the boys could be liable for the motorcyclist's death on a theory of negligence. Considering all of the facts, the court determined that the boys' relationship to the driver, as passengers in his car, was close enough to extend a minimal duty to summon assistance for the helpless motorcyclist. The court noted the minuscule time and effort it would have cost the boys to place just *one* emergency call with the potential to save a man's life (in addition to the *forty-four* calls they made to friends and others in the aftermath of the accident). Similar to the California court, the New Jersey court explained that "evolving notions of duty . . . are no longer tethered to rigid formalisms or static historical justifications. . . . The determination of the existence of duty is ultimately a question of fairness and public policy."[21]

Tort liability rules can and should be reformed when existing rules operate to the detriment of society. Implicit bias is detrimental to society because it oppresses and disenfranchises entire segments of society by machinery that is invisible and often institutional. Tort law should respond. Where implicit bias manifests in conduct that meets the elements of a tort claim, a tort rule that exposes the implicit bias and expresses its wrongfulness could advance egalitarian policy. Tort remedies for implicit bias could deter behavior caused by such bias through both the rational actor assumption (by assessing a cost) and through the law's expressive norm-regulating function (by making a social statement). Assuming that most Americans consciously self-identify as egalitarian, expressing the existence of implicit bias could further individual self-actualization by healing cognitive dissonance. That is, once implicit bias is exposed, most people will seek to avoid perpetrating behavior driven by

---

[17] *Id.* at 447 (quoting RESTATEMENT (SECOND) OF TORTS § 314 cmt. c (1965)).

[18] *Id.* at 450.

[19] *Id.* at 454 n.11.

[20] Podias v. Mairs, 394 N.J. Super. 338, 926 A.2d 859 (App. Div. 2007).

[21] *Id.* at 349.

implicit bias and to align their self-identity with their actions.[22] Publicizing the injurious effects of implicit bias could advance social justice and might even instigate a "norm cascade" that can result from new legal rules that converge with a public consensus.[23]

II. EXAMPLES OF TORTIOUS CONDUCT CAUSED BY IMPLICIT BIAS

Before turning to the challenges of creating enhanced penalties for implicit bias, a few examples of how implicit bias can inspire tortious conduct will help contextualize the tort remedy proposed in this chapter. These examples are intended to illustrate a few of the many ways in which implicit bias plays out in daily life.

Example 1: Employer, a law school, makes tenure-track hiring decisions based on initial candidate interviews with an appointments committee, which makes recommendations to the faculty. Students also interview candidates and make recommendations. A special faculty meeting is called to discuss and vote on candidates. Official criteria for hiring and promotion are candidates' academic and publication records, teaching evaluations, and community service, but there is no requirement that hiring decisions address any of these criteria. Any faculty member can request "blind voting," so that faculty members vote anonymously on candidates, and such requests are routinely made. The hiring proceedings are undocumented and unrecorded.

The law school, situated in a major multicultural city, has a dearth of Hispanic professors, but officially claims to be an equal opportunity employer. Rico Suarez is a very strong 30-year-old candidate who attended Harvard Law School and has a publication record superior to anyone presently on the faculty. His teaching evaluations are excellent, and he has a demonstrated commitment to community service, including serving on a national board to advance college opportunities for inner-city youth. The hiring committee recommended hiring Suarez over all of the other candidates.

During faculty discussions, Richard White, a senior faculty member, stated that a student told him that Suarez "inappropriately touched" a female student on the shoulder during student interviews with the candidate, but the statement was never substantiated. In response, the dean pointed out that the law school could not tolerate a sexual harassment claim by a student against a professor. Another faculty member mistakenly referred to Suarez as "Rico Suave," which elicited an uproar of laughter. The meeting was interrupted during discussions about Suarez by the arrival of dinner, and the meeting was adjourned.

At the next faculty meeting, the discussion of candidates continued, and when Suarez's name was brought up, the faculty members agreed that he had already been

---

[22] *See* Deana A. Pollard, *Implicit Bias and Self-Critical Analysis: The Case for a Qualified Evidentiary Equal Employment Opportunity Privilege*, 74 WASH. L. REV. 913, 922–25 (1999).
[23] *See* Sunstein, *supra* note 6, at 2035.

discussed. Ultimately, Suarez was rejected by the faculty in favor of Randy Smith, a Caucasian candidate who received an offer for a tenure-track position. Smith's academic and publication records were objectively inferior to Suarez's, and he had lower teaching evaluations and no demonstrated community service. After Smith accepted the offer, it came to light that it was Smith, not Suarez, who had touched a female student's shoulder during student interviews, but it was determined that White made an "honest" mistake in confusing the two candidates. A member of the appointments committee disclosed to Suarez the inaccurate statement that he had touched a student, as well as the "Rico Suave" slip, and apologized to Suarez for the mistake that appeared to have cost him the job opportunity. The truth is that Suarez is devoutly Catholic and is married to his high school girlfriend.

Suarez files a lawsuit against the law school for arbitrary, unstructured, and negligent hiring practices that enable and support the application of implicit biases relative to hiring decisions. Suarez claims that stereotypes that Hispanic men are "macho" womanizers caused him to lose a tenure-track contract worth millions of dollars and a lifetime of job security. Suarez seeks injunctive relief in the form of instatement to the next available tenure-track position and an injunction mandating changes to the hiring processes, including a requirement that candidates' qualifications are directly compared in accordance with the law school's official hiring criteria, that faculty hiring decisions are recorded, and that all voting is transparent.

Example 2: Plaintiff, a naturally blonde and very attractive young woman, is one of a dozen newly hired associate attorneys in a prestigious New York law firm. Plaintiff is asked to second-chair a very interesting, high-profile excessive force case against the New York Police Department (NYPD) for a law firm partner, who is male. Defendant, another new associate, makes statements to several other associates that Plaintiff was given the assignment because she is "dating" the partner, based on the fact that the Defendant witnessed Plaintiff and the partner go to lunch together alone on several occasions. Defendant and several other associates discuss Defendant's perceptions over lunch, during which other associates make statements that Plaintiff routinely makes "dumb" comments and comes off as "spoiled and conceited." Thereafter, the associates ostracize Plaintiff at work, which causes Plaintiff to suffer debilitating emotional distress and to resign from the law firm.

Plaintiff discovers the statements made about her by Defendant and the other associates. The truth is that the partner originally took Plaintiff to lunch to discuss the case because they share a law school alma mater, Columbia Law School. At the initial lunch, the partner discovered that Plaintiff's father works for the NYPD, and the partner felt that Plaintiff may have insight into police culture, which would help with discovery and trial strategy. Partner therefore chose Plaintiff to second-chair the trial and took her to a series of "power lunches" to brief her on the case. Partner and Plaintiff had a strictly professional relationship. Plaintiff sues Defendant for defamation and intentional infliction of emotional distress and alleges that implicit bias that attractive blonde women are unintelligent, spoiled, conceited, and promis-cuous caused Defendant's defamatory statements and other misconduct.[24] Plaintiff seeks emotional distress and reputation damages, lost wages, and exemplary damages based on the operation of implicit bias that caused her to be victimized by the other associates.

Example 3: In the same week, two couples move into a neighborhood of single-family homes in which all existing neighbors live in traditional civil unions (i.e., heterosexual marriages). One of the new couples is a husband and wife, and the other is a gay couple. A few weeks after the new couples move in, Neighbor's lawnmower is stolen from his backyard, although it had been stored in the backyard for several years without incident prior to the theft. Both the heterosexual new couple and the gay couple have large, unlocked storage units in their backyards. Neighbor suspects that the gay couple is responsible for the theft of his lawnmower, so he enters their backyard when they are not home and inspects their storage unit, but does not find the lawnmower. The gay couple discovers Neighbor's actions and sues for trespass to land and invasion of privacy. The gay couple asserts that Neighbor's suspicion resulted from unconscious bias that gays are deviant and not trustworthy.[25]

III. PROPOSED TORT REMEDIES TO EXPOSE, DETER, AND REDRESS IMPLICIT BIAS

In fashioning tort remedies to redress the problem of implicit bias, it is impor-tant to stay focused on the main objectives: to expose the problem, instigate intro-spection and discourse concerning its harmful social effects, and engage the law's norm-regulating potential. Comprehensive equitable remedies, such as institutional injunctions, redress wrongful group practices, as opposed to redressing a single wrongful practice, and so highlight the depth of the injustice. Such injunctions are particularly prominent in cases of social injustice such as civil rights infringe-ment. Exemplary damages typically express and highlight the wrongfulness of certain types of socially destructive conduct that the government has a special interest in quelling. Both tort remedies are suggested to publicize the *social* problem of implicit bias through *individual* tort lawsuits.

A. *Equitable Remedies*

Complicated and clandestine social mechanisms that result in widespread injustice call for creative solutions. Implicit bias is ubiquitous and systematic, yet largely

---

[24] The concept that attractive people are spoiled and get ahead easily may be exacerbated by Deborah L. Rhodes's book, THE BEAUTY BIAS (2010), which documents only the benefits of beauty and fails to consider the harassment and negative stereotypes that also attend physical beauty.

[25] *See, e.g.,* Russell A. Ward, *Typifications of Homosexuals,* 20 THE SOC. Q. 411 (1979), *available at* http://www.media-awareness.ca/english/issues/stereotyping/gays_and_lesbians/gay_news.cfm.

invisible. Many times, it cannot be proven to have caused injury in a particular case, despite the availability of statistical proof of its destructive influence. Judges have broad discretion to fashion equitable remedies, such as injunctions, which are personal orders to the defendant to perform a specified act or to avoid specified conduct. Restructuring institutional practices by means of broad-based injunctive relief in individual lawsuits may be necessary to advance social justice relative to implicit bias. Injunctions are enforceable by the court's contempt power, unlike a defendant's failure to pay damages awards, so they tend to be effective.

Many important social disparities can be traced to employment opportunities (or lack thereof) and their financial ramifications. The employment context is ripe with potential to further social justice through tort remedies for implicit bias–inspired practices. For example, decentralized and subjective hiring and promotion processes provide fertile ground for implicit bias–inspired injustices, because their influence can be hard to detect and responsibility for employment decisions is diffused and unaccountable. Thus, in the employment context, courts have engaged their equitable powers to order changes in hiring or promotion policies, such as prohibiting unrecorded selection panel deliberations[26] and certain managerial individuals from making promotional appointments except under a court-approved plan.[27] Institutional injunctions could also be used in other areas in which implicit bias clearly manifests, such as jury selection and deliberation processes. This section exemplifies how an injunction could work in the employment setting.

Implicit bias is enabled, even encouraged, by hiring and promotion processes that are structurally amorphous and decentralized, rather than more accountable processes based on a candidate's *verifiable* qualifications, including educational background, years of experience, and reference statements. Patterns of disparate outcomes and statistical analyses can reveal discrimination against certain minority groups where there is no evidence of intent or even a hostile work environment. Therefore, a conceptualization of workplace dynamics that focuses on the way in which implicit bias operates in the context of organizational structure, promotional practices, and group dynamics is needed to replace the typical focus on isolated incidents of discrimination resulting from defendants' discriminatory intent or purpose.[28] Based on the same type of evidence that proves a Title VII disparate impact case, tort principles could hold employers directly liable for hiring or promotional structures that enable implicit bias to manifest in patterns of racial or other unfair disparate employment decisions, perhaps on a theory of negligence.

Institutional dynamics and implicit bias–enabling employment processes can be short-circuited by carefully tailored equitable remedies that interrupt or bypass the

---

[26] *See, e.g.*, Perez v. F.B.I., 714 F. Supp. 1414 (W.D. Tex. 1989), *aff'd mem.*, 956 F.2d 265 (5th Cir. 1992).

[27] *See, e.g.*, U.S. v. City of Montgomery, 744 F. Supp. 1074 (M.D. Ala. 1989).

[28] *See, e.g.*, Tristin K. Green, *Discrimination In Workplace Dynamics: Toward A Structural Account of Disparate Treatment Theory* 38 Harv. C.R.- C.L. L. Rev. 91 (2003).

dynamics that lend themselves to manifesting implicit bias–infused decisions. With this in mind, when an employer's hiring or promotional structure results in palpable racial disparities in opportunities, company-wide equitable remedies should be available when even one employee proves that implicit bias more likely than not caused injury. That is, if an employer's hiring or promotional structure creates an unreasonable and foreseeable risk of lost opportunities (and lost wages) for a particular, identifiable group subject to implicit bias, a negligence cause of action could result. Unlike typical existing disparate impact remedies, broader equitable remedies modifying the entire corporate hiring structure could be used in recognition that the harm extends beyond the particular plaintiff at hand.

Accordingly, where an employee can establish the elements of a tort to establish liability, the employer could be placed under an affirmative duty to address the broader social issue and to restructure its hiring or promotional scheme to minimize the operation of implicit bias, in addition to compensating the individual grievant. A court could issue an affirmative injunction to require the employer to alter its hiring or promotional practices, to implement objective criteria for hiring or promotion, to create safeguards and monitoring systems to identify and avoid implicit biased decision-making, and to make sure that clearly identifiable people who have been educated on the dynamics of implicit bias are held accountable for decisions. In this way, individual lawsuits could instigate institutional remedies and would send a message to other employers who wish to avoid the potential embarrassment of being told by a court how to structure their internal processes to avoid systematic injustice.

B. *Exemplary Damages*

Exemplary damages constitute a statement that the tortious conduct to which they attach is not merely a civil infraction necessitating cost-shifting to make the tort victim whole, but rather civil conduct that the government seeks to expose and discourage because of its more pronounced threat of oppression. Exemplary damages express social disapproval.

Exemplary damages are sums additional to compensatory damages that are imposed for the general purpose of retribution or deterrence. They may be awarded as parasitic damages to any cognizable harm, including nominal damages. An award of exemplary damages typically requires a bad state of mind such as a malicious, oppressive, or other morally culpable intent. However, broadly speaking, exemplary damages attach to an "antisocial mental state."[29] Implicit bias can fairly be characterized as an antisocial state of mind that the government has a special interest in exposing and redressing.[30] Just as hate-inspired crimes are likely to "produce

---

[29] DOBBS, *supra* note 1, at 1064 (2000) (citing Smith v. Wade, 461 U.S. 30 (1983)).

[30] The U.S. Supreme Court has long recognized that the government has a special duty to protect "discrete and insular minorities" who are known to be the target of majoritarian bias. *See* United States v. Carolene Products Co., 304 U.S. 144, 153 n.4 (1938) (suggesting a higher level of scrutiny

retaliatory crimes, inflict distinct emotional harms on their victims and incite community unrest,"[31] manifestations of implicit bias are particularly oppressive because they are ubiquitous, lead to hidden yet heartfelt injustice, and inflict the same sort of distinct emotional harm as hate crimes. Indeed, because it is more prevalent, yet invisible, implicit bias–inspired conduct may pose a greater danger to society than hate crimes.

Allowing exemplary damages for tortious conduct caused by implicit bias could bring great publicity to this social problem; doing so could also punish and deter its manifestations by assessing a social "cost" to those whose implicit bias causes cognizable injury to others. For example, in the corporate setting, proof of institutional discrimination resulting from organizational processes that lend themselves to outcomes consistent with racial stereotypes could justify an exemplary damages award to draw more attention to the problem and to encourage other employers to take heed and review their organizational processes. An exemplary damages award could draw attention to unfair employment decisions caused by implicit bias more effectively than equitable remedies alone. Another example is where implicit bias can be shown to have caused a dignitary tort, such as where a company decides to "investigate" an employee or business associate based on implicit assumptions concerning character – such as those consistent with black men or homosexual stereotypes.

Exemplary damages awards could be avoided by persons or institutions who demonstrate a desire to avoid future injustices resulting from implicit bias. Defendants could be given the opportunity to attend (or require that their employees attend) implicit bias training classes in lieu of exemplary damages. Such an exception could further social justice without assessing punitive measures against defendants who respond to the allegations in good faith; these training classes would be similar to criminal diversion programs that focus on education or rehabilitation as opposed to punitive consequences.[32] A tort rule providing for an award of exemplary damages or mandatory educational training may effectuate social change through various mechanisms, and an education-based diversion program may appease dissenters considerably.

C. *Strict Liability*

Because behavior caused by implicit bias is by definition unintentional and unknowing, its theory of punishment is necessarily strict liability. Its punishment through

---

where a law discriminates against minorities, which paved the way for the heightened level of scrutiny in substantive due process cases and the adoption of "strict scrutiny" in race-based equal protection challenges).

[31] Wisconsin v. Mitchell, 508 U.S. 476, 488 (1993).

[32] See A.B.A., *Standard 14–4.1, Diversion and Other Alternative Resolutions*, in ABA STANDARDS FOR CRIMINAL JUSTICE: PLEAS OF GUILTY (3d ed. 1999); Bordenkircher v. Hayes, 434 U.S. 357 (1978) (diversion programs are not unconstitutional conditions).

tort liability must therefore be justified by reference to social policy as opposed to the fault principle, a subject discussed in more detail in the latter portion of this chapter. There is some legal precedent for the appropriateness of enhanced penalties for tortious behavior inspired by bias. The closest analogy is enhanced criminal penalties for crimes motivated by hate, although there are obvious distinctions in terms of intent and proof of bias. Just as free-floating hate is not actionable, a remedy for implicit bias should be dependent on a predicate tort, rendering the penalty for implicit bias a derivative damages claim or equitable remedy parasitic to otherwise cognizable tortious conduct. Intentional, dignitary, and negligence-based torts can result from implicit bias. When implicit bias is shown to be a cause of tortious conduct, enhanced or creative remedies specific to this socially destructive aspect of causation should be available.

Courts could award enhanced tort penalties for torts inspired by implicit bias, or state legislatures could respond to the problem by passing laws, as many states have done relative to exemplary damages generally. Because an exemplary damages award based on the social effects of implicit bias[33] inherently does not connote moral culpability or social stigma per se, it need not be proven by clear and convincing evidence, because the defendant's state of mind and character are not at issue. An implicit bias enhancement penalty law that could be adopted by state legislatures might read something like this:

> In a tort action where it is proven by a preponderance of evidence that the defendant's tortious conduct was inspired by implicit bias, in addition to actual or nominal damages, the plaintiff may recover exemplary damages to stimulate public discourse and social awareness concerning the injustices that result from implicit bias. A defendant shall not be liable for such exemplary damages if the defendant agrees to enter an implicit bias educational training program.

IV. CHALLENGES TO AN ENHANCED PENALTY FOR IMPLICIT BIAS–INSPIRED TORTS

Three issues should be considered before tort remedies for implicit bias should be established. First, how could a plaintiff establish the content of the implicit bias that led to the commission of a tort against him or her? Second, is strict liability for

---

[33] For example, research on the effects of African American names (such as Lakisha and Jamal) appearing on job applicant resumes compared with white names (such as Emily and Greg) indicate significant differences in callback rates, even controlling for differences in education, work experience, and zip code. *See* Marianne Bertrand and Sendhil Mullainathan, *Are Emily and Greg More Employable than Lakisha and Jamal? A Field Experiment on Labor Market Discrimination*, 94 AM. ECON. REV. 991 (2004). In live job interviews, race similarly influences an applicant's chances of success. *See, e.g.*, Pollard, *supra* note 22, at 956–58 (discussing differences in interview styles depending on the applicant's race).

implicit bias socially desirable? Third, does the First Amendment preclude special tort remedies for implicit bias?

A. *Proving Implicit Bias*

Regarding the first issue, people harbor an infinite number of biases against other people that can never be fully cataloged, such as those based on salient childhood experiences that society generally does not share. However, there are some clearly established stereotypes generally held by members of our society. These common stereotypes result from common experiences, including media messages, norms, and jokes. This explains why even members of the class subject to a negative stereotype are known to exhibit the same stereotypes as society generally, despite such being contrary to their personal best interests.[34] Identifying a commonly held stereotype, and then demonstrating that it more likely than not inspired the defendant's tortious conduct, should be sufficient proof that, but for the implicit bias, the tort would not have been committed.

Stereotypes can be identified through a variety of sources. The first is common knowledge, a matter distinctly within a jury's discretion. Common stereotypes include the following: black men are angry and violent, Hispanic men are chauvinistic womanizers, and pretty blonde women are stupid – hence the common phrases, "angry black man," "machismo," and "dumb blonde." Gay stereotypes may not be quite as well known, but gays have been characterized overtly as immoral, both in political and religious commentary and the mainstream media. For example, Yale history professor George Chauncey offered expert testimony in a gay couple's challenge to California Proposition 8's definition of marriage (a union between opposite-sex couples only) that the proponents of Proposition 8 propagated stereotypes that gays are "perverts" who prey on young children or entice straight people into "sick" behavior. Similarly, the portrayal of gays and lesbians in the media and major films, such as *The Silence of the Lambs* and *Basic Instinct*, manifest notions that gays and lesbians are deviant, even psychopathic and murderous, and a threat to society. The emotional effect and salience of these media messages are enhanced by the charisma of the actors involved, providing memorable fodder for the availability heuristic[35] concerning gays in the same way that Pamela Anderson and O. J. Simpson provide salient examples of the dumb blonde woman and angry black man stereotypes. Society is probably sufficiently aware of these commonly held

---

[34] *See* Charles Lawrence III, *Unconscious Racism Revisited: Reflections on the Impact and Origins of "The Id, The Ego, and Equal Protection,"* 40 CONN. L. REV. 931, 957 (2008); KENNETH B. CLARK, THE EFFECT OF PREJUDICE AND DISCRIMINATION ON PERSONALITY DEVELOPMENT, WHITE HOUSE MIDCENTURY CONFERENCE ON CHILDREN AND YOUTH (1950); KENNETH B. CLARK, PREJUDICE AND YOUR CHILD (2d ed. 1955) (black and white doll studies).

[35] *See* Amos Tversky & Daniel Kahneman, *Availability: A Heuristic for Judging Frequency and Probability,* 5 COG. PSYCH. 207–32 (1973).

stereotypes to determine whether they played a role in a tort lawsuit, considering all of the evidence.

A second source of proof could be expert witnesses. Psychologists who study implicit bias have found certain biases fairly consistently across society. Such experts could explain to a jury why certain implicit biases are commonly held and explain their probable origin and content. This would provide sufficient information to allow a jury to reach an opinion about the probable cause of discriminatory conduct caused by implicit bias.

B. *Is Strict Liability for Harm Caused by Implicit Bias Socially Desirable?*

Because strict liability is liability without fault, it must be justified based on social policy, as it has been in other areas of contemporary strict liability. The question is whether implicit bias constitutes enough of a threat to our social order to warrant liability in the absence of fault.

There is no way to quantify the social harm that results from implicit bias. It manifests every minute of every day in an infinite number of social interactions. For some members of our society who occupy a class against whom implicit bias is most harshly applied – such as black men and gay men – the social effects may be constant, palpable, and financially and emotionally devastating. Tortious conduct caused by implicit bias is a distinctly oppressive form of civil misconduct because it targets and oppresses a person based on his or her largely immutable characteristics. The harm to society resulting from implicit bias-inspired torts is different and more dangerous than general tortious misconduct because it tends to oppress persons sharing the characteristic of the tort victim and can exacerbate bias. Thus, the implicit bias–inspired tort emanates harm beyond the victim and has an oppressive ripple effect on society. Tortious conduct that manifests and renders tangible implicit bias based on race, religion, gender, color, national origin, ancestry, disability, sexual orientation, and other immutable characteristics should be punished effectively through appropriate equitable relief tailored to the mechanism of injustice or exemplary damages, based on its widespread and socially oppressive effects.

The fact that proof of implicit bias may be difficult to pinpoint in a particular case should not present an obstacle to strict liability. Early courts deemed emotional injury too "metaphysical," "evanescent," "intangible," "speculative," and "peculiar," such that "toughening of the mental hide" was more appropriate than a legal remedy.[36] Yet, juries routinely awarded sums for intangible pain and suffering, and eventually emotional distress damages were recognized as parasitic damages, the doorway to their eventual independent recognition. Implicit bias may be more amenable to proof than emotional distress, because members of a society with different levels of

---

[36] *See* PROSSER & KEETON ON TORTS, *supra* note 3, at 55–56.

emotional vulnerability largely share the same socially constructed and perpetuated implicit biases and everyone understands injustice, probably more readily than another's emotional injury. Similarly, where direct proof of why or how a product is unreasonably unsafe is not available, res ipsa loquitur can bridge the evidentiary gap to support strict liability. Where the role that implicit bias played in tortious conduct sufficiently "speaks for itself," a remedy should lie despite a lack of fault in the traditional tort sense or clear proof of precisely *how* the implicit bias caused injury.

Strict liability for exemplary damages is an unusual concept, but it is not novel. Principals can be liable for exemplary damages arising from their agents' conduct based on vicarious liability, a form of strict liability. The Second Restatement of Agency provides four separate bases for a principal's vicarious liability for exemplary damages based on an agent's misconduct. The most relevant basis is where the principal "ratifies or approves" the tortious act punishable by exemplary damages.[37] In the Title VII context, to further Congress's antidiscrimination policy, the Supreme Court has limited general agency principles allowing employer liability for exemplary damages. It limited exemplary damages to instances where the employer failed to take "good faith efforts to comply with Title VII,"[38] noting Title VII's prophylactic primary objective of *preventing* employment discrimination, not redressing it.[39] In essence, the pervasiveness of employment discrimination justifies vicarious liability for exemplary damages where necessary to motivate employers to engage in self-critical analysis and to adopt antidiscrimination policies. By the same token, vicarious liability for exemplary damages under Title VII is denied where an employer has made a "good faith" attempt to comply with Title VII, to encourage employers to educate themselves about the law, and to address employment discrimination proactively. Because implicit bias is also a pervasive threat to society, exemplary damages based on a theory of strict liability may be justified where an employer "ratifies" implicit bias by failing to undertake "good faith" efforts to eradicate this social problem in the face of evidence that implicit bias plays a role in disparate employment outcomes.

Allowing creative equitable remedies or enhanced penalties for tortious conduct caused by implicit bias would no doubt garner much attention. A media frenzy would likely result from the first injunction to restructure hiring practices in a large corporate employer or the first exemplary damages award based on implicit bias. This would stimulate open discussion and perhaps robust and heated debate, and it would cause people to question themselves, one another, and existing social norms – a fundamental value of American culture and the cornerstone of the

---

[37] *See* Kolstad v. American Dental Association, 527 U.S. 526, 542–43 (1999) (quoting Restatement (Second) of Agency § 217C (1957). *See also* Restatement (Second) of Torts § 909 (1979) (same).

[38] Kolstad v. American Dental Association, 527 U.S. 526, 545 (1999).

[39] *Id.* at 544–46.

First Amendment's protection of speech. Tort law's ability to address the pervasive social problem of implicit bias will no doubt be challenged, because "implicit bias" intuitively sounds resistant to modification through civil sanctions. Yet increasing the social cost of socially injurious behavior has been shown to affect norms in other contexts not intuitively amenable to behavior modification, such as drunk driving attendant to alcohol abuse, which often attends addiction that supersedes reasoned judgment.[40]

Legal rules are most effective in producing norms when they converge with a public consensus, even if the public was previously unaware of the consensus.[41] That is, publicizing an underrecognized consensus can operate to establish strong norms consistent with public sentiment, which is what happened with drunk driving and public smoking.[42] Considering the public's ignorance about implicit bias, it can hardly be said that a consensus concerning implicit bias currently exists. However, adopting new legal rules that spark public debate can give rise to a public consensus, which likely will be that the social effects of implicit bias are unfair and un-American. Publicizing a new legal rule that tortious behavior caused by implicit bias could expose tortfeasors to court-ordered corporate/behavioral modifications and enhanced penalties may effectively instigate public debate and lead to consensus-building.

Strict liability has also been justified based on "systematic" or repeated activity that poses nonreciprocal risks to society, because injury eventually ensues. The nature of implicit bias and the way in which stereotypes are called into play after even a slight interaction with a person subject to the stereotype make clear that implicit bias indeed operates systematically and repeatedly against certain members of society in particular, causing many harms that will never be redressed. This strengthens the case for imposing strict liability for implicit bias where it can be proven to have caused injury.

C. Does Tort Liability for Implicit Bias Implicate the First Amendment?

The First Amendment must be considered any time that tort liability arises from speech. Tortious behavior caused by implicit bias resulted in part from speech in two of the examples given earlier. Because some implicit bias–inspired torts will arise from speech, some First Amendment analysis is necessary. A brief history of the Supreme Court's rulings on speech torts and criminal regulation of hate speech and hate crime is helpful.

---

[40] *See* Pollard, *supra* note 9, at 815–17 (discussing the efficacy of California's campaign against drunk driving, which effectively changed driving behavior).

[41] *See, e.g.*, McAdams, *supra* note 6, at 358 (a norm arises where there is a consensus about the positive or negative esteem worthiness of engaging in a behavior, there is some risk of being caught engaging in the behavior, and the existence of the consensus and the risk of being caught are publicized).

[42] *See* Pollard, *supra* note 9, at 812–24 nn.209, 219–24, 249 (discussing social norm changes resulting from new laws concerning public smoking and drunk driving).

Historically, tortious speech such as defamation was not subject to First Amendment protection. However, in 1964, the Supreme Court determined that tort liability constitutes state action, warranting some First Amendment protection against tort liability for speech. In a series of cases beginning with *New York Times v. Sullivan*,[43] the Court "constitutionalized" speech torts by raising the burdens of proof necessary to state a claim, thereby reducing the number of speech tort claims that can survive First Amendment scrutiny and enhancing speech protection. All tort liability for speech must meet the Court's constitutional restrictions, the parameters of which continue to evolve.

The Court's rulings on criminal penalties for hate speech and hate crime help clarify that the proposed tort remedies for implicit bias are constitutional. The Court determined in *R.A.V. v. City of St. Paul* that viewpoint-based punishment for hate speech is unconstitutional even when the speech falls within a class of *unprotected* speech.[44] However, the Court decided the following year in *Wisconsin v. Mitchell* that enhanced penalties for hate-motivated crimes do not present a First Amendment problem because the enhanced penalties relate to criminal *conduct* regardless of any expressive *content*, such as where the defendant chose the victim based on the victim's race, religion, color, disability, sexual orientation, national origin, or ancestry.[45] That is, a criminal penalty enhancement is constitutional if it is based on an illegal act that the state has a special interest in deterring where the penalty is unrelated to any expressive component. Although many illegal acts could be characterized as expressive in nature, such as shooting a member of the U.S. Congress to express outrage about congressional policy, the Supreme Court has long rejected the concept that violent crimes are protected just because they may express political or other opinion.[46] Similarly, federal courts have long recognized that speech that embodies a crime or tort is similarly unprotected under the "speech acts" doctrine.[47] As clarified by the Supreme Court in *R.A.V. v. City of St. Paul*, "Where the government does not target conduct on the basis of its expressive content, acts are not shielded from regulation merely because they express a discriminatory idea or philosophy."[48]

Torts caused by speech that reveals implicit bias should be distinguished from other torts caused by implicit bias, although neither presents a First Amendment problem. Where a government seeks to expose and punish implicit bias that causes tortious *conduct* that is itself unprotected by the First Amendment, the government's motive is both content and viewpoint neutral, and the First Amendment is not

---

43 376 U.S. 254 (1964).
44 R.A.V. v. City of St. Paul, 505 U.S. 377 (1992). *Cf.* Richard Delgado, *Words that Wound: A Tort Action for Racial Insults, Epithets, and Name-Calling*, 17 HARV. C.R.- C.L. L. REV. 133 (1982).
45 Wisconsin v. Mitchell, 508 U.S. 476, 481 n.1 (1993).
46 *Id.* at 484.
47 *See, e.g.*, Rice v. Paladin, 123 F.3d 233 (4th Cir. 1997).
48 R.A.V., 505 U.S. at 390.

violated, in accordance with *Wisconsin v. Mitchell*. Indeed, tort remedies for conduct caused by implicit bias present even less of a First Amendment concern than enhanced penalties for hate crimes, because implicit bias is, by definition, unexpressed and unintended: no race-based "hate" is intended. In *Wisconsin v. Mitchell*, the sticky issue that persuaded the Wisconsin Supreme Court to find that the hate-crime–enhanced penalty was unconstitutional was its potential for "chilling" racist speech. That is, a prosecutor could use prior racist statements to prove that a crime was motivated by hate, so people might avoid making First Amendment protected racist statements for fear that the statements could later be used as evidence against them in a subsequent hate-crime prosecution.[49]

The Supreme Court rejected this analysis, pointing out that the First Amendment generally does not prohibit the evidentiary use of speech to prove a crime, motive, or intent.[50] The tort remedies proposed herein present no First Amendment threat and circumvent the Wisconsin Supreme Court's concerns because, although prior racist statements may prove *conscious* bias, they do not prove *implicit* bias and would therefore be irrelevant to the issue of whether implicit bias caused a tort.[51] To the extent that expressed, conscious bias motivates tortious conduct, an enhanced penalty presumably would be governed by *Wisconsin v. Mitchell*, a concept Justice Kagan referred to as "hate torts" nearly twenty years ago,[52] but not subject to the tort remedies proposed herein.

For implicit bias–inspired speech, the analysis is similar. The proposed tort remedies apply only to tortious speech caused by *implicit* bias, not racist or other consciously biased speech. That is, speech that may be subject to the proposed tort remedies is tortious *but not overtly biased*, so no expression of bias protected by the First Amendment enters the marketplace of ideas. Rather, the bias "sneaks out of the brain" and affects judgment and behavior beyond conscious awareness, rendering it unworthy of First Amendment protection because it bypasses conscious intellectual processes.[53] To the extent that racist or other consciously biased speech allegedly constitutes a tort per se, any enhanced penalty – and indeed liability itself – is probably precluded by *R.A.V. v. City of St. Paul*. Tortious speech caused by implicit bias circumvents the concerns expressed in *R.A.V. v. City of St. Paul* so that, provided that the Court's general First Amendment limits to imposing civil liability for speech are not violated, tort remedies for bias-inspired speech pose no First Amendment issue.

---

[49] Mitchell, 508 U.S. at 481–82.

[50] *Id.* at 489.

[51] Clearly, overtly prejudiced people probably also harbor implicit bias. However, some research has shown that "high-prejudiced people" and "low-prejudiced people" can demonstrate equal activation of implicit stereotypes, rendering conscious prejudice irrelevant as well as more prejudicial than probative.

[52] *See* Elena Kagan, *Regulation of Hate Speech After R.A.V.*, 60 U. Chi. L. Rev. 873, 887 (1993).

[53] *See* Waller v. Osbourne, 763 F. Supp. 1144, 1148–49 (M.D. Ga. 1991).

V. CONCLUDING REMARKS

It is uncivilized for any society to allow a subset of the population to bear most or all of the costs of social dysfunction. Implicit bias poses a constant, pervasive threat to society and causes much silent suffering. People who are not subject to common stereotypes and do not feel the sting of unfair assumptions and bias-inspired injustice may not understand what all the fuss is about, which is precisely why implicit bias must be brought into the public spotlight. If we, as a society, are ever to create a more civilized and fair society, it should be accomplished though introspection and open discourse. Engaging legal doctrine to expose the problem of implicit bias and commence public and private debate may be a starting point to advance self-actualization, individual liberty, collective unity, and a more egalitarian future for America. Tort liability potentially is one means of furthering these goals.

5

Employment Law

Implicit Bias in Employment Litigation

Judge Nancy Gertner and Melissa Hart

Every employment discrimination lawsuit tells at least two stories – stories that are about judgment, discretion, and even bias. One story starts long before litigation, with workplace relationships and decisions. The parties end up in court only after one of the actors, the defendant, decided that the other, the plaintiff, will be fired or not hired, demoted, or not given a raise. Those decisions invariably involve personal judgments – even biases that are explicit or implicit. Once an adverse employment action is challenged in court, however, a new story, with yet another set of decision-makers takes over. Even then, the decisions that judges must make about how to interpret the information presented in court leave room for discretion, judgment, and a new opportunity for bias.

Judges rarely recognize the part they play in this second story line. A few years ago at an annual event held in Massachusetts, a plaintiff's attorney asked a panel of district court judges, "Why are federal judges so hostile to employment discrimination claims?" Most of the judges protested that they were not personally biased against these claims; they were merely applying the law. However, U.S. District Judge Nancy Gertner (one of the authors) agreed with the lawyer, rather than her colleagues, holding that both the law and often those applying it reflect a deep skepticism about claims of discrimination that necessarily affects litigation outcomes.

Judges exercise enormous discretion in civil litigation in general, a discretion that has only increased with recent decisions of the Supreme Court. The Court has directed that a judge considering a motion to dismiss should exercise "common sense" in evaluating the plaintiff's claim in light of other "plausible" explanations for a defendant's conduct.[1] The trial court's "common sense" view of what is or is not "plausible" affects employment litigation perhaps more than any other type of litigation. Studies have shown that judicial biases significantly influence summary judgment outcomes in such cases. Indeed, many commentators have noted that

[1] Ashcroft v. Iqbal, 129 S. Ct. 1937 (2009).

employment discrimination plaintiffs face an unusually difficult uphill battle. As a general matter, doctrinal developments in the past two decades have quite consistently made it more difficult for plaintiffs to assert their claims of discrimination. In addition, many of these doctrines have increased the role of judicial judgment – and the possibility of the court's implicit bias – in the life cycle of an employment discrimination case.

This chapter explores the range of discretion and the possibility of bias not in the workplace, but in the courtroom. We examine how the development of employment discrimination law, particularly in recent years, has made the finding and the remediation of bias – of all kinds – ever more difficult. Both the legal doctrine and its application by trial and appellate judges reflect the often unrealistic search for a rogue, guilty decision-maker in the workplace, whose biases are overt. Anything short of that – any more subtle form of discrimination – will not pass muster. If you believe that the battle for equality is largely over, if you cannot imagine that discrimination can masquerade behind ostensibly neutral words or that even sexist or racist remarks reflect the actor's true discriminatory intent, you will rarely find claims of discrimination to be plausible. Your "common sense" will always tell you otherwise.

Part I begins by examining the persistence of gender and racial disparity in the workplace despite the fact that laws prohibiting discrimination have been on the books for decades. Social science offers an explanation in the form of studies that describe the role implicit bias plays in those continuing inequities just as the legal system seems especially resistant to integrating their insights. Part II explores the ways in which doctrinal developments for assessing evidence in employment discrimination cases – the procedural mechanisms that guide the cases through the system – are a one-way ratchet that makes it harder and harder to prove that discrimination occurred and that enables the judge to enact his or her biases.

I. THE PERSISTENCE OF WORKPLACE DISCRIMINATION, THE ROLE OF IMPLICIT BIAS, AND THE INSIGHTS OFFERED BY SOCIAL SCIENCE

Federal law has prohibited race discrimination in employment for more than forty-five years,[2] yet evidence from multiple sources reveals significant continuing racial and gender disparities in workplace opportunity. Recent studies confirm that these disparities are substantially attributable to bias on the part of decision-makers. Indeed, the more recent studies build on the decades-old consensus among social scientists

---

[2] Title VII of the Civil Rights Act of 1964, which prohibits discrimination based on race, sex, religion, and national origin, went into effect in 1965. *See* 42 U.S.C. § 2000e (2006). Other federal laws prohibiting discrimination based on age and disability have followed. *See* The Age Discrimination in Employment Act of 1967 (ADEA), Pub. L. No. 90–202 (codified as amended at 29 U.S.C. § 621 (2006)); The Americans with Disabilities Act of 1990 (ADA), Pub. L. No. 101–336 (codified as amended at 42 U.S.C. § 12101 (2006)).

about the cognitive processes that produce bias and stereotyping and the ways that workplace policies operate to make these biases more or less significant in the allocation of opportunity. Yet just as litigants have sought to incorporate the insights of social science into their litigation strategy, the distance between legal analysis and social scientific analysis has widened.

A. *Evidence of Continued Discrimination at Work*

The persistence of discrimination in employment is reflected not only in the ever-growing number of charges of discrimination filed with the Equal Employment Opportunity Commission (EEOC) – almost 36,000 charges of race discrimination filed in 2010 – but also in statistics that show disparities in income and opportunity. Indeed "[e]very measure of economic success reveals significant racial inequality in the U.S. labor market."[3] The most recent EEOC data, for example, show that people of color make up 34 percent of the private sector workforce, but hold only 11 percent of senior or executive positions.[4] In large law firms, people of color constitute 12.4 percent of the associate pool, but only 6 percent of partners.[5] And on the federal bench, 84 percent of the judges are white, and a significant percentage of the ninety-four federal district courts in the country have never had a judge who was a person of color.[6]

In 2010, the median weekly earnings for full-time employees varied significantly by race and gender: for white men, the average was $850 a week, whereas for black men that number dropped to $633 and Hispanic men earned an average $560 each week.[7] Among women, the median weekly earnings were $684 for white women, $592 for black women, and $508 for Hispanic women.

In 2009, the Bureau of Labor Statistics reported that the unemployment rate for black male college graduates 25 and older was nearly twice that of white male college graduates – 8.4 percent compared with 4.4 percent.[8]

Social psychologists, organizational behavioralists, and labor economists offer a range of possible explanations for these continuing disparities. Central to these

---

[3] Marianne Bertrand & Sendhil Mullainathan, *Are Emily and Greg More Employable than Lakisha and Jamal? A Field Experiment on Labor Market Discrimination*, 94 Am. Econ. Rev. 991 (2004).

[4] Equal Employment Opportunity Commission, 2009 Job Patterns for Minorities and Women in Private Industry (2009), *available at* http://www1.eeoc.gov/eeoc/statistics/employment/jobpat-eeo1/2009/index.cfm#select_label.

[5] *Law Firm Diversity Among Associates Erodes in 2010*, Nat. Assoc. for L. Placement (November 4, 2010), http://www.nalp.org/2010lawfirmdiversity.

[6] Carl Tobias, *Diversity on the Federal Bench*, Nat. L. J., October 12, 2009, *available at* http://www.law.com/jsp/nlj/PubArticleNLJ.jsp?id=1202434429480.

[7] U.S. Dept. of Labor, Median Weekly Earnings of Full-Time Wage and Salary Workers by Sex, Race and Hispanic or Latino ethnicity, 1979–2010 annual averages 41 (2011), http://www.bls.gov/cps/cpsrace2010.pdf.

[8] Michael Luo, *In Job Hunt, College Degree Can't Close Racial Gap*, N.Y. Times, Dec. 1, 2009, *available at* www.nytimes.com/2009/12/01/us/01race.html.

explanations is the conclusion, supported by empirical evidence, that racial and gender bias – whether implicit or otherwise – continues to play a significant role in the allocation of job opportunities. Two recent studies that focused specifically on the role played by race in employment decisions found that it was a significant factor. In one study, researchers sent out sets of resumes with identical qualifications, giving half of the "applicants" names traditionally associated with African Americans – "Lakisha" and "Jamal" – and half names without a specific ethnic association, such as "Greg" and "Emily."[9] They found a 50 percent gap in callback rates between the white and black resumes. This gap – which meant that a white candidate received one callback for every ten resumes submitted, whereas a black candidates had to send out fifteen resumes for the single callback – existed across occupations and industries.[10] The researchers estimated that "a white name yields as many more callbacks as an additional eight years of experience."[11]

In another study, a group of labor economists found that the race of the hiring manager has a significant effect on the race of new hires.[12] This study used data from a large U.S. retailer to examine how a change in the race of a manager affects the likelihood of black employees being hired. "The estimates suggest that when a black manager is replaced by a non-black manager in a typical store, the share of new hires that is black falls roughly from 21 to 17 percent, and the share that is white rises from 60 to 64 percent."[13] The researchers isolated other common traits in supervisors and employees and found that racial bias was by far the most likely explanation for the decision patterns.

B. Insights from Social Science about the Relationship between Workplace Policies and Intrusion of Bias

In addition to studies that specifically identify racial dynamics in work decisions, there is a long history of social science analyses focused on explaining how organizational culture and structure relate to the extent of bias in a workplace. Extensive research on the formation of corporate cultures has identified the ways in which organizations reflect both formal and informal cultures, some created very explicitly and some generated more organically.[14] Corporate cultures provide a context within which supervisors and employees determine what is permissible and what is

---

[9] Bertrand & Mullainathan, *supra* note 3.

[10] *Id.*

[11] *Id.*

[12] Laura Guiliano et al., *Manager Race and the Race of New Hires*, 27 J. Lab. Econ. 589 (2009).

[13] *Id. See also* Anne Lawton, *The Meritocracy Myth and the Illusion of Equal Employment Opportunity*, 85 Minn. L. Rev. 587, 600–01 (2000) (describing studies that show both race and gender disparities, particularly in more highly paid, prestigious fields).

[14] *See, e.g.*, J. N. Baron & D. M. Kreps, Strategic Human Resources: Frameworks For General Managers 19–20 (1999); E. H. Schein, Organizational Culture and Leadership (4th ed. 2010).

not. "Case study research on workplaces shows that internal policies and practices play a significant role in shaping the culture of the workplace, and that workplace cultures may in turn help to sustain or minimize bias."[15] Although cultural contexts may not control individual decision-makers, researchers have found that they have a considerable influence in shaping decisions.

Of particular importance to the role implicit bias plays in employment discrimination, case studies have shown that corporate cultures that include unguided managerial discretion tend to permit greater consideration of irrelevant factors such as race and gender in the allocation of workplace benefits and opportunities.[16] In contrast, employers with more formalized and transparent decision-making practices and more oversight have less disparity and less bias in workplace decisions.[17]

Over the past several decades, social scientists have testified as expert witnesses in employment discrimination cases, offering to explain to judges and juries how these phenomena operate to permit bias to infiltrate workplace decisions. One of the earliest and most famous cases was a sex discrimination case, *Price Waterhouse v. Hopkins*.[18] Ann Hopkins was a candidate for partnership at Price Waterhouse in 1982. At the time she was considered, the company had 7 female and 655 male partners, and Hopkins was the only woman being considered for partnership that year.[19] Although she had an extremely successful business record at the firm, some described her as abrasive and as particularly hard on staff members. Her lack of interpersonal skills was of major concern to many evaluating her candidacy.[20] In discussions among the men considering Hopkins's candidacy, she was described as "macho," advised to take "a course at charm school," and to "walk more femininely, talk more femininely, dress more femininely, wear make-up, have her hair styled, and wear jewelry."[21]

---

[15] Brief for American Sociological Association and the Law and Society Association, as Amici Curiae Supporting Respondents at 8, Wal-Mart Stores, Inc. v. Dukes, 131 S. Ct. 2541 (2011).

[16] *See, e.g.*, N. Dasgupta, *Implicit Ingroup Favoritism, Outgroup Favoritism, and Their Behavioral Manifestations*, 17 SOC. JUST. RES. 143 (2004); M. Hewstone et al., *Intergroup Bias*, 53 ANN. REV. PSYCH. 575 (2002); C. N. Macrae & G. V. Bodenhausen, *Social Cognition: Thinking Categorically About Others*, 51 ANN. REV. PSYCH. 93 (2000). It bears mentioning that, although consideration of race may be a result of implicit or unconscious bias, it may also be the result of explicit, though unstated prejudice. *See* Ralph Richard Banks & Richard Thompson Ford, *(How) Does Unconscious Bias Matter? Law Politics and Racial Inequality*, 58 EMORY L.J. 1053, 1059 (2009) ("The unconscious bias approach not only discounts the persistence of knowing discrimination, it elides the substantive inequalities that fuel conscious and unconscious bias alike.").

[17] *See, e.g.*, FRANK DOBBIN, INVENTING EQUAL OPPORTUNITY (2009); Alexandra Kalev et al., *Best Practices or Best Guesses? Assessing the Efficacy of Corporate Affirmative Action and Diversity Policies*, 71 AM. SOC. REV. 589 (2006); J. A. Kmec, *White Hiring Agents' Organizational Practices and Out-Group Hiring*, 35 SOC. SCI. RES. 668 (2005); L. B. Edelman & S. Petterson, *Symbols and Substance in Organizational Response to Civil Rights Law*, 17 RES. SOC. STRATIFICATION & MOBILITY 107 (1999).

[18] 490 U.S. 228 (1989).

[19] *Id.* at 233.

[20] *Id.* at 233–35.

[21] *Id.* at 235.

After examining the decision-making process used for partner selection at Price Waterhouse, psychologist Susan Fiske, Hopkins's expert witness, reviewed the extensive literature on sex stereotyping and analyzed the aspects of the Price-Waterhouse partnership process that permitted sex stereotyping to influence the decision not to award Hopkins a partnership.[22] Fiske focused particularly on Hopkins's status as the only woman in the pool of candidates, the subjectivity of the evaluation process, and the language – both explicitly discriminatory and more subtly biased – used to describe her.[23]

Although similar testimony has been offered in harassment cases and in class action litigation in recent years,[24] its appropriateness has become a topic of increasing controversy in both academic and litigation settings.[25] The debate came to a head in the Supreme Court's 2011 decision in *Wal-Mart v. Dukes*, in which the Court's majority was highly critical of the expert testimony offered by plaintiffs to show how excessively subjective decision-making can lead to impermissible disparities in pay and promotions.[26]

The *Wal-Mart* decision highlighted the differences between the conclusions reached in court decisions and the kinds of conclusions reached by social scientists. In *Wal-Mart*, organizational behavioralist Dr. William Bielby testified about the structural dynamics of workplace decision-making and the social science evidence demonstrating how the kinds of policies adopted by Wal-Mart made the company vulnerable to the intrusion of significant bias in workplace decisions.[27] Indeed, Dr. Bielby's testimony was similar to that offered decades earlier by Dr. Fiske in *Price Waterhouse*, applying the insights of social science to the ways in which both organizations and individuals contributed to biased decision-making.

The Supreme Court rejected Dr. Bielby's testimony, asserting that it "does nothing to advance [plaintiffs'] case." Dr. Bielby had acknowledged at his deposition that his expertise allowed him to offer information about the risks presented by the policies Wal-Mart had adopted, but that he could not specifically "calculate whether 0.5 percent or 95 percent of the employment decisions at Wal–Mart might be determined by stereotyped thinking."[28] In the view of the Supreme Court majority, that was "the essential question on which respondents' theory of commonality [in its class certification motion] depends. If Bielby admittedly has no answer to that question, we can safely disregard what he has to say. It is worlds away from significant proof that Wal–Mart operated under a general policy of discrimination."[29] The

---

[22] *See* Hopkins v. Price Waterhouse, Inc., 618 F.Supp. 1109, 1117–18 (D.D.C. 1985).

[23] *Id.* at 235–36.

[24] *See* Melissa Hart & Paul Secunda, *A Matter of Context: Social Framework Evidence in Employment Discrimination Class Actions*, 78 FORDHAM L. REV. 37, 45–50 (2009).

[25] *Id.* at 51–66.

[26] 131 S.Ct. 2541 (2011).

[27] *Id.* at 2562.

[28] Dukes v. Wal-Mart, Inc., 222 F.R.D. 189, 192 (N.D. Cal. 2004).

[29] Wal-Mart, 131 S.Ct. at 2563.

Court's observations are troubling, to say the least. Human behavior – and surely proof of discriminatory intent – cannot be reduced to numerical percentages. To suggest that nothing short of mathematical precision justifies this kind of testimony fundamentally underestimates its considerable value. As one court held in admitting social frameworks evidence, such testimony "does not tell the jury what to decide in any given case; it only tells them what to consider."[30]

Moreover, the search for the "general policy of discrimination" is perhaps even more troubling. It reflects the view that redressing discrimination in the twenty-first century is about ferreting out overt discrimination, the offending policy, or the overt discriminator. For those willing to listen, the social science research has been explaining for years that discrimination is much more complicated than that.

Future courts considering expert evidence from social scientists may choose to limit *Wal-Mart* to its particular facts. After all, the Court did not broadly condemn the use of social science testimony, but rather criticized the use of that specific testimony to justify class action treatment. Undoubtedly, defendants will argue that the Court's criticisms can be generalized to all employment discrimination cases, that the insights of social science just do not answer the same question that a lawsuit seeks to resolve. If employment discrimination law continues in its present direction, it is likely that many courts will agree with those arguments.

II. LEGAL DEVELOPMENTS THAT EXCLUDE CLAIMS OF IMPLICIT BIAS IN THE WORKPLACE, ALL THE WHILE PERMITTING ITS INTRUSION IN COURTS

Although there is a great deal of consensus among social psychologists and organizational behavioralists about the role implicit bias plays in decision-making, there is no similar consensus among legal scholars or courts about the extent to which employment law should reflect this phenomenon.

The scholarly debate has focused predominantly on Title VII's prohibition against discrimination "because of" race or some other protected characteristic as it applies in individual discrimination claims. Many scholars have argued that current law prohibits such acts of discrimination, observing that the question of whether bias is conscious or unconscious is irrelevant to the question whether the evidence demonstrates discrimination.[31] The law prohibits acts taken "because of" discrimination without specifying whether that discrimination must be conscious or explicit. Others assert that the law prohibits – and should prohibit – only conscious

---

[30] Tuli v. Brigham & Women's Hosp., Inc., 592 F. Supp. 2d. 208 (D.Mass. 2009).

[31] *See, e.g.*, Tristin K. Green & Alexandra Kalev, *Discrimination-Reducing Measures at the Relational Level*, 59 HASTINGS L.J. 1435 (2008); Melissa Hart, *Subjective Decisionmaking and Unconscious Discrimination*, 56 ALA. L. REV. 741 (2005); Linda Hamilton Krieger, *The Content of Our Categories: A Cognitive Bias Approach to Discrimination and Equal Employment Opportunity*, 47 STAN. L. REV. 1161, 1164 (1995).

discriminatory animus. These scholars argue that plaintiffs overreach when they seek to hold employers accountable for stereotyping they do not know they are engaged in and that, in any event, the operation of implicit bias in the workplace is far from certain.[32]

To a large extent, this debate misses the mark. It ignores the legal doctrines that already exist and that target workplace policies whose net effect is to enable implicit bias to operate in job decisions; namely, disparate impact and pattern and practice claims. To be sure, recent decisions of the Supreme Court may be interpreted as undermining or at least narrowing such claims.[33] In this environment, the individual disparate treatment claim may well be the most viable route for employment discrimination plaintiffs. Yet the same questions persist even in the individual cases – whether the law requires a search for the overt discriminator, ignoring more subtle forms of discrimination, and what kind of evidence can be used to show how bias operates in the workplace at issue.

In any event, whatever standard applies, the critical question is how is it applied by this important decision-maker – the judge. "Plaintiffs' attempts to convey their stories fall on deaf ears as courts find ways of rationalizing any of the various challenges made to an employers' business justification."[34] Implicit bias not only plays a role in the underlying story that gives rise to an employment discrimination claim. Even more troubling, an examination of the doctrines courts have developed to evaluate the evidence suggests that it plays at least as significant a role in the second story – the story of the way the claims fare in litigation.

It has been widely noted that employment discrimination plaintiffs do not do well in federal courts.[35] In fact, very few employment discrimination cases get to trial. Some claims never make it past the initial stages of litigation, when defendants ask judges to dismiss because the facts pled by the plaintiff do not state a claim for legal relief. Others survive that first stage, only to be dismissed at summary judgment. The cases are fact intensive and while disputes of fact should mean the denial of summary judgment, discrimination cases are different. The result often depends entirely on how the judge perceives the facts and the overall narrative. These perceptions, rarely overturned on appeal even on de novo review, spell the difference between defeat for a plaintiff or the case moving forward to a jury.[36] Indeed, research on national jury verdicts suggests that, if an employment discrimination plaintiff can get past

---

[32] Amy L. Wax, *The Discriminating Mind: Find It, Prove It*, 40 CONN. L. REV. 979, 985 (2008).

[33] *See, e.g.*, Ricci v. DeStefano, 129 S.Ct. 2658 (2009); Wal-Mart Stores, Inc. v. Dukes, 131 S.Ct. 2541 (2011).

[34] Natasha T. Martin, *Pretext in Peril*, 75 MO. L. REV. 313, 317 (2010).

[35] *See, e.g.*, Elizabeth M. Schneider, *The Changing Shape of Federal Civil Pretrial Practice: The Disparate Impact on Civil Rights and Employment Discrimination Cases*, 158 U. PA. L. REV. 517 (2010); Kevin M. Clermont & Stewart J. Schwab, *Employment Discrimination Plaintiffs in Federal Court: From Bad to Worse?*, 3 HARV. L. & POL'Y REV. 103, 131–32 (2009); Michael Selmi, *Why Are Employment Discrimination Cases So Hard to Win?*, 61 LA. L. REV. 555, 557 (2001).

[36] *See, e.g.*, Pat K. Chew, *Seeing Subtle Racism*, 2 STAN. J. C.R. & C.L. 183, 185–86 (2010).

judicial dismissal and make it to a jury, she or he has a significant chance of winning a verdict.[37]

A. *Plausibility Pleading and Judicial "Common Sense"*

The Supreme Court's 2009 decision in *Ashcroft v. Iqbal* directed district courts evaluating motions to dismiss to "draw on [their] judicial experience and common sense" in assessing whether a plaintiff's allegations met the threshold of stating a "plausible claim for relief."[38] The Court observed that this plausibility requirement demands something more than pleadings that are "merely consistent with" liability.[39] Instead, when a judge evaluates a complaint, she or he should ask – as the Court itself did in *Iqbal* – whether alternative explanations for the events complained of are more likely than the allegations made by the plaintiff.[40]

The *Iqbal* standard is most likely to influence outcomes in cases that turn on allegations of discriminatory intent.[41] Because intent is typically proven by circumstantial evidence, the judge is obliged to draw inferences about the meaning of the evidence and, in particular, about the likelihood that bias was a motivating factor in the defendant's actions. Specifically, a judge is supposed to consider whether discrimination or some other explanation more "plausibly" explains the facts.

By placing the judge's own "common sense" at the heart of the decision whether to dismiss a discrimination claim at an early stage of litigation, the *Iqbal* standard risks increasing the impact of a judge's implicit biases on the outcome of employment disputes. Indeed, there is little difference between judicial "common sense" and the very cognitive processes that social scientists have identified as producing stereotyping and bias. When the legal standard itself incorporates reliance on that kind of judgment, it places corresponding importance on the identities of the judges themselves.

Much recent legal scholarship has sought to assess whether the *Iqbal* standard has in fact increased the number of employment discrimination cases that are dismissed on the pleadings. Several studies have found that courts applying *Iqbal* are more likely to grant a motion to dismiss in a civil rights case than they were under the old pleading standards.[42] Even when cases are not dismissed outright, *Iqbal*'s command that judges use their "common sense" in evaluating plaintiffs' claims puts a judge's

[37] Joseph Seiner, *After Iqbal*, 45 WAKE FOREST L. REV. 179, 199–200 (2010).

[38] 129 S. Ct. 1937, 1950 (2009).

[39] *Id.* at 1949.

[40] *Id.* at 1951–52.

[41] *See, e.g.,* Stephen Burbank & Stephen Subrin, *Litigation and Democracy: Restoring a Realistic Prospect of Trial*, 46 HARV. C.R.-C.L. L. REV. 399, 408 (2011).

[42] Seiner, *supra* note 38 at 179; Patricia Hatamyar, *The Tao of Pleading: Do Twombly and Iqbal Matter Empirically?*, 59 AM. U. L. REV. (2010); Howard M. Wasserman, *Iqbal, Procedural Mismatches, and Civil Rights Litigation*, 14 LEWIS & CLARK L. REV. 157 (2010).

own perspective front and center in the analysis from the outset. Although the judge was always part of the story, this standard legitimizes an even larger role.

B. *Summary Judgment and the Meaning of Evidence*

A case thrown out on the pleadings will not go through any of the factual development permitted by discovery in civil litigation. Even those cases that make it through discovery are more likely to be rejected by a judge at summary judgment than to get to a jury. Recent studies show that more than 70 percent of summary judgment motions in employment discrimination cases are granted.[43] Once again, the attitudes of judges considering these cases – the biases and assumptions they bring to their analysis – may be determinative.

In one of its earliest cases interpreting Title VII,[44] the Supreme Court set out a structure for the presentation of evidence that would, ideally, help uncover impermissible motivations for employment actions. Initially, the plaintiff must meet the basic requirements of a prima facie case designed to eliminate some obvious nondiscriminatory explanations for an adverse action.[45] The defendant is then responsible for offering some legitimate, nondiscriminatory explanation for the events at issue.[46] Finally, the plaintiff carries the ultimate burden of proving that the adverse action took place under circumstances suggesting discrimination.[47] A plaintiff can meet this ultimate burden in a variety of ways. He or she may find "direct" evidence of discrimination in the form of a statement by the employer that the decision was made for discriminatory reasons, a very rare occurrence. Instead, most evidence is circumstantial evidence demonstrating that the defendant's proffered explanation for the decision is dishonest by pointing to similarly situated workers who were treated differently under similar circumstances, identifying discriminatory comments or behavior in the workplace, or pointing to the plaintiff's qualifications in relation to his or her coworkers. This skeletal proof structure is fleshed out in each individual case with the particular facts of the challenged employment decision.

Although every case is as unique as the facts that underlie it, numerous doctrines have developed to address some of the more typical types of evidence that plaintiffs

---

[43] *See* JOE CECIL & GEORGE CORT, FEDERAL JUDICIAL CENTER, ESTIMATES OF SUMMARY JUDGMENT ACTIVITY IN FISCAL YEAR 2006 (2007); Elizabeth M. Schneider, *The Dangers of Summary Judgment: Gender and Federal Civil Litigation*, 59 RUTGERS L. REV. 705, 709 n.22 (2007); Ann C. McGinley, *Credulous Courts and the Tortured Trilogy: The Improper Use of Summary Judgment in Title VII and ADEA Cases*, 34 B.C. L. REV. 203, 205–06 (1993) (arguing that "the increased inappropriate use of summary judgment" has "silently curtail[ed] workers' civil rights claims" and that the "misapplication of civil procedural rules to employment discrimination cases threatens substantive anti-discrimination law").

[44] McDonnell-Douglas Corp. v. Green, 411 U.S. 792, 802 (1973).

[45] Tex. Dep't of Cmty. Affairs v. Burdine, 450 U.S. 248 (1981).

[46] *Id.*

[47] *See* Reeves v. Sanderson Plumbing Prods., Inc., 530 U.S. 133 (2000).

and defendants offer in litigation. These judicially created doctrines are simply shorthand descriptive tools that judges use to characterize their understanding of the evidence presented by the parties. In many cases, they provide new opportunities for the stereotypes and assumptions of judges to filter cases out of litigation at early stages. Moreover, these doctrines often run counter to the insights of social science about how workplace dynamics actually operate. Three tools for evaluating evidence in particular – "stray remarks," "honest belief," and "same decision-maker" – all discount or ignore the way that cognitive processes operate.

1. Stray Remarks

The doctrine most likely to exclude evidence that may show bias – implicit or explicit – on the part of the decision-maker is the "stray remarks" doctrine. The notion that stray remarks in the workplace might not themselves prove discrimination derives from Justice Sandra Day O'Connor's concurring opinion in *Price Waterhouse v. Hopkins*.[48] In that case, which addressed "mixed-motive" discrimination in Title VII jurisprudence, Justice O'Connor was concerned that "stray remarks," as she defined them, should not be considered "direct evidence" of discrimination for the purpose of applying the "mixed-motive" approach, which was a more forgiving standard for discrimination claims.

The doctrine has unfortunately morphed over the years from its original use to distinguish direct from circumstantial evidence in mixed-motive cases into a tool for discounting, and even excluding, evidence that a judge determines to be more prejudicial than probative.[49] For example, in *Straughn v. Delta Air Lines*, the First Circuit characterized its stray remarks analysis as follows:

> Although statements directly related to the challenged employment action may be highly probative in the pretext inquiry... mere generalized "stray remarks," arguably probative of *bias* against a protected class, normally are not *probative of pretext* absent some discernible evidentiary basis for assessing their temporal and contextual relevance.[50]

Under this approach, comments that are "arguably probative of bias" may now not be "probative of pretext" unless they were (a) related to the employment, (b) made close in time to the employment decision, (c) uttered by decision makers or those in a position to influence the decision maker, and (d) unambiguous. Other courts have drawn similar conclusions.[51]

---

[48] 490 U.S. 228 (1989).

[49] *See, e.g.*, Henry v. Wyeth Pharm., Inc., 616 F.3d 134, 149–50 (2d Cir. 2010); Morgan v. N.Y. Life Ins. Co., 559 F.3d 425, 432 (6th Cir. 2009); Joseph v. Publix Super Markets., Inc., 151 Fed. App'x. 760, 769 (11th Cir. 2005).

[50] 250 F.3d 23, 36 (1st Cir. 2001) (internal citations omitted) (emphasis in original).

[51] *See, e.g.*, Hemsworth v. Quotesmith.Com, Inc., 476 F.3d 487, 491 (7th Cir. 2007); Wallace v. Methodist Hosp. Sys., 271 F.3d 212, 222 (5th Cir. 2001).

Yet Justice O'Connor's passing reference in her concurrence to "stray remarks" hardly justifies this approach. Indeed, the Supreme Court made it clear more than a decade ago that courts must consider *all* of the evidence in evaluating a claim of discrimination.[52] Further, weighing the evidence – including its temporal proximity to the employment decision and the speaker of the remark – is the job of the jury, not a judge.[53] A remark that may seem "stray" to a judge may strike the jury as evidence that the decision-maker harbored biases that influenced the employment decision. More broadly, it may reflect a culture in the organization, a culture that privileges negative remarks about minorities or women. Just because a remark appears "ambiguous" to the judge from his or her exalted perch does not mean that it did not have a clearer resonance in the context of the workplace give and take.[54]

Indeed, it is ironic that at a time when social scientists are identifying implicit biases in the way evaluators deal with "Lakisha" or "Tyrone," courts are discounting or, worse, excluding evidence of explicit bias.

2. Honest Belief

In some employment discrimination cases, a defendant offers an explanation for the adverse employment decision that the plaintiff then demonstrates is utterly lacking any factual basis. Imagine, for example, a black employee who is fired for theft, but who can demonstrate that she did not in fact steal a thing. In a majority of the federal circuits, a plaintiff in an employment discrimination case will not survive summary judgment when the employer articulates reasons for the plaintiff's termination and "the company honestly believe[s] in those reasons . . . even if the reasons are foolish or trivial or baseless."[55] Courts adhering to this version of the honest belief rule apply it aggressively at the summary judgment stage of employment discrimination cases, resulting in the dismissal of scores of cases without juror consideration of whether biases implicit or not may have played a role in the decision-makers' thought processes.

The doctrine is "plainly inconsistent with what empirical social psychologists have learned over the past twenty years about the manner in which stereotypes,

---

[52] Reeves, 530 U.S. 133 (2000).

[53] *Id.* at 152–53.

[54] Diaz v. Jiten Hotel Mgmt., Inc., 762 F. Supp. 2d 319 (D .Mass. 2011).

[55] Kariotis v. Navistar Int'l Transp. Corp., 131 F.3d 672, 676 (7th Cir. 1997) (internal citation omitted). *See also* Ruiz v. Posadas de San Juan Assocs., 124 F.3d 243, 248 (1st Cir. 1997); Hawkins v. PepsiCo, Inc., 203 F.3d 274, 279–80 (4th Cir. 2000); Deines v. Tex. Dep't of Protective & Regulatory Servs., 164 F.3d 277, 280–81 (5th Cir. 1999); Eurle-Wehle v. United Parcel Serv., Inc., 181 F.3d 898, 900 (8th Cir. 1999); Villiarimo v. Aloha Island Air, Inc., 281 F.3d 1054, 1063 (9th Cir. 2002); Piercy v. Maketa, 480 F.3d 1192, 1200–01 (10th Cir. 2007); Jones v. Gerwens, 874 F.2d 1534, 1540 (11th Cir. 1989); Woodruff v. Peters, 482 F.3d 521, 531 (D.C. Cir. 2007). The Sixth Circuit has departed from the majority approach, adopting a formulation of the honest belief rule that requires the employer to establish "its reasonable reliance on particularized facts that were before it at the time the decision was made" for the honest belief rule to defeat a plaintiff's discrimination claims. Smith v. Chrysler Corp., 155 F.3d 799, 807 (6th Cir. 1998).

functioning not as consciously held beliefs but as implicit expectancies, can cause a decision maker to discriminate against members of the stereotyped group."[56] A court that was taking seriously the possibility that implicit bias infects workplace decision-making would allow the jury to consider whether the defendant believed the plaintiff stole because of assumptions that he or she made about the trustworthiness of African American employees. Indeed, a small number of federal courts have recognized that there may be circumstances in which an employer acts honestly but "without awareness of the extent to which [its] judgments are influenced by ingrained discriminatory attitudes."[57]

3. Same Decision-Maker

Another doctrine that is sometimes used to dismiss a plaintiff's case at summary judgment is the "same decision-maker" or "same actor" defense. As first articulated by the Fourth Circuit in a 1991 decision, the doctrine developed because "[i]t hardly makes sense to hire workers from a group one dislikes (thereby incurring the psychological costs of associating with them), only to fire them once they are on the job."[58] The assumption behind this doctrine is that whatever bias a person has will manifest itself the same way at every stage of the employment relationship. That assumption is flawed; in fact, cognitive bias does not necessarily operate consistently, but instead may vary depending on circumstances.[59]

A majority of federal circuits have adopted some version of the same decision-maker defense.[60] However, some courts have recognized that the psychological assumption behind the theory may be an unreasonable one in many circumstances. As the Seventh Circuit observed, "a manager might hire a person of a certain race expecting [him] not to rise to a position in the company where daily contact with the manager would be necessary. . . . Similarly, if an employee were the first African-American hired, an employer might be unaware of his own stereotypical views

---

[56] Linda Hamilton Krieger & Susan T. Fiske, *Behavioral Realism in Employment Discrimination Law: Implicit Bias and Disparate Treatment*, 94 CAL. L. REV. 997, 1035 (2006); *see also* Anne Lawton, *The Meritocracy Myth and the Illusion of Equal Employment Opportunity*, 85 MINN. L. REV. 587, 616 (2000) (arguing that "[the] 'honest belief' standard has made it virtually impossible for a plaintiff to prevail on an employer's motion for summary judgment absent direct evidence of the employer's discriminatory intent").

[57] Henry v. Wyeth Pharm., Inc., 616 F.3d 134, 157–58 (2d Cir. 2010). *See also* Bernhard v. Nexstar Broad. Group, Inc., No. 04–3157, 2005 U.S. App. LEXIS 18870, at *8 (3d Cir. May 4, 2005) (declining to apply the honest belief doctrine); Obike v. Applied EPI, Inc., No. Civ. 02–1653(JRT/FLN), 2004 WL 741657, at *4–5 (D. Minn. Mar. 24, 2004) (same).

[58] Proud v. Stone, 945 F.2d 796, 797 (4th Cir. 1991) (quoting John J. Donohue & Peter Siegelman, *The Changing Nature of Employment Discrimination*, 43 STAN. L. REV. 983, 1017 (1991)).

[59] *See, e.g.* Linda Hamilton Krieger, *Civil Rights Perestroika: Intergroup Relations After Affirmative Action*, 86 CAL. L. REV. 1251, 1314–16 (1998).

[60] Natasha T. Martin, *Immunity for Hire: How the Same-Actor Doctrine Sustains Discrimination in the Contemporary Workplace*, 40 CONN. L. REV. 1117, 1128–29 (2008).

of African-Americans at the time of hiring."[61] Like the "honest belief" and "stray remarks" doctrines, the creation of a general rule that assumes a plaintiff's case is less valid when the same decision-maker was involved in both the hiring and the firing plainly makes it harder for an employment discrimination plaintiff to pursue the claim.

All three doctrines rest on flawed assumptions about human behavior that make them particularly inappropriate as general rules for evaluating evidence. The very fact that these doctrines gained a foothold in employment discrimination reflects a reluctance on the part of the federal judiciary to take seriously the role that implicit bias plays in discrimination.

III. CONCLUSION

Perceptions of the pervasiveness of employment discrimination as a continuing workplace problem vary widely. One survey of U.S. workers concluded that "race is the most significant determinant in how people perceive and experience discrimination in the workplace, as well as what they believe employers should do to address such incidents and attitudes."[62] In describing this racial divide in how Americans view the problem of discrimination, Professor Russell Robinson points to, among other evidence, polls taken between 1996 and 2003 showing dramatic "perceptual segregation."[63] These studies consistently found that half or more than half of African American respondents see significant continuing discrimination in the workplace, in contrast to only a small percentage of whites.[64] A 2003 Gallup poll found that "two-thirds of non-blacks say they are satisfied with the way blacks are treated," but almost the same percentage (59%) of blacks feel that black people are not treated well.[65] In 2011, researchers conducted a national survey and found that a significant percentage of white people believe not only that anti-black bias is no longer a

---

[61] *See, e.g.,* Johnson v. Zema Sys. Corp., 170 F.3d 734, 745 (7th Cir. 1999). *See also* Antonio v. Sygma Network, Inc., 458 F.3d 1177, 1183 (10th Cir. 2006) (noting that the jury should be permitted to decide the significance of the fact that the same person hired and fired a plaintiff); Williams v. Vitro Servs. Corp., 144 F.3d 1438, 1443 (11th Cir. 1998) (same).

[62] K.A. Dixon et al., A Workplace Divided: How Americans View Discrimination and Race on the Job (2002), *available at* http://www.issuelab.org/research/workplace_divided_how_americans_view_discrimination_and_race_on_the_job_a?utm_source=feedburner&utm_medium=feed&utm_campaign=Feed%3A+issuelab_race_and_ethnicity+%28IssueLab%3A+Race+and+Ethnicity%29; www.heldrich.rutgers.edu/uploadedFiles/Publications/Work_Trends_020107.pdf.

[63] Russell K. Robinson, *Perceptual Segregation*, 108 Colum. L. Rev. 1093, 1126–27 (2008).

[64] The percentage of whites seeing discrimination against African Americans varied, depending on the question asked, between 4 and 43%. *Id.*

[65] Steve Crabtree, *Worlds Apart? Treatment of Groups in Society*, Gallup Poll News Service, July 15, 2003, *available at* http://www.gallup.com/poll/8851/Worlds-Apart-Treatment-Groups-Society.aspx. *See also* David Benjamin Oppenheimer, *Understanding Affirmative Action*, 23 Hastings Const. L. Q. 921, 946–73 (1996) (describing national surveys over the past fifty years of racial stereotypes about blacks held by white Americans that "support the view that overt racism has lost favor socially, but racist attitudes lie close beneath the surface of our society"). *Id.* at 947.

serious problem in the United States but also that anti-white bias has become the more serious problem.[66]

Perhaps not surprisingly, in light of these surveys, research has also shown that a judge's race is likely to have an impact on his or her perceptions of the significance of racial harassment;[67] similarly, a judge's gender will affect her or his understanding of the significance of allegations in gender discrimination claims.[68] In short, the identity of the judge resolving a dispute matters. Ideally, the federal courts should include judges with a broad range of experiences and who understand how different their experiences likely are from those of most of the plaintiffs or defendants appearing before them. Even more essential is that judges recognize that their "common sense" is neither neutral nor objective.

Judges like to think they are "free of bias, even-handed, and open-minded."[69] Yet research on implicit bias and cognitive processes teaches that they cannot be entirely free of bias any more than any other person can be. The biases – implicit and otherwise – of judges reviewing discrimination claims may well play as much a role in the story of employment discrimination litigation as the biases that triggered the lawsuit.

---

[66] Michael Norton & Samuel Sommers, *Whites See Racism as a Zero-Sum Game That They Are Now Losing*, 6 PERSPECTIVES SOC. SCI. 215 (2011).

[67] *See also* Pat Chew & Robert E. Kelley, *Myth of the Color-Blind Judge: An Empirical Analysis of Racial Harassment Cases*, 86 WASH. U. L. REV. 1117, 1156–63 (2009).

[68] *See* Pat K. Chew, *Judges' Gender and Employment Discrimination Cases: Emerging Evidence-Based Empirical Conclusions*, 14 J. GENDER, RACE & JUSTICE 359 (2011).

[69] Judge Michael B. Hyman, *What the Blindfold Hides*, 48 JUDGES' J. 32 (2009).

6

Health Law

Cognitive Bias in Medical Decision-Making

Michele Goodwin and Naomi Duke

On any given day in the United States, disparities in the quality of health care and health outcomes for racial and ethnic minority groups in comparison to whites are evidenced in our nation's hospitals and clinics. These disparities are not fully explained by differences in patient education, income, insurance status, expressed preference for treatments, and severity of disease. Compelling research indicates that even for African Americans able to gain access to health care services, disparities persist in diagnostic screening and general medical care, mental health diagnosis and treatment, pain management, HIV-related care, and treatments for cancer, heart disease, diabetes, and kidney disease.[1]

For example, despite the implementation of standardized pain assessment in health care settings, disparities in pain management persist by race and ethnicity. African Americans and Hispanics are more likely to have their pain undertreated than non-Hispanic whites. Even with adjustment for multiple confounders, studies reveal the consistent under-treatment of African Americans and members of other marginalized racial and ethnic groups experiencing cancer pain, postoperative pain, chest pain, chronic low back pain, and other acute pain who present in emergency, primary care, inpatient hospital, and nursing home settings.[2]

Data regarding the management of heart disease reveal similar disparities in care along race and ethnic lines. Compared to white patients, African Americans are

---

[1] *See* M. van Ryn & S. S. Fu, *Paved with Good Intentions: Do Public Health and Human Service Providers Contribute to Race/Ethnic Disparities in Health?* 93 AM. J. PUB. HEALTH 248 (2003); Council on Ethical and Judicial Affairs, *Black-White Disparities in Health Care*, 263 J. AM MED. ASS'N 2344 (1990); *see* BRIAN D. SMEDLEY ET AL., UNEQUAL TREATMENT: CONFRONTING RACE AND ETHNIC DISPARITIES IN HEALTH CARE (FREE EXECUTIVE SUMMARY) (2003), *available at* http://www.allhealth. org/briefingmaterials/UnequalTreatment-56.pdf.

[2] C.R. Green et al., *The Unequal Burden of Pain: Confronting Racial and Ethnic Disparities in Pain*, 4 PAIN MED. 277 (2003); V.L. Shavers et al., *Race, Ethnicity, and Pain Among the U.S. Adult Population*, 21 J. HEALTH CARE FOR THE POOR & UNDERSERVED 177 (2010); A. Cintron. & R.S. Morrison., *Pain and Ethnicity in the United States: A Systematic Review*, 9 J. PALLIATIVE MED. 1454 (2006).

less likely to receive cardiac catheterization for acute myocardial infarction.[3] They are also significantly less likely to undergo coronary artery bypass grafting even after controlling for appropriateness and medical necessity.[4] These findings are not related to patient refusal or other demographic factors.[5] Thus, despite platitudes purporting the arrival of post-racialism in the United States, in this century, race and ethnic categorization still matter in defining Americans' health. Regrettably, these differentials in health can be compared to segregated health care systems of the past.

Medical researchers and scholars have helped build a credible tier of research that chronicles these health disparities, and health law reporters have garnered national praise for their books on the topic. Missing from this very important body of scholarship, however, is a theory to explain why biases occur. The emerging science of implicit racial bias might illume explanations for this deeply troubling history of disparate medical treatment and outcomes between racial minorities and whites in the United States. As Chapter 1 explained in detail, implicit bias references stereotypes and shared beliefs about a group that often result from positive or negative portrayals of the group in a shared environment. The stereotypic beliefs facilitate the development of attitudes marking preference of one group over another in personal and professional interactions.

Racial stereotyping persists despite rigorous, explicit debunking of myths portraying African Americans as racially inferior, of lower intelligence, dilatory, apathetic toward employment, harnessing a propensity for violent behavior, and as having a notorious preference for government subsidies. Even studies revealing that white women are more likely to smoke during pregnancy and consume alcohol than their African American counterparts, or that white youth are more likely to consume illicit drugs than African American and Latino teenagers, or that rates of drinking are highest among white teens have failed to dismantle these deeply entrenched, common misperceptions. In the medical context, implicit racial bias can result in the use of group membership instead of individual qualities to make judgments about a patient's motivations and health status.

This chapter takes up the issue of cognitive bias in medicine, focusing specifically on the role of implicit racial bias in maintaining inequities in health and health care. Practicing medicine requires physicians to diagnosis conditions on the basis of ambiguous symptoms, sometimes under severe time pressure, and often with the patient's well-being in jeopardy. Such uncertainty requires physicians to make decisions based on probability assessments, which in turn require physicians to assign meaning to a host of variables that pertain to the patient. Too often, racial background is one such variable. Our claim is that the interaction between a physician and a

---

[3] A.G. Bertoni et al., *Racial and Ethnic Disparities in Cardiac Catheterization for Acute Myocardial Infarction in the United States, 1995–2001*, 97 J. NAT'L MED. ASS'N 317 (2005).

[4] E.L. Hannan et al., *Access to Coronary Artery Bypass Surgery by Race/Ethnicity and Gender Among Patients Who Are Appropriate for Surgery*, 37 MED. CARE 68 (1999).

[5] *Id.*

black patient can trigger a cascade of stereotypes about black people (for example, that black people eat diets richer in fried foods than white people or black women will not exercise), which in turn become part of the context in which a diagnosis is made. Similarly, a stereotype that black patients do not adhere to their medication regimen as faithfully as white patients do could influence how the physician opts to treat a diagnosed condition. In both scenarios – one where stereotypic knowledge about black citizens could alter the diagnosis and the other where the same could alter treatment – the point is the same: physicians apply group stereotypes to individual patients without conscious regard for whether those stereotypes are accurate and, even if they are, whether the particular patient at issue is a counter-typical example. In the medical context, the answers to those questions – which physicians are not usually privy to because implicit biases frequently operate without conscious awareness – literally can mean the difference between life and death.

Not only can implicit racial bias influence individual decisions about a particular patient, but also those individual decisions can aggregate over the course of the client–patient relationship and risk resulting in substantively different treatment for similarly situated patients of different ethnicities. Similarly, as these biases aggregate to change the landscape of a particular case, they also begin to alter the direction of the entire medical field. We contend that implicit racial bias can help explain the widening health disparity gap, patient accounts of poor quality of care, and physician decision-making. Indeed, implicit bias may help explain a deeply troubling history of disparate medical treatment and outcomes between racial minorities and whites in the United States.

This chapter proceeds in five parts. Part I provides a brief overview of implicit bias and its relevance for medicine and efforts to better understand sources for the persistence in health disparities in the United States. Part II examines medical decision-making and situates the threat of implicit bias within this context. Part III briefly reviews the historical context of racial discrimination in the American health care system, while Part IV brings the discussion full circle by providing the most recent evidence linking implicit bias, medical decision-making, and disparate health. The latter section argues that, even in an age of expanded development in medical technology and greater strides to promote equity, remnants of a segregated health system remain in the form of differences in health outcome and treatment opportunity. In Part V, the chapter concludes with suggested interventions to redress implicit bias: (1) medical education and diversification of the workforce, (2) innovation in medical professional evaluation and monitoring, and (3) rethinking Title VI of the Civil Rights Act of 1964 as legal remedy.

I. IMPLICIT BIAS

We begin this chapter by framing and defining the terminology employed herein, offering consistent, though tailored descriptions of what constitutes an implicit bias or racial disparity in health care delivery. By doing so, we recognize that instances and patterns of discrimination can be stylized or uniquely situated according to specific spheres or interactions. To this end, we avoid generic terminology conflations and definitions. In other words, discrimination in medical delivery or access should not be conflated with unequal treatment in other services, such as legal services, housing accommodations, or education, although each might be proven to emanate from racial bias. Our framing denotes the particularities located within implicit health care biases and discrimination.

Implicit biases are likened to rapid, automatic, heuristic-driven actions producing unequal treatment.[6] Such biases are largely unconscious in nature, representing cognitive and neural processes shaped by sociocultural learning that apply positive and negative valence to demographic categories, most notably race and ethnicity. In a persuasive article published by the Stanford Law Review, Professor Charles Lawrence described unconscious discrimination and bias as being readily traceable to historical and contemporary notions of American society.[7] Indeed, conflict arising between historically rooted and reinforced unconscious preferences and a prevailing contemporary social ethic of egalitarianism relegates prejudice and stereotypes related to race to the subconscious.[8] Thus, when evidence confirms systematic disparities in health outcomes by demographic groups that are not attributable to (or caused by) income, health status, education level, and insurance status, researchers should consider implicit bias as a relevant influence in medical decision-making.

The Institute of Medicine defines disparities in care "as racial and ethnic differences in the quality of health care that are not due to access-related factors or clinical needs, [patient] preferences, and appropriateness of intervention."[9] From this definition, disparities are derived on two levels in the American medical system: (1) macro-level health care systems and the regulatory climate and (2) micro-level discriminatory behavior occurring in the exchange at the patient–provider level.[10] Accordingly, discrimination taking place during the patient–provider exchange reflects "differences in care that result from biases, prejudices, stereotyping, and uncertainty in clinical communication and medical decision-making."[11] In the context of implicit bias, differentials in care are not the result of unjust or unethical intent, but they do result in disparate impact.

Examples of implicit bias may be observed at the macro and micro levels. Most obviously, the impact of implicit bias at the systems level can be seen in disparate geographic positioning for health care facilities, highlighting tensions in access

---

[6] Christine Jolls & Cass R. Sunstein, *The Law of Implicit Bias*, 94 CAL. L. REV. 969 (2006).
[7] Charles R. Lawrence III, *The Id, the Ego, and Equal Protection: Reckoning with Unconscious Racism*, 39 STAN. L. REV. 317 (1987).
[8] *Id.*
[9] SMEDLEY ET AL., *supra* note 1, at 3–4.
[10] *Id.*
[11] *Id.*

between rural communities and cities as well as inner-cities versus elite or segregated urban communities. But, the effects of implicit bias at the macro level extend to institutional limitations placed on resource allocation for interpreter and translation services, institutional restrictions placed on the number of patients seen by payer status, and rigid time structures ordering the medical visit.

Likewise, analyses from the provider perspective yield examples of implicit bias's micro-level impact. The health care provider begins the medical visit with sincere intentions to provide relief for the suffering described by a patient. Implicit personal preferences and biases, not readily accessible, then affect the nonverbal body language of the provider, which is readily interpreted by the patient. The patient interaction may or may not support underlying biases, but overlying time constraints prohibit thoughtful consideration of unconscious opinions and objective determinants that have come into play. Objective evidence may be missed in favor of cognitive shortcuts, population-based heuristics, and social categorizations, which may be further consonant with underlying preformed opinions. The cognitive shortcuts form the basis for medical decision-making, diagnostic judgments, and recommendations regarding treatment modalities.

II. MEDICAL DECISION-MAKING AND CARE OF THE PATIENT

The prevailing American view understands medical providers as rational actors, objectively weighing the patient's history and clinical findings to arrive at the maximum likelihood diagnosis and a definitive treatment recommendation. This medical model is consistent with an American notion of an "equal playing field," imagined with egalitarian norms and values. However, as we argue in Part II, the realities of medical decision-making reveal more nuanced and complex dynamics driven by economic and social factors, which alone explain some, but not all racial disparities. For example, medical models and service delivery are burdened by several competing interests and well documented, if not mundane, realities. This includes the need for rapid assessment as a function of increasing demands to see more patients in a finite period of time, which creates perverse incentives.

Some of the externalities resulting from problematic service models are obvious such as physicians engaging in medical shortcuts (sometimes pushed by hospital, clinical, or HMO management), shuffling patients in and out as expeditiously as possible, and making less informed, making time-pressured "guesses" as to the underlying medical dilemmas associated with patients, and providing episodic care versus methodical, consistent treatment, because patients make fewer visits in light of financial constraints. Such pressures produce physician cognitive fatigue and patient physical fatigue.

The dynamics above individually and collectively illume the environmental (and economic) pressures that attend contemporary medical delivery. These factors do not operate in isolation of formal medical decision-making models. Rather, to better understand what causes cognitive biases to occur necessitates thinking about and acknowledging the constraints and externalities of medical delivery and cost optimalization alongside grappling with the contours of formal medical decision-making models.

Health care and sociological literatures identify several distinct medical decision-making models, including (1) paternalism, (2) informed decision-making, (3) professional-as-agent, and (4) shared decision-making.[12] Among clinical practice guidelines, shared decision-making is increasingly advocated as the standard of care and a quality of care measure, and there is good reason for this, especially when considering the fundamental goals of this model. Indeed, the foundational elements in a shared decision-making model include attention to dismantling the physician–patient hierarchy by (1) permitting shared decision-making beyond the patient and clinician, thereby providing flexibility for inclusion of more than two individuals (e.g., family and/or friends and multiple health providers); (2) communication of information by both the clinician and patient; (3) consensus with regard to the preferred treatment as a result of mutual exchange and commitment; and (4) final agreement and joint responsibility regarding the treatment to be implemented – a negotiated agreement.[13] Given this model's deliberate effort to promote patient decision-making inclusion, it comes as no surprise that patient advocacy groups perceive shared decision-making as the "best" model for physician–patient interaction as it promotes informed consent, informed choice, and patient autonomy and control.[14] As the nature of health care morphs from a focus on acute care to one of chronic disease management, shared decision-making and patient involvement become essential for effective health care management.[15]

However, shared medical decision-making does not operate in a vacuum, divorced from the economic and social externalities described supra. Even as doctors acknowledge the benefits of this model,[16] and may perceive their conduct as falling within this framework, implicit bias may be present in their conduct and thus undermine the health care goals they wish to achieve. We argue that implicit bias threatens the foundation for mutual exchange between the provider and patient, because

---

[12] The paternalistic model assumes a passive role for the patient with the physician as dominant, an expert, and a decision-maker. The informed model incorporates information sharing, generally from physician to patient; once informed, the patient is able to make medical decisions because he or she now possesses requisite information and personal value judgments. In the professional-as-agent model, the physician makes the treatment decision as if acting on behalf of the patient. This model assumes the physician has some insight into the patient's inclination regarding future health, consent notwithstanding. The shared decision-making model features two-way exchange for information as well as treatment preference. *See* Cathy Charles et al., *Shared Decision-Making in the Medical Encounter: What Does It Mean? (Or It Takes at Least Two to Tango)*, 44 Soc. Sci. Med. 681 (1997).

[13] *Id.*

[14] *Id.*

[15] Charles et al., *supra* note 12.

[16] *Id.*

the integrity of medical decision-making is compromised across multiple paradigms for health care delivery, all of which include aspects of shared decision-making.[17] Examined in this way, implicit biases may be the cause for some health care disparities, despite attention to physicians adopting particularly egalitarian medical decision-making models.

We apply the research of Drs. Michelle van Ryn and Steven Fu in situating implicit bias as a contributing factor to health care disparities in the medical decision-making context. Integrating social cognition and provider behavior research literatures, van Ryn and Fu offer several theories to account for the way in which health care and human service providers may influence and contribute to racial and ethnic disparities in care and treatment.[18] Their research suggests that providers' conscious and unconscious beliefs about patients (i.e., help seekers) influence the effects of patients' race and ethnicity on provider behavior.[19] Van Ryn and Fu make the following important observation:

> [P]roviders may influence help seekers' views of themselves and their relation to the world (society, culture, community). For example, providers may intentionally or unintentionally reflect and reinforce societal messages regarding help seekers' fundamental value, self-reliance, competence, and deservingness. Providers may both have and intentionally or unintentionally communicate lower expectations for patients in disadvantaged social positions... than for their more advantaged counterparts.... [P]roviders are powerful gatekeepers and may influence health disparities via such mechanisms as differential access to treatments or services and loss of benefits and rights.

The important takeaway is this: implicit bias operates as a significant threat to the patient–provider interaction, with direct impact on medical decision-making,

---

[17] Several paradigms exist as models for health care delivery: (1) relationship-centered care, anchored in four principles: relationships in care must include the personhood of all individuals; emotions and their expression are central to establishing relationships; context for reciprocity of effect; and moral value exists in relationship development and maintenance; *see* L.A. Cooper et al., *Delving Below the Surface*, 21 J. GEN. INTERN. MED. S21 (2006); (2) patient-centered care, anchored in four principles: respect and consideration for patients' cultural traditions, personal preferences, values, and family traditions; team approach and collaboration between patients, families, and providers in clinical decisions; support for patient self-care and monitoring; and efficiency and coordination of transitions; *see* INSTITUTE FOR HEALTHCARE IMPROVEMENT, www.ihi.org (last visited on February 7, 2011); and (3) family-centered care, pediatric framework anchored in seven principles: respect for child and his or her family; honoring sociodemographic and culture diversity that affects families' experience and perception of care; identifying and building of strengths of child and family; support and facilitation of choice for child and family; flexibility in care models that facilitates responsiveness to cultural beliefs and values of child and family; unbiased and open lines of communication that are affirming; and provision of formal and informal support to child and family throughout child development; *see* American Academy of Pediatrics Institute for Family-Centered Care, *Family-Centered Care and the Pediatrician's Role*, 112 PEDIATRICS 691 (2003).

[18] Ryn & Fu, *supra* note 1.

[19] *Id.*

the physician–patient relationship, and the quality of care delivered. Implicit bias in the medical context can result in providers bypassing or limiting in-depth questioning during medical assessments; miscalculating the interactional and cognitive competence of the patient; discouraging or limiting patient questions; ignoring, overlooking, or minimizing a patient's description of concerns; failing to recognize the cultural relevance assigned to symptoms by the patient; assigning demographic characteristics to infer causality for clinical manifestations; and miscalculating patient decision-making capacity. Individually, any of these factors can significantly undermine patient health. Collectively, they reveal the deadly potential of implicit bias.

III. HISTORY AND THE AMERICAN MEDICAL SYSTEM

The exploitation of African Americans and other minority groups by ways of medical experimentation, medical neglect, and substandard care occupies an important, if not fully understood space in U.S. history, spanning the antebellum period through Jim Crow and up to contemporary medicine. From experimentation performed on slaves to forced sterilization resulting from racist and classist notions of fitness and feeble-mindedness, a disquieting irony exists. Despite assertions of biological difference between blacks and whites, racial inferiority myths did not preclude the use of blacks in experiments and research activities for the betterment of a medical profession historically focused on servicing the larger white majority. As medical evidence demonstrates, African Americans still do not benefit fully from a medical system that many of their forbears sacrificed to create.

In the pre–Civil War time period, "[s]laves found themselves as subjects of medical experiments [as] physicians needed bodies and . . . the state considered [slaves] property[,] . . . [denying] them the legal right to refuse to participate."[20] Alongside slaves, other indigent, transient, and immigrant groups became source material for medical advancement,[21] but blacks were especially easy targets given their slave status. The unpaid, coerced manipulation of their bodies conferred benefits to others that were never intended to be realized for blacks. For example, the exploitation of blacks and other marginalized groups as a source of teaching material for white trainees contributed to the development and maintenance of medical institutions, which later excluded blacks from treatment even in life and death medical emergencies.[22] Indeed, preference for the use of black bodies for dissection prompted grave robbing and the delivery of executed black prisoners to medical societies.[23]

---

[20] Vanessa Northington Gamble, *Under the Shadow of Tuskegee: African Americans and Health Care*, 87 Am. J. Pub. Health 1773, 1774 (1997).
[21] Todd L. Slavit, *The Use of Blacks for Medical Experimentation and Demonstration in the Old South*, 48 J. S. Hist. 331 (1982).
[22] *Id.*
[23] *Id.*

For African Americans, post–Civil War times were marked by arduous experiences and the medical sphere provided no exception or relief. Grave pillaging from black cemeteries persisted as a means to supply bodies for elite medical schools and legalized segregation further exacerbated discrimination against the living.[24] Despite slavery's abolition, blacks continued to be characterized by inferior status in all walks of life, including restriction from health facilities servicing white patients.

In response to wide-spread medical discrimination, blacks endeavored to train clinical professionals and build health care facilities within their own communities. However, the segregated health system maintained a poorer health standard for blacks as compared to whites throughout the mid-twentieth century. Congress's enactment of the Hospital Survey and Construction Act (Hill-Burton Act) in 1946,[25] which allocated money for the improvement of the states' hospital systems, did little to change the status quo. In fact, the legislation was instrumental in maintaining divided and disparate care. It prohibited the use of funds for facilities that discriminated on the basis of race, color, national origin, or creed, but did little in the way of desegregating medical facilities or changing attitudes about race as a sociological and legal rather than biological construct. In this way, medicine mirrored public education's "separate, but equal" mythology, which produced inequitable services and institutions for blacks.[26]

Nearly twenty years after the passage of Hospital Survey and Construction Act, the momentum for civil rights action against the American health care system was realized in *Simkins v. Moses H. Cone Memorial Hospital*,[27] in which the U.S. Fourth Circuit Court of Appeals declared segregated health care in Hill-Burton hospitals to be unconstitutional. In essence, the court declared that, on receipt of federal funds, hospitals built with Hill-Burton money operated as state actors, making them subject to the Fifth and Fourteenth Amendment prohibitions against racial discrimination.[28] The *Simkins* decision along with a richly developed civil rights jurisprudence established the precedent that helped usher in the Civil Rights Act of 1964.[29]

---

[24] Gamble, *supra* note 20; David C. Humphrey, *Dissection and Discrimination: The Social Origins of Cadavers in America, 1760–1915*, 49 BULL. N.Y. ACAD. MED. 819 (1973); Slavit, *supra* note 21.

[25] 42 U.S.C.S. § 291 (2006). The purpose of the Hill-Burton Act was to assist states in the construction and modernization of public and other nonprofit medical facilities. This assistance included the development of diagnostic, preventive, treatment, and rehabilitative services as well as the promotion of research and the useful application of experimental results.

[26] Brown v. Bd. of Ed. of Topeka, 347 U.S. 483, 483 (1954). In 1954, the U.S. Supreme Court declared states laws permitting separate but equal public schools unconstitutional. The unanimous Court declared that "separate educational facilities were inherently unequal."

[27] 323 F. 2d 959 (1963).

[28] *Id.*

[29] Sidney D. Watson, *Race, Ethnicity and Quality of Care: Inequalities and Incentives*, 27 AM. J. L. MED. 203 (2001).

Title VI of the Civil Rights Act of 1964[30] prohibited racial discrimination as a condition of receiving federal funds, the impact of which was not fully realized until Congress authorized the Medicare and Medicaid programs in 1965. In the immediate aftermath of Medicare certification, the promise of racial and ethnic equality in health care was dramatic: "[i]n less than four months, the lure of federal Medicare dollars transformed and desegregated American health care without massive resistance, public demonstrations or protests."[31]

However, with all that the Medicare Title VI certification process promised, including relative ease in the transition to integration;[32] there were mixed realities. Scholars point to the absence of accountability or sanction for previous discrimination. Substantial evidence proves this problem persists. Also, unlike the arduous process of public education systems in their integration efforts, hospitals as private entities had the luxury of making sensitive and politically charged decisions behind closed doors.[33] And ironically, the Hill-Burton Act's strong, unambiguous financial incentive arguably undermined competition, by applying to all hospitals, thereby driving down competition by eliminating the possibility that some hospitals would elect to remain segregated.[34]

Despite the promise of equality and parity provided for in Title VI legislation, significant limitations in the implementation and reach of Medicare certification facilitated the persistence of segregation within the larger medical system. For example, physicians were exempted from compliance with Title VI. Many nursing home facilities failed to comply with the Civil Rights Act.[35] Vestiges of a two-tier health system remained in the form of public and private hospitals and clinics. This was further compounded by delayed and disparate Medicaid reimbursement, which prompted restriction on the numbers of Medicaid patients seen by health care providers, ultimately incentivizing physicians to avoid the treatment of minority patients.[36] And finally, prejudices and stereotypes served to justify variation in service delivery.[37]

---

[30] 42 U.S.C. § 2000d (2006). Title VI addressed the equal protection and nondiscrimination rights of the Constitution. It established as federal policy that programs and activities receiving federal assistance will not discriminate on the basis of race, color, and national origin.

[31] Watson, *supra* note 29, at 215.

[32] The "white only" signs were removed and hospitals began admitting black patients.

[33] Watson, *supra* note 29.

[34] The federal government applied Title VI requirements to all hospitals.

[35] As Professor Yearby noted, the struggle continues in the 21st century. Ruqaiijah Yearby, *Striving for Equality, but Settling for the Status Quo in Health Care: Is Title VI More Illusory than Real?* 59 RUTGERS L. REV. 429, 446 (2007).

[36] *See also* David Barton Smith, *Eliminating Disparities in Treatment and the Struggle to End Segregation*, 775 COMMONWEALTH FUND i, vi (2005). As Professor Smith noted, "[P]roviders have expanded profitable services in areas with the most advantageous payer mix. This has tended to increase services in predominantly white, affluent suburban areas and reduce services in less affluent, predominantly minority, inner-city areas."

[37] Watson, *supra* note 29.

The tacit two-tier system lingers and serves as a telling reminder of the culture in which the American medical system was shaped. Professor Marianne Lado's in-depth research on the closure and relocation of urban health care facilities to suburban areas throughout the 1970s–1990s, concludes quite simply that "over decades, many African American communities are simply underserved, left out of the mainstream of medicine and unable to take advantage of pharmaceutical and technological advances."[38] The rise in managed care organizations has presented challenges for Medicaid recipients in accessing care, including alternate-day scheduling for those patients who receive this benefit,[39] modified listings for the availability of providers based on Medicaid vs. commercial status, and differential marketing of services by neighborhood.[40] The two-tier system has relegated the health concerns of blacks and other marginalized groups to the "underfunded, overcrowded, inferior, public health-care sector."[41]

IV. IMPLICIT BIAS, MEDICAL DECISION-MAKING, AND HEALTH DISPARITIES

Old and negative racial attitudes developed, nurtured, and promoted within the U.S. medical and legal systems are not easily overcome or eviscerated. When norms shift, explicit, unbiased, and positive attitudes may surface; however previous opinions are stored in memory and serve as an unconscious reference point for behavior.[42] Thus, "[b]elow the waterline of conscious categorization and presupposition, stereotypes and prejudice have free reign, shielded from human awareness. Medical judgment informed by such stereotypes is bound to yield racially disparate results, even absent conscious intent."[43]

There is mounting contemporary evidence pointing to the use of demographically based stereotyped schemas across clinical settings. Provider assumptions about patients' honesty, motivations, and level of suffering directly affect diagnostic and

---

[38] Marianne Engelman Lado, *Unfinished Agenda: The Need for Civil Rights Litigation to Address Race Discrimination and Inequalities in Health Care Delivery*, 6 Tex. F. on C.L. & C.R. 1, 10 (2001).

[39] *Id.* Professor Lado provided an example of disparate treatment of Medicaid patients by managed care organizations, noting that "[f]rom 1995 through 1997, LDF [National Association for the Advancement of Colored People Legal Defense & Educational Fund, Inc.] received complaints that physicians in one state that had implemented a mandatory managed care program for Medicaid recipients, routinely scheduled appointments with Medicaid enrollees on different days than their commercial enrollees."

[40] *Id.*

[41] W. Michael Byrd & Linda A. Clayton, *An American Health Dilemma: A History of Blacks in the Health System*, 84 J. Nat'l. Med. Assoc. 189, 189 (1992).

[42] John F. Dovidio, *On the Nature of Contemporary Prejudice: The Third Wave*, 57 J. Soc. Issues 829 (2001).

[43] M. Gregg Bloche, *Race and Discretion in American Medicine*, 1 Yale J. Health Pol'y L. & Ethics 95, 104 (2001).

treatment practices.[44] These assumptions may be linked to loss of empathy for and devaluation of groups along racial lines.

For example, a study involving a sample of post-angiogram patients traced the relationship between race and socioeconomic status to physician perceptions and medical decision-making. After adjusting for patient age, sex, frailty/sickness, depression, self-efficacy, social assertiveness, and physician characteristics (age, sex, race, specialty), researchers found that a patient's race is associated with physician assessments of patient intelligence, physical feelings of affiliation toward a patient, and beliefs about a patient's likelihood of risk behavior and adherence to medical advice.[45] Compared to white patients, black patients with coronary artery disease were more likely to be perceived as at risk for noncompliance with cardiovascular rehabilitation, substance abuse, and having inadequate social support.[46] Black patients were also more likely to be described as less intelligent, and physicians reported weaker feelings of affiliation toward these patients.[47]

The authors found that a patient's socioeconomic status (SES) is associated with physician perception of patients' personality, abilities, behavioral propensities, and role demands.[48] Patients of lower SES were perceived to be less intelligent and to exhibit more negative personality characteristics.[49] Lower SES status was also correlated with other stereotypes, including physician belief that these patients were at greater risk for noncompliance with cardiovascular rehabilitation, that low SES populations desire a physically inactive lifestyle, have low career demands, less responsibility for care of a family member, and lack adequate social support.[50] One explanation for the study's findings is that "physicians' understanding of epidemiologic evidence regarding population-based likelihoods may function as stereotypes, and be applied to assessments and perceptions of individuals regardless of actual individual characteristics."[51] Recognizing the high correlation between race and SES, the study authors asserted that physicians' negative attributions toward black patients and those of low SES may have a devastating cumulative effect on the clinical encounter.[52]

In a subsequent study using the same data on post-angiogram patients, Dr. Michelle van Ryn and colleagues noted that when controlling for clinical factors, insurance status, and physician characteristics, black men were almost half as likely as white men to receive recommendation for coronary artery bypass surgery despite

---

[44] *Id.*

[45] Michelle van Ryn & Jane Burke, *The Effect of Patient Race and Socioeconomic Status on Physicians' Perceptions of Patients*, 50 Soc. Sci. Med. 813 (2000).

[46] *Id.*

[47] *Id.*

[48] *Id.*

[49] Negative characteristics included lack of self-control and irrationality. *Id.*

[50] *Id.*

[51] Ryn & Burke, *supra* note 45.

[52] *Id.* at 813.

clinical guidelines documenting it to be the appropriate management of heart disease for the sampled groups.[53] The authors argue that disparities in treatment for coronary artery disease are partially mediated by physicians' race-based perceptions of social and behavioral characteristics of the patients.[54]

Implicit racial bias is implicated in other health categories, including differential recommendations by emergency medicine and internal medicine resident physicians for thrombolysis in the treatment of acute coronary syndromes in simulated clinical vignettes.[55] On measures of explicit bias, physicians expressed equal preference for white and black patients and rated the two patient groups as equally cooperative with medical procedures.[56] However, with increasing implicit bias in favor of white patients, the likelihood of treating white patients and not treating black patients with thrombolysis for equivalent symptoms of acute myocardial infarction rises.[57]

In a study of more than 2,500 voluntary physician visitors to the public *Project Implicit* website,[58] Dr. Janice Sabin and colleagues demonstrate that patterns of implicit and explicit attitudes toward race mirror those of large, diverse samples of individuals in the United States.[59] In general, physicians held implicit preferences for whites above blacks.[60] African American physicians showed no implicit racial bias, but had a wide variation in pro-white and pro-black associations.[61] Male physicians consistently demonstrated a preference for whites through implicit and explicit measures.[62] Consistent with previous findings in social cognition, implicit and explicit attitudes were noted to be related, but distinct concepts.[63] Based on these findings, the authors conclude that "[i]t is plausible that during medical decision-making, even among those with egalitarian values, implicit social attitudes and stereotypes stored in memory may be retrieved automatically without awareness and may influence medical care, albeit unintentionally."[64]

A more recent study, focusing on the clinical encounter from the patient's perspective, indicates a clear connection between perceived bias, risk to shared

---

[53] Michelle van Ryn et al., *Physicians' Perceptions of Patients' Social and Behavioral Characteristics and Race Disparities in Treatment Recommendations for Men with Coronary Artery Disease*, 96 Am. J. Pub. Health 351 (2006).

[54] *Id.*

[55] Alexander R. Green et al., *Implicit Bias Among Physicians and Its Prediction of Thrombolysis Decisions for Black and White Patients*, 22 J. Gen. Intern. Med. 1231 (2007).

[56] *Id.*

[57] *Id.*

[58] Implicit Association Test (IAT), www.implicit.harvard.edu (last visited February 13, 2011).

[59] Janice A. Sabin et al., *Physicians' Implicit and Explicit Attitudes About Race by MD Race, Ethnicity, and Gender*, 20 J. Health Care for the Poor & Underserved 896 (2009).

[60] *Id.*

[61] *Id.*

[62] *Id.*

[63] *Id.*

[64] *Id.* at 896, 906–907 (2009).

decision-making, and the potential for disparate health outcome. In a qualitative study involving African American diabetic patients, Dr. Monica Peek and colleagues found that a number of race-related factors identified by patients, including physician bias and discrimination and cultural discordance, affect shared decision-making opportunities in clinical care.[65] Biases and discrimination identified by patients included less information sharing, more domineering tone by the physician, poor active listening, and physicians' unwillingness to consider patient preferences for treatment plans.[66] Mistrust of physicians figured significantly in patient-responses, which ultimately undermines the physician–patient relationship and quality of care. When patients do not trust their patients they will not communicate freely or fully with their care providers. Peek's research confirms this. Patients were less likely to fully disclose symptoms, they felt unable to question physician authority, and were ambivalent about prescribed treatment plans.[67]

The relevance of implicit bias to patient behavior is well substantiated by the research of Dr. Louis Penner and his colleagues. In their field study documenting the impact of physicians' explicit and implicit racial biases on the medical encounter, they found that black patients responded especially negatively to encounters with providers high in implicit bias and low in explicit bias relative to other combinations of expressions of bias.[68] Their research notes "[t]o the extent that [provider] advocacy efforts are adversely influenced by race-related impressions and lesser personal engagement, racial minority status translates into disadvantage in negotiating medical bureaucracy, and thus into disparate real-world access to clinical services despite formal equality."[69]

If our argument is correct, that implicit bias in the delivery of medicine persists across race and SES lines, what factors contribute to the bias and what can be done to reduce the likelihood of implicit bias? Several external environmental characteristics increase the likelihood of implicit bias in medical decision-making. They include instances of greater clinical uncertainty, physician fatigue and cognitive strain, increased workload resulting in reduced clinical encounter times, more hurried decision-making and linguistic discrepancies resulting in failures of communication.[70] These encounter characteristics produce an increased likelihood

---

[65] Monica E. Peek et al., *Race and Shared Decision-making: Perspectives of African Americans with Diabetes*, 71 SOC. SCI. MED. 1 (2010).

[66] *Id.*

[67] *Id.*

[68] Louis A. Penner et al., *Aversive Racism and Medical Interactions with Black Patients: A Field Study*, 46 J. EXP. SOC. PSYCHOL. 436 (2010).

[69] Bloche, *supra* note 43, at 106.

[70] Sabin et al., *supra* note 59; Janice A. Sabin et al., *Physician Implicit Attitudes and Stereotypes About Race and Quality of Medical Care*, 46 MED. CARE 678 (2008); Nathan Bostick et al., *Physicians' Ethical Responsibilities in Addressing Racial and Ethnic Healthcare Disparities*, 98 J. NAT'L. MED. ASSOC. 1329 (2006).

of discriminatory action because providers lack the motivation or cognitive reserve to monitor and manage clinical behaviors.[71]

V. PRESCRIPTIONS FOR THE FUTURE

This chapter concludes by turning to prescriptions. In previous sections, the chapter examined what distinguishes implicit bias in the health care context and how medical decision-making may become corrupted by endogenous and exogenous pressures and forces. At the crux of this chapter, as well as thematically explored throughout this book, are questions about cognitive, implicit connections to entrenched racial biases. The authors in this book, as well as our colleagues in the field, exhaustively document and record the ways in which race mattered and continues to in society. That record is strong, but no longer requires convincing. Therefore, we conclude this chapter on a pragmatic note, to examine the extent to which law, rules, or creating new norms will offer anything relevant to addressing implicit bias in medicine.

A. *Physician Training and Diversity*

Increasing diversity within the health care curriculum as well as among staff and students at medical schools remains an urgent need. Inarguably, medical education should reflect the diversity of a global society. Yet this important goal and directive at some institutions is often half-heartedly implemented. For example, rather than a broad-scale integration of race and medicine into medical school curricula, often one-time, noncompulsory courses are used to substitute for what might otherwise be a sustained or substantial educational dialogue and nuanced curriculum.

Much of the work focused on eliminating bias in the medical context promotes improving cultural competency of services and awareness of health disparities in the clinical setting.[72] To the extent that the ultimate goal is to create a health care delivery model that is free of systematic influences that produce barriers to the achievement of full health by certain groups, cultural competency and disparity awareness training and strategies to eliminate implicit bias are easily replicable tools that can be deployed to address the problem. However, given that cultural competency training is often delivered in a group setting, by consultants rather than

---

[71] John F. Dovidio et al., *Disparities and Distrust: The Implications of Psychological Processes for Understanding Racial Disparities in Health and Health Care*, 67 Soc. Sci. Med. 478 (2008).

[72] *See, e.g.*, a well-received program created by the Society for General Internal Medicine. Health Disparities Education: Beyond Cultural Competency, *Resources*, Society for General Internal Medicine Disparities Task Force, *available at* www.sgim.org/index.cfm?pageId=269 (last visited March 5, 2011). *See also* U.S. Department of Health and Human Services, OPHS Office of Minority Health National Standards on Culturally and Linguistically Appropriate Services (2001), *available at* http://minorityhealth.hhs.gov/assets/pdf/checked/finalreport.pdf.

full-time, tenured track professors, and as a self-limited program or workshop, these types of interventions in their current form, although needed, likely fall short of what is pragmatically useful to fully address implicit bias.

Consider, for example, that two common results of an institution's cultural competency or diversity training are the production of health materials and administrative documents in multiple languages and the provision and expansion of interpreter services. Despite best intentions, for the medical student already expressing egalitarian attitudes, these types of initiatives or exercises unlikely stimulate a deeper level of self-awareness that facilitates change. Such prepackaged exercises rarely achieve broad change.

Indeed, even with the use of special, "one-stop" shopping diversity courses, the quality of such courses are questionable – as there are no diversity accreditation bodies. Thus, if we can agree that a sensible way to attack implicit bias is at its early roots, medical schools must endeavor to diversify their curricula, and should be held accountable for a training methodology that matches real-world – a diverse world's – challenges.

Secondly, increasing faculty diversity[73] remains an urgent need. Because research focused on the malleability of implicit bias suggests that a change in social context and presentation of counter-stereotypic information can reduce automatic preferences and labels, diversifying medical and nursing school faculty is essential – not simply for the benefit of faculty and students of color, but for that of white faculty and students and the multitude of patients who will be served by them all.[74]

B. *Monitoring*

Monitoring and enforcement serve an important role in shifting behavior. To this end, surveying patients is frequently used to guide quality improvement initiatives in the clinical setting. However, surveys are often administered, collected, reviewed, and summarized at the aggregate level and then filed away, thus limiting their impact on patients' individual experiences on the quality of care provided during the clinical encounter. How to counter this predictable result? Increased intentionality in the design of a patient satisfaction survey combined with an implementation blueprint could enhance and reinforce self-system awareness, self-righting, and institutional

---

[73] The Maternal and Child Health Bureau maintains a collaborative focused on developing a workforce that reflects the racial and ethnic diversity of the U.S. population. *See* Health Resources and Services Administration, *Maternal and Child Health, Diversity Training and Peer Collaborative*, U.S. Dep't of Health and Human Services, http://mchb.hrsa.gov/training/grantee_resources_dtpc.asp (last visited March 5, 2011).

[74] Nilanjana Dasgupta & Anthony G. Greenwald, *On the Malleability of Automatic Attitudes: Combating Automatic Prejudice with Images of Admired and Disliked Individuals*, 81 J. Pers. Soc. Psychol. 800 (2001). *See* Irene V. Blair, *The Malleability of Automatic Stereotypes and Prejudice*, 6 Pers. Soc. Psychol. Rev. 242 (2002) for review of research on influences and malleability of automatic biases.

accountability. Three survey components are essential to effectively understand what is meaningful (and breached) in the physician–patient relationship : (1) perceptions and experiences of verbal and nonverbal behaviors by providers, (2) ratings of provider trust, and (3) measurement of the degree of shared decision-making taking place during encounters.[75]

Additionally, we recommend institution-level data collection to examine patient diagnoses, treatment, and outcomes stratified by race, ethnicity, and other demographic markers including payer status. Systematic discrepancies between treatment decisions and recommended action based on evidence in clinical guidelines could provide a basis for individual corrective action with supervisory oversight.

C. *Litigation: Return to Title VI of the Civil Rights Act?*

Title VI of the Civil Rights Act is a logical tool to combat racial discrimination. Its disparate treatment provision seemingly fits or is applicable to cases of discrimination where empirical data demonstrates a racial disparity – or so we might think. However, successful efforts to heighten proof requirements under the law have chipped away at its scope to combat racial discrimination. Scholars and practitioners who claim disparity itself proves racial discrimination have received a chilly reception from courts. However, implicit bias is the result of historically rooted factors that produce subconscious motivations. Because the behaviors operate at the subconscious-level, meeting the proof requirement (intentionality) and litigating such cases will be difficult under current civil rights laws. While numbers may not "lie," proving intention to cause discrimination, despite proof of a disparity, is an uphill battle. Because Title VI addresses intentional discriminatory behavior, implicit bias would seem to fall squarely outside of the scope of that law.

As a result, formidable challenges exist in litigating discrimination cases based on implicit bias. Despite empirical data that might point strongly to implicit bias causing discrimination, the proof requirements outlined in contemporary jurisprudence make adjudicating such cases a significant emotional and economic gamble for plaintiffs.

That said, current research in social psychology may hold future promise, and could prove useful to litigating future cases of implicit bias. Researchers are developing frameworks to understand the degree to which implicit biases may be controlled once identified. This research raises interesting questions as to whether a bias continues as "subconscious" after identification or whether a continued bias supplemented by disparate treatment becomes intentional after its identification and disclosure.[76]

---

[75] For a discussion of multiples of types of survey and interview formats with the potential for measurement of shared decision-making *see* Cathy Charles et al., *supra* note 12.

[76] Michael S. Shin, *Redressing Wounds: Finding a Legal Framework to Remedy Racial Disparities in Medical Care*, 90 CALIF. L. REV. 2047 (2002).

Analyzed in light of earlier recommendations that patient surveys be implemented and that macro-level investment in enforcement (i.e., sharing patient feedback and survey results with physicians) occur, a new way to approach Title VI emerges or at least it could shift the burden of proof of non-intent to discriminate to the provider. Some lawyers see this work as holding significant promise in the civil rights domain.

VI. CONCLUSION

The U.S. Supreme Court's enforcement of civil rights throughout the mid-twentieth century did much to remove overt reference to race and ethnicity as a marker for differential treatment in the American health care system. However, research in the last two decades points to the significance of hidden and unconscious biases as a source of enduring inequities in health status for blacks and other marginalized groups as compared to whites. Implicit bias is a barrier to the achievement of comparable levels of health among advantaged and disadvantaged groups in the United States. Accountability measures are of critical importance in reducing the contribution of implicit bias to disparate medical decision-making and treatment in medicine. Despite strides in improving access to care for some, implicit bias poses a barrier to full access to care and appropriate quality of care for others.

7

Education Law

Unconscious Racism and the Conversation about the Racial Achievement Gap

Charles R. Lawrence III

"What's happened to us?" My friend Tom asks this question with the intimate tone of one sibling speaking to another about a family problem.

"I just read that 60 percent of black males in D.C. drop out of high school," he says. "Can that be true? Have we let things get that bad?" Tom looks up from the sink where he is rinsing dishes before putting them in the dishwasher. He is waiting for my answer.

I am not sure how to begin. I could finesse and tell him that I need to consult the latest data on the dropout rate. Yet Tom's question poses a greater challenge. He is not really asking a question at all, at least not one that solicits my expertise as an academic who teaches and writes about race and education policy. Instead, he is initiating a conversation. Over the course of our thirty-year friendship, Tom and I have found ourselves in some version of this conversation more times than I can easily count. It is a conversation about what our parents' generation used to call "the state of the race."

Tom wants to know my opinion on what the media pundits and policy wonks call "the racial achievement gap" or, less euphemistically, "the black–white achievement gap." He has seen some of the flood of newspaper and magazine articles that tell a story of a wide and persistent gap between the academic performance of white and black children and ask the rhetorical question, "Why?" Tom is way too smart to think that I or anyone else has a single simple answer to this question. He is really asking me to think out loud with him about how *we* should respond. I use the word "we" here in the same way Tom has used the word "us" in his first question. We both understand that we are speaking, as our parents would, about what should be the collective response of "the race."

Tom Williamson is a lawyer. In 1982 he became the second African American to make partner at Covington and Burling, one of Washington, D.C.'s, largest and most prestigious law firms. A graduate of Harvard College and Berkeley Law School, Tom was a Rhodes Scholar and close friend of Bill Clinton while they both studied at Oxford. During President Clinton's first administration he served as the Department of Labor's Solicitor. At the time of our conversation, Tom had been elected to Covington's management committee. For his entire life Tom has negotiated the complicated and often treacherous terrain of America's most elite academic and professional institutions, often sitting in classrooms and meetings where he saw no other black face.

Tom's father was an officer in the U.S. Army and the first in his family to attend college. In 1952, he bought a modest home in Piedmont, California, a white upper middle class enclave surrounded by the mostly black city of Oakland. At Piedmont High Tom excelled in the classroom and on the ball field, learning well the lessons of token membership that would serve him so well at Harvard, Oxford, and Covington. Chief among these were his father's admonitions that he must be twice as good as his white classmates in everything he did and that in each success and failure he represented not just himself but "the race."

I recite this brief biography because it informs my understanding of Tom's question and my own response. My friend and I share the formative experience of having lived much of our lives as token blacks in elite white institutions. I too heard a father's instruction to excel and understood that any failure would be attributed not just to me but also to "the race."

I know that when Tom asks, "What's happened to us?" he is asking a very complex question that follows directly from the dual meaning of our fathers' counsel. Their first charge was to recognize the meaning of the dominant (read white) American narrative about the racial achievement gap, to understand that this narrative presumes black inferiority and so requires us to rebut that presumption not just once but again and again. Tom is asking how we make that rebuttal. How do we demonstrate that what has happened to us (the gap in achievement between white children and black children) should not be seen as evidence to support the ideology that asserts black inferiority?

The second charge from our fathers was that we must accept responsibility for the condition of our brothers and sisters. We must find a way to do something about the achievement gap, if only because white folks will not find it in their interest to right this wrong.

In this chapter I endeavor to answer my friend's question or, more modestly, to capture and articulate some part of the content of that late-night conversation. I begin with the history and ideology that create the context for the conversation about race and academic achievement. I use the word "conversation" here to speak of the public conversation within which my conversation with my friend takes place – the conversation that is taking place in academic journals, in newspapers, on TV talk shows, and around dinner tables when our white colleagues gather with friends.

In 1987, in an article titled "The Id, the Ego, and Equal Protection: Reckoning with Unconscious Racism,"[1] I wrote that we are all racists, that we share a common history and cultural heritage in which racism has played and still plays a dominant role. We internalize the lessons and beliefs of white supremacy and act on those lessons, often without awareness of those beliefs. The injury of segregation and racism is achieved not only by the legal, economic, and institutional structures that deny subordinated people of color access to power and material well-being but also through ideology – the beliefs that give those structures and practices meaning, the stories that are told to teach us who does not belong and who may not enter, and to explain and justify that denial of entry and belonging.

In 1954, the Supreme Court declared that segregated schools were inherently unequal. The decision in *Brown v. Board of Education*[2] relied on the Court's finding that the segregation of black pupils "generates a feeling of inferiority as to their status in the community."[3] The injury of segregation is found in its social meaning – in the story that segregation tells to black children and to the rest of us and in its designation of a superior and an inferior caste. Segregated schools were symbols of America's beliefs about race. As Justice Harlan observed almost sixty years earlier in his dissent from the "separate but equal" doctrine of *Plessy v. Ferguson*, "segregation proceeds on the ground that colored citizens are inferior and degraded."[4]

Our conversation about the causes and cures for the racial achievement gap inflicts the same defamatory and psychic injury on black and brown children. It is a conversation that tells a story, and the story it tells sends a message to these children that conveys the same meaning as did the segregated schools declared unconstitutional in *Brown v. Board of Education*.

If we listen to the conversation about the racial achievement gap we hear two core arguments or stories, each of which contains and conveys a particular ideology, worldview, and politics. The first story tells us that the racial gap in academic achievement is caused by inherent racial difference. Blacks achieve less well in academic endeavors because they are intellectually inferior. Nature, biology, and the genes they have inherited from their parents and grandparents have made them this way, and there is little we can do to change this essential racial difference. I call this the *nature story*. The second story explains the achievement gap by pointing to structures and conditions of inequality, to the material and social environments that burden black children and keep them from achieving academically. To eliminate the racial achievement gap we must eliminate these structures and conditions. I call this the *structure story*.

---

[1] Charles R. Lawrence III, *The Id, the Ego and Equal Protection: Reckoning with Unconscious Racism* 39 STAN. L. REV. 317 (1987). *See also* Charles R. Lawrence III, *Unconscious Racism Revisited: Reflections on the Impact and Origins of "The Id, the Ego and Equal Protection,"* 40 CONN. L. REV. 931 (2008).

[2] Brown v. Bd. of Educ., 347 U.S. 483 (1954).

[3] *Id.* at 494.

[4] Plessy v. Ferguson, 163 U.S. 537, 560 (1896) (Harlan, J., dissenting).

A third story has emerged as perhaps the most often-told story. I call this the *culture story*. Those who tell the culture story say they do not blame black genes, but neither do they believe that environmental conditions alone can account for the achievement gap. The *culture story* is a story about individuals whose behavior is determined by the beliefs, values, norms, and socialization of the families, groups, or communities to which they belong.

Most often I tell the *structure story* because I believe that story as a matter of both faith and science. Yet the story I want to tell in this chapter, the story I was looking for that night in my conversation with my friend Tom, is more complicated and truer than the simple *structure story*. I want to ask how we hear these stories, what we think they mean, and what we believe about them.

I want to ask what those meanings and beliefs teach us about how the science of implicit bias can help us understand the causes of the achievement gap and to realize our responsibility for doing something about it. When I say "implicit bias" I mean to encompass all of the attitudes and beliefs that an individual possesses that are not the product of consciously held positions, whether or not those attitudes and beliefs overlap with explicit beliefs.[5] I want to emphasize the importance of querying *where* and *why* the implicit biases that we capture by using Implicit Association Tests, among other means, come from.[6]

Much of the knowledge that operates implicitly inside the heads of individuals stems from the three dominant stories (nature, structure, culture) discussed later, which in turn stem from the persistent existence of white supremacy in our society (and not from the inevitable consequences of categorization). Moreover, these stories we hear in the conversation about the racial achievement gap are intimately related to one another: we cannot hear one without hearing the others. The story of superior and inferior races, the story of structural oppression, and the story of the cultures that may shape behavior and academic performance are one story, and that story is about ***us***.

When I say "***us***" I intend two meanings. First, I mean that the stories told about the achievement gap are about ***us*** – about the black and brown folk who are pictured at the bottom of the gap, about my people. That was Tom's meaning when he asked, "What's happening to us?" Yet I also use the word to mean ***all*** of us. We are all the ***us*** in this story because there can be no story told about slaves that is not also a story about the slave holder, no story about a colonized people that is not also a story about the colonizer.

I. STORY ONE (THE NATURE STORY): "THEY'RE JUST DIFFERENT (READ: INFERIOR)"

The first core argument about the achievement gap holds that African American children perform less well in school because they are in some essential way different

---

[5] *See* Lawrence, *Unconscious Racism Revisited, supra* note 1, at 931–78.

[6] I have written elsewhere about the consequences of not asking where and why. *See Id.* at 961.

from other children. Partisans of this position argue that we inherit our intelligence from our parents and grandparents, that our ability to learn to read, write, compute, and engage in the tasks of information acquisition and analysis is passed from parent to child in the genes. Nature determines a child's intelligence and school performance. If black children perform less well in school, it is evidence that blacks, as a group or as a race, have fewer or weaker intelligence genes than whites. If nature creates the racial achievement gap, there is little that the schools or other social interventions can do to close it. Moreover, if nature, rather than society, has created the gap, this is the order that nature or God intended, or it is a rational and efficient order. Whether we look to the heavens or the market, we should feel no moral responsibility for changing the status quo.[7]

In the eighteenth and nineteenth centuries, European and American intellectuals relied on craniometry to explain and defend racial hierarchy. They measured people's heads and compared them to those of gorillas, chimpanzees, and orangutans. Samuel Morton, a physician from Philadelphia and founder of craniometry, argued that brain size correlated directly with intelligence. He amassed the largest collection of skulls in the world and claimed his research revealed that Africans have the smallest brains, whereas whites have the largest – which evidenced the intellectual superiority of whites. Morton's widely influential book, *Types of Mankind*,[8] published in 1854, went through nine editions before the end of the century and served as fodder for those looking to justify white superiority. It also established the new "scientific method" for proving racial differences through mathematical measurements of various parts of the human anatomy. By the end of the nineteenth century, the entire society "understood that science had proved 'the Negro' to be inferior and a separate order of being."[9]

In the twentieth century, intelligence testing replaced measuring skulls as the "science" that proved that blacks belonged at the bottom of the social, political, and economic ladder. H. H. Goddard was first to establish the idea that intelligence could be measured along a single linear scale. He coined the word "moron" and wrote, "The people who are doing drudgery are, as a rule, in their proper places."[10] The Immigration Restriction Act of 1924, which restricted immigrants who were *not from*

---

7 The most prominent recent example of this claim can be found in RICHARD J. HERRNSTEIN & CHARLES MURRAY, THE BELL CURVE: INTELLIGENCE AND CLASS STRUCTURE IN AMERICAN LIFE (1994).

8 *See* JOSIAH CLARK NOTT ET AL., TYPES OF MANKIND: OR, ETHNOLOGICAL RESEARCHES: BASED UPON THE ANCIENT MONUMENTS, PAINTINGS, SCULPTURES, AND CRANIA OF RACES, AND UPON THEIR NATURAL, GEOGRAPHICAL, PHILOLOGICAL AND BIBLICAL HISTORY (1854). TYPES OF MANKIND, published in 1854, asserted that the races of man were separately created species and that each possessed a constant and undeviating physical and moral nature. The book went through nine editions before the end of the century and served as fodder for those looking to justify white superiority. It also established the new "scientific method" for proving racial differences through seemingly mathematical measurements of various parts of the human anatomy.

9 Audrey Smedley, *Science and the Idea of Race: A Brief History*, in RACE AND INTELLIGENCE: SEPARATING SCIENCE FROM MYTH (Jefferson M. Fish ed., 2002).

10 HENRY H. GODDARD, PSYCHOLOGY OF THE NORMAL AND SUBNORMAL 246 (1919).

western or northern Europe, marked the first victory of the eugenics movement. As Stephen Jay Gould has noted, "We have never . . . had any hard data on genetically based differences in intelligence among human groups. Speculation, however, has never let data stand in its way: and when men of power need such an assertion to justify their actions, there will always be scientists available to supply it."[11]

In 1969 psychometrician Arthur Jensen argued in the *Harvard Education Review* that IQ was genetically determined and that the government should end Head Start and other programs aimed at increasing the academic performance of minorities.[12] As late as 1994, Richard Herrnstein and Charles Murray's best seller, *The Bell Curve*, reiterated the scientific racism of Goddard and Jensen, arguing that IQ scores proved African American mental deficiency and proposing that Americans with the lowest IQs be sequestered in "high tech" versions of reservations "while the rest of America tries to go about its business."[13]

II. STORY TWO (THE STRUCTURAL STORY): "IT'S SOCIETY'S FAULT"

The second core argument responds to the first. The causes of the achievement gap can be found in the lived reality of children assaulted, wounded, and dying from the structural conditions of de facto hypersegregation and poverty in a nation still deeply divided by race.[14] We structuralists argue that the environmental causes are evident. If those at the bottom of the gap are denied prenatal care, access to health care, adequate nutrition, and decent housing, we should not be surprised if they do less well in school than those who receive these necessities in abundance. If children are exposed to substance abuse at an early age, grow up in single-parent households, live in crime-ridden neighborhoods, and attend the poorest schools with the least qualified teachers it is predictable that they would do less well on tests than children who are not exposed to these risks factors. In a recent study by the Educational Testing Service, researchers found that birthweight, lead poisoning, hunger and nutrition, television watching, parent availability, and student mobility were all factors that contribute significantly to the achievement gap.[15]

---

[11] Stephen Jay Gould, *Racist Arguments and IQ*, in RACE AND IQ (Ashley Montagu ed., 1975, expanded edition 1999).

[12] A. R. Jensen, *How Much Can We Boost IQ and Scholastic Achievement*, 39 HARV. EDUC. REV. 1 (1969).

[13] Herrnstein & Murray, *supra* note 7, at 526. *But see* THE BELL CURVE WARS: RACE, INTELLIGENCE AND THE FUTURE OF AMERICA (Steven Fraser ed., 1994); STEPHEN JAY GOULD, THE MISMEASURE OF MAN (1996).

[14] *See generally* DOUGLAS MASSEY & NANCY DENTON, AMERICAN APARTHEID: SEGREGATION AND THE MAKING OF THE UNDERCLASS (1993).

[15] *See* Charles R. Lawrence III, *Who Is the Child Left Behind? The Racial Meaning of the New School Reform*, 39 SUFFOLK U. L. REV. 699, 718 n.56 (2006) *citing* PAUL E. BARTON, PARSING THE ACHIEVEMENT GAP: BASELINES FOR TRACKING PROGRESS (2003), http://www.ets.org/MediaResearch/ pdflPICPARSING.pdf. *See, e.g.*, John M. Flora, *High Mobility Linked to Low Test Scores*, INDIANAPO-LIS STAR, Mar. 4, 1999, at NI (linking high levels of student mobility common to underprivileged youth and lower test scores); Marge Christensen Gould & Hennan Gould, *A Clear Vision for Equity*

I will not go on with this testimony to the accuracy of the structural story because my purpose here is not to assert that story's truth. Rather I want to ask you to listen to the way the story is told. I want to interrogate the meaning we give to this story when we tell and hear it together with the other stories in the conversation. Is its meaning infected by the nature story of measured and inferior brains? Does the structural story participate in the injury identified in *Brown*?

As you may have guessed from the rhetorical tone of my questions, I want to suggest that it does. Too often, we tell the structural story in a way that renders our young people passive objects to the structures of racism as if they had neither the capacity nor the will to resist or fight back against those oppressive structures. Our inclination to deny agency to black and brown children, to have little faith in their resources, reveals the work that racism's story of inherent limitation has done. This is why the conservative charge that liberals engage in the racism of "low expectations" has such resonance with significant numbers of black folk. We often hear a tone of fatalism in the structural story, particularly when liberal participants in the policy debates use the story to suggest that the changes needed are beyond our capacity.

When we make the pragmatic argument that we must accept piecemeal and inadequate reforms because there is no political will to make structural change, I fear that we have accepted the status quo so easily because we have lived with inequality for so long that it seems natural – that we have lost our sense of outrage because we believe some part of the nature story that says this is where poor black children are supposed to be.

III. STORY THREE (THE CULTURE STORY): "IT'S YOUR PEOPLE'S FAULT"

Go into any inner city neighborhood and folks will tell you that government alone can't teach kids to learn. *They* know that parents have to parent, that children can't achieve unless we raise their expectations and turn off the television sets and eradicate the slander that says a black youth with a book is acting white.[16]

Our own brother-president, Barack Obama, spoke those words. Why is he telling us about what inner city folks know? "[T]hat the government alone can't teach kids to learn," "that parents have to parent," and that they have "to turn off the[ir] television sets." What does he mean when he speaks of "the slander that says a black youth with a book is acting white?" Although he does not use the words "achievement

and Opportunity: Diagnosis and Treatment of Vision Disorders in Poor Children Improves Academic Achievement, 85 PHI DELTA KAPPAN 4, 324 (2003) (discussing high rate of undiagnosed vision problems among impoverished children); Richard Rothstein, *Social Class Leaves Its Imprint*, EDUC. WK., May 19, 2004 (discussing the effects of health problems, housing issues, and economic security on student performance).

16 Senator Barack Obama, Keynote Address at the 2004 Democratic National Convention (July 27, 2004).

gap," we readily understand Obama's words within the context of that conversation. He enters this conversation by invoking the culture story.

Those who tell the culture story seek to distance themselves from Jensen, Herrnstein, and Murray, but they also find environmental explanations unsatisfactory. They see human behavior as the product of beliefs, values, norms, and socialization and look to the moral codes that operate within particular families, communities, or groups for explanations of why some children do less well in school.

I first heard the culture story when Daniel Patrick Moynihan, the secretary of labor under President Lyndon Johnson, argued that the problems of crime, drugs, out-of-wedlock babies, and increasing welfare rolls in poor black communities could be traced to a community culture of poverty that legitimized immoral behavior and encouraged economic dependence. *The Negro Family: The Case for National Action*,[17] known as the Moynihan Report, made the term "culture of poverty" a household phrase[18] and was later invoked as a rationale for cutting government programs. The culture story, filled with the familiar tropes of indolence, ignorance, and immorality, sounded suspiciously like the nature story with a new title. I was certain that most Americans heard it that way. So I listen to this story with a skeptic's ear.

At the same time, I have seen black children engage in behaviors that make them complicit in their own failure. I have watched little black boys, who were my daughter's kindergarten classmates in Washington, D.C., change from eager bright-eyed learners to adolescents who acted as if they cared little about school success or the consequences of failure. I know the studies of home language environments of black children that found that lower levels of verbal exchange between parent and child lowered children's IQ scores.[19]

The late John Ogbu, an anthropologist who taught for many years at the University of California, Berkeley, was the most influential scholar to tell the culture story.[20] Ogbu's extensive research and scholarship focused on how the dynamics of minority communities influenced the school performance of minority children. In a 1986 article, coauthored with Signithia Fordham, he introduced the notion of opposition

---

[17] Office of Policy Planning and Research, United States Department of Labor, The Negro Family: The Case for National Action (1965), *available at* http://www.dol.gov/oasam/programs/history/webid-meynihan.htm.

[18] Patricia Cohen, *'Culture of Poverty' Makes a Comeback*, N.Y. Times, Oct. 17, 2010 (noting a recent resurgence of research and scholarship on culture and poverty).

[19] Diana Slaughter & Edgar Epps, *The Home Environment and Academic Achievement of Black American Children and Youth: An Overview*, 56 J. Negro Educ. 1 (1987). Endya B. Stewart, *Family-and Individual-Level Predictors of Academic Success for African American Students: A Longitudinal Path Analysis Utilizing National Data*, 36 J. Black Stud. 597 (2006).

[20] *See generally* John U. Ogbu, Minority Education and Caste: The American System in Cross Cultural Perspective (1978); Margaret A. Gibson & John U. Ogbu, Minority status and Schooling: A Comparative Study of Immigrant and Involuntary Minorities (1991); John U. Ogbu, Black American Students in an Affluent Suburb: A Study of Academic Disengagement (2003).

to "acting white" or oppositional behavior.[21] Obama's reference to "acting white" alludes to this article and to the academic and political controversy provoked by this article and the body of Ogbu's work. According to Ogbu, many black American children perceive that education is not a vehicle to social mobility and opportunity, and therefore they develop negative attitudes toward schooling. Ogbu suggested that the history of discrimination has created community-based folk theories that even those who work hard will never reap rewards equivalent to whites and that these cultural belief systems contribute to self-defeating behaviors.

I assign an article by Ogbu to my classes because his work is complicated, nuanced, and foundational to the social science of race and education.[22] Yet more than that I want my students to experience how Ogbu's words are given meaning by the larger narrative of which they are a part. I want them to see how journalists have portrayed him,[23] to examine how they themselves read his words, and to appreciate how that reading may be influenced by their own predispositions and by the master narrative.

In the article I assign, Ogbu seeks to explain the differences in academic performance of children from different nonwhite minority groups. His theory posits three types of minorities:

1. "Autonomous minorities, such as Jews and Mormons in the United States, . . . are victims of prejudice and pillory but not of stratification. . . . They usually have a cultural frame of reference which demonstrates and encourages academic success . . ."

2. "Immigrant minorities are people who have moved more or less voluntarily from their land of origin . . . because they believed that such a move would result in improved economic well-being, better overall opportunities, and/or greater political freedom. . . . These immigrants usually experience initial problems of adjustment in school, but their problems are not characterized by persistent adjustment difficulties or low academic performance . . ."

3. "Involuntary or caste-like minorities are people who did not initially choose to become members of a society; rather they were brought into that society through slavery, conquest, or colonization. African Americans, Mexican Americans, American Indians, and native Hawaiians are examples . . . In America, involuntary minorities' perspectives of undeserved and institutionalized oppression or discrimination influence the ways they respond to white Americans and to societal institutions which whites control. In general, America's involuntary minorities experience persistent problems in school adjustment and academic performance."[24]

---

[21] SIGNITHIA FORDHAM & JOHN OGBU, BLACK STUDENTS' SCHOOL SUCCESS: COPING WITH THE BURDEN OF ACTING WHITE (1986).

[22] I assigned John Ogbu, *Minority Education in Comparative Perspective*, 59 J. NEGRO EDUC. 1 (1990).

[23] *See, e.g.*, Felicia Lee, *Why Are Black Students Lagging?*, N.Y. TIMES, Nov. 30, 2002.

[24] Ogbu, *supra* note 22, at 46–47.

The ways these groups perceive and respond to their treatment by white Americans and to schools are influenced by the expectations they bring with them. For example, the Chinese and the Punjab, whom Ogbu studied in California,

> interpreted the cultural and language differences they encountered as barriers to be overcome and not as a threat to their own language and identities. In contrast, involuntary minorities often believe cultural differences are markers of identity that should be maintained. America's involuntary minorities may perceive learning or speaking Standard English and practicing other aspects of white middle class culture as threatening to their own minority culture.[25]

I ask my students who Ogbu thinks is responsible for the gap because I want them to think about the word "responsible" in several ways. The first is *responsible* as fault or blame; the second is *responsible* as causation, without any implication of moral judgment; and the third is *responsible* for cure or remedy – for doing something about closing the gap.

Listen to two student responses to the Ogbu article:

> Student #1: I feel that much of Ogbu's negative cultural argument is a thinly veiled attempt to disassociate himself from black America. His perspective is strongly influenced by his Nigerian-born immigrant background. In his work I keep hearing him say, I am an immigrant, I am part of the immigrant "positive, dual-status, upward-mobility" mentality, I am not a part of this "negative" black America. Ogbu's work has been easily subverted to reaffirm the argument that some (black) children just can't be taught, that they are not worth teaching because they don't value education, that this is just the way things are meant to be and they can't be changed.[26]

> Student #2: In the school where I taught in Baltimore some of my smartest students dropped out of school the quickest. Partially this was based on the fact that they were bored out of their skulls (thanks to low expectations and inexperienced teachers). Partially it is because a smart kid (especially boys) can make a lot of money selling drugs. Quite frankly if you saw people who look like you succeed at dealing but never succeed by going to college, which would seem like the better option? Ogbu is right that there are differences in levels of expectations in various ethnic groups, but I don't think it relates to dislike of being white. It seems more like a rational appraisal of how the world (as they know it) works.[27]

The first student, an African American woman, hears the old racist stereotypes from the nature story in Ogbu's description of involuntary immigrant culture. She hears him saying, "This is who you people are," and she wants to respond, "We're not all like that." She feels Ogbu's need to distance himself from this image of blackness.

---

[25] *Id.* at 47.
[26] Student reflection piece on file with author.
[27] Student reflection piece on file with author.

"This is a typical move for black immigrants like Africans and West Indians," she says. They want to distance themselves from the narrative of inferiority that America has told about black folk.

The second student, a white woman who taught in Teach for America before coming to law school, reads Ogbu as a structuralist. She hears him objectively describing black students' rational response to the oppressive structures of urban poverty. "Wouldn't you choose dealing drugs over school if faced with the same options?," she asks. Ogbu might consider this reading closer to his intended meaning. He describes himself as a structuralist, noting for example that Koreans take on the attributes of involuntary minorities (i.e., they act "black") in Japan, where they perceive the discrimination against them as permanent, whereas in the United States they act like voluntary minorities.

President Obama seems to read Ogbu much as the first student does, as blaming black Americans for the achievement gap. At least he is concerned that his audience hears the story from nature. "We're not like that," he says, when he tells his audience we black folks know that "parents have to parent" and that our children can't achieve unless we have "high expectations" and "turn off our television sets." Yet his words are also directed to the second student who says, "Look at the environment, what do you expect?" He hears racism in the voice of this liberal teacher who *expects* her student will choose to deal drugs over school. He calls on black folk to "eradicate the slander that says a black youth with a book is acting white." There is an important, if subtle, difference between Obama's message and the structural message that places blame on the environment and says the resulting behavior is to be expected, if not inevitable. He believes our children and their parents have agency, that they have the capacity to fight against the structures and ideology of racism if we will have faith in them and fight with them.

I want to explore why we hear the culture story in these two very different ways. So I ask my students whether they hear this story as more like the story from nature or more like the structural story. I ask how they think most Americans hear the culture story. What do we think it means when Ogbu says that Jews and Mormons have a culture that "encourages academic success," or when sociolinguist Martha Ward reports that, among lower income black families, children are expected to be "seen and not heard," that there are "few educational toys, and little direct language instruction?"[28] Is culture something about the people themselves, or is it something about the environment?

One student responds that when we hear people describe a racial group's culture we think about something that "comes from the *inside*" – that there is something about Jews themselves that makes them good at school and something about blacks that makes them not so good at school. To call this "something" their culture means, "You people are just like that." There are nods of agreement around the classroom.

[28] MARTHA WARD, THEM CHILDREN: A STUDY IN LANGUAGE LEARNING (1972).

We cannot hear the culture story without at the same time hearing the nature story, which still dominates the master narrative: that essentialist story about race and intelligence influences the meaning we give the culture story. Too often we respond to the racist story that keeps whispering in our ears by denying we hear it.

One way we do this is by rejecting the evidence of culture that Ogbu offers. We say, "We're not all like that," or we minimize the behavior's impact on school performance or romanticize it, as in "It's a black thing. You wouldn't understand." Yet these responses fail to answer the racist whisper of the nature story, and in offering them; we abandon our children to their own self-destruction.

A better answer to the nature story is one that explains how culture is related to structural conditions of inequality. One can read and interpret "culture" in two ways:

1. as an essential characteristic of individuals and racial groups (nature)
2. as responsive to relationships and structures of inequality (environment)

Sociologist William Julius Wilson calls the liberal response to the nature story "incomplete" because it does not "capture the impact of relational, organizational, and collective processes that embody the social structure of inequality."[29] These processes include the operation and organization of schools; residential racial segregation; social isolation in poor neighborhoods; discrimination in hiring, promotions, and other avenues of mobility; and ideologies of group differences shared by members of society and institutionalized in organizational practices and norms.

These structural mechanisms of racism and inequality operate in the domain of collective experience. The unequal conditions of housing, schools, employment, and incarceration, as well as the racist ideology that characterizes blacks as less intelligent, work against blacks, Hawaiians, Mexicans, Samoans, and Filipinos as groups. Culture, the modes of behavior and outlook that are shared within each of these communities, is most fully understood as an expression of social relations within these communities and between these communities and the organizational and the institutional structures of inequality that oppress them. Culture serves as both a tool of and as a constraint on these social relations.

For example, research on teacher expectations has found that teachers share ideologies of group differences, including those that highlight social and cultural differences.[30] These ideologies justify or prescribe what educators believe are "appropriate" ways of handling the education of black and white students. For black students these ideologies often result in teacher expectations and practices that undermine academic achievement. The nature story causes teachers to employ curricula and

---

[29] William Julius Wilson, *The Role of the Environment in the Black-White Test Score Gap*, in THE BLACK-WHITE TEST SCORE GAP 508 (Christopher Jenks & Meredith Phillips eds., 1998).

[30] Ronald F. Ferguson, *Teachers' Perceptions and Expectations and the Black-White Test Score Gap*, in THE BLACK-WHITE TEST SCORE GAP 273–317 (Christopher Jenks & Meredith Phillips eds., 1998).

pedagogy, modes of socialization, and modes of discipline that fail to engage or challenge or show respect for black students. Even more importantly, black and brown students see and feel the teachers' racism, even when the teachers themselves do not, and the students hear and internalize the story from nature that is contained in the different way they are taught.

IV. WHERE DO WE GO FROM HERE? HELPING OUR CHILDREN FIGHT BACK

African American students must achieve in the face of racism. Because our society and our schools devalue them by virtue of their social identity as African Americans, it is no wonder that so few of them perform to their full potential. These simple truths are seldom spoken in the national conversation on race and academic achievement. If we are truly committed to closing the achievement gap, we must first challenge the conversation that denies black students' gifts and then offer models for achieving excellence that confront racist stigma and stereotype.

What must African American students bring to the task of academic achievement? What commitment must they have, what social, emotional, and physical resources, and what support from others are required when African American intellectual inferiority is so much taken for granted that even well-intentioned individuals routinely register doubts about black intellectual competence?

Ideology must be countered with opposing ideology. There must be an oppositional narrative of intellectual gifts, of resistance and achievement that challenges racist ideology. African Americans have such a narrative, a tradition of storytelling that contains a philosophy of education: "Freedom for literacy and literacy for freedom, racial uplift, citizenship, and leadership."[31]

The great abolitionist Frederick Douglass's autobiographical account of his discovery of the power of literacy provides a compelling example of this tradition. Douglass recounts his master's discovery that his wife had been teaching Douglass to read. Douglass was most struck not by the vehemence with which his master forbade his wife to teach him but by the reasons given. Education would "spoil a nigger," make him unfit to be a slave, discontent, unhappy, and unmanageable. The power of this narrative is not just in the content of the lesson – education as liberation – but also in the act of Douglass telling his own story, the former slave supremely articulate, subverting the ideology that claimed slaves were incapable of consciousness:

> From that moment, I understood the pathway from slavery to freedom.... The decided manner with which he spoke, and strove to impress his wife with the evil consequences of giving me instructions served to convince me that he was deeply sensible of the truths he was uttering.... What he most feared, I most desired. What

[31] THERESA PERRY ET AL., YOUNG GIFTED AND BLACK: PROMOTING HIGH ACHIEVEMENT AMONG AFRICAN AMERICAN STUDENTS 85 (2005).

he most loved I most hated. That which to him was a great evil, to be carefully shunned, was to me a great good, to be diligently sought, and the argument which he so warmly waged against my learning to read, only seemed to inspire me with a desire and determination to learn.[32]

The lesson this narrative prescribes is that schools must foster in African American students "identities of achievement," and "intentionally socialize" students to the behaviors that are necessary for them to be achievers.

Of course, the lesson of achievement as a form of resistance to racism is more complicated today than it was in Douglass's time or even fifty years ago. When there were "white" and "colored" signs on bathrooms and drinking fountains, the message those signs conveyed was clear, and the responsibility to disprove the message was the whole community's imperative. The segregated Mississippi schools my parents attended were intentionally organized in opposition to the ideology of black intellectual inferiority. Well-spoken, well-mannered, well-dressed teachers saw their vocation as racial uplift. "He always expected us to perform at the highest level," says my mother of Mr. Bowman, her principal and math teacher at Magnolia High in Vicksburg. In the 1950s my sisters and I attended predominantly white schools in suburban New York. Our parents told us we must excel because we represented not just ourselves and our family but also the race. The narrative of achievement as ideological battle made sense because the ideological battle lines were clear.

Today, African American students live in a more confusing world. They experience the slights, stereotypes, and exclusions of racism, but civil rights laws have made racial discrimination illegal, and most white Americans embrace the ideal of racial equality. Yet, these laws have eliminated neither the structures of racism nor the beliefs and practices that whisper stories of inherent inferiority in young people's ears.

Many of my law students – bright, high-achieving African American young people – worry that affirmative action may stigmatize them. When they do not know the full extent of racism's history and enduring effects, when racist ideology is coded or unconscious, they may blame their black classmates or even themselves for reinforcing the stereotypes that discount their talents. Some suffer from anxiety at the threat of being prejudged because they are black.

Claude Steele's research on "stereotype threat" provides useful insight into how black students' awareness of negative stereotypes about black intellectual ability depresses their academic performance relative to that of white students. Steele sought to understand the persistent underperformance of African American college students from the middle class. The gaps between these students and their white classmates in standardized test scores, college grades, and graduation rates could

---

[32] Frederick Douglass, Narrative of the Life of Frederick Douglass, An American Slave (1845).

not be explained by social and economic deprivation, and Steele was skeptical of theories that pointed to factors relating to the students themselves, such as poor motivation, a distracting peer culture, lack of motivation, or Herrnstein and Murray's ignominious suggestion in *The Bell Curve* of genes. I suspect that none of these rang true for Steele because he had taught too many brilliant, highly motivated black students at Stanford whose performance could not be explained by these theories.

Steele was convinced, however, that something racial must be depressing the performance of these students. He and his colleagues began not by asking how the intelligence, motivation, or peer culture of the black students themselves might explain their troubles; rather they examined aspects of the world the students encountered at school.

Steele tells a story about one of his students at Stanford:

> A normally energetic black student who had broken up with his longtime girlfriend and had since learned that she, a Hispanic, was now dating a white student. This hit him hard. Not long after hearing about his girlfriend, he sat through an hour's discussion of *The Bell Curve* in his psychology class, during which the possible genetic inferiority of his race was openly considered. Then he overheard students at lunch arguing that affirmative action allowed in too many under-qualified blacks.[33]

By this young man's own account he had experienced very little of what he thought of as racial discrimination, but Steele wondered if the features of his world contained in this story might have a bearing on his academic life. In several years of carefully controlled research Steele and his colleagues identified a phenomenon they call "stereotype threat" – the threat of being viewed through the lens of negative stereotype or the fear of doing something that would inadvertently confirm that stereotype.

Steele gave an extremely difficult Graduate Record Exam in English literature to black and white Stanford students who were statistically matched in ability. The students were told that this was a test of their "verbal ability." Steele's hypothesis was that this characterization of the test would trigger the black students' fear that their performance on it might confirm the stereotype about the inferior intellectual ability of African Americans and that this anxiety would in turn depress their performance. Indeed, this is precisely what happened, with blacks performing a full standard deviation below whites when they were told the test was "diagnostic" of their intellectual ability.

Steele then administered the same test to another matched group of black and white students. This time he told them that the test was part of a laboratory experiment to study how certain problems are solved. Steele emphasized that the task did *not*

---

[33] PERRY ET AL., *supra* note 31.

measure a person's level of intellectual ability. This simple instruction profoundly changed the meaning of the test. It removed the "spotlight anxiety," and the black students' performance rose to match that of equally qualified whites.

In a series of experiments further refining his hypothesis, Steele found that the most achievement-oriented, skilled, motivated, and confident students were the ones most impaired by stereotype threat. What made black students more susceptible to stereotype threat was not weaker academic identity and skills, but stronger academic identity and skills. Black students' performance was thus impaired because they were trying too hard to disprove or distance themselves from the stereotype rather than not trying hard enough.

Steele's prescription for overcoming stereotype threat and its detrimental effects is to, as far as possible, remove the threat. The first step is to acknowledge the existence of societal racial stereotypes and recognize the many cues from teachers, students, and institutional practices and policies that can evoke a sense of threat. Schools and universities must then adopt policies and implement programs that refute that threat or its relevance to the target. Steele argues that "the success of black students may depend less on expectations and motivation – things that are thought to drive academic performance – than on trust that stereotypes about their group will not have a limiting effect on their school world."[34]

Yet trust is the flip side of expectations. Black children will trust their teachers to treat them without reference to societal stereotypes about black intellectual inferiority only when those teachers acknowledge the existence of those stereotypes and show that nonetheless they expect much of their student's intellectual gifts. Steele's own research confirms the importance of high expectations. In a study of how teachers could overcome stereotype threat when giving feedback on written work across a racial divide, Steele found that black students trusted and could accept criticism from professors who explicitly conveyed that they were using high standards and that they believed the students could meet those standards.

Unfortunately the achievement gap debate is less about a search for ways to improve the educational opportunities of poor black and brown children than it is about the reinforcement of beliefs about their intelligence. This belief system, rooted in slavery, colonization, and the ideology of white supremacy, has led academics and professional educators to begin with a search for black students' deficiencies as the explanation for their academic failure or success. Language and cultural diversity, poverty, crime, and drug-ridden neighborhoods may determine a student's *opportunity* to learn. They do not, however, determine his or her *capacity* to learn. The search for student deficiencies diverts attention from the gap in opportunity, from income inequality, and from inadequacy of resources for schools. Moreover, when the black–white achievement gap is a conversation about black students' deficiencies and incapacity, we are sidetracked from what ought to be our primary

---

[34] *Id.*

mission – closing the gap between the current performance of African American students and their potential to perform at levels of excellence.

There are models of exemplary teachers and schools that have created cultures of excellence and produced high achievement among African American students – schools where calculus is taught to fifth graders and teachers who use the Socratic method to teach logarithms. At the University Laboratory School in Hawaiʻi, teachers use poetry and journal writing to help a diverse student body achieve the state's highest verbal test scores, and the Kumu Hula (a teacher of Hawaiian dance and culture) invites her students to participate in a demonstration to protest the sale of ceded lands. Thus students at an indigenous Hawaiian-culture–based public charter school rebuild ʻauwai and loʻi[35] while learning the history of U.S. occupation and colonial imperialism and the science and economics of sustainable ecological systems. They are taught by educators who respect prior knowledge and engage in critical analysis, who treat their children as scholars, and who join with them to fight the structures and ideologies of racism and colonialism.

This teaching challenges the common assumptions held by educators about teaching and learning that are central to the prevailing approach to research and to school reform that seeks to close the achievement gap – assumptions about methodology, student mental capacity, student mental health, and behavioral characteristics that provide the rationale for what Asa Hilliard called the "brutal pessimism" about African American students' potential.

One of the things that makes an honest conversation about the achievement gap especially hard is the difficulty of talking about how the African American community and other subordinated communities of color participate in the modern-day stigmatization and miseducation of our children. In a conversation where victim-blaming is a recurrent theme, we are reluctant to reinforce a message that distracts us from the central task of naming racism and the savage inequalities of opportunity as the primary causes of the achievement gap.

However, African Americans are not immune to the disease of racism. I have heard black teachers call their students "stupid" and "ignorant" or say, "What do you expect from kids like this?" I have heard black parents chastise their children with these same demeaning words and heard the words repeated as children taunt each other on the playground. I want to be clear that the abusive adults in our community are a minority. I have heard the same abuse issue from the mouths of white parents in upscale suburban malls. I also know that when black adults speak like this to children, the adults are parroting their own teachers and parents, reenacting the

---

35 J. Noelani Goodyear-Kaopua, *Rebuilding the ʻAuwai: Connecting Ecology, Economy and Education in Hawaiian Schools*, 5 ALTERNATIVE 46 (2009), http://socialsciences.people.hawaii.edu/publications_lib/Goodyear-Ka%27opua%20AlterNative%202009%205%282%29%2046–77.pdf. ʻAuwai is the Hawaiian name for the system of irrigation ditches Kanaka Maoli (Native Hawaiians) developed in precolonial Hawaii to enable sustainable, prolific wetland taro cultivation. Loʻi kalo is the Hawaiian name for wetland taro fields.

destruction of their own psyches, the stunting of their own gifts. This is how racism is internalized and perpetuated.[36]

Few of us will speak openly of our doubts about the intellectual capacities of black children and teachers, but the discourse among educators and education policymakers evidences the continued vitality of such beliefs. The academic and professional literature is "filled with student, family and cultural deficit theories, proposed minimum competency remedies, reflecting a terrible pessimism about the power of (black) teachers, schools and children."[37] More importantly, these views shape our educational practices – the way black children are spoken to, disciplined, and taught. When children are told to "shut up and sit down," when the toilets in the bathroom are broken and the classroom ceiling leaks, when there are no gifted or Advanced Placement classes, or when black students are discouraged from taking them, these practices and conditions, like segregation, are symbols of racist ideology. They "generate feelings of inferiority."

If we are to close the achievement gap we must address the deep structural inequalities that are its chief causes in a society still profoundly segregated by race, wealth, and social capital. Educators must create cultures of excellence and high expectations in schools for black and brown students – cultures that define success by superior achievement rather than marginal improvement. We must recruit and nurture school leaders and teachers who are committed to the project of excellence – scholars who believe black students are partners in the scholarly endeavor. We must educate and organize our communities to insist on excellence in their schools; to demand the resources necessary to that task; and to reject the fraudulent reforms of watered-down standards, high-stakes testing, commercial rote-learning programs, and phony school choice. We know what excellent schools look like. We know how to reproduce them. The challenge is political. Can we create the political will to change when the achievement gap is a condition of the oppressors' privilege?

There is no such thing as a neutral educational process. Education either functions to integrate our children into the logic of the current oppressive system and bring about conformity to it, or it becomes what the revolutionary Brazilian educator

---

[36] "Self-depreciation is another characteristic of the oppressed, which derives from their internalization of the opinion the oppressors hold of them. So often do they hear that they are good for nothing, know nothing, and are incapable of learning anything – that they are sick, lazy, and unproductive – that in the end they become convinced of their own unfitness." PAULO FREIRE, PEDAGOGY OF THE OPPRESSED 45 (Myra Bergman Ramos trans., 1970).

"The analysis we are undertaking is psychological. It remains, nevertheless, evident that for us the true disalienation of the black man implies a brutal awareness of the social and economic realities. The inferiority complex can be ascribed to a double process: First, economic. Then, internalization or rather epidermalization of this inferiority." FRANZ FANON, BLACK SKIN WHITE MASKS xvi (Richard Philcox trans., 2007). "[T]he black schoolboy who is constantly asked to recite, 'our ancestors the Gauls,' identifies himself with the explorer, the civilizing colonizer, the white man who brings truth to the savages, a lily-white truth. The identification process means that the black child subjectively adopts a white man's attitude." *Id.* at 2.

[37] ASA HILLIARD, in YOUNG GIFTED AND BLACK, *supra* note 31, at 143.

Paulo Friere called the "practice of freedom"[38]: the means by which the oppressed become critical thinkers and discover how to participate in the transformation of their world. Friere teaches two lessons that are central to this pedagogic practice: Education, liberation, and humanization are inseparable, and the teacher must trust in the students' ability to do this work. These lessons are essential to promoting high achievement among African American, Latino, Hawaiian, and Pacific Island students. Students must understand the relationship between their education and the struggle for liberation, and teachers must believe in students' capacity for becoming full participants in their own liberation and humanization.

[38] FREIRE, *supra* note 36.

8

Communications Law

Bits of Bias

Jerry Kang

Scientists have demonstrated that implicit biases are pervasive, large in magnitude, and have real-world consequences.[1] What can we do about them? One principal strategy is to decrease implicit biases in our minds (the other is to disrupt their causal link to behavior). To decrease bias, we should understand its source. Put crudely, is it nature or nurture? I argue that its source is mostly nurture, and of a specific sort – via vicarious experiences with outgroups mediated by electronic media. These vicarious interactions, fed to us via entertainment, news, social media, and computer-mediated communities, strengthen particular mental associations. If these vicarious experiences are indeed a substantial source of implicit bias, what might policymakers do in the shadow of the First Amendment?

I. WHERE DOES IMPLICIT BIAS COME FROM?

A. Nature

Perhaps implicit biases are "hardwired" into our DNA and into our brains as a product of evolution. In support of this position, one might cite research revealing that certain biases are shared by other primates. Consider, for example, the recent work by Neha Mahajan, Mahzarin Banaji, and colleagues, who studied intergroup biases of rhesus macaques, a primate species that diverged from our evolutionary line between twenty-five and thirty million years ago.[2] Deploying an ingenious variation of the Implicit Association Test, the researchers discovered that

Thanks to Jonathan Feingold for able research assistance. © by author.

[1] *See generally* Kristin A. Lane et al., *Implicit Social Cognition and the Law*, 3 ANN. REV. LAW SOC. SCI. 19.1 (2007).

[2] *See generally* Neha Mahajan et al., *The Evolution of Intergroup Bias: Perceptions and Attitudes in Rhesus Macaques*, 100 J. PERSONALITY & SOC. PSYCH. 387 (2011).

these monkeys distinguished between photographs of ingroup and outgroup members automatically and stared longer at outgroup monkeys (M = 10.83 s vs. 6.58 s; p = .004).[3] This behavior was consistent with the hypothesis that greater threats would prompt longer stares. Moreover, this longer span of attention could not be explained by unfamiliarity. Even "familiar" monkeys (monkeys that at adolescence had recently exited the ingroup to join an outgroup) prompted longer stares. In addition, the male monkeys (although not females) showed an implicit attitudinal preference in favor of the ingroup: they associated ingroup members more with favorable items (i.e., fruits) and outgroup members more with less favorable items (i.e., spiders; $F(5,185)$ = 3.06, p = .011).[4]

Such findings are fascinating. As the authors explain, they provide the "first systematic evidence that [intergroup] interactions are likely to be subserved by nearly identical cognitive mechanisms in human and nonhuman primates."[5] At the same time, these findings should not be overread. The fact that ingroup preference might be "natural" in primates does not say much about the particularities of how human ingroups are constructed and which ingroups are made salient. In other words, even if it is natural for us to like ourselves and to dislike others generally, that psychology does not tell us which specific groups to like, for what reasons, and with what intensity. That specificity is provided instead by our history, culture, and politics.

The upshot here is that even if broad cognitive tendencies are given to us by nature – that is, to categorize human beings into groups and to prefer ingroups – something else fills in the particular details of where to draw the boundaries and with what content. For example, in the early 1900s in Asia, a person of Japanese descent did not view a person of Korean descent as an ingroup member. By contrast, in the 2010s, in the United States, both Japanese Americans and Korean Americans might view themselves as sharing an ingroup identity of Asian American. In the early 1900s in California, the stereotype associated with a Chinese face might be that of an illegal immigrant. By contrast, in the early 1980s, the stereotype might be that of the model minority. These various differences could not have been produced by natural selection.

This understanding of cultural malleability is entirely consistent with evidence that implicit biases are highly reactive to the environment.[6] For example, Nilanjana Dasgupta and Anthony Greenwald found that implicit attitudes could be altered through exposure to counter-typical exemplars.[7] Participants were given a "general

---

3 *See id.* at 391, 392 Fig. 2.
4 *See id.* at 399.
5 *Id.* at 401.
6 *See generally* Irene V. Blair, *The Malleability of Automatic Stereotype*, 6 Pers. & Soc. Psychol. Rev. 242 (2002) (literature review).
7 Nilanjana Dasgupta & Anthony G. Greenwald, *On the Malleability of Automatic Attitudes: Combating Automatic Prejudice with Images of Admired and Disliked Individuals*, 81 J. Personality & Soc. Psych. 800, 807 (2001).

knowledge" questionnaire that was either pro-Black, pro-White, or race-neutral. The pro-Black condition exposed participants to people like Martin Luther King Jr. ("good") and Charles Manson, the serial killer ("bad"). For the pro-White condition group, the valences were flipped (e.g., Louis Farrakhan as "bad" and John F. Kennedy as "good"). Those participants who answered the pro-Black questionnaire had substantially decreased Implicit Association Test (IAT) race bias scores[8] – although follow-up studies have found much smaller effects.[9]

Not only famous counter-typical people can change our implicit biases but also the context in which we see ordinary folk. For example, Bernd Wittenbrink, Charles Judd, and Bernadette Park have demonstrated that exposure to a positive depiction of Blacks (a movie segment of an outdoor barbeque from the film *Poetic Justice*) decreases implicit bias scores more than exposure to a negative depiction (a clip from the film *Black & White & Red All Over* showing Black characters arguing over a gang-related incident).[10] Similarly, racial attitudes were less biased on a priming procedure when Black faces were viewed in a "church" context than in an "urban street corner" context.[11]

In sum, even if nature provides the broad cognitive canvas, nurture paints the detailed pictures – regarding who is inside and outside, what attributes they have, and who counts as friend or foe. The task now is to determine where these pictures come from.

B. *Nurture*

A first hypothesis is that these mental pictures originate from direct social interactions with other human beings. For example, what we think about Native Americans might come from actual, face-to-face interactions with Native Americans. This would, however, require that such direct encounters actually take place. My focus is on race and ethnicity, and the truth is that notwithstanding substantial movement toward integration, American residential neighborhoods remain racially segregated.[12] Accordingly, direct interracial experiences may not be common for many of us. Indirect, or vicarious experiences, with other social groups delivered through the media may be far more frequent. In other words, we learn about others

---

[8] The IAT effect changed nearly 50% as compared to the control (IAT effect M = 78 ms versus 174 ms, $p = .01$), and remained for more than twenty-four hours.

[9] *See* Jennifer A. Joy-Gaba & Brian A. Nosek, *The Surprisingly Limited Malleability of Implicit Racial Evaluations*, 41 SOCIAL PSYCH. 137, 141 (2010) (finding an effect size approximately 70% smaller).

[10] *See* B. Wittenbrink et al., *Spontaneous Prejudice in Context: Variability in Automatically Activated Attitudes*, 81 J. PERSONALITY & SOC. PSYCHOL. 815, 818–19 (2001).

[11] *Id.* at 823.

[12] *See generally* WILLIAM H. FREY & DOWELL MYERS, RACIAL SEGREGATION IN US METROPOLITAN AREAS AND CITIES, 1990–2000: PATTERNS, TRENDS, AND EXPLANATIONS (APRIL 2005); DOUGLAS S. MASSEY & NANCY A. DENTON, AMERICAN APARTHEID: SEGREGATION AND THE MAKING OF THE UNDERCLASS 81, 109–44 (1993).

by being told stories about them – through movies, news, music, and electronically mediated communications.

1. Entertainment

A vast literature in media studies has documented how *entertainment* media trade on stereotypes in both fiction and reality-based genres.[13] Over-the-top stereotypes have been Hollywood mainstays for decades, and consuming such content influences our attitudes and stereotypes.[14]

Even if you believe that outlandish portrayals have largely disappeared from the media, biases can still be transmitted through more subtle vectors. For example, Max Weisbuch and colleagues examined how race bias could be transmitted via nonverbal behavior on television shows.[15] By coding the body language of characters in eleven popular TV shows (while removing audio and cropping out the target character), they discovered that Black target characters received more negative body language (from the other characters in the show) than White target characters of equivalent social status ($M = 0.16$ vs. -0.04; $p < 0.047$). Interestingly, the transcripts of the shows' dialogue showed no discernible bias. Moreover, when asked explicitly, reviewers familiar with the shows did not rate the Black and White target characters differently in their perceived attractiveness, sociability, kindness, and intelligence.

More disturbing is the potential impact of these TV shows on viewers. Weisbuch et al. found a correlation between exposure to nonverbal race bias via these TV shows and the viewers' IAT score: $r(51) = 0.28$, $p = 0.047$.[16] To probe for causation and not merely correlation, the researchers explored whether a specific "treatment" of a video clip (with either pro-Black or pro-White body language) could alter IAT scores in viewers in an experimental setting. They discovered that those participants exposed to the pro-White treatment displayed higher IAT scores (in other words, displayed a stronger pro-White attitude) than those who were exposed to the pro-Black treatment (IAT $M = .70$ vs. $.43$, $p = .05$).[17] Disconcertingly, the biased behavior within these treatment videos was invisible: when participants were explicitly tasked to determine whether a particular treatment video was either pro-Black or pro-White, their accuracy was no better than chance.

---

[13] *See, e.g.*, Srividya Ramasubramanian, *Television Viewing, Racial Attitudes, and Policy Preferences: Exploring the Role of Social Identity and Intergroup Emotions in Influencing Support for Affirmative Action*, 77 COMM. MONOGRAPHS 102, 103–04 (2010) (briefly summarizing literature).

[14] *See id.* at 111–12, tbls1–2 (showing correlations between "perceived stereotypes on television" and personally held stereotypical beliefs and prejudicial feelings). Personally held biases also correlated negatively with self-reported support for affirmative action policies.

[15] *See* Max Weisbuch, et al., *The Subtle Transmission of Race Bias via Televised Nonverbal Behavior*, 326 SCIENCE 1711 (2009).

[16] *See id.* at 1712.

[17] *See id.* at 1713 and Supporting Online Material at 7–8, *available at* www.sciencemag.org/cgi/content/full/326/5960/1711/DC1.

2. News

If entertainment media transmit bias explicitly and implicitly, do news programs do the same? Unfortunately, local news programs often showcase violent and sensational crime stories.[18] For example, the Pew Project for Excellence in Journalism's annual study of local news programming consistently finds that local newscasts spend approximately 25% of their time on crime stories.[19] As often said, "if it bleeds, it leads." Violent crime news stories frequently involve racial minorities, especially African Americans, in part because racial minorities are arrested for violent crimes more frequently, on a per capita basis, than Whites.[20]

Even holding arrest rates constant, certain minorities appear to be overrepresented as perpetrators and underrepresented as victims on television news.[21] Travis Dixon and Daniel Linz examined local news broadcasts in Los Angeles and Orange Counties in California and computed differentials between television crime rates and real-world crime rates. They found, for example, that Blacks were portrayed as victims of homicide only 23% of the time, whereas their victimization rate was 28%. Whites were portrayed as victims 43% of the time on the news, although their actual victimization rate was 13%.[22] On the perpetrator side, TV news portrayed Blacks as perpetrators 36% of the time, although the actual arrest rate percentage for Blacks was 21%.[23]

This steady diet of stories and images has predictable consequences. For example, Travis Dixon and Keith Maddox examined the relationship between skin color of the perpetrator in a crime news clip and the emotional discomfort of the viewers.[24] They found generally that participants who saw a dark-skinned Black perpetrator

---

[18] Network news is less obsessed with violent crime than is local news. That said, consumption of network news has also been correlated with personal stereotype endorsement about African Americans (e.g., that they are intimidating or impoverished). *See, e.g.,* Travis L. Dixon, *Network News and Racial Beliefs: Exploring the Connection Between National Television News Exposure and Stereotypical Perceptions of African Americans*, 58 J. COMM. 321, 329 tbl.4 (2008).

[19] Tom Rosenstiel et al., *Local TV News Project 1998: What Works, What Flops, and Why*, JOURNALISM.ORG (March 1, 1999), http://www.journalism.org/node/377. The Project for Excellence in Journalism (PEJ) is an affiliate of the Columbia University Graduate School of Journalism. *See also* Wally Dean & Lee Ann Brady, *After 9/11, Has Anything Changed?*, in ON THE ROAD TO IRRELEVANCE 95 (2002) ("the actions of cops, criminals, suspects, crime victims, family members, and lawyers made up 27 percent of all stories") (study by PEJ).

[20] *See* Jerry Kang, *Trojan Horses of Race*, 118 HARV. L. REV. 1489 (2005) search for "FBI, U.S. DEP'T OF JUSTICE, CRIME IN THE UNITED STATES 2002: UNIFORM CRIME REPORTS") (summarizing literature) [hereinafter, Kang, *Trojan Horses*].

[21] *See* Travis L. Dixon & Daniel Linz, *Race and the Misrepresentation of Victimization on Local Television News*, 27 COMM. RESEARCH 547 (2000).

[22] *Id.* at 561 tbl.3.

[23] *Id.* tbl.4. Interestingly, Latinos were drastically underrepresented as both homicide victims (19% TV versus 54% actual) and arrested perpetrators (23% TV and 47% actual).

[24] Travis L. Dixon & Keith B. Maddox, *Skin Tone, Crime News and Social Reality Judgments*, 35 J. APPLIED SOC. PSYCH. 1555 (2006).

registered higher emotional concern about the crime story than those participants who saw a White perpetrator (M = 3.84 vs. 2.91; $p <. 05$). Interestingly, they also found a significant interaction between skin tone and news consumption. Heavy news viewers (as defined by a median split) responded more emotionally to the dark-skinned perpetrator than to the White perpetrator (M = 4.51 v. 2.67; $p < .01$); light news viewers showed no difference between the two.[25]

Consistent with such findings are studies that show potential political and voting consequences of local news crime coverage. In one study, political scientists Frank Gilliam and Shanto Iyengar created variations of a local newscast: a control version with no crime story, a crime story with a Black-suspect mug shot, and a crime story with a White-suspect mug shot.[26] The Black and White suspects were represented by the same morphed photograph that differed only in skin hue. In the ten-minute newscast, the image of the suspect appeared for only five seconds. When exposed to the Black suspect, White participants showed 6% more support for punitive remedies than did the control group, which saw no crime story. There was no statistically significant difference in such support when participants saw the White suspect.

3. Virtual Worlds

In contrast to television entertainment or news, Internet enthusiasts might have more utopian hopes for new media – the brave new virtual worlds of online gaming and social interaction. Unfortunately, even in virtual spaces, both race and racism persist. First, when individuals play as human (indeed anthropomorphic) characters, these characters are racialized. In other words, these avatars reveal those features that we culturally employ to map individuals into racial categories.[27]

Second, the racial politics of the real world – including resentment of racialized others who invade an ingroup's "territory" – bleeds into cyberspace. Black avatars have been subject to hate speech.[28] A hijab-wearing character was pushed into the sea and thus "killed" by a character dressed as a policeman.[29] Sometimes violence gets more pogrom-like. Lisa Nakamura has commented thoughtfully about the racist (virtual) violence committed in the *World of Warcraft* game against Chinese players

---

[25] *Id.* at 1562.

[26] Franklin D. Gilliam, Jr. & Shanto Iyengar, *Prime Suspects: The Influence of Local Television News on the Viewing Public*, 44 AM. J. POL. SCI. 560, 563–67 (2000).

[27] A virtual census of characters in 150 videogames on nine platforms conducted in 2005–06 found overrepresentation of males (85.23% in games versus 50.9% in actual population) and Whites (80.5% versus 75.1%). *See* Williams et al., *The Virtual Census: Representations of Gender, Race and Age in Video Games*, 11 NEWS MEDIA & SOC'Y 815, 825–26 (2009).

[28] *See, e.g.*, Jerry Kang, *Cyber-Race*, 113 HARV. L. REV. 1130, 1133–34 (2000) (showing transcript of attack, which involved racial epithets) [hereinafter Kang, *Cyber-Race*].

[29] *See* Methal R. Mohammed, *Cultural Identity in Virtual Reality (VR): A Case Study of a Muslim Woman with Hijab in Second Life (SL)*, 3 J. VIRTUAL WORLDS RES. 4, 7 (2009).

working as "gold" farmers, who produce virtual online goods sold on eBay for real dollars.[30]

If we focus more on implicit bias, virtual media researchers have collected evidence of online discrimination as a function of an avatar's skin color – despite everyone's conscious recognition that the avatar is a complete fabrication. For example, Paul Eastwick and Wendi Gardner studied whether certain "social influence" tactics that work in the real world would also work in a virtual world. The persuasion literature has documented the efficacy of both the foot-in-the-door (FITD) and the door-in-the-face (DITF) techniques. The FITD technique asks someone for a small favor and then follows up with a larger request. The effectiveness of this technique turns on the desire for consistency on the part of the target (the person who was solicited). By saying "yes" to the small favor, the target has affirmed the trait of helpfulness. To remain consistent, the target is then more likely to agree to the larger favor.

The DITF technique works in the opposite direction: the first request is intentionally designed to overreach, but after rejection, the second, smaller ask is more likely to be granted. This technique trades not on consistency but on reciprocity. The second, more reasonable request is viewed as a concession from the original demand, for which there ought to be reciprocity from the target. This motive to reciprocate is an affiliative phenomenon, driven by some sense of obligation to the requester. Thus the qualities of the requester, such as his or her attractiveness, have been shown to moderate DITF's effectiveness.

Eastwick and Gardner attempted both techniques in the virtual world, but did so using two different avatars: one with the lightest skin possible ("milk") in the virtual world There.com and the other with the darkest skin possible ("espresso"). The FITD technique (which turns on self-perception) worked, as in the real world, regardless of race. However, the DITF technique (which turns on reciprocity) only worked for the White avatar.[31] Consider what this finding means. It seems unlikely that anyone (except a self-avowed racist) would explicitly predict that he or she would respond differently to a request for a favor in a virtual world simply because of that avatar's made-up "race." Yet, this is precisely what was found.

We have reached sobering conclusions. First, even if certain basic cognitive tendencies drive us to prefer the ingroup, the specific details of how such tendencies play out in the real world are socially constructed. Second, the specific content of implicit biases comes from environmental experiences, which are substantially vicarious and electronically mediated. Of course, we cannot determine the precise percentage of implicit biases that can be attributed to vicarious electronic media as opposed to all other sources. In particular, we cannot deny the potency of

---

[30] Lisa Nakamura, *Don't Hate the Player, Hate the Game: The Racialization of Labor in World of Warcraft*, 26 CRITICAL STUD. MEDIA COMM. 128 (2009).

[31] Paul W. Eastwick & Wendi L. Gardner, *Is It a Game: Evidence for Social Influence in the Virtual World*, 4 SOC. INFLUENCE 18, 26 (2009).

real-world interactions that teach us implicitly, daily, who occupies the higher rungs of power and influence. That said, the research described supports the conclusion that vicarious experiences remain significant influences.

II. SOLUTIONS

Suppose that we as a society become persuaded that vicarious experiences are a substantial source of implicit bias. Private parties could then voluntarily respond in whatever ways they think appropriate to reduce the transmission of implicit bias. Unfortunately, there is reason to be skeptical that radical change will occur in a field like entertainment. Just as sex and violence sell, so do comforting schemas. An even harder question is whether the state can do anything by force of law. Would the First Amendment block any governmental attempt to decrease implicit biases?

A. *Broadcast: Do No Harm*

If any legal intervention is constitutionally plausible, it would be within the communications medium of broadcasting, which has historically tolerated the most regulation.[32] As the Communications Act of 1934 makes clear, the electromagnetic spectrum that broadcasters use is not private property, but rather is government property held in the public trust. The United States licenses that spectrum to private parties who use it for private gain, but in exchange must at least pay lip service to the "public interest."[33]

Because of this use of public property for private gain, as well as spectrum scarcity[34] and broadcast's pervasiveness,[35] broadcast ownership, structure, and content have been substantially regulated. The Federal Communications Commission (FCC) has promulgated (and the courts have enforced) regulations that restrict the broadcast of content deemed "bad" because of obscenity,[36] indecency,[37] and excessive commercialization.[38] Specific to antiracism, the FCC, at the instruction of the courts, has revoked the broadcast licenses of stations that favored segregation and aired anti-Black racial epithets.[39] Conversely, it has also promulgated regulations that promote content deemed "good" through informational programming

---

[32] Part II.A draws heavily on Kang, *Trojan Horses, supra* note 20.

[33] *See*, e.g., 47 U.S.C. § 303 (2000).

[34] *See* Red Lion Broad. Co. v. FCC, 395 U.S. 367, 390–92 (1969).

[35] *See* FCC v. Pacifica Found., 438 U.S. 729–30, 748–49 (1978).

[36] *See*, e.g., 18 U.S.C. § 1464 (2000) (criminalizing radio communication of "obscene, indecent, or profane" content); 47 C.F.R. § 73.3999(a) (2003) (prohibiting the broadcast of obscene material).

[37] *See*, e.g., 18 U.S.C. § 1464; *see also Pacifica*, 438 U.S. at 748–51.

[38] *See* The Revision of Programming and Commercialization Policies, Ascertainment Requirements, and Program Log Requirements for Commercial Television Stations, 98 F.C.C.2d 1076, 1101 (1984).

[39] *See*, e.g., Office of Communication of the United Church of Christ v. FCC, 425 F.2d 543, 547–50 (D.C. Cir. 1969).

guidelines,[40] community ascertainment requirements,[41] and children's educational television guidelines.[42] Specific to questions of race, the FCC has also tried to promote "good" and diverse content by increasing minority ownership of stations through affirmative action. The point of this partial inventory is not to defend each regulation on its merits. Instead, it is to demonstrate how much we regulate broadcast content despite the First Amendment.

1. Redefining the Public Interest

To repeat, the touchstone for governmental management of broadcast is the public interest standard. This vague standard has been decomposed into three parts: diversity, competition, and localism. What is important for purposes of this discussion is to recognize that the FCC has operationalized large chunks of both the diversity and localism standards in terms of local news. In an important order revising mass media ownership policy, the FCC wrote this about diversity:

> Although all content in visual and aural media have the potential to express viewpoints, we find that viewpoint diversity is *most easily measured* through news and public affairs programming. Not only is news programming *more easily measured* than other types of content containing viewpoints, but it relates most directly to the Commission's core policy objective of facilitating robust democratic discourse in the media. Accordingly, we have sought in this proceeding to measure how certain ownership structures affect news output.[43]

As for localism, the FCC focused on "programming responsive to local needs and interests, and *local news quantity and quality*."[44] The regulatory history on how we ended up here is less important than the final destination: local news has become a critical component of the FCC's public interest analysis, at least in the media ownership context. It is only a slight exaggeration to say that one pursues the public interest by airing local news.

Yet what is on local news? As we already learned, crime stories. And we have seen what consumption of these stories might cause. Indeed, it is not too much of a stretch to analogize local news programs, dense with images of racial minorities committing violent crimes in one's own community, to Trojan Horse viruses. Local news provides

---

[40] Until the broadcast deregulation of the early 1980s, broadcast stations were required to show at least 5% local programming, 5% informational programming (news and public affairs), or 10% total nonentertainment programming. *See* The Revision of Programming and Commercialization Policies, Ascertainment Requirements, and Program Log Requirements for Commercial Television Stations, 98 F.C.C.2d 1076, 1078 (1984).

[41] *See id.* at 1097 (describing then-existing ascertainment requirements).

[42] Congress passed the Children's Television Act (CTA) of 1990. *See* Pub. L. No. 101–437, 104 Stat. 996 (codified as amended at 47 U.S.C. § § 303(a), 303(b), 394 (2000)).

[43] *Id.* In the Matter of 2002 Biennial Regulatory Review, 18 F.C.C.R. 13,620 (2003), aff'd in part and remanded, Prometheus Radio Project v. FCC, 373 F.3d 372 (3d Cir. 2004).

[44] *Id.* (emphasis added).

useful information that we seek. We invite it into our homes, in through the gates of our minds, and accept it at face value, as an accurate representation of newsworthy events. Yet something lurks within those newscasts that increases implicit bias.

If this is empirically demonstrable, then the FCC should follow the Hippocratic Oath and "do no harm." Concretely, it should break the operational linkage between the public interest standard and the number of hours of local news aired. The argument here is not to suppress local news. Instead, it is simply to stop fetishizing it, as currently conceived. There are better metrics. Here are two concrete suggestions.

First, the FCC could measure the number of bona fide investigative journalists that the broadcast station employs. Increasing the numbers of such journalists would promote the values of diversity and localism better than simply counting the number of hours of local news. As we enter a media environment in which repackaging, aggregating, and opining replace actual news gathering, it makes even more sense to encourage investigative journalist "boots on the ground." What we need and want are trained professionals digging up sources and facts.

Second, the FCC should more directly credit substantive content, in the form of debiasing public service announcements (d-PSAs), as contributing to the public interest. These announcements could strive to communicate messages that in substance and form fight against prejudice and stereotyping. The malleability studies discussed earlier provide design suggestions for these d-PSAs.

If this approach seems inconsistent with government "neutrality," we should recognize that modern broadcast policy is anything but neutral. In terms of suppressing "bad" content, think again about indecency policy. In terms of promoting "good" content, think about the federally funded Corporation for Public Broadcasting (CPB), which subsidizes the broadcast networks PBS and NPR. Congress explicitly charged the CPB to "address the needs of racial and ethnic minorities, new immigrant populations, people for whom English is a second language, and adults who lack basic reading skills."[45] In addition, Congress made clear that "it is in the public interest to encourage the development of programming that involves creative risks and that addresses the needs of unserved and underserved audiences, particularly children and minorities."[46] Another analogy is to children's educational television programming rules, which strongly encourage broadcasters to show three hours of such programming per week.[47]

B. *Integration: Promote Social Contact*

Let us now turn to new media, including the virtual online worlds accessible through the Internet. In sharp contrast to television and radio broadcast, the Internet is given

[45] 47 U.S.C. § 396(m)(1).
[46] 47 U.S.C. §396(a)(6).
[47] *See In the Matter of Policies and Rules Concerning Children's Television Programming*, 11 F.C.C.R. 10,660, 10,718–21 (1996).

full First Amendment respect, no weaker than print.[48] Accordingly, the plausible interventions here cannot involve direct government regulation. Instead, the appeal is to programmers, designers, entrepreneurs, and corporations to create voluntarily virtual worlds that help decrease racial bias. How might this be done? One way is to promote intergroup social contact.

In a recent meta-analysis of the social contact hypothesis,[49] Thomas Pettigrew and Linda Tropp reviewed 515 studies using 713 independent samples that encompassed a quarter-million people from 38 nations. They found that intergroup contact correlates negatively with prejudice (average $r = -0.215$; $p < .0001$). To check whether the causal sequence might be operating in reverse (i.e., whether less prejudiced people sought out greater intergroup contact), the researchers distinguished studies by the degree of choice that people had to engage in such contact. They saw no significant correlation between the choice to interact and the magnitude of decrease in prejudice ($r = .005$, $p = .89$).[50] The bottom line then is that social integration does decrease intergroup bias. Can the Internet be leveraged to promote such social integration?[51]

Arguably, cyberspace has the potential both to increase the quantity and to improve the quality of interracial contact. As for quantity, cyberspace makes geographical proximity less relevant, thereby partially lifting residential segregation's chokehold on interracial social contact. In addition, cyberspace makes it easier to talk to strangers because individuals are less fearful. One strategy that virtual community operators could explicitly follow is to promote chance encounters with other people. Consider the following two possible interfaces for a graphical world. In World 1, one can move instantly between locations by clicking on a menu of available rooms; by contrast, in World 2, the only way to move from room to room is by walking your avatar (even if quickly) through intervening hallways and public spaces. World 2 is a superior integration space because walking increases the number of common spaces regularly traversed. Along the way, we might encounter interesting people and unexpected places to explore – something less likely to happen if we simply "teleport" from location to location. For similar reasons, many people in real space prefer walkable cities to those that require driving.

As for quality, social psychologists have identified the following environmental attributes as especially valuable in decreasing biases: (1) exposure to disconfirming data, (2) interaction among people of equal status, (3) cooperation, (4) nonsuperficial contact, and (5) equality norms.[52] These discoveries provide guidance for smart

---

[48] Reno v. ACLU, 521 U.S. 844 (1997).

[49] Thomas F. Pettigrew & Linda R. Tropp, *A Meta-Analytic Test and Reformulation of Intergroup Contact Theory*, 90 J. PERSONALITY & SOC. PSYCHOL. 751 (2006).

[50] *See id.*

[51] The following borrows substantially from Kang, *Cyber-Race, supra* note 28.

[52] Norman Miller & Marilynn B. Brewer, *The Social Psychology of Desegregation: An Introduction*, in GROUPS IN CONTACT: THE PSYCHOLOGY OF DESEGREGATION 1, 2 (Norman Miller & Marilynn B. Brewer eds., 1984).

design of virtual spaces.[53] One concrete strategy is to encourage team games in which groups compete against each other for prizes, virtual or real. What is essential here is that the teams form somewhat randomly, so that individuals do not stick only to those players they already know. The hope is that by repeatedly playing these games in teams, with individuals of other races, we might alter – even if slightly – racial attitudes and stereotypes for the better.

If this sounds farfetched, consider online games such as *World of Warcraft* (WoW) or *EverQuest*. As incredible as it may seem, there are millions of players across the globe who spend dozens of hours per week in this virtual online environment. The relationships made within these games are not trivial, at least according to self-reports; in one survey, 60 percent of men and 75 percent of women regard the friendships that they have made in *EverQuest* to be as significant as those in real life.[54] Various scholars have tried to theorize why relationships mediated through avatars online might feel even more intense than relationships in real life. It might be that online participants engage in greater self-disclosure because of anonymity and safety. In addition, they can ignore the constraints of real-life physical appearance and focus more on the substantive content of messages.[55]

User interface designers are well aware that the underlying social architecture of an online community must be engineered. In real life, for example, the human voice carries only so far. However, online, the spatial reach of "speech" is a function of how a game or virtual world is designed. For instance, *EverQuest* allows various chat channels, including the ability to communicate to everyone within one's zone or guild. By contrast, in another online world, *Dark Age of Camelot*, there is no easy way to communicate with such a large number of players.[56] As another example of social engineering, *EverQuest* forces cooperation among players because each type of character has peculiar strengths and weaknesses that must be complemented by other characters with different strengths and weaknesses. In addition, as Nick Yee has described, *EverQuest* makes possible and arguably encourages certain acts of altruism. Thus, we see how one virtual world has created some of those very conditions likely to help decrease intergroup hostility. As anecdotal evidence, consider the following statement by one *EverQuest* player:

> In EQ [EverQuest], we engage in difficult, sometimes dangerous and often life-threatening struggles. Even though it isn't RL [real-life] – you learn a lot about the character of the person playing the game. Some are selfish and greedy in EQ and you figure they are similar in RL – others are eager to help and think of others over themselves – and I have found them to be the same in RL. The difference between

53 *See also* Yair Amichai-Hamburger & Katelyn Y. A. McKenna, *The Contact Hypothesis Reconsidered: Interacting via the Internet*, 11 J. Computer-Mediated Comm. 825 (2006) (discussing ways in which the Internet can promote those conditions necessary to decrease intergroup hostility).

54 *See* Nick Yee, *Befriending Ogres and Wood-Elves: Relationship Formation and the Social Architect of Norath*, 9 Int'l J. Computer Game Res. 1 (2009).

55 *See* Amichai-Hamburger & McKenna, *supra* note 53, at 836.

56 *See* Yee, *supra* note 54.

these friendships and RL is the ability to watch someone in action before allowing them into your life. Also, the fact that we are all unable to see our real faces prior to becoming friends – we can't prejudge someone on the basis of their looks.[57]

What is interesting is that because online interaction is computer mediated, certain aspects of that interaction can be tweaked in ways that are impossible in real life. For instance, as the previous quotation demonstrates, there can be a selective delay in real-life social category disclosure. In other words, it might take a while before a player finds out that another one is a member of a particular race. As has been discussed, there is troubling evidence that, despite good intentions, stereotypes are triggered simply by exposure to the object of the stereotype. Therefore even though debiasing through social integration requires participants to reveal their real-life social categories eventually, a strategic delay of such information could allow for different sorts of social interactions to take place online.

Even more interesting tweaks are identified by Yee. For instance, there is evidence that eye contact influences social interactions. The game, *Star Wars Galaxies*, automatically maintains eye contact between relevant characters. In contrast to the real world, where one can maintain eye contact practically with only one person at a time, no such physical constraint exists in the virtual world. If one avatar is speaking to an audience of five other players, the scene can be painted slightly differently on each person's computer screen such that the avatar maintains eye contact with each member of the audience.

Again, many readers might be skeptical that such interactions in cyberspace could influence what happens in the real world. Yet there is increasing evidence that virtual experience can influence real-life behavior. In one experiment, Nick Yee and Jeremy Bailenson explored whether participants' embodiment (through an immersive 3D virtual world technology) in either an attractive or unattractive avatar would influence social behavior in the real world.[58] They discovered that participants embodied in attractive avatars subsequently behaved differently on a dating website: they exaggerated less about their own height (M = 0.17 vs. 1.17 inches, $p = .05$) and selected more attractive partners as potential dates (M = 10.47 vs. 9.43, with M representing the sum of two partners selected on a 1–7 attractiveness scale; $p = .01$) on the dating site.[59]

III. CONCLUSION

We have more than circumstantial evidence to believe that implicit biases come significantly from the media we consume. Through the media, we engage in vicarious

---

[57] *Id.*

[58] Nick Yee & Jeremy N. Bailenson, *The Difference Between Being and Seeing: The Relative Contribution of Self-Perception and Priming to Behavioral Changes via Digital Self-Representation*, 12 MEDIA PSYCHOL. 195 (2009).

[59] *See id.* at 204–05.

experiences that reinforce often negative attitudes of the outgroup and strengthen particular stereotypes. Recognition of this phenomenon, especially if it can be measured through scientific instruments, could prompt change. Much of this reform would have to be voluntary on the part of those who produce entertainment and news. Intriguingly, those who create the social architecture of virtual worlds might be able to design debiasing environments that promote the type of social contact that decreases intergroup hostility. In the meantime, the law should not encourage content that exacerbates implicit biases by equating the "public interest" in broadcast to more "local news."

9

Corporations Law

Biased Corporate Decision-Making?

Justin D. Levinson

Despite the high stakes of today's global economic climate, corporations have not lived up to the challenge of operating in a manner that recognizes their vast impact on people's lives. Instead, they have been accused of making decisions that disregard the welfare of workers, denigrate the environment, and ignore other social responsibilities.[1] Yet what drives corporate decisions that seem to further disadvantage already challenged groups? Is it always a rational pursuit of profit and corporate growth? Or might there be a more nuanced explanation that explains why corporations, for example, hire a particular executive, select an employee benefit plan, build a plant in a certain neighborhood, or donate to a specific charity? Research on implicit bias provides one potential explanation: corporate "persons," like real people, make decisions in automatically biased ways, often without their awareness. In turn, these decisions adversely affect already disadvantaged groups within society.

Corporate laws have yet to grapple with the problem of implicit bias.[2] This chapter begins an implicit bias based exploration of corporate law in two ways. First, in recognition of the early state of knowledge of implicit bias in corporate decision-making, the chapter proposes that the same empirical methods that have taught scholars about implicit bias in other areas can be implemented to learn more about bias in the corporate law setting. To that end, it presents an empirical study

The author would like to thank and acknowledge Danielle M. Young for her guidance during the design and statistical analysis of the empirical studies, and Chloe Dooley, who assisted with data collection.

[1] *See, e.g.* Kent Greenfield, *The Place of Workers in Corporate Law*, 39 B.C. L. Rev. 283 (1998); Dan Greenwood, *Torts in Corporate Law: Do Corporations Have a Fiduciary Duty to Commit Torts?*, *in* Tortious Liability Emerging Trends (M.N. Bhavani ed. 2008); Cheryl L. Wade, *For-Profit Corporations That Perform Public Functions: Politics, Profit, and Poverty*, 51 Rutgers L. Rev. 323 (1999).

[2] *See generally* Antony Page, *Unconscious Bias and the Limits of Director Independence*, 2009 Ill. L. Rev. 237.

that investigated the following question: If a corporation is truly a legal person, what kind of person is it? Moreover, is it the kind of person particularly likely to discriminate? The chapter then turns to two broader questions that help define the relationship between corporations and implicit bias: First, how might implicit bias infect corporate decision-making in unintentional yet powerful ways, and second, how can the law minimize the continuing harm of implicit bias without straying from needed corporate protections?

The first section of this chapter employs the Implicit Association Test, one of the core empirical methods that have expanded knowledge of implicit bias, and directs it at examining how people perceive the characteristics of corporations as corporate persons. The studies I conducted, which serve as a starting point for empirical research of implicit bias in corporate decision-making, reveal that people implicitly associate corporations with older whites and explicitly perceive them as somewhat resembling old (racist) white men.

The second section of this chapter takes a more traditional (nonempirical) approach in examining more broadly how corporations may make biased decisions based on stereotypes related to group membership, focusing on the specific examples of executive compensation and charitable giving. It outlines the corporate safety net of the business judgment rule, the primary protective mechanism insulating officers and directors from liability for a wide range of corporate decisions. It then evaluates whether, in unique circumstances, courts might choose to limit the applicability of the business judgment rule when officers and directors engage in a series of transactions that are both economically detrimental to shareholders and reinforce racial and gender hierarchies. Finally, it considers the implementation of an alternative remedy – implicit bias training for officers and directors – that might lead to future decision-making benefits both in increasing profit and in mitigating bias.

I. WHAT KIND OF "LEGAL PERSON" IS A CORPORATION? AN EMPIRICAL ANALYSIS

Empirical research from the field of implicit social cognition has provided compelling reasons to consider how implicit bias might operate in corporate decision-making. Yet, most empirical research on implicit bias sits outside the corporate realm. One should ask, then, whether new, targeted empirical studies could be developed to test unique hypotheses related to racial and gender bias in corporate decision-making. In addition to exploring empirically the influence of bias on the range of decisions considered in Part II of this chapter, including executive compensation and charitable giving, implicit social cognition methods can allow for the investigation of a wide range of questions. In that spirit, inspired by discourse surrounding the doctrine of corporate personhood, I conducted an empirical study designed to explore implicit perceptions of the corporate person. Specifically,

I hypothesized that, as legal persons, corporations are perceived most like natural persons who would be described as older (racist) white men.

The principle of corporate personhood is one of the most fundamental and controversial doctrines of corporate law. Some of the doctrine's strengths – including that it gives corporations the ability to enter into contracts, to sue, and be sued – make the function of corporate personhood seem beneficial and noncontroversial. Yet its weaknesses, such as the narrowly construed profit-driven purpose of corporations, as well as the *Citizens United* protections relating to political campaign donations,[3] expose the corporation to well-deserved scrutiny. This tension between the benefits of corporate personhood and its simultaneous potential for abuse has caused some commentators to ask this question: If the corporation is really a person, what kind of person is it? Empirical methods, including those used by implicit social cognition researchers to expose implicit racial bias, may provide an avenue to answer this question.

Responses to the fundamental query surrounding the true identity of the corporate person have focused on the corporation's narrow-sighted concern for shareholder wealth generation at the expense of workers and the surrounding community. This perspective has led some, such as in the documentary film *The Corporation*, to argue that a corporation harbors a corporate "personality" similar to the personality of a psychopath and therefore has no moral conscience.[4] This perspective, rooted in an examination of a corporate person's pathology, loosely relies on the American Psychiatric Association's *Diagnostic and Statistical Manual of Mental Disorders* in an attempt to "diagnose" the mental illness of the corporate form. It thus answers the question not of what kind of person a corporation is, but what might be wrong with it.

However, another perspective – the implicit social cognition perspective – may help reveal more about the corporate person in the context of race and gender. Similar to the pathology-driven inquiry, this perspective approaches the corporation as a legal person and asks what kind of person it is. Unlike the clinical approach, however, the implicit bias perspective can rely on well-developed empirical methodology to test, for example, whether members of the public hold implicit associations between corporate "people" and a whole range of attributes, including race, gender, and age.

Using social cognition methods, I devised a two-part study to tackle the question of whether people perceive corporate persons as a type of person who automatically, yet systematically, discriminates. Specifically, the study tested the hypothesis that people perceive corporations as older (even racist) white men.[5]

---

[3] Citizens United v. Fed. Election Comm'n, 130 S.Ct. 876 (2010).
[4] *The Corporation* (Big Picture Media 2003).
[5] Because asking corporations, "what kind of person are you," would likely not yield accurate results, I set out to test empirically how people perceive corporations. Although using implicit methods is

A. Study One: Implicit Associations of Corporate Persons

The first study employed Implicit Association Tests (IATs) to test how people implicitly perceive corporations as analogous to natural persons. IATs, which are explained in detail in Chapter 1, often pair "an attitude object (such as a racial group) with an evaluative dimension (good or bad) and test how response accuracy and speed indicate implicit and automatic attitudes and stereotypes."[6] For this study, three separate IATs were designed: a Corporation/Race IAT (to test implicit associations between corporations and white or black), a Corporation/Gender IAT (to test implicit associations between corporations and male or female), and a Corporation/Age IAT (to test implicit associations between corporations and old or young).[7]

Measures and Materials: I hypothesized that participants would implicitly associate corporations with white, male, and old, thus indicating that people implicitly perceive corporations as old white men. I conducted the study on the campus of a large university, using volunteer participants.[8]

The IATs were presented in counterbalanced order so that order-based effects could be eliminated. The first measure tested was the Corporation/Race IAT. I was specifically interested in whether people would implicitly associate corporations with white compared to black. Thus, the Corporation/Race IAT requires participants to group together words representing corporations (business, shareholders, corporation, stockholders, and for-profit) with white and black faces. For purposes of this study, I used photos of only white male and black male faces.[9]

The second measure tested was the Corporation/Gender IAT. This test examined whether people would implicitly associate corporations with male compared to female. The Corporation/Gender IAT requires participants to group together words

---

a far from foolproof way to determine the true identity of a corporation, it is likely to offer some clues. As the research in Chapter 1 and elsewhere in this volume demonstrates, implicit attitudes can be based on stereotypes. Thus testing people's implicit perceptions of corporations has potential shortcomings and should only be looked at as a starting point for social cognition research on corporations.

6 *See* Justin D. Levinson et al., *Implicit Racial Bias: A Social Science Overview*, *supra* ch. 1.

7 These IATs were designed as single-category IATs. *See* Andrew Karpinski & Ross B. Steinman, *The Single Category Implicit Association Test as a Measure of Implicit Social Cognition*, 91 J. PERSONALITY & SOC. PSYCHOL. 16 (2006). An advantage of single-category IATs is that they allow researchers to understand implicit associations with more specificity. For example, a two-category IAT designed with my hypothesis in mind might test whether people implicitly associate old people with corporations and young people with nonprofits. Such a design has advantages, but one drawback is that even with statistically significant results, researchers can have trouble determining conclusively whether the significant result is driven by a strong association between one of the pairs (nonprofit and young, for example) or strong associations between both pairs. Single-category IATs are straightforward tests that allow for simple conclusions.

8 Some volunteers were thanked with candy bars, although candy bars were not replenished after they ran out, and it appeared as though participants were not particularly interested in the candy.

9 The photos used had been pretested and matched by other researchers for attractiveness and race stereotypicality.

representing corporations with male and female first names.[10] The third measure tested was the Corporation/Age IAT, which evaluated whether people implicitly associate corporations with old compared to young. The Corporation/Age IAT requires participants to group together words representing corporations with words representing old and young.[11]

Thirty-nine participants completed the study.[12] The mean age was 24.13 years old. Twenty-three of the participants were male, and sixteen were female. The participant pool was ethnically diverse. Nearly half of the participants (n = 19) identified themselves as Asian American, 26 percent (n = 10) identified themselves as white/European American, 13 percent (n = 5) identified themselves as Pacific Islanders, and another 13 percent (n = 5) identified themselves as multiracial. Sixty-four percent of the participants were currently enrolled as undergraduates. Others held postgraduate degrees, including two with PhDs. Six participants had completed some graduate school.

Results: As predicted, the first IAT – the Corporation/Race IAT – confirmed the hypothesis that people hold implicit biases associating corporations with white.[13] Participants displayed a significant association between Corporation and white compared to Corporation and black, producing a significant IAT effect (D = .117, t(38) = 2.22, p < .05). The results support the conclusion that people implicitly associate corporations with whites and, because the photos were only of black and white men, with white men in particular. The second IAT – the Corporation/Gender IAT – did not produce a significant effect. Although participants were slightly faster to associate Corporations with male names compared to Corporations with female names, the IAT effect was not significant (D = .04, t(38) = .663, p > 0.1). The third IAT – the Corporation/Age IAT – confirmed the hypothesis that people implicitly associate corporations and old. Participants were faster to associate Corporations with old compared to Corporations with young, producing a significant IAT effect (D = .366, t(38) = 9.722, p < .01).

Taken together, the results of Study One indicate that people hold implicit associations between corporations and members of certain groups, namely older whites.

---

[10] The male names were Josh, Peter, Ian, Andrew, and Brandon. The female names were Emily, Donna, Debbie, Katherine, and Jane.

[11] The words representing old were old, seasoned, senior, experienced, and established. The words representing young were fresh, new, young, youthful, and junior.

[12] Using the recommended protocol for single-category IATs, data were eliminated for participants whose responses were more than 20% incorrect or had more than 10% of their responses under 300 ms (a speed too fast for even the fastest diligent participant).

[13] In computing the results, I followed the scoring algorithms suggested by Greenwald and his colleagues. *See* Anthony G. Greenwald et al., *Understanding and Using the Implicit Association Test: I. An Improved Scoring Algorithm*, 85 J. PERSONALITY & SOC. PSYCHOL. 197 (2003), modified for the single-category IAT. In this algorithm, mean latencies are computed for each block, and complimentary blocks are subtracted from each other (e.g., corporations-white are subtracted from corporations-black). These difference scores are divided by their inclusive standard deviation score, and the average of these two scores is called *D*.

These findings offer an initial clue in identifying the perceived characteristics of the corporate person. Following up on these results, I conducted a second study using a different methodology.

B. *Study Two: Shared Traits of Corporations and Racist Old White Men*

The second study examined what traits and characteristics people attribute to corporations. I hypothesized that people would attribute to corporations the same traits they attribute to racist old white men and specifically that corporations would be judged to be more similar to racist old white men than to young egalitarian people of color.

Methods and Materials: To test this hypothesis, I conducted a two-step study. The first step consisted of a pretest that asked participants to rate the character traits of old racist white men and young egalitarian people of color. Participants were given a list of forty traits[14] and were asked to rate how much each trait represented old racist white men, young egalitarian people of color, or neither. Participants rated the traits on a scale ranging from −3, indicating that the word was extremely representative of young egalitarian people of color; to 0, which was neutral; to 3, indicating that the word was extremely representative of old racist white men.

Results of the pretest were calculated to look for consensus as to which traits were perceived to be representative of the two groups. Based on mean scores and standard deviations, seven words were selected for each category. Participants believed that old racist white men were best characterized by the following words: cutthroat, greedy, hierarchical, narrow-minded, selfish, stern, and unethical; young egalitarian people of color were characterized by these words: careful, caring, diverse, egalitarian, fair, open-minded, and just. These fourteen words were then selected for inclusion in the next portion of the study.

In the second portion of the study, a separate group of participants was asked to evaluate how much the pretested characteristics were representative of corporations.[15] By using the pretested traits, it became possible to determine whether people rated corporations more as sharing the traits of old racist white men or of young egalitarian people of color. Participants rated each trait, presented among a list of various neutral traits, on a scale ranging from −3 to 3 (−3 representing "extremely unrepresentative of corporations," 0 representing neutral, and 3 representing "extremely representative of corporations"). Responses were aggregated into two indices consisting of the pretested traits: one representing old racist white men and the other representing young egalitarian people of color.

---

[14] Examples were angry, deliberate, engaging, entitled, fair, hard working, influential, intense, nurturing, powerful, and stern.

[15] Participants in both portions of the second study were recruited from a psychology course at a large university. Participants received bonus credit for participating.

As in Study One, the participant pool for both portions of Study Two was quite diverse.[16] Twenty-four participants, all undergraduate students, completed the pretest portion of Study Two. Fifty-eight participants, also undergraduate students, completed the second portion of the study.

Results: Participants attributed the same characteristics to corporations that were separately attributed to old racist white men. This result was confirmed by a paired samples *t*-test, $T (2,57) = 2.321, p < .05$, indicating that people associated corporations with old racist white men more than with young egalitarian people of color.

Taken together, the studies show that people perceive both implicitly (through the IAT) and explicitly (through a questionnaire) that corporations are similar to older whites and, in the second study, even to old racist white men. Although preliminary, the studies provide a new look at corporate personhood.

II. BIASED CORPORATE DECISION-MAKING: RACIAL INEQUALITY AT SHAREHOLDER EXPENSE

If corporations, like other persons, are susceptible to implicit biases in decision-making, how might these biases manifest in the corporate context? Consider a short list of decisions a board or board committee might make at a single meeting: appoint corporate auditors, hire consultants to advise regarding a potential layoff, approve the hiring of a new chief financial officer, weigh issuance of additional equity and/or debt securities, make a charitable contribution to the opera, and finalize the appointment of a new director. Although not every board decision has the potential to be infected by implicit bias, many do. For example, the hiring of a business consultant to help orchestrate a layoff is a step that many corporations take when trying to weather tough economic times. Yet, few corporations consider how the evaluation process involved in orchestrating a layoff may become skewed by the automatic and nonconscious influence of stereotypes related to employees (those held by both supervisors and consultants).[17] Research has shown, for example, that layoff criteria differ for Caucasians and African Americans, a finding that supports the contention that implicit bias could be driving corporate layoff disparities.[18]

Similarly, when issuing debt securities, corporations must choose underwriters and legal counsel to facilitate their transaction. These decisions, which are frequently made quickly by the board or the general counsel's office, are similarly susceptible

---

[16] Participants in Study Two were slightly younger than those in Study One. They were similarly diverse in terms of ethnicity.

[17] *See generally* George Wilson & Debra Branch McBrier, *Race and Loss of Privilege: African American/ White Differences in the Determinants of Job Layoffs from Upper-Tier Occupations*, 20 Soc. Forum 301 (2005) (finding that the corporate layoff criteria for Caucasians and African Americans are often different).

[18] *See Id.*

to implicit biases in the way that competent services by investment banking and legal professionals are judged.[19] For example, statistics show that minority lawyers at large law firms have had less success in attracting and retaining large corporate clients,[20] a finding that could potentially be traced to decision-makers' implicit racial stereotypes. Although the entire range of corporate decisions should be examined fully in light of implicit bias, this chapter begins the discussion by considering two areas in which implicit bias may function in corporation decision-making. These areas, although preliminary and in need of empirical study, can then be critiqued within the legal framework regarding board fiduciary duty protection.

A. *Excessive Executive Compensation*

Big Thyme Corporation, a Fortune 500 company, hires Paul Thurston as its chief operating officer (COO). Thurston receives an annual salary of $4 million, plus a large stock option that could end up paying as much as $40 million a year. The board approves the hiring and compensation package, even though the prior CEO and COO each left the company having underperformed and holding compensation packages worth more than $50 million each. All senior executives at Big Thyme, including the departed two and Mr. Thurston, are white men in their fifties and sixties. A careful analysis by several compensation experts finds that, although the company did hire a compensation consultant, the corporation gave larger compensation packages than were necessary or standard in the industry to all three executives. Big Thyme has never hired a person of color as a senior executive, and few women hold senior management positions.

Corporations may display discriminatory implicit biases in making executive compensation decisions. Specifically, implicit bias might affect board and managerial evaluations of a candidate's ability, dedication, value, and professionalism such that stereotype-consistent candidates (the prototypical white male executive with a distinguished graying look) may be overpaid and stereotype-inconsistent candidates (men of color and women) may be underhired and underpaid. Likely because of a slew of overpaid executives (most of whom are, not surprisingly, stereotype consistent), executive compensation has become a hot button issue during today's volatile economic times. Public outrage at the massive salaries and large equity-based bonuses offered to executives despite high unemployment rates has caused scholars to reexamine broad board protections in awarding lucrative executive contracts.[21]

---

[19] E. Macey Russell, address at Harvard Law School Summit: Achievable Next-Generation Strategies for Diversity and Inclusion (May 6, 2011).

[20] Brent L. Henry & E. Macey Russell, *Developing Great Minority Lawyers for the Next Generation*, J. Am. Corp. Couns. (2010).

[21] Lawrence A. Cunningham, *A New Legal Theory to Test Executive Pay: Contractual Unconscionability*, 94 Iowa L. Rev. (forthcoming 2011).

Although the role of implicit bias in executive compensation has yet to be studied empirically,[22] empirical studies do provide support for the contention that racial stereotypes play a role at least in hiring and that implicit racial bias can lead to these race-based decisions. A study by Marianne Bertrand and Sendhil Mullainathan tested whether employers in Chicago and Boston responded differently to resumes submitted by candidates they perceived as white or black.[23] The researchers created fictitious resumes, varied the amount of job experience embodied in the resumes, and manipulated whether the resumes had white-sounding or African American–sounding candidate names. They then mailed the resumes in response to real job listings and measured the number of interview calls the hypothetical candidates received (on voicemail accounts they created for the study). The results of the study showed that employers called more candidates with white-sounding names than candidates with African American–sounding names. In fact, the researchers found that having a white-sounding name was equivalent to having eight years of additional work experience.

Additional research has confirmed that racially biased results like those in the resume study can be predicted by implicit bias. In a Swedish study, Dan Olof Rooth employed a similar resume methodology to Bertrand and Mulinathan. However, he took his study further by tracking down the employers' recruiters and convincing many to participate in his study of implicit bias.[24] As predicted, he found that the recruiters who held stronger implicit ethnic biases (against Arab Muslim–named candidates) were more likely to call candidates with Swedish white–sounding names than those with Arab Muslim–sounding names.[25] Rooth later collaborated with Jens Agerstrom to replicate his study using implicit stereotypes of obesity in the workplace setting.[26] Much as in Rooth's first study, the researchers found that employer recruiters with more anti-obesity implicit bias were less likely to call candidates who were obese. Furthermore, recruiters' self-reported (explicit) stereotypes did not predict their behavior.

These studies highlight the way implicit bias can automatically skew hiring decisions, even among decision-makers who view themselves as egalitarian. In light of the findings, one might ask whether related corporate decisions, such as how much

---

[22] Some corporate law scholars, including Antony Page, have suggested the possibility that unconscious biases affect executive compensation and other corporate board decisions, but empirical studies have yet to pursue this possibility. *See* Page, *supra* note 2 (providing a detailed discussion of the ways in which various cognitive biases may affect directorial decision-making).

[23] Marianne Bertrand & Sendhil Mullainathan, *Are Emily and Greg More Employable than Lakisha and Jamal? A Field Experiment on Labor Market Discrimination*, 94 Am. Econ. Rev. 991 (2004).

[24] Dan-Olof Rooth, *Implicit Discrimination in Hiring: Real World Evidence*, in IZA Discussion Papers (2007), *available at* http://papers.ssrn.com/sol3/ papers.cfm?abstract_id=984432.

[25] In Rooth's study, he compared resumes with white Swedish–sounding names with those with Arab-sounding names.

[26] Jens Agerstrom & Dan-Olof Rooth, *The Role of Automatic Obesity Stereotypes in Real Hiring Discrimination*, 96 J. Applied Psychol. 790 (2011).

to pay high-level executives, might suffer from similar implicit biases. If race and gender become a proxy for experience or competence, as the studies show is likely, even good faith compensation decisions will reflect this bias. Corporations could be expected, then, to routinely overpay older white male executives (at shareholder expense) and to underhire and underpay deserving women and minority executive candidates (likely leading to shareholder loss). To confirm this type of systemic disparity in executive hiring and compensation, new empirical projects should combine the hiring studies' creative methods with the focus of other studies that have examined the role of stereotypes in high-level positions, much as in a 2011 study that found that men implicitly associate males with traits of successful managers and females with traits of unsuccessful managers.[27]

B. *Biased Charitable Giving*

> Loan-Me-Money, Inc., a highly profitable check-cashing and advance lending institution, makes three charitable donations over a two-year period. The company donates $1 million to Ivy League University, $2 million to the city opera, and $1 million to the Modern Art Museum. Almost all of the company's revenue comes from its 241 retail outlets, which are exclusively located within inner cities and other economically depressed areas around the East Coast and Midwest.

Beyond compensation decisions, implicit bias may affect other corporate decisions, such as a board's decision to make charitable contributions to certain organizations. Although corporate charitable contributions are lauded as socially beneficial and are obviously a critical piece of funding for a range of nonprofit entities, it is nonetheless possible that corporations make charity-related decisions in inefficient ways fueled by implicit bias. Specifically, board members may irrationally be drawn to support charities that seem more worthy or appealing to them, as ingroup members, rather than those appealing to business clients and the relevant economic community.

Studies have shown that people allocate resources to ingroup members in the charity context because outgroup members are perceived as being less worthy of charitable donation. In one such study, Christina Fong and Erzo Luttmer tested whether people's charitable giving would be predicted by their perceptions of the race of the charity's beneficiaries (as well as the worthiness of the beneficiaries).[28] One thousand adult participants were told that there was a 10 percent chance that they would receive one hundred dollars and were asked whether they would give

---

[27] See Ioana M. Latu et al., *What We "Say" and What We "Think" About Female Managers: Explicit Versus Implicit Associations of Women with Success*, 35 PSYCHOL. WOMEN Q. 152 (2011). *See also* Justin D. Levinson & Danielle Young, *Implicit Gender Bias in the Legal Profession: An Empirical Study*, 18 DUKE J. GENDER L. & POL'Y 1 (2010).

[28] Christina M. Fong & Erzo F. P. Luttmer, *Do Fairness and Race Matter in Generosity? Evidence from a Nationally Representative Charity Experiment*, J. PUBLIC ECON. (forthcoming, 2011).

some of that money, if they won it, to a described charity. The charity was then described, and the participants saw photos of the beneficiaries of its services. The researchers found that when white participants saw photos of black beneficiaries, these participants rated the beneficiaries as less worthy; this decreased worthiness predicted a decrease in the amount that the participants agreed to give to the charity.

Empirical research has also confirmed that implicit bias can cause people to allocate resources in racially biased ways, findings that should be considered both in the executive compensation and the charity context. Laurie Rudman and Richard Ashmore, for example, found that implicit bias drives decisions to allocate economic resources to various groups. The researchers first administered a series of IATs to participants, including those testing implicit attitudes and stereotypes of blacks, Jews, and Asians.[29] Later, the participants (who were university students) completed a survey asking for help in administering a mandatory 20 percent budget cut to university student organizations. They were given a list of the current funding levels of student organizations and were asked to implement the cut. The researchers then compared the student-participants' IAT scores with their recommended budget cuts for each student organization; they found that scores on the stereotype IATs predicted economic discrimination. That is, participants with stronger negative implicit biases regarding blacks, Jews, and Asians were the most likely to cut the budgets of black, Jewish, and Asian student organizations. Furthermore, asking the participants their (explicit) attitudes toward these groups did not serve as a good predictor of their fund allocation. The results of the study demonstrate the way implicit biases about certain groups can affect how a limited amount of resources are allocated.

In light of the findings of these two studies, one could hypothesize that corporate decisions regarding charitable contributions are affected in discriminatory ways by a board's implicit biases. Specifically, one could predict that corporations make more than an optimal share of donations to charities that do not serve people of color, even when it would be in the company's best interest to make donations to charities that do so. For example, in the case of Loan-Me-Money, Inc., the company makes almost all of its profits in areas that have large minority populations. If the company makes a series of charitable donations to elite charities that tend to serve wealthy members of the (largely white) community outside of the company's target market, one could legitimately question first the economic efficiency of that transaction for the business, and second (in light of the research described earlier), whether implicit biases may have factored into the giving decisions. Although the company's decision would almost surely pass scrutiny under corporate law's business judgment

---

[29] Laurie A. Rudman & Richard D. Ashmore, *Discrimination and the Implicit Association Test*, 10 Group Processes & Intergroup Rel. 359 (2007).

rule (for example, by asserting that opera patrons have helped fund the company or that the donation helps the company's reputation), additional scrutiny may be warranted.

C. Should Fiduciary Duties Protect against Implicit Racial and Gender Bias?

As I have hypothesized, corporate boards may automatically and even unconsciously make decisions to allocate resources to those executives and charities associated with positive stereotypes, instead of those with negative stereotypes, and that this allocation, due to stereotypes, exceeds necessary or optimal amounts. What legal protections should be offered to a board that allocates excessive resources in this stereotype-consistent way? Fortunately for directors, the business judgment rule provides broad protection for a variety of decisions, both in executive compensation and charitable giving. The various rationales for the business judgment rule are strong and widely accepted, including that companies should be able to recruit the best board members and officers, boards should be encouraged to make the best decisions (even if risky), capital markets would be hindered by constant fiduciary duty suits against public companies, and hindsight bias will often make decent directorial decisions look awful in hindsight (and therefore in need of additional protection).[30] These powerful supports for the business judgment rule have tended to overpower detracting points of view, even in the case of massive payments made to ineffective managers at the expense of the corporation. Thus lawsuits challenging board decisions, in the absence of conflict of interest, almost always fail.

Yet is it possible for the business judgment rule to be implemented in a way that would protect directors in the vast majority of business decisions and yet address irrational decisions tainted by implicit bias in a meaningful way? And if so, how? This section provides an overview of the current legal treatment of executive compensation and charity cases and begins the discussion of the ways that corporate law might address harms driven by implicit bias. Although the analysis reveals that there are no simple ways to allow for implicit bias challenges consistent with existing doctrine, it is nonetheless important to begin the discussion of how corporate laws may eventually allow for narrow circumstances in which inefficient and bias-driven decisions can be challenged. One aggressive possibility, for example, would be to consider removing business judgment protection in limited instances and allow suits alleging a stereotype-related inefficient allocation of resources to proceed on their merits. As this section discusses, such a move, although unlikely, might occur through a limited expansion of duty of loyalty violations based on "self-dealing."

---

[30] *See, e.g.*, Jeffrey J. Rachlinski, *A Positive Psychological Theory of Judging in Hindsight*, 65 U. CHI. L. REV. 571 (1998).

This type of remedy would shift the burden to the corporation to demonstrate the good faith and inherent fairness of the transaction.

1. Protection for Executive Compensation Decisions

Corporate laws governing executive compensation provide limited remedies for shareholder challenges to transactions based on implicit bias, even when such transactions continue an outrageous shift of wealth away from the corporation and into the hands of senior managers. Despite shared moral outrage over some infamous compensation packages, ranging from $210 million for Home Depot's CEO to Citigroup's leader's $68 million on the heels of a federal bailout,[31] corporate law provides no meaningful remedy. Shareholders suing under corporate law desiring to prove corporate waste must first overcome the protections of the business judgment rule.

Yet courts have set an incredibly high threshold. In a case involving Disney's hiring and later termination of Michael Ovitz, a situation in which the company parted with more than $130 million in exchange for approximately one year of corporate service, the Delaware Supreme Court was unwilling to find that the company's directors breached their fiduciary duties.[32] In fact, simply hiring an independent compensation consultant (something Disney did) and carefully reviewing potential gains from stock option grants (which Disney did not do) can essentially insulate a board from liability in deciding to spend any amount of money and stock on a senior manager. As Lawrence Cunningham has explained, "[M]assive salaries are outside the doctrine of waste because they so easily meet a long-standing test the Supreme Court stated in 1933 that defines 'waste' as occurring when there is 'no relation' between what the corporation gives and gets."[33] Thus, the corporate law approach to executive compensation provides little hope not only to shareholders who watch hundreds of millions disappear but also to shareholders who see excessive corporate money being consistently paid to older white male executives and former executives.[34]

2. Protection for Charitable Contribution Decisions

Similar to the failures of corporate law governing executive compensation, corporate law relating to charitable contributions fails to provide real choices for shareholders wishing to challenge a pattern of biased and inefficient charitable donations. The

[31] *See* Cunningham, *supra* note 21, at 8.
[32] In re The Walt Disney Co. Derivative Litigation, 906 A.2d 27 (Del. Supr. 2006).
[33] *See* Cunningham, *supra* note 21, at 30 (citing Rogers v. Hill, 289 U.S. 582, 591–92 (1933)).
[34] Not all corporate executives are white males, of course, and there are certainly instances in which nonwhite males receive large amounts of compensation. However, senior executives remain disproportionately white male.

A.P. Smith Manufacturing Co. v. Barlow decision is a classic example of the broad protection given to directors in making charitable contributions.[35] In that case, the directors of a company that manufactured fire hydrants and valves donated money to Princeton University. The New Jersey Supreme Court upheld this donation, first announcing the strong public policy in favor of charitable giving and, second, reinforcing the board's ability to exercise business judgment. Although the court provided the broad outline for a successful claim (no pet charities, indiscriminate giving, etc.), it essentially created a rule whereby boards, to withstand a challenge to a charitable gift, only have to claim that somewhere, somehow, the corporation benefited from the donation.

One winning argument for the company, then, might have been that giving to an Ivy League school improves the quality of the workforce and therefore will ultimately benefit the corporation. Another winner might have been that making the donation generates valuable public relations. Regardless of the reason given, it is not hard to justify a decision to act charitably. Yet should it always be so simple? If charitable donations are excessively given to elite, white-dominated charities because of the operation of ingroup biases and other stereotypes, might a more careful legal inquiry be preferable? The serious risk, of course, is fewer charitable contributions. Yet the bias-combating gains of an effective remedy would likely include more deliberative boards, greater corporate efficiency, and an opening for nontraditionally cash-rich charities.

Solutions offered for the more commonly explored failures of corporate law to protect shareholder wealth have made some progress in addressing lavish and irrational spending, but do not create a clear pathway for addressing implicit bias in corporate decision-making. For example, in response to excessive executive compensation, the Dodd-Frank Act of 2010 took steps to protect shareholders, including requiring more involvement of independent directors as well as expanding disclosure requirements.[36] Scholars have taken a different approach in suggesting ways to limit abuses of executive compensation. Lawrence Cunningham, for example, suggests that plaintiffs avoid corporate law altogether and instead pursue their claims under state contract law unconscionability doctrine. Although these measures may provide some potential relief for shareholders or at least may encourage corporations to be less reckless in compensating senior managers, they provide little indication that an implicit-bias–related wealth shift could be mitigated in a meaningful way.

As this analysis has revealed, an implicit bias competent solution both for inefficient and excessive executive compensation and for excessive ingroup charitable giving seems elusive in light of a powerful business judgment rule. To find a potential winning argument for implicit bias challenges then, one might look to other

---

[35] 13 N.J. 145, 98 A.2d 581 (1953), *appeal dismissed*, 346 U.S. 861 (1953).
[36] Dodd-Frank Wall Street Reform and Consumer Protection Act, Pub. L. No. 111-203, §§ 951–956, 124 Stat. 1376, 1899–906 (2010).

situations in which courts have disregarded the business judgment rule. Courts have cast aside the rule in unique situations in which fairness is implicated. It could be contended that a similar step may be implicated for the most egregious corporate offenders.

3. Potential Expansion of the Duty of Loyalty

The duty of loyalty strives to protect shareholders from self-dealing officers and directors. When a corporate officer or director stands to benefit from a transaction at the expense of the corporation, that officer or director will be required to prove the good faith and inherent fairness of the transaction. The hallmark of a duty of loyalty claim is that the corporation has lost economic value while an officer or director stands to gain at the corporation's expense. Although the duty of loyalty tends to be invoked in cases where corporations are harmed to the obvious benefit of an officer or director, a suit relying on loyalty-like fairness principles to combat implicit bias might be one possible pathway for implicit bias related claims. In such a suit, if a corporation has made a clear series of inefficient economic decisions in a stereotype-consistent manner, the shareholders would claim that the decisions should not be given business judgment protection. Rather, they would argue that the decisions should be considered under an "inherent fairness" standard, accompanied by a shifted burden of proof, as are cases related to the duty of loyalty.

The major challenge that shareholders would face in bringing a duty of loyalty styled claim for implicit bias based inefficiencies would be demonstrating the board's conflict of interest. In a duty of loyalty case, a director's benefit is usually easy to spot. For example, consider the classic examples of a CEO and director creating a new advertising line to benefit his spouse's career[37] or a director seizing an opportunity for a personal investment without sharing that benefit with the company.[38] In a case involving implicit bias, however, a director's conflict of interest is not so obvious.

Some courts and the Model Business Corporation Act (MBCA) have adopted fairly broad interpretations of self-dealing, although likely not broad enough to sustain an implicit bias based claim. The MBCA provides that a director may face a self-dealing allegation when the corporation conducts business with a "related person." MBCA Section 8.60 (5) defines a related person fairly broadly, including a "child, step child, parent, step parent, grandparent, sibling, step sibling, half sibling, aunt, uncle, niece or nephew (or spouse of any thereof)." Although a claim of implicit bias would likely fail without showing the specific benefit to an insider's family member as defined in the MBCA, psychological theory provides at least some support for a claim that,

---

[37] Bayer v. Beran, 49 N.Y.S.2d 2 (Sup. Ct. 1944). In that case, the defense convinced the court that the hiring was indeed fair and did not burden the business.

[38] In re eBay, Inc. S'holders Litig., No. C.A. 19988-NC, 2004 WL 253521, at *1 (Del. Ch. Jan. 23, 2004) (corporate officers and directors alleged to breach duty of loyalty by failing to offer directed share investment opportunities to the corporation).

not so different from an individual's desire to help his or her own extended family, people act with an implicit desire to maintain the social and racial status quo. [39] One such psychological theory, known as system justification theory, has documented the many ways people are unconsciously driven to maintain the status quo, and it could help explain why board members may consistently favor ingroup members in their decisions, almost as if they were extended family.

A second hurdle for bringing a self-dealing styled claim based on implicit bias relates to whether the directors must consciously favor the ingroup in their decisions or whether unconscious favoritism would be enough to allow a claim. On this issue, some courts have applied broad interpretations of self-dealing that allow for even unconscious preference to fall outside of legal protection. For example, in the case of *Albright v. Jefferson County National Bank*, Chief Judge Lehman stated, "Included within its scope is every situation in which a trustee chooses to deal with another in such close relation with the trustee that possible advantage to such other person might influence, consciously or *unconsciously*, the judgment of the trustee."[40] Despite the favorability of this approach for a shareholder's claim based on implicit, or unconscious desires, for the reasons discussed earlier, a shareholder claim would still be a long shot to succeed on duty of loyalty grounds under traditional constructions. It is therefore important to consider other potential remedies for implicit bias in corporate decision-making.

4. Other Remedies: Corporate Training

Even though corporations are unlikely to be held liable in court for implicit bias influenced decisions, they may nonetheless choose to address the serious harms of implicit bias by providing training for directors, officers, and other decision-makers. Research has shown that, although implicit biases are extremely powerful, there are some ways to at least temporarily diminish their strength. Might it be possible, then, to "de-bias" or otherwise train corporate decision-makers to minimize the effects of implicit bias in corporate decisions? If so, the benefits both to corporations and society could be significant.

Empirical studies provide hope that implicit biases can be reduced in the corporate setting, given the right training program and directors and officers who are internally motivated to avoid bias. One fascinating study conducted in a naturally occurring

---

[39] For more on the unconscious need to support the status quo, see John T. Jost et al., *A Decade of System Justification Theory: Accumulated Evidence of Conscious and Unconscious Bolstering of the Status Quo*, 6 POL. PSYCHOL. 881, 912 (2004); Levinson, *SuperBias: The Collision of Behavioral Economics and Implicit Social Cognition*, AKRON LAW REV. (forthcoming 2012) [hereinafter, Levinson, *SuperBias*].

[40] Bayer v. Beran, 49 N.Y.S.2d 2, 7 (1944) citing Albright v. Jefferson Cnty. Nat'l Bank, 292 N.Y. 31, 39 (1944) (emphasis added). Courts in related contexts, such as in determining directorial independence, have similarly indicated that conscious awareness may not be the proper standard for establishing a conflict of interest. *See* Page, *supra* note 2 at 286 (citing *In re* Oracle Corp. Derivative Litig., 824 A.2d 917, 920 (Del. Ch. 2003)).

environment found that long-term exposure to women in counter-stereotypic roles reduced implicit gender biases.[41] In this study, researchers found that women students who were measured for implicit bias before and after a year of college study (in either all-women or coeducational colleges) displayed significantly less implicit gender bias when they had been taught by female math and science professors. This style of reduction in implicit bias, rather than fleeting, has the potential to be meaningful and long lasting.

Other studies have shown that biases can be at least temporarily decreased through training or other novel methods. For example, researchers found that teaching study participants to recognize and differentiate features in African American faces reduced participants' later negative implicit racial biases when looking at those faces.[42] In a separate study, social scientists found that showing positive media portrayals of people in counter-stereotypic roles (for example, a female CEO) can temporarily reduce negative implicit attitudes.[43] Interestingly, however, not all people are equally likely to respond to such interventions.[44] People who are internally motivated to be egalitarian – those who embrace equality and fairness as part of their personal values – are more likely to show training benefits and would stand to benefit most from well-designed, professional implicit bias reduction training.[45] Even with the right program and executives, however, it is unclear how long the bias reduction effects of short-term interventions last; it is possible that they may only last for seconds or minutes.[46] The studies, however, provide hope for corporations that are willing to make a sophisticated commitment to reduce corporate implicit bias through carefully developed and properly implemented training programs.

Thus, a corporation's implementation of a meaningful implicit bias reduction program that carefully draws on social scientific knowledge would be likely to at least somewhat reduce implicit bias, perhaps while increasing overall decision

---

[41] *See* Nilanjana Dasgupta & Shaki Asgari, *Seeing Is Believing: Exposure to Counterstereotypic Women Leaders and Its Effect on the Malleability of Automatic Gender Stereotyping*, 40 J. EXPERIMENTAL SOC. PSYCHOL. 642 (2004).

[42] Sophie Lebrecht et al., *Perceptual Other-Race Training Reduces Implicit Racial Bias*, 4 PLUS ONE e4215 (2009).

[43] Nilanjana Dasgupta & Anthony G. Greenwald, *On the Malleability of Automatic Attitudes: Combating Automatic Prejudice with Images of Admired and Disliked Individuals*, 81 J. PERSONALITY & SOC. PSYCHOL. 800 (2001).

[44] Nilanjana Dasgupta & Luis Rivera, *From Automatic Antigay Prejudice to Behavior: The Moderating Role of Conscious Beliefs About Gender and Behavioral Control*, 91 J. PERSONALITY & SOC. PSYCHOL. 268 (2006); Karen Gonsalkorale et al., *Accounting for Successful Control of Implicit Racial Bias: The Roles of Association Activation, Response Monitoring, and Overcoming Bias*, PERSONALITY & SOC. PSYCHOL. BULL. (forthcoming 2011).

[45] Those who are externally motivated to avoid bias, people who embrace equality because it is considered socially desirable, are less likely to be helped simply by learning about implicit bias.

[46] This temporary nature of de-biasing underscores the continuing need to focus on longer term remedies to implicit bias. As I have argued elsewhere, the best way to eliminate implicit biases is through a pathway to social change. *See* Justin D. Levinson, *Forgotten Racial Equality: Implicit Bias, Decisionmaking, and Misremembering*, 57 DUKE L. J. 345 (2007).

efficiency.[47] To be most effective, such a program should contain at minimum four core elements. First, it must include key decision-makers, including board members and corporate officers. Second, it should consist of more than a single training, because a continuing commitment to bias reduction will increase the likelihood of continued benefits. Third, it should be supplemented with meaningful voluntary corporate disclosure of information, such as human resources records and charitable giving information; this access to information will allow decision-makers to self-reflect on the potential bias-related impact of corporate decisions.[48] Fourth, in collaboration with the training-based elements of the program, corporations should embrace a corporate culture that combats implicit bias by valuing diversity in multiple ways, including by hiring people in counter-typical roles.[49]

IV. CONCLUSION

This chapter's discussion and empirical investigation of implicit bias in corporate decision-making are first steps in examining the nexus between implicit social cognition and corporate law. Further examination of corporate decision-making may show, for example, that business judgment protection should be selectively peeled away in unique circumstances or that large-scale bias training is even more necessary than is currently known. Future research, particularly empirical studies, should continue to investigate both whether corporate persons may in fact act in a biased manner similar to older white men and whether corporations generally are likely to make decisions that can be predicted by implicit bias.[50] Legal scholars should continue to consider potential remedies for decisions that, individually and collectively, result in subordination of already disadvantaged groups. Until then, however, corporations may be playing an implicit bias infused role in the global marketplace.

---

[47] For more on the connection between implicit racial biases and other cognitive biases, particularly economic ones, see Levinson, *SuperBias, supra* note 39.

[48] A more modest step in the context of charitable donations, even without implicit bias training, would be to require corporations to regularly report to shareholders on their charitable activity in a way that highlights the nexus between the corporation's business and the charity. Although this would not place more bite into a legal challenge related to a pattern of seemingly inefficient donations, it would at least have the potential to raise bias awareness on the part of the board as well as shareholders. This kind of monitoring function has support in various areas of law.

[49] For more on counter-stereotypes, see Jerry Kang & Mahzarin R. Banaji, *Fair Measures: A Behavioral Realist Revision of "Affirmative Action,"* 94 CAL. L. REV. 1063 (2006).

[50] Researchers, for example, might test whether priming company-specific norms prior to a decision-making process will elicit heightened implicit racial bias in decision-making.

10

Tax Law

Implicit Bias and the Earned Income Tax Credit

Dorothy A. Brown

The purpose of the earned income tax credit (EITC) is to eliminate tax-related incentives to remain on welfare. It operates by reimbursing low-income workers for income and Social Security tax withholdings that are not withheld from welfare payments. One persistent problem associated with the EITC is the large number of tax returns with EITC-related errors – referred to as the "error rate." The inappropriate payments that flowed from the public treasury as a result of these errors are estimated at more than $10 billion for 2006 alone.

President Bill Clinton and the Republican Congress battled in the mid-1990s over the EITC's future. Republican President Gerald Ford signed the EITC into law in 1975 in part to reduce "the welfare rolls," but it was the Republican Congress that wished to abolish the EITC and President Clinton who wanted to save it. The choice to reform or abolish the EITC depended on why the error rate occurred and how readily the problem could be redressed.

The first theory to explain the error rate is that, because of the EITC's complexity, it is easy to make a mistake in calculating the credit. For instance, the Internal Revenue Service (IRS) informational booklet explaining the EITC is more than fifty pages long and includes several worksheets. The solution for the problem of complexity would be to simplify the EITC to reduce error rates. The second theory to explain the error rate is that it is the result of taxpayer fraud. Under this theory, taxpayers want something for nothing, so they cheat and claim an EITC amount that they know they are ineligible to receive. The solution to a problem based on fraud would be to increase audits of low-income taxpayers to crack down on the fraud.

I would like to thank the editors for their extremely helpful suggestions. I would also like to thank the participants at the Tulane Tax Roundtable. Finally, I thank Daniel M. Reach and Ryan M. Richards for excellent research assistance.

The political compromise between President Clinton and the Republican Congress was to single out EITC taxpayers for audit, an enforcement mechanism that cost taxpayers $1 billion over five years. This chapter examines the role that implicit racial bias might have played in the decision to spend $1 billion dollars to audit EITC recipients as opposed to simplifying the EITC filing process. Implicit racial bias refers to the process of employing preexisting knowledge about race (i.e., stereotypes) to make sense of something new (the EITC error rate) without conscious thought. The widespread impact of implicit bias on daily decision-making has been documented extensively over the past decade, especially in contexts in which decision-makers are given great discretion.

So why did Congress (and the president) choose to conduct audits of claimants rather than to simplify the EITC application process? Implicit bias likely is responsible in significant part for that choice. Given that the error rate stemmed from ambiguous behavior (meaning that we do not know whether complexity or cheating is to blame) and in the absence of empirical data, the question of whether EITC recipients were cheating or not depended on *who* our legislators believed these people to be. Most welfare recipients are white. Yet Americans tend to associate welfare policies with black Americans. Indeed, scholars have suggested that "opposition to welfare may be *specifically rooted* in the [erroneous] perception that welfare recipients are overwhelmingly black."[1] Perceiving welfare as a program for black people does not in itself explain why Congress would choose to audit rather than to simplify. Rather the decision as to which remedy to choose depended on how Congress perceived black welfare recipients.

Survey data collected by Professor Mark Peffley and his colleagues contemporaneous to the policy shift showed that a "substantial portion" of Americans agreed that blacks are "lazy," "irresponsible," and "lacking discipline."[2] Peffley found that "a very sizable number of whites – as many as one in every two – openly endorse frankly negative characterizations of 'most' blacks."[3] These openly reported attitudes likely were the tip of the iceberg. The implicit bias literature demonstrates beyond any real doubt that the hidden biases that people hold toward black Americans differ in number and strength from those that are openly reported. Indeed, it is often the egalitarian-minded citizens – those who know better than to say openly (and perhaps do not consciously believe) that blacks are lazy, irresponsible, and lacking discipline – who show the greatest divergence between explicitly reported racial attitudes and those that measures such as the Implicit Association Test reveal them to hold. Perhaps it is *because* welfare reform is so "implicitly racialized" that scholars find

---

[1] Christopher M. Federico, *When Do Welfare Attitudes Become Racialized? The Paradoxical Effects of Education*, 48 Am. J. Pol. Sci. 374, 387 (2004) (emphasis added).

[2] Mark Peffley et al., *Racial Stereotypes and Whites' Political Views of Blacks in the Context of Welfare and Crime*, 41 Am. J. Pol. Sci. 30 (1997).

[3] *Id.*

"the relationship between [racial] perceptions and opposition to welfare appears to be *stronger*" among the college-educated.[4]

The central argument is that members of Congress – educated and egalitarian-minded as they might be – are people just like the rest of us. In the context of welfare, which many commentators believe the EITC to be a form of, legislators are primed to think in racial terms. The decision to audit was made in the context of viewing welfare as a policy for black people and viewing black people as lazy, irresponsible, and lacking discipline. This activation of racial stereotyping of welfare made the welfare cheat explanation easier for politicians to believe.

Although this chapter focuses on implicit bias related to the EITC, one could easily imagine how implicit racial bias in the broader context of tax policy would be an area of fruitful further study. Congress enacts tax laws, and one could expect to see an implicit bias in favor of middle-class taxpayers, a group that by and large represents the lifestyles of members of Congress. For example, why does Congress decide that homeowners, but not renters, are eligible to receive a tax break? The greatest beneficiaries of the tax breaks for homeownership are middle and upper middle income taxpayers.[5] In contrast, lower income taxpayers and the majority of blacks and Latinos are most likely to be renters and not eligible for the tax break.

Further, the joint return provision of the Internal Revenue Code favors single wage–earner heterosexual households. Some couples pay higher taxes as a result of getting married, whereas others get a tax cut. White married couples are more likely to be single wage–earner couples than black married couples. Therefore when blacks marry their taxes are more likely to go up; in contrast, when whites marry, their taxes are more likely to be reduced.[6]

Implicit bias in the EITC context has led to three problems. First, instead of auditing the tax returns of lazy, disproportionately black welfare cheats (the perception of who is on welfare), the IRS most likely audited the tax returns of many hard-working white taxpayers, because contrary to conventional wisdom the typical EITC claimant is white – not black.

Second, when Congress concluded the problem was fraud and targeted $1 billion of auditing dollars solely on EITC-claimants, other non-EITC taxpayers who were actually committing fraud were allowed to do so without fear of reprisal. Implicit bias has thus prevented decision-makers from cracking down on real taxpayer fraud, committed especially by the wealthy.

---

[4] *Id* at 686. *See also* Federico, *supra* note 1, at 374–91 (2004) ("[B]lack stereotypes are now a major covert theme in discussions of welfare; those with the highest levels of cognitive ability may be more likely to represent welfare recipients in terms of the categories suggested by these discussions.") (Internal citation omitted). [emphasis added].

[5] Dorothy A. Brown, *Shades of the American Dream*, 87 Wash. U. L. Rev. 329 (2010).

[6] Dorothy A. Brown, *Race, Class, and Gender Essentialism in Tax Literature: The Joint Return*, 54 Wash. & Lee L. Rev. 1469 (1997).

Third, by focusing on audits and not simplifying the EITC, implicit bias has left the error rate pretty much intact.[7] Had Congress instead simplified the EITC, the error rate would have decreased significantly without costing taxpayers more than $1 billion. Simplification would have had the added benefit of reducing the very high percentage of EITC taxpayers who spend precious dollars on tax return preparers and refund anticipation loans because of the EITC's complexity. Further, if the credit were easier to claim, those eligible for it but who do not file for the EITC might be encouraged to do so. Implicit bias has gotten in the way of meaningful tax reform and has cost those least able to pay significant amounts of money.

I. THE EITC

Republican President Gerald Ford established the EITC in 1975. The legislative history tells us that it was designed to "refund" the income and Social Security taxes withheld from taxpayers' paychecks, thereby providing them with an incentive to get off of welfare and into the workforce. Specifically, the legislative history describes the EITC's "most significant objective" as "encouraging people to obtain employment, reducing the unemployment rate and *reducing the welfare rolls*."[8] It estimates a $0.1 billion reduction in welfare payments "resulting from the increase in income for those receiving the [earned income tax] credit."[9]

The EITC was made a permanent part of the Internal Revenue Code in 1978. The EITC is a refundable credit for the working poor, which means low-income taxpayers may receive a tax refund in excess of their income tax withholding and, in certain instances, in excess of their Social Security withholding. Only taxpayers with wages or "earned income" are eligible for the EITC, and they can only have a limited amount of investment income and still remain eligible. One way to look at the EITC is as an alternative to increasing the minimum wage. More than two-thirds of EITC claimants do not receive a net transfer payment,[10] but use the EITC to offset their income, Social Security, and excise taxes that they have actually paid. Accordingly, less than one-third receive an EITC greater than the taxes they pay.

According to the Center on Budget and Policy Priorities in 2009, the EITC lifted about 6.6 million people out of poverty, about half of whom were children. Without the EITC, the poverty rate among children would have been almost one-third higher.

---

[7] Leslie Book, *Symposium: Closing the Tax Gap: Refund Anticipation Loans and the Tax Gap*, 20 Stan. L. & Pol'y Rev 85, 93–94 (2009) ("Estimates of EITC error rate approximate twenty-five to thirty-five percent, despite the government's significant efforts over the past ten years to increase compliance.").

[8] S. Rep. No. 94-36, at 33 (1975) (emphasis added). *See also* Dorothy A. Brown, *Race and Class Matters*, 107 Colum. L. Rev. 790, 817 (2007); Dorothy A. Brown, *The Tax Treatment of Children: Separate But Unequal*, 54 Emory L. J. 755 (2005) [hereinafter Brown, *Children*].

[9] *Id.* at 35.

[10] Lawrence Zelenak, *Tax or Welfare? The Administration of the Earned Income Tax Credit*, 52 UCLA L. Rev. 1867, 1910 n.180 (2005).

As originally enacted the EITC did not increase for family size.[11] The Senate Finance Committee did not want to increase the EITC for each additional child out of concern for providing an "economic incentive for having additional children."[12] It was not until 1990 that the EITC was amended to allow increased credit amounts for additional children. Currently, the maximum EITC depends on whether the taxpayer has no children, one child, two children, or three or more children.

Similarly, it was not until 2001 that an adjustment was made to the calculation of the EITC to take marriage into account. A marriage penalty exists where for the same household income, two singles receive a higher EITC than they would if they were married. The marriage penalties associated with the EITC are severe and have been well known for many years. President Bush signed into law the first EITC adjustment for marital status in 2001, and there have been subsequent amendments. Although the adjustment for marriage reduces the marriage penalties associated with the EITC, it does not eliminate them because the income level at which the EITC phase-out begins for married couples is not double the amount for singles. As a result, married dual-income wage earners are penalized. Consider the following example as described by Professor Waters Lindsey:

> [F]or an unmarried couple with two children, where each parent earns $ 14,000 in wages and each parent claims a child as an exemption and for EITC purposes for taxable year 2009, each parent will receive the maximum EITC of $3043 for a combined EITC of $6086. In contrast, due to the marriage penalty, a married couple with two children receives a smaller EITC . . . the married couple's EITC is only $3642, substantially less than the combined EITC of $6086 for the unmarried couple. As a result, there remains a substantial marriage penalty under the EITC.[13]

As earned income rises, the credit increases. When income reaches the "earned income amount" the maximum EITC is reached. As income rises past the "earned income amount" the credit remains the same until the "threshold phase-out amount" of income is reached. At that point for each additional dollar of earned income, the credit amount decreases – or is phased out – until the credit becomes zero. When income reaches the "phase-out ends" income level, the EITC is zero. Consider the following three examples.

Example #1: Sally has two children and is the head of her household. She earns $10,000 of wages for the year. Her EITC will be $4,000.[14] Sally's income is not in excess of the earned income amount ($12,780); therefore for each dollar she earns, her EITC amount increases.

---

[11] Brown, *Children*, *supra* note 8, at 766.

[12] S. Rep. No. 1230, at 425–26 (1972).

[13] Vada Waters Lindsey, *Encouraging Savings Under the Earned Income Tax Credit*, 44 U. Mich. J. L. Ref. 83, 102 (2010) (citations omitted).

[14] Because her income of $10,000 is less than the "earned income amount," her EITC calculation is relatively simple: $10,000 multiplied by the credit percentage of 40% = $4,000.

Example #2: Jerry and Maria Smith are married with two children and have earned income of $25,000. The Smiths will not receive the maximum EITC of $5,112 for families with two children for the following reason: their earned income of $25,000 is greater than the point at which the EITC is reduced for every additional dollar earned – here $21,770. Instead the Smiths' EITC will be $4,431.76.[15] For every dollar they earn in excess of $21,770, the Smiths lose a portion of their EITC. Because $25,000 is well below the point at which the Smiths lose their entire credit (the married phase-out amount of $46,044), they still receive a significant EITC.

Example #3: Bob is head of his household, has one child, and earns $25,000 of income. Bob will not receive the maximum credit of $3,094 because $25,000 is greater than the threshold phase-out amount of $16,690. For every dollar he earns between $16,690 and $25,000 he is losing part of his EITC. He will receive a credit of $1,766.06,[16] significantly below the maximum EITC.

Current law still reflects EITC's legislative history, which seeks to discourage the working poor from having children. For example, the maximum EITC for households with two children is not double the amount for households with one child, nor is the maximum EITC for households with three or more children triple the amount for those with one child. In contrast, the middle-class Child Tax Credit (CTC) increases proportionately to the number of children. The CTC for two children is double the amount for one child, and it triples for a family with three children. According to the legislative history surrounding the CTC, those levels reflect the fact that, for each additional child, a family's financial well-being is under some additional stress.[17] Yet the same could be said about low-income taxpayers.

In addition, the EITC is reduced once household income reaches $16,690 for all households with children, regardless of the number of children. The CTC reflects more fully the fact that a family has a reduced ability to pay taxes as family size increases. Although the EITC does provide a larger credit based on the existence and number of children in the household, it could be more generous by recognizing, as the CTC does, that $16,690 does not go as far if you have three children than if you have one child or even two children.

Finally, as the examples showed, the EITC is extraordinarily complicated. The EITC's complexity was documented by a Government Accounting Office (GAO) study that found that EITC errors were made not only by taxpayers but also by tax preparers and IRS staff.[18] Because the EITC is so complicated, 72 percent

---

[15] $12,780 × 40% = $5,112 − [(21.06%) × ($25,000 − 21,770) = 680.238] = $4,431.76.

[16] $9100 × 34% = $3094 − [(15.98%) × ($25,000 − $16,690) − $1,327.93] = $1,766.06.

[17] S. Rep. No. 105-33, at 3 (1997) ("[T]he individual income tax structure does not reduce tax liability by enough to reflect a family's reduced ability to pay taxes as family size increases."); *see also* H. R. Rep. No. 105-48, at 310 (1997).

[18] *See* U.S. Gen. Accounting Office, Tax Administration: Continuing Problems Affect Otherwise Successful 1994 Filing Season 2 (1994), *available at* http://www.gao.gov/archive/1995/gg95005.pdf [hereinafter Gen. Accounting Office, Continuing Problems] ("The Earned Income

of low-income taxpayers pay for tax return preparation, at an estimated cost of $1.75 billion annually.[19] This figure is in contrast to only 60 percent of all taxpayers who pay tax preparers.[20] Thus EITC claimants use some of their EITC dollars to pay for tax services – at a higher percentage than the typical taxpayer.

II. EITC BECOMES WELFARE . . . AGAIN . . . AND SUFFERS BACKLASH

Then this Congress took a dramatic step: Instead of taxing people with modest incomes into poverty, we helped them to work their way out of poverty by dramatically increasing the earned-income tax credit. It will lift 15 million working families out of poverty, rewarding work over welfare, making it possible for people to be successful workers and successful parents. *Now that's real welfare reform.*[21]

– President Bill Clinton

In his 1994 State of the Union address, President Clinton echoed the EITC legislative history from almost two decades earlier by equating current EITC claimants with former welfare recipients. Later that year, the Republicans took over Congress. An early Republican legislative agenda item was "reforming" welfare, which occurred in 1996. In 1997, the CTC was enacted for the benefit of middle-class children and was expressly denied to certain families eligible for the EITC.

When politicians refer to taxpayers as welfare recipients, they are playing the race card to some extent.[22] American opposition to welfare is due in large part to the belief that welfare recipients are disproportionately black because blacks are not as committed to work as others.[23] Professor Dorothy Roberts has described how welfare conveys the imagery "of the lazy welfare mother who breeds children at the expense of taxpayers in order to increase the amount of her welfare check."[24] Her description sounds eerily familiar in this context. First, the EITC as originally enacted did not

---

Credit (EIC) was the source of many errors by taxpayers and tax practitioners in preparing returns. Those errors, *along with errors by IRS staff* in following IRS procedures for handling EIC claims, increased IRS' [sic] error resolution workload and delayed taxpayers' receipt of benefits." (emphasis added)).

[19] ALAN BERUBE ET AL., THE PRICE OF PAYING TAXES: HOW TAX PREPARATION AND REFUND LOAN FEES ERODE THE BENEFITS OF THE EITC (2002), *available at* http://www.brookings.edu/es/urban/publications/berubekimeitc.pdf.

[20] David Marzahl, Executive Director, Center for Economic Progress, Presentation to the President's Advisory Panel on Federal Tax Reform: Issues, Challenges and Opportunities: Low Income Taxpayers and the Tax Code, at 7 (2005).

[21] Address Before a Joint Session of Congress on the State of the Union, 1 Pub. Papers 126, 129 (Jan. 25, 1994) (emphasis added).

[22] KENNETH J. NEUBECK & NOEL A. CAZENAVE, WELFARE RACISM: PLAYING THE RACE CARD AGAINST AMERICA'S POOR 90 (2001) ("The racialization of welfare has reached the point where politicians can now exploit racial animus to promote their political ambitions and goals simply by speaking the word *welfare*.").

[23] Brown, *Children*, *supra* note 8, at 795.

[24] Dorothy E. Roberts, *Racism and Patriarchy in the Meaning of Motherhood*, 1 AM. U. J. GENDER & L. 1, 25 (1993).

increase with the number of children so as to not "encourage" taxpayers to have additional children. Second, Congress held the notion that taxpayers engaged in fraudulent behavior by cheating on their tax returns so as to increase the amount of their tax refund. It is ironic that Clinton equated taxpayers, who are only eligible for the EITC because they work for a living, with welfare recipients who can receive welfare without working.

The irony was not lost on certain Democratic members of Congress when discussing payments to farmers in 1996 – coincidentally the same year that welfare reform was enacted.[25] Rep. Barney Frank (D-Mass.) compared the payments to farmers with Aid to Families with Dependent Children (AFDC), stating, "I would not necessarily mind welfare for farmers, but they get 7 years of welfare, the AFDC recipients get 5, and of course there is no work requirements [sic]."[26] Democratic members of Congress who referred to the payments to farmers as "welfare" were severely chastised by Republicans and Democrats alike. Rep. Roberts (R-Kans.) stated that "farm programs are not welfare and partisan statements equating farm programs with welfare do a disservice to farmers and ranchers."[27] Sen. Harkin (D-Iowa) stated that "[f]armers work very hard for their money. They are proud people. They want to get their income from the market and not from the mailbox."[28] Given the racial breakdown of farmers, this discourse should not be surprising.

Professor Jim Chen has described government subsidies to farmers as "an almost perfectly race-matched system of affirmative action for whites."[29] American farm owners are 98% white[30] and are presumed to be hard working and not desirous of handouts. Those who receive the EITC are perceived differently. When a government subsidy disproportionately benefits whites, they are receiving the money because they are "hard working." However, when a government subsidy goes to blacks, they are receiving the money because they are "lazy" and not "hard working."

Congress decided not to extend the full range of CTC benefits to EITC taxpayers in 1997. During that debate, Republican members of Congress referred to the EITC as welfare. House Speaker Newt Gingrich (R-Ga.) stated that giving "an additional $500-per-child tax credit to those who pay no taxes is welfare, plain and simple."[31] Rep. Jack Kingston (R-Ga.) stated that giving the CTC to low-income taxpayers would be giving "another welfare benefit to people who are not paying taxes."[32] Rep. Bill Archer (R-Tex.) reportedly said that extending the CTC to low-income

---

[25] Brown, *Children, supra* note 8, at 797–801.
[26] *Id.* at 797–98 n.201.
[27] *Id.* at 798 n.202.
[28] *Id.* at 799 n.210.
[29] Jim Chen, *Of Agriculture's First Disobedience and its Fruit*, 48 Vand. L. Rev. 1261, 1307 (1995).
[30] *Id.* at 1306–07.
[31] 143 Cong. Rec., E1365 (daily ed. July 8, 1997).
[32] *Id.* at H3895 (daily ed. June 18, 1997).

taxpayers would amount to "a welfare payment."[33] Very few Democrats came out in support of EITC taxpayers. Rep. Ken Bentsen (D-Tex.) was one who did by arguing that Congress was denying "the full $500 per child tax credit to 15 million working, taxpaying, wage-earning parents because it doesn't let them count the credit against their payroll taxes."[34] In addition to members of Congress, Republican Treasury Secretary Paul O'Neill stated "that the IRS must 'examine the devil out of' those receiving the [earned income] tax credit, which, to be frank, is a form of welfare."[35]

In 1998, Congress authorized the IRS to begin an EITC compliance initiative that targeted EITC taxpayers for increased audits. The increased audits were the result of a political compromise between President Clinton and the Republican Congress in exchange for not repealing the EITC.[36] Since 1998, well over $1 billion has been spent on the effort. Ironically, this compliance initiative came only a few years after Congress ordered the IRS to stop doing random taxpayer audits because of the "excessive burdens and intrusion" imposed on taxpayers.[37] Apparently what is burdensome for the average taxpayer can be ignored when dealing with EITC taxpayers.

EITC overpayment estimates range anywhere from 27 percent to 31 percent. Congress, observing the ambiguous behavior – namely, the high error rate – and concluding that fraud was the culprit, has conducted numerous hearings and requested an overwhelming number of GAO reports, most of which focus on noncompliance issues.[38]

EITC noncompliance has been defined to include "erroneous [EITC] claims caused by negligence, mistakes, confusion, and fraud."[39] However, most of the GAO reports did not consider taxpayers who were eligible to receive EITCs but did

---

[33] Richard W. Stevenson, *Main G.O.P. Tax Writer Balks at a Credit that Clinton Wants*, N.Y. TIMES, July 17, 1997, at A18 ("The Republican, Representative Bill Archer of Texas, the chairman of the Ways and Means Committee, said he would not include the costs of providing the proposed $500 per child credit to low-income working families who have no Federal income tax liability. . . . Instead, Mr. Archer said, he would consider it a welfare payment, not a tax cut.").

[34] 143 CONG. REC. H4804 (daily ed. June 24, 1997).

[35] John W. Lee, *Transaction Costs Relating to Acquisition or Enhancement of Intangible Property: A Populist, Political, but Practical Perspective*, 22 VA. TAX REV. 273, 293–94 n.106 (2002) (citations omitted).

[36] DAVID CAY JOHNSTON, PERFECTLY LEGAL 132 (2003); *See also* Lee, *supra* note 35 at 273, 293 ("Declines in audit rates commenced in 1968," but "accelerated in 1995, after Congress, by then controlled by Republicans, cut [the Service's] spending sharply and required the agency to devote more resources to customer service. . . . Congress also directed the Service to devote more audit resources to EITC issues largely for political reasons.").

[37] Robert Greenstein, *The New Procedures for the Earned Income Tax Credit*, 99 TAX NOTES 1525, 1528 (2003).

[38] *See* Brown, *Children, supra* note 8, at 773 n.74 (citing 17 different GAO reports).

[39] U.S. GEN. ACCOUNTING OFFICE, EARNED INCOME CREDIT: NONCOMPLIANCE AND POTENTIAL ELIGIBILITY REVISIONS 1, 4 n.2. (1995) [hereinafter GAO REPORT, POTENTIAL ELIGIBILITY REVISIONS].

not claim them; according to one study, "for every three households that claimed the credit, there was an additional eligible household that did not."[40] Thus considerable numbers of eligible EITC taxpayers are not taking advantage of this credit.

In the IRS Data Book is a table titled "Costs Incurred by the Internal Revenue Service, by Budget Activity," which for years had a separate line for the EITC.[41] The remarkable feature of the table was that it singled out *no other tax provision*. If we wanted to find out how much, if any, the IRS spends on denying unlawful tax shelters to high-income taxpayers or to corporations, we could not do so because that data are not stated separately.

The Improper Payments Information Act of 2002[42] requires each federal agency to identify all programs that "may be susceptible to significant improper payments" and the steps it has taken to reduce such payments.[43] However, the Office of Management and Budget (OMB) interpreted this act to require the IRS to notify it of improper payments associated with only one tax provision – the EITC.[44] The EITC is the only tax provision about which the OMB has requested improper payment information.

During 2003, a second set of debates occurred around the decision to expand the CTC to include certain EITC claimants. Rep. Spencer Bachus (R-Ala.) stated that "increasing the child tax credit to [EITC recipients] who don't pay income taxes amounts to turning the tax code 'into a welfare system.'"[45] Rep. Robert Portman (R-Ohio) stated that the EITC "is not a tax issue – it's a government transfer payment to people who do not pay income taxes."[46] Rep. Ernest Istook (R-Okla.), chairman of the Appropriations subcommittee that has authority over the IRS budget, stated, "The problem is that welfare payments are being mislabeled as tax rebates, [t]o end the confusion, we should stop putting the 'tax refund' label on government checks that are actually public assistance."[47] Finally, then–House Majority Leader Tom

---

[40] U.S. Gen. Accounting Office, Major Management Challenges and Program Risks: Department of the Treasury 11, 12 (2003) [hereinafter GAO Report, Major Management Challenges].

[41] *See, e.g.,* Internal Revenue Service, 1999 Data Book 39 tbl.33 (1999). The IRS singled out the EITC until FY 2007. Since then, table 28 has listed only general enforcement costs.

[42] Pub. L. No. 107–300, 116 Stat. 2350 (2002); *See also* Zelenak, *supra* note 10, at 1896–97.

[43] Zelenak, *supra* note 10, at 1896–97.

[44] *Id.* at 1897. It remains unclear whether OMB will continue to interpret the law this way after the passage of The Improper Payments Elimination and Recovery Act of 2010 (IPERA), Pub. L. No. 111-204 (2010).

[45] Bruce Alpert, *Demos See Tax Debate as Fodder in Campaign; GOP Calls Complaints a Class Warfare Tactic,* Times-Picayune (New Orleans), June 15, 2003, at 16.

[46] David Firestone, *Fight or Flight? G.O.P. Split Over Tax Credits,* N.Y. Times, June 8, 2003, at A23.

[47] Chris Casteel, *Senators Explain Votes, Say Low-Income Families off Tax Roles,* Daily Oklahoman, June 7, 2003, at 30. Representative Istook was in the news several years ago on a non-EITC tax matter: the congressman inserted a provision into a 2004 spending bill that would have given legislators and their staff assistants the ability to examine income tax returns. David E. Rosenbaum, *G.O.P. Says Motive for Tax Clause in Budget Bill Was Misread,* N.Y. Times, Nov. 22, 2004, at A22.

DeLay (R-Tex.) stated, "To me, it's a little difficult to give tax relief to people that don't pay income tax."[48] Congressman Delay ignored the fact that all wage earners pay Social Security and Medicare taxes.

In August 2003, the IRS announced that it was subjecting 25,000 EITC claimants to precertification,[49] which requires EITC claimants to provide additional documentation to the IRS that they are eligible for the credit.[50] EITC claimants had to prove that they had a child who qualified them for the larger credit amount.[51] No other taxpayers had to file additional forms to receive a refund.

The IRS issued preliminary results from the first set of precertification claimants in May 2004, including information that almost 20 percent of the taxpayers did not claim the EITC on their 2003 return.[52] The IRS could not determine whether failure to claim the credit was the result of ineligible taxpayers choosing not to file or of eligible taxpayers being deterred from filing.[53] No other tax provision requires precertification, although all welfare-type programs do so.[54] The results of precertification were decreased participation in the EITC and increased burdens on taxpayers. As a result, the IRS stopped the precertification program.[55]

The error rate still hovers around 25%. In 2009, for EITC claims totaling $43 billion, the IRS paid out between $10 and 12 billion in error.[56] Because the high error rate has been attributed to taxpayer fraud, the focus on reducing the error rate has been primarily on enforcement – specifically increased audits and precertification. Yet these measures have done very little to reduce the problem. Implicit bias has caused Congress to ignore the obvious; namely, that simplicity is the only thing that will decrease the error rate, because most errors are due not to fraud but to the EITC's complexity.

III. HARMS OF IMPLICIT BIAS

This section describes three primary harms that implicit bias in the EITC context has wrought on different taxpayer groups. First, targeting the EITC for special

---

[48] David Firestone, *DeLay Rebuffs Move to Restore Lost Tax Credit*, N.Y. TIMES, June 4, 2003, at A1.

[49] Zelenak, *supra* note 10, at 1871–72.

[50] *See* I.R.S. Announcement 2003–40, IRS, http://www.irs.gov/newsroom/article/0,,id=110298,00.html (last updated January 14, 2009).

[51] Robert Greenstein, *The New Procedures for the Earned Income Tax Credit*, 99 TAX NOTES 1525, 1528, 1525 (2003).

[52] Zelenak, *supra* note 10, at 1871.

[53] *Id.* at 1872.

[54] *Id.* at 1884.

[55] NINA E. OLSON, RUNNING SOCIAL PROGRAMS THROUGH THE TAX SYSTEM 84 (2009), *available at* http://www.irs.gov/pub/irs-utl/vol2_socialprograms.pdf.

[56] TREASURY INSPECTOR GEN. FOR TAX ADMIN., THE EARNED INCOME TAX CREDIT PROGRAM HAS MADE ADVANCES; HOWEVER, ALTERNATIVES TO TRADITIONAL COMPLIANCE METHODS ARE NEEDED TO STOP BILLIONS OF DOLLARS IN ERRONEOUS PAYMENTS (2008), *available at* http://www.treasury.gov/tigta/auditreports/2009reports/200940024fr.pdf.

government audits and scrutiny has primarily harmed hard-working white taxpayers. Further by focusing solely on errors made by existing EITC filers, limited efforts were made to reach out to those who are eligible but have not filed for their EITC, a failure that also has a racial impact.

Second, by focusing solely on EITC taxpayers, Congress and the IRS have ignored far larger instances of tax fraud. The IRS estimates that there is a gap between taxes owed and unpaid by individuals and corporations of almost $300 billion.[57] Even if all errors in the EITC were to magically disappear tomorrow, the tax gap would remain largely intact. Noncompliance by corporations, high-income individuals, and cash-based business owners are each instances where additional audit dollars would bear much fruit but have been largely ignored.

Finally, by concluding that the ambiguous behavior of high error rates is due to fraud and not complexity, there has been little reduction in the error rate even after more than a decade of effort. Congress has missed an opportunity to simplify the EITC, which would not only reduce the error rate but also would put more EITC dollars in the hands of EITC taxpayers and potentially encourage new EITC filers who are eligible but not currently filing, thereby lifting even more hard-working Americans out of poverty.

A. Who Are EITC Taxpayers?

One study showed that 54 percent of those eligible for the EITC were white, 24 percent were black, almost 18 percent were Latino/a, and 3.6 percent were "other."[58] It is likely therefore that the majority of EITC taxpayers who were audited by the IRS were white. When members of Congress told the IRS to audit EITC taxpayers it is unlikely that they had in mind auditing lots of white taxpayers.

In addition, by focusing on those who were claiming the EITC fraudulently, Congress largely ignored the significant percentage of taxpayers who were eligible for the EITC but were not applying for it. A study using the 2002 National Survey of America's Families showed that only 58 percent of all low-income parents had heard of the EITC.[59] Whereas the knowledge gap between black parents and white parents was relatively small (68% vs. 73%), the gap between Latino parents and white parents was extremely large (27% vs. 73%). More outreach dollars, coupled

[57] U.S. Department of the Treasury, Update on Reducing the Federal Tax Gap and Improving Voluntary Compliance (2009), *available at* http://www.irs.gov/pub/newsroom/tax_gap_report_-final_version.pdf.

[58] Jeffrey B. Liebman, *Who Are the Ineligible Earned Income Tax Credit Recipients?*, in Making Work Pay: The Earned Income Tax Credit and its Impact on America's Families 286–87 (Bruce D. Meyer & Douglas Holtz-Eakin eds., 2001).

[59] Elaine Maag, Disparities in Knowledge of the EITC 1323 (2005), *available at* http://www.taxpolicycenter.org/UploadedPDF/1000752_Tax_Facts_3–14–05.pdf. The Urban Institute has not polled on this question since 2002. The GAO Report, *infra* note 58, also relies on data from 2002.

with simplification, would probably allow additional eligible taxpayers to file and receive their EITC.

B. *Tax Gap Is More than the EITC*

By focusing virtually all auditing efforts at lowering the EITC error rate in recent years, the tax gap between taxes owed but unpaid grew unabated. Although the IRS estimate of the EITC noncompliance rate is high, its noncompliance rate is not the highest of all such rates. The IRS estimates that the gap between taxes owed but unpaid by individual and corporate taxpayers is more than $300 billion.[60] In addition, the IRS states that its most current enforcement efforts only resulted in the collection of about 16% of the tax gap.[61] Underreported income by self-employed taxpayers totaled nearly $68 billion of the more than $300 billion tax gap.[62] In contrast, the estimated tax gap for the EITC approaches $12 billion.[63] The EITC represents less than *one-half of 1 percent* of the total tax gap.

The IRS estimates that self-employed individuals generally underreport their income by 64%, and self-employed individuals who operate in a cash business underreport their income by 89%.[64] Small corporations and sole proprietors constitute 29% of the tax gap.[65] Thus, significant noncompliance areas that generate greater revenue losses than are estimated for the EITC go unaudited.[66] Because Congress has been obsessed with the EITC error rate, other tax cheats have been allowed to continue without fear of reprisal.

[60] *See* U.S. Gen. Accounting Office, *Tax Gap*: IRS Can Improve Efforts to Address *Tax* Evasion by Networks of Businesses and Related Entities 7 (2010), *available at* http://www.gao.gov/new. items/d10968.pdf (The report indicates that IRS anticipates recovery sufficient to decrease the tax gap to $290 billion).

[61] IRS Updates Tax Gap Estimates, IRS (February 14, 2006), http://www.irs.gov/newsroom/article/ 0,,id=154496,00.html ("IRS enforcement activities, coupled with other late payments, recover about $55 billion of the tax gap [$345 billion], leaving a net tax gap of $290 billion.").

[62] U.S. Gen. Accounting Office, *Tax Gap*: Limiting Sole Proprietor Loss Deductions Could Improve Compliance but Would Also Limit Some Legitimate Losses 5 (2009), *available at* http://www.gao.gov/new.items/d09815.pdf.

[63] U.S. Gen. Accounting Office, Support for Low Income Individuals and Families: A Review of Recent GAO Work 7 (2010), *available at* http://www.gao.gov/new.items/d10342r.pdf ("IRS estimates on overpayments have ranged from 24 to 32 percent of dollars claimed at a cost of up to $12 billion per year.").

[64] GAO Report, Potential Eligibility Revisions, *supra* note 39, at 4–5.

[65] U.S. Gen. Accounting Office, *Tax Gap*: Many Actions Taken, but a Cohesive Compliance Strategy Needed 2, 7 (1994) ("As a starting point, IRS could focus more of its efforts on highly noncompliant groups, such as small corporations and sole proprietors, who make up 29 percent of the tax gap.").

[66] *See* Philip J. Harmelink et al., *The Challenge of the EITC*, 100 Tax Notes 955, 960 (2003) (showing that individual noncompliance was estimated at $132 billion, offshore noncompliance at $70 billion, corporate noncompliance at $46 billion, and partnership noncompliance at $30 billion, compared with the estimates for EITC noncompliance, which was placed at $10 billion).

C. Simplification

Because of the complexity of the EITC, tax return preparers, IRS personnel, and others are more prone to make mistakes when filing the return. In tax year 2003, 71 percent of EITC tax returns were filed by paid professionals.[67] In fact, EITC filers, who should have the simplest returns, are more likely to use paid return preparers than middle and upper income taxpayers. Because of congressional inaction in simplifying the EITC, hard-working low-income taxpayers have had to pay a part of their credit to tax return preparers.

A cottage industry in the form of refund anticipation loans (RALs) disproportionately used by EITC filers has developed. For the 2005 tax year, 63 percent of RAL recipients were EITC taxpayers, even though they made up only 17 percent of individual taxpayers.[68] One estimate places the cost of RAL loan fees at $570 million per year for EITC taxpayers.[69] A 2002 study by the Brookings Institution found that electronic tax filing and preparation services proliferate in neighborhoods where large numbers of families claim the EITC.[70] EITC taxpayers are not only targeted by the IRS but also are easy prey for others.

Given the EITC's complexity, one wonders what simplification would look like. Currently the IRS produces a chart that calculates tax liability for incomes below a certain level so that all taxpayers have to do is check their income level, marital status, and family size to see how much taxes they owe. The IRS could create such a chart for the EITC, showing credit amounts for different income amounts, different marital statuses, and different numbers of children. If the IRS did more of the heavy lifting, taxpayers would not have to and would be less likely to use tax return preparers and RALs.

Consider how simplification in other contexts has produced dramatic results. Dr. Atul Gawande explains how something as simple as a checklist decreased deaths during surgery at Columbia Presbyterian Hospital.[71] Put another way, complexity kills. When discussing EITC claimants, additional money that would no longer have to be spent on tax return preparers could produce equally significant outcomes. If we were dealing with white farmers in Idaho who were receiving government funds at a level 25–30% higher than they were entitled to, what would be the result? Would

---

[67] Stephen D. Holt, *Keeping It in Context: Earned Income Tax Credit Compliance and Treatment of the Working Poor*, 6 CONN. PUB. INT. L. J. 183, 199 (2007).

[68] CHI CHI WU & JEAN ANN FOX, ONE STEP FORWARD, ONE STEP BACK: PROGRESS SEEN IN EFFORTS AGAINST HIGH-PRICED REFUND ANTICIPATION LOANS, BUT EVEN MORE ABUSIVE PRODUCTS INTRO-DUCED, 11 (2007), *available at* http://www.consumerfed.org/elements/www.consumerfed.org/file/finance/RAL_Report_2007020507.pdf.

[69] *Id.*

[70] *See* Berube, et al., *supra* note 19, at 1 ("High-EITC zip codes are home to 50 percent more electronic tax preparation services per filer than low-EITC zip codes.").

[71] ATUL GAWANDE, THE CHECKLIST MANIFESTO (2009).

we assume that the farmers are lazy and decide to audit them, or would we assume that the farmers are hard working and decide to simplify the program?

IV. CONCLUSION

In President Obama's January 2011 State of the Union address, he called for simplifying the tax code. There is no better place to start than with the EITC. Yet implicit bias has largely gotten in the way of EITC simplification. Implicit bias allows members of Congress to make judgments based on the high error rates and conclude they occur due to fraud and not complexity. Members of Congress see lazy, welfare cheats instead of the reality of hard-working taxpayers struggling to make ends meet while trying their best to calculate their proper share of EITC benefits – or trusting tax return preparers to do it for them. The EITC lifts millions of Americans and their families out of poverty every year. Implicit bias has gotten in the way of simplification for far too long. America's working poor deserve better. The time for change is now.

11

Intellectual Property

Implicit Racial and Gender Bias in Right of Publicity Cases and Intellectual Property Law Generally

Danielle M. Conway

I. CONNECTING RACE AND GENDER TO INTELLECTUAL PROPERTY LAW

Intellectual property (IP) rights have a tremendous impact on the production, control, and direction of culture and identity in American society. The dominant players in the entertainment and advertising industries seek to control wealth and to profit from the ability to influence the direction of culture and identity in American society; for example, institutional copyright holders are concerned with maintaining the status quo that favors their interests over those who have been historically disenfranchised and oppressed by the unauthorized and uncompensated exploitation of their personas and identities. These dominant players, the "haves," continue to benefit from the head start they achieved as a result of their white privilege that afforded them the ability to serve as the architects of the current intellectual property law regime favoring print, broadcast, and digital media interests.

No longer is overt racism or sexism necessary to maintain the status quo in favor of institutional copyright holders; instead, two of the more pernicious influences on directing outcomes in intellectual property law cases are, first and foremost, the belief that American copyright law is superior to publicity rights law and, second, the unconscious deployment of highly subjective beliefs and stereotypes by decision-makers who are required to settle disputes between institutional copyright holders and disenfranchised publicity rights holders, many of whom are African American and women. These well-meaning decision-makers, practitioners, and even scholarly commentators are convinced that intellectual property law is immune from implicit race and gender bias. In an attempt to respond to the cacophonous claims that intellectual property protection and enforcement regimes in America are race neutral, this chapter presents the theory that implicit bias is present and operating in the intellectual property law sphere generally and in the right of publicity sector specifically. Understanding how implicit bias functions in intellectual property domains will allow us to address to what extent intellectual property law and its application can respond to the reality of implicit bias and then to accept the challenge of taking steps to address what forms of distributive justice are appropriate for rights holders whose social and economic interests have been marginalized, disenfranchised, and subordinated by unconscious biases permeating this sphere of law.

The right of publicity provides celebrities and noncelebrities alike control over the commercial value of their personas or identities. The relatively recent emergence and general recognition of the right of publicity reflect an American societal determination that the individual's interest in the associative value of his or her persona merits distinct legal protection. Courts and commentators also have addressed the unique aspects of the right of publicity by extolling that the persona, particularly those of celebrities, has important expressive and communicative impacts on society. As one commentator has summarized,

> Entertainment and sports celebrities are the leading players in our Public Drama. We tell tales, both tall and cautionary, about them. We monitor their comings and goings, their missteps and heartbreaks. *We copy their mannerisms, their styles, and their modes of conversation and of consumption. Whether or not celebrities are "the chief agents of moral change in the United States," they certainly are widely used – far more than are our institutionally anchored elites – to symbolize individual aspirations, group identities and cultural values.* Their images are thus important expressive and communicative resources: the peculiar, yet familiar idiom in which we conduct a fair portion of our cultural business and everyday conversation.[1]

There is a palpable conflict between institutional copyright holders and publicity rights holders regarding which right will prevail, particularly when these rights overlap, as with the use of photographs, videos, and sound recordings where the copyright holder and the publicity rights holder are not one and the same. Thus, the narrative invoked by powerful institutional copyright holders is that, despite their obvious head start in exploiting their copyrights (and often misappropriating the publicity rights of others in so doing), enforcing another's publicity rights deprives them, their licensees, and even the general public of the rights expressly granted by the U.S. Constitution and the Copyright Act and thereby limits the value of their copyrighted works. In essence, institutional copyright holders have painted themselves as victims harmed by those who have recently recognized the social utility that publicity rights offer them as they seek to protect their persona and identities from unauthorized exploitation. Although it is true that the commercial value of a person's identity often results from success in endeavors such as entertainment or sports that offer their own substantial rewards, in an age of institutional entertainment conglomerates that have harnessed the power of valuable expressive content, including identity, to define and

---

[1] *See* Comedy III Prods., Inc. v. Gary Saderup, Inc., 25 Cal. 4th 387, 397, 106 Cal. Rptr. 2d 126 (2001) (emphasis added).

direct societal shifts and norms through the wielding of copyright monopolies, one of the only available intellectual property-based means for protecting the proprietary interests of an individual and her persona is the right of publicity.

Thus, fair and equitable mechanisms to protect and enforce this individual right, which normatively must be free from both overt racism and implicit bias, are essential to responding to the seemingly limitless power exerted by institutional copyright holders in their ongoing efforts to impose their vision of American culture. In the shadows of institutional copyright holders lurk core questions about basic fairness for those who seek to protect the value of their identities, as against those who would continue a legacy of unauthorized exploitation. As the law grapples to balance the power that institutional copyright holders wield against the publicity rights of individuals, it must also mediate between the rapidly developing forms of content that are copyrightable and the equally evolving technologies for appropriating identity. Too often ignored in the chaos of competing intellectual property interests are the basic value judgments about what characteristics and traits the right of publicity should cover and whether protection for publicity rights will be doled out fairly and equitably, regardless of the race and gender of the parties or whether subjective judgments based on stereotypes will factor into decisions regarding protection and enforcement of publicity rights.

The cost of conceding the underlying values is best illustrated by the relationship between intellectual property law and indigenous communities. In many indigenous communities, the assets, resources, and knowledge that have originated and evolved with indigenous peoples through experiences with their environments form the basis of indigenous identity and community values.[2] Being disenfranchised from indigenous assets, resources, and knowledge or having the same misused, misap-propriated, and commodified causes indigenous identities to become hostage to external forces, perceptions, and influences that relegate indigenous peoples to subordinate or nonexistent positions at the fringes of society and the economy. In far too many indigenous communities, identity – as manifested through cultural assets such as art, dance, and traditional knowledge and practices – is all that remains with indigenous peoples after colonization. The same concerns – although perhaps not always to the same degree – are at issue with treatment of African Americans and women in American society. These concerns force us to question whether our intellectual property laws are complicit in providing a legal vehicle for the exploitation, devaluation, and promotion of derogatory stereotypes that serve to fuel further oppression against indigenous, minority, and women artists at the hands of institutional entertainment and advertising entities.

---

[2] *See generally* Danielle M. Conway, *Indigenizing Intellectual Property Law: Customary Law, Legal Pluralism, and the Protection of Indigenous Peoples' Rights, Identity, and Resources*, 15 TEX. WES-LEYAN L. REV. 207 (2009); Danielle M. Conway, *Promoting Indigenous Innovation, Enterprise, and Entrepreneurship through the Licensing of Article 31 Indigenous Assets and Resources*, SMU L. REV. (forthcoming 2011).

This chapter explores these questions through an implicit race bias lens. Implicit race bias is a term that describes biases that are generally outside the awareness and control of a person – in essence, biases that lurk beneath the human consciousness – which disproportionately affect people in meaningful ways. Implicit biases are hidden, reflexive associations that affect decision-making in all contexts, such as employment decisions, judicial decisions, or social decisions and interactions. In right of publicity cases, these snap judgments may result in either copyright interests being treated more favorably than publicity rights interests without a proper balancing assessment, or producing situations in which publicity rights holders belonging to a specific group are deemed less worthy of protection due to either the types of misappropriating uses made of these individuals' identities or personas or a decision-maker's lack of capacity to identify with publicity rights holders who do not look like them. Similarly, as further research should explore, implicit bias likely affects a range of other intellectual property topics: patent law where African American and women inventors may not be perceived as equally inventive as their white counterparts; copyright law where individuals belonging to this segment of society may not be deemed as producers or creators of original works of authorship or, even more offensive, may have their works of authorship imitated, co-opted, and repackaged for mainstream (white) audiences without any ensuing compensation; or trademark law where images and symbols of or associated with African Americans and women are used to project negative, false, and psychically injurious stereotypes that continue to marginalize members of these groups.

The proper application and enforcement of the right of publicity have the potential to generate net positive effects for the development of American culture in general and for African Americans and women in particular. To realize these potential benefits, it is imperative to study and address how implicit bias affects decision-making in right of publicity cases. Eradicating implicit bias in right of publicity cases (and more broadly in IP law) provides an opportunity to promote a long-awaited balance of interests between institutional industry actors and individual content providers that will augur well for a more inclusive environment, which will in turn facilitate growth and expansion of real, as opposed to manufactured, American culture. To get to this point, implicit bias must first be unearthed and then addressed in the discipline of intellectual property law, which far too long has been cloaked by a presumption of race and gender neutrality.

II. EXPOSING THE MYTH OF RACE AND GENDER NEUTRALITY IN INTELLECTUAL PROPERTY LAW

For several reasons the intersection between implicit bias and intellectual property law has yet to be made universally evident. First, IP law is overly characterized as race and gender neutral. Second, it is perceived as implicating the rights and obligations of primarily institutional holders of subject matter and not nearly so much the contributions of collaborators, artisans, or laborers. Again, this dichotomous treatment between authors and inventors and those from whom they take knowledge and labor remains invisible in the process of distributing rewards and incentives. Third, IP law has largely escaped having its doctrines and practices scrutinized by critical race and feminist theorists most likely because its most fervent proponents, those who have benefited from a head start in garnering the intangible spoils, have been über successful in creating the impression that this particular segment of the law is premised on that which is rational, objective, dispassionate, and neutral.

Despite its origins in feudal Europe and in the colonial Americas before, yet including, the adoption and ratification of the U.S. Constitution – eras marked by flawed, unequal, and often harsh governance – IP law is perceived to be a rational and equitable means of rewarding and incentivizing invention and knowledge creation by inventors and authors. Its application is assumed to be objective, dispassionate, and (race and gender) neutral. And yet the U.S. Constitution has never been race and/or gender neutral with respect to IP law.

The *original* U.S. Constitution, said to be a model for democracy, liberty, and respect for man's fundamental rights, embodied a philosophy of overt exclusion, separatism, and discriminatory racial and gender dysfunction. Professor K. J. Greene pointedly remarked that "[t]he original U.S. Constitution excluded both black women and men from the blessings of liberty."[3] This original document also housed Article I, § 8, cl. 8, better known as the patent and copyright clause. This clause, lofty in ideals coveting innovation, knowledge creation, cultural dissemination, and access to the power that comes with harnessing information and technology, provides that Congress has the power

> "to promote the progress of science and useful arts, by securing for limited times to authors and inventors the exclusive right to their respective writings and discoveries."

It should always be remembered that this clause, unanimous in its adoption by our forefathers, was developed at a time and in a context when all men and women were neither equal nor were they considered by those who benefited from this provision as being human beings. Professor Keith Aoki has highlighted the fact that "during the antebellum era . . . slaves were not legally recognized as possessing creative and inventive agency of their own."[4] According to Professor Aoki, it was "inconceivable that slaves could own a patent, even though a slave may have invented the cotton gin, which eventually was used in extending the economic life of plantation slavery."

Focusing on the notion of inconceivability primes these questions: Who could not conceive of such a circumstance? What beliefs, attitudes, and stereotypes supported this notion of inconceivability? Who benefits, either explicitly or implicitly, from holding fast to harmful race- and/or gender-tinged beliefs, attitudes, and stereotypes?

---

[3] K.J. Greene, *Intellectual Property at the Intersection of Race and Gender: Lady Sings the Blues*, 16 Am. U. J. Gender Soc. Pol'y & L. 365 (2007–08).

[4] Keith Aoki, *Distributive and Syncretic Motives in Intellectual Property Law (With Special Reference to Coercion, Agency, and Development)*, 40 U.C. Davis L. Rev. 717, 719 (2007).

Professor Aoki offered yet another illustration in the discussion about J. E. Stuart and his slave, Ned. Because slaves were victim to overt bias, their inventions, such as Ned's double plow, were deemed property of slave owners. Stuart unapologetically professed that "the Patent laws were passed to encourage inventions of a useful character on the Part of the Political to the exclusion of the [servile] race, who by reason of the general Stupidity, are concerned without the range of both the letter, [and] the Spirit of the law."[5] Thus the race- and gender-neutral conceptions of IP law are distortions of the actual history of the law and policy of intellectual property protection and enforcement.

Some might frame this discussion as historically important yet inapposite to the current intellectual property law protection and enforcement regime. In essence, there exists a romantic vision that society has evolved, as a result of the Reconstruction Amendments, civil rights era struggles and victories, and the innovation and technological transformation that marks the 21st century, to promote and provide neutral incentives for all innovators, inventors, and creators, regardless of race or gender. Yet questions remain as to how the beliefs, attitudes, and stereotypes about the inconceivability of the black slave as inventor and creator affect modern society generally and what other areas of IP law have been infected by this pretextual neutral narrative promoted by proponents of the U.S. intellectual property law regime under which multiple layers of implicit bias flow wide and deep.

The race- and gender-neutrality narrative of intellectual property law is ripe for analysis and deconstruction, especially if we are to address the implicit bias engrained at every level of the intellectual property protection and enforcement regime. I propose that implicit bias exists and is prevalent in the substance and doctrine of intellectual property law, separate and distinct from general litigation, just as much as it exists and is prevalent in employment law, criminal law, or discrimination law.

My approach in this chapter is to analyze publicity rights law, as opposed to the other more conventional disciplines in the intellectual property sphere that were developed under the original U.S. Constitution in a time of overt racism, and then to offer observations about judicial decision-making and juror fact-finding, to a lesser degree, that have been influenced by both the pretextual neutral narrative encasing intellectual property law jurisprudence and the pervasive impact of implicit bias on publicity rights outcomes.

III. IMPLICIT BIAS IN RIGHT OF PUBLICITY LITIGATION

The right of publicity is a relatively new intellectual property right that owes a substantial part of its existence to new media channels introduced in the early 20th century. From television, to magazines, to web pages, to movies, media are a

---

[5] *Id.* at 743 (citing Dorothy C. Yancy, *The Stuart Double Plow and Double Scraper: The Invention of a Slave*, 69 J. Negro Hist. 1, 49 (1984)).

tremendous force in both informing the American public and defining American attitudes, beliefs, and stereotypes. Messages delivered from industry through multimedia outlets shape and control the direction of American culture. This content derives from the prominence of sports and entertainment figures whose identities have become valuable commodities in the conveyance of advertisers' messages to the American consumer. As such, the right of publicity is a vital mechanism to create balance between content providers and advertisers in the media-driven construction of American culture. In the context of race and gender, the right of publicity also has significance as a post-Reconstruction era cause of action prominently figuring in the development of legal mechanisms to respond to a long history of institutional and systemic racism that has been manifested through countless misappropriations of the creative outputs of African Americans and women. The right of publicity offers a means to achieve distributive justice by providing individuals with the tools and the ability to reap the economic benefits associated with the exploitation of identity and persona in American culture. The right of publicity can be viewed as restoring a form of property right in individuals, especially African Americans and women, who for so much of their existence in American society have been deprived of the means to accumulate wealth and to amass social and cultural capital.

The discussion that follows illustrates how implicit race bias can affect assessment of the relative value of physical attributes and comparative strength of a person's claim to the control of his or her identity against strong institutional copyright interests. To assess just how implicit bias functions in judicial decision-making, I compare the language used to describe the litigants and their claims in four prominent right of publicity cases. The nature of right of publicity claims requires that judicial decision-makers consider the "worth" or "value" of intensely personal characteristics or attributes. This type of comparative worth processing activates stereotypical knowledge about the racial and/or gender group of which the plaintiff is a member. If the stereotypes are favorable (e.g., white males are industrious and intelligent) then the value of the claimed characteristic or attribute or persona at the center of the right of publicity claim is assessed more favorably. Of course, when the value of the thing to be protected is higher, the likelihood that it will survive judicial scrutiny (especially against claims of preemption wielded by powerful institutional copyright holders) is correspondingly higher. At the same time, if the activated stereotypes are negative (e.g., blonde women are ditzy) then the plaintiff's claim is devalued, and the relative weight given to the rights of the institutional copyright holder is artificially inflated. I use the word "artificially" to denote that these stereotype-driven assessments of the relative worth of claims does not necessarily – or even remotely – correspond to the actual uniqueness of the claimed attribute or characteristic or industriousness behind a claimed persona.

Consider the vastly different descriptions of Vanna White, a celebrated game show hostess, or June Toney, a highly successful black model, with John Facenda,

a venerated sports announcer, or Russell Christoff, the "distinguished" face behind
Folgers Coffee.

A. *Vanna White Castigated – John Facenda Venerated: Uncloaking Implicit
Race and Gender Bias in Contextual Identity Right of Publicity Cases*

 Vanna White is one of the most memorable
hostesses to ever grace the television screen.
During her years as the hostess of the popular
game show *Wheel of Fortune*, White adorned
the set; interacted with the male host, the
contestants, and the members of the audience; and revealed the letters as contestants
attempted to solve the puzzle. Her name and identity were so well known that
Samsung chose to use her likeness in a series of advertisements about videocassette
recorders. Driving the theme that Samsung products would be used well into the
21st century the "ad depicted a robot, dressed in a [blonde] wig, gown, and jewelry
which [the advertising company] consciously selected to resemble White's hair and
dress. The robot was posed next to a game board . . . instantly recognizable as the
Wheel of Fortune game show set, in a stance for which White is famous." White did
not consent to this use of her identity. In fact, "[u]nlike the other [male] celebrities
used in the campaign, White neither consented to the ads, nor was she paid."

Although White "won" her case on appeal, the road toward that relative victory
was filled with judicial rebuke for her efforts to enforce her right of publicity.
First, the district court granted Samsung summary judgment, reasoning that White
failed to show that Samsung appropriated her "name or likeness." The dissenting
opinions at the appellate court cast Samsung as the "true" victim of overprotection
of the right of publicity in favor of a woman who did not "see the humor" in being
allegedly "spoofed" or "parodied." Specifically, the dissent criticized the majority for
"confus[ing] Vanna White, the person, with the role she has assumed as the current
hostess on the 'Wheel of Fortune' television game show" and stated further that
"those things which Vanna White claims identify her are not unique to her. They
are, instead, attributes of the *role* she plays. The representation of those attributes,
therefore, does not constitute a representation of Vanna White." The dissent went
on to devalue her persona with the following:

> Vanna White is a one-role celebrity. She is famous solely for appearing as the hostess
> on the "Wheel of Fortune" television show. There is nothing unique about Vanna
> White or the attributes which she claims identify her. Although she appears to be an
> attractive woman, her face and her figure are no more distinctive than that of other
> equally comely women. She performs her role as hostess on "Wheel of Fortune"
> in a simple and straight-forward manner. Her work does not require her to display
> whatever artistic talent she may possess.

The devaluation and disdain in this diatribe for women who seek employment in Hollywood as hostesses are palpable. On one level, the role of hostess or set adorner would rarely if ever be filled by a male model or actor; thus, he would not be described as having a fungible identity or in this case no identity at all (i.e., White's "face and her figure are no more distinctive than that of other equally comely women"). On another level, the dissent reads into the right of publicity a requirement of distinctiveness and artistic talent that nowhere appears in the elements of the cause of action. In this way, the dissent discounts the existence and value of White's persona based on an assumption that she has not displayed unique qualities or artistic talent in establishing her identity, and therefore she is not worthy of receiving protection against a multinational corporation that would financially benefit in quite a substantial way from exploiting what the dissent deems valueless.

In castigating the majority opinion and White herself, Judge Kozinski's dissent argued that it is the *Wheel of Fortune* game board, not Vanna White, which evokes White's image. As he wrote, "once you include the game board, anybody standing beside it – a brunette woman, a man wearing women's clothing, a monkey in a wig and gown – would evoke White's image, precisely the way the robot did.... The panel is giving White an exclusive right not in what she looks like or who she is, but in what she does for a living."[6] This criticism is hypocritical, especially considering that American society approves of the social construct that masculine identities and corresponding roles permit men to define themselves by their profession, while at the same time women identifying themselves by their profession are denigrated and, if Judge Kozinski had his way, unable to protect a legally recognized right.

The dissent views Samsung, a multinational corporation and institutional copyright holder, as a victim and exposes a bias premised on the superiority of copyright interests over publicity rights while also accusing White of free-riding based on the assumption that she undeservedly benefits from an identity that she likely was not even responsible for creating.

No, this case does not represent a win for Vanna White or for women trying to protect their publicity rights. Instead, it represents how implicit bias in right of publicity cases threatens the most important individual property rights in the digital information age – the right to control one's own essence, identity, and persona.

Unlike *White v. Samsung*, the language and narrative of *Facenda v. N.F.L. Films* is filled with an almost embarrassing overflow of praise and reverence for a white, male sports announcer and his justifiable efforts to champion his identity over and above the institutional copyright interests of NFL Films.

---

[6] White v. Samsung Elecs. Am., Inc., 989 F.2d 1512, 1515 (9th Cir. 1993). (dissenting opinion).

The district court in *Facenda* granted summary judgment to John Facenda Jr. on his claim (in his own right and on behalf of his father's estate) that the NFL made unauthorized use of Facenda's name or likeness when using a 13-second recording of the voice of the late Mr. Facenda in a film, *The Making of Madden*, about the sports computer-simulation game "Madden NFL 06." The unquestioning acceptance of the legitimacy of Facenda's postmortem right of publicity is telling. The district court concluded that the "NFL [did] not own an unrestricted copyright in Facenda's recordings. Instead, the NFL's use of the recordings [wa]s limited by the Blanket Release's provision precluding their use to endorse a product or service. Because of this limitation, the copyright law would not be relevant to NFL's use of Facenda's voice in the Making of Madden."

The reverence for Facenda and the laudatory narrative used to describe him and his proprietary interest in his voice are unmistakable. Consider the following findings that the district court made:

> John Facenda, who passed away in 1984, was a Philadelphia television news anchor-man, and the narrator of NFL Films' game footage and highlight reels. Plaintiff has provided evidence showing Facenda's popularity in both roles, and the strength of the identification between his voice and NFL Films. Barry Wolper, chief financial officer for NFL films conceded at his deposition that he had heard Facenda's voice described as "legendary" and that he, personally, would characterize Facenda's as a "legendary voice." Moreover, certain lines of narration, as delivered by Facenda, "have achieved classic status." . . . NFL presented Facenda's legacy to the public as something to be treated with reverence. In 1994, it released a video of compiled clips entitled "The Legendary John Facenda" or "The Legendary Voice of John Facenda." . . . Thus, although John Facenda is not a "legend" in the same category as, say, Hercules, or John Henry, Plaintiff has shown that he was, and remains, a very popular figure among football fans; that he was strongly associated with NFL Films; and that his voice/delivery is the major basis of his appeal.[7]

The district court determined that although Facenda's appearance was brief, it added some commercial value to *The Making of Madden* that also belied the NFL's claims of incidental use. The Court of Appeals for the Third Circuit agreed with the district court's right of publicity analysis. Far from being seen as a threat to the public interest from the overprotection of intellectual property rights, Facenda was viewed as merely preserving his right to control his identity.

The court of appeals recognized that *Facenda* presented dueling intellectual property rights: the right of publicity versus copyright law. The narrative in *Facenda* represents a far different approach from the one taken in *White*. The Third Circuit's narrative is full of healthy respect and admiration for the famous and legendary voice

---

[7] Facenda v. N.F.L. Films, Inc., 488 F. Supp. 2d 491, 494 (E.D. Pa. 2007) *aff'd in part, vacated in part by* 542 F.3d 1007 (3d Cir. 2008).

of Facenda, and the court depicts Facenda as a legendary talent who is simply trying to guard his proprietary interest against overreaching by NFL.

B. *June Toney Obscure – Russell Christoff Distinguished: Implicit Bias in Misappropriation of Likeness Publicity Rights Cases*

The flattery given to Facenda's "legendary" voice is reminiscent of the description of the "distinguished appearance" of Russell Christoff, who won a $15.6 million jury verdict for Nestlé USA's misappropriation of the model turned kindergarten schoolteacher's right of publicity, which the jury (and later the appellate court) determined was violated when Nestlé USA used his image without authorization on its Taster's Choice coffee labels.[8]

In 1986, Christoff was paid $250 for his time and received a contract governing the use of his image, which was signed by his agent and by Nestlé Canada. The contract provided that, if Nestlé Canada used the picture on a label it was designing for a brick of coffee, Christoff would be paid $2,000 plus an agency commission.[9] Christoff's contract also provided that the price for any other use of Christoff's image would require further negotiations. Without informing Christoff or paying him according to the terms of the contract, Nestlé Canada used Christoff's image on the coffee brick. Fifteen years later, Nestlé USA obtained his photo from Nestlé Canada and featured it on Taster's Choice labels, newspaper coupons, and magazine ads in twenty-two countries.[10] Christoff had forgotten about the photo but when he finally noticed his image, he sued, alleging that Nestlé violated his statutory and common law rights of publicity.

When discussing the unauthorized use of Christoff's identity, even Nestlé itself took a most respectful tone when describing its actions:

> A decision was made to use Christoff's image because of his "distinguished" look and because he could create continuity with the original "taster" to whom the parties refer as Taster No. 1. Steele believed that she had authority to use Christoff's image because she knew it had been widely used in Canada. Steele never investigated the scope of the consent and never asked Christoff if he consented to the use of his image. Steele explained that "in talking to my colleague at Nestlé Canada, I believed that we had usage rights for the photo. So, I didn't think there was any need to [contact Christoff]."[11]

---

[8] Christoff v. Nestle USA, Inc., No. BC 36163, 2005 WL 5490764 (Trial Order) (Feb. 27, 2005), *rev'd by* 62 Cal. Rptr. 3d 122 (Ct. App. 2007).

[9] Christoff v. Nestle USA, Inc., 62 Cal. Rptr. 3d 122 (Ct. App. 2007).

[10] *Id*. at 127.

[11] *Id*. at 126–27.

Compare the praise heaped on Facenda and Russell with the linguistic treatment of June Toney. Ms. Toney authorized Johnson Products Company to use her likeness on the packaging of a hair-relaxer product from November 1995 to November 2000. She also authorized the use of her likeness in national magazine advertisements run from November 1995 to November 1996. The agreement anticipated future negotiation of additional uses of her likeness, which were governed by an express requirement to negotiate the terms of those uses separately. In August 2000, L'Oreal acquired the product line from a successor in interest to Johnson, and five months later Wella Corporation acquired the same from L'Oreal. Without renegotiating its use with Toney, L'Oreal and Wella used Toney's likeness in connection with packaging and promotion of the product line beyond the authorized time period. Although, like Vanna White, Toney ultimately won her case, the record is devoid of any judicial reverence, or mere respect, for Ms. Toney's interests, especially considering the pervasiveness of her image in the African American community.

Why? Why do we read about Facenda's "legendary voice" among football fans and Christoff's "distinguished appearance" among coffee consumers, and at the same time we read Judge Kozinski's disdain for Vanna White's claim that her persona is protected and we see no effusive praise for June Toney's characteristics? Why was the NFL's 13-second use of Facenda's voice on NFL products (or Nestle's use of Christoff's distinguished "appearance") seen as more deserving of protection from misappropriation than White's (or Toney's) identity? One answer could be that the judges who decided *Facenda* could identify more readily with sports broadcasting as a legitimate, masculine profession as opposed to White's profession of adorning a game-show stage. Another (and more cogent) reason for the distinguishing treatment is that reflexive, gender-based snap judgments were made about the seriousness of the respective claims based on who was bringing the publicity rights actions and what aspects of identity were being protected (e.g., the masculine, revered voice of a legend versus the generic appearance of a "comely woman," who should be able to see the humor in being spoofed without being compensated). And yet, what is the practical difference between a "voice" and an "appearance" (which, in any event, is a wildly uncharitable reduction of Vanna White's persona)? Both are innate. In fact, if anything, maintaining one's appearance (through, for example, diet and exercise) requires *more* industry than maintaining the tenor of one's voice. So the idea that a woman's persona is reduced to her appearance, and that her appearance is not unique and industrious in the same way that a sports announcer's voice is unique and industrious, does not hold water. In addition, because its grounding is not rooted in any sort of empirical (or even analytical) analysis, the illicit operation of implicit gender bias likely contributed to its formation.

IV. CONCLUSION

A starting point for addressing implicit bias in intellectual property law cases is to first accept that this area of the law is not race and gender neutral. The next step is to confront the legal fiction that institutional copyright interests are superior to publicity rights interests. Further, decision-makers should become aware of the disparate and discriminatory treatment that certain groups in society have suffered because of the structure of American copyright law. Finally, decision-makers should seek to probe the facts of each publicity rights case as thoroughly as was done for the plaintiffs in *Facenda v. N.F.L. Films* and *Russell Christoff v. Nestle USA, Incorporated*, with the goal of applying procedural and substantive rules to achieve distributive justice for publicity rights holders whose interests for far too long have been eclipsed by and subordinated to the interests of institutional copyright holders.

12

Environmental Law

A Tale of Two Neighborhoods: Implicit Bias and Environmental Decision-Making

Rachel D. Godsil

PROLOGUE: AN ENVIRONMENTAL JUSTICE STORY

For many people, Southampton, located on the Atlantic coast of Long Island, conjures up images of white, sandy beaches, quaint villages, and affluent summer visitors. East New York, Brooklyn, known during the 1980s and 1990s as the murder capital of New York City, elicits very different images: gangs, street violence, urban blight. Thomas Polsinelli, owner of Atlas Bio-Energy Corporation, owned a tract of land in each.

The two-acre tract in Southampton was fairly remote and adjacent to a railroad trestle; no homes or apartments or shops were located within a mile radius. The East New York tract was smaller, a half-acre, and, although zoned industrial, was located in a densely populated neighborhood. Atlas sought to benefit from the government's interest in (and funding for) alternative energy sources and developed a plan to construct a waste-wood to energy incinerator. The corporation initially concluded that the Southampton site was the better location for the waste-wood incinerator and submitted a proposal simultaneously to the state government energy fund for a start-up grant and to Southampton's town council. The state energy fund was very enthusiastic and approved Atlas for a grant. Atlas also negotiated a $6 million agreement to sell the energy. The township's reaction was quite different. The proposal was advertised in the local newspaper, and more than 200 residents showed up to protest the plan. Atlas quickly withdrew the proposal and decided to build the incinerator on its other property.

Concluding that community outreach was risky, Polsinelli decided to proceed with construction in his East New York site without seeking any environmental approvals from the city or state. Southampton was (and is) overwhelmingly white and affluent. East New York was (and is) overwhelmingly black, Latino, and poor. Did race influence Atlas's decision? Was Polsinelli a racist?

I. INTRODUCTION

The controversy over the proposed incinerator in East New York took place in 1995. I joined the NAACP Legal Defense Fund as the challenge to the incinerator began and worked with East New York residents and other organizations to form the East New York Community Committee against the Incinerator. The East New York story is one of many examples of communities of color challenging noxious land uses during a time in which evidence that people of color are more likely to be burdened by pollution and less likely to benefit from civic amenities galvanized the environmental justice movement in the late 1980s and 1990s.[1] Although many of these individual challenges were successful, people of color are still suffering the health-threatening impacts of pollution.

Using implicit social cognition as a lens, this chapter explores how race operates in contexts like the attempt to build the East New York incinerator and how to determine whether race influences decision-making. This lens provides a way to understand whether a beach town inhabited by affluent, white residents may be treated differently than a densely populated urban neighborhood even by those who hold consciously egalitarian values. This chapter also sets forth the civil rights jurisprudence in which a government or private act may be influenced by race without triggering a cognizable lawsuit.

In the East New York fight against the incinerator, we used several legal strategies that were race neutral as well as a political strategy that was highly racialized. This chapter concludes with a discussion of whether existing efforts to address environmental justice through state laws and modifications of federal environmental laws have been sufficiently protective of our most vulnerable communities or whether other strategies are necessary to overcome the implicit biases and structural barriers to equality.

A. *Racial Attitudes, Implicit Social Cognition, and Structural Racialization*

Atlas Corporation's belated application to the New York Department of Environmental Conservation (DEC) for a permit to locate an incinerator in East New York was initially approved without any environmental review. Many community members in East New York considered the decisions by both Atlas and the DEC to be racist, pure and simple. The memory of the battle remains fresh. The community resident who led the fight, former Black Panther Charles Barron, is now the City Council

---

[1] *See generally* CONFRONTING ENVIRONMENTAL RACISM: VOICES FROM THE GRASS ROOTS (Robert D. Bullard ed., 1993).

member for the area. Lending his support to another Brooklyn neighborhood's 2009 fight against a medical-waste transfer station, Barron argued:

> We have land transfer stations in the district, we have bus depots in the district.... They wanted to build a wood-burning incinerator in the district. This is racism in the rawest terms. They can take this somewhere else. There is someplace in the city where there are no residents, no day care centers, no schools.[2]

State Senator John Sampson agreed:

> This wouldn't happen on Fifth Avenue.... It wouldn't happen on the East Side. It wouldn't happen on the West Side of Manhattan. It's interesting that the only other facility of its kind is in the South Bronx, and we know what the health conditions there are.[3]

Barron's comment suggests that the decision to site a noxious land use in a black or Latino neighborhood is a product of hostility or animosity toward residents of these communities – that other options are available where no people will be harmed, but the decision-makers instead choose to burden a community of color. Sampson's claim is slightly different; he seems to be suggesting that decision-makers are reluctant or unwilling to burden an affluent white community with noxious land uses, which leaves them the only option of burdening a poor community of color. Is the distinction salient? Do most whites harbor the kind of active hostility that Barron suggests?

Not consciously. In the new millennium, most people in the United States of all races and ethnicities support the idea that all people are equal regardless of race and that laws should protect us all. Because most people consider themselves to be egalitarian, however, they are unwilling to acknowledge or perhaps are even unaware of the complexity of their attitudes and behaviors. Accordingly, the concept of implicit social cognition is a useful frame for understanding how someone can simultaneously embrace egalitarian values and yet harbor biases about a particular group.

Also important are the structural barriers to equal treatment that Sampson may have been alluding to in his suggestion that politicians are unlikely to locate certain kinds of facilities in affluent white neighborhoods. The overlap between race and poverty is not total. In total numbers, more white people are poor than blacks and Latinos (15.1 million whites compared to 9.2 blacks and 9.1 Latinos of any race); however, a significantly greater proportion of blacks and Latinos are poor (24% and 21%, respectively) than whites (10%).[4] Additionally, income disparities reflect only

---

[2] Helen Klein *Waste Station Fallout – Many Allege "Environmental Racism,"* YOURNABE.COM (January 22, 2009), http://www.yournabe.com/articles/2009/01/22/brooklyn/doc497922250632363199923.txt.
[3] *Id.*
[4] Current Population Survey (CPS), Annual Social and Economic (ASEC) Supplement, Below 100% of Poverty – White Alone, U.S. CENSUS BUREAU (2007). http://pubdb3.census.gov/macro/032008/

a facet of the wealth and opportunity gap between whites and people of color.[5] For purposes of environmental justice, the most significant structural dimension is residential segregation.[6] Although residential segregation is slowly waning in the United States, blacks and Latinos are vastly more likely to live in segregated communities and in communities with high concentrations of poverty than are whites, even holding income constant.[7]

Many who focus on civil rights issues in law and other disciplines are familiar with the structural barriers to equality described briefly here. However, they are less familiar with the role of the psychological constructs, both in creating obstacles to overcome the structural barriers and in their effect on micro and macro decisions that affect individuals and communities. In this chapter, therefore, I explore the link between structural racialization (a term coined by john powell[8]) and implicit bias and how the two work in concert to produce entrenched inequality.

As other chapters in this book have explained, we all engage in implicit cognition in order to function in the world. We automatically draw on "schemas" to impose order on the vast amount of sensory input we perceive on a constant basis.[9] How do we know what to do when we hear a ringing sound from a small device? Because we automatically place the small device into our schema for "cell phone," we answer it without stopping to consider alternative actions that the ringing might require. However, when imposed on groups of people rather than objects, these schemas – or categories – run the risk of becoming stereotypes.

Stereotypes are problematic: they cause us to make assumptions (both negative and positive) about people based on superficial characteristics. They often have the effect of distorting our judgments about individuals and tend to be self-perpetuating and therefore deeply entrenched. Race, not surprisingly, creates some of the most powerfully entrenched stereotypes. Implicit bias, then, refers to the phenomenon in which negative stereotypes or associations about different groups are automatically activated in people's minds, regardless of the conscious views the individual might

pov/new01_100_02.htm; *see also* Current Population Survey (CPS), Annual Social and Economic (ASEC) Supplement, Below 100% of Poverty – Black Alone, U.S. CENSUS BUREAU (2007), http://pubdb3.census.gov/macro/032008/pov/new01_100_06.htm.

5 *See, e.g.*, Thomas M. Shapiro et al., *The Racial Wealth Gap Increases Fourfold*, Institute on Assets and Social Policy (May 2010), http://iasp.brandeis.edu/pdfs/Racial-Wealth-Gap-Brief.pdf (finding a wealth gap of $95,000 between whites and blacks).

6 *See* Rachel D. Godsil, *Viewing the Cathedral from Behind the Color Line: Property Rules, Liability Rules, and Environmental Racism*, 53 EMORY L. J. 1809 (2004).

7 *Residential Segregation of Blacks or African Americans: 1980–2000*, in U.S. CENSUS BUREAU, CENSUS 1980, 1990, AND 2000 SUMMARY FILE 1, http://www.census.gov/hhes/www/housing/housing_patterns/pdf/ch5.pdf.

8 *See, e.g.*, Jason Reece et al., *The Geography of Opportunity Mapping to Promote Equitable Community Development and Fair Housing in King County, WA* (April 2009), http://4909e99d35cada63e7f757471b7243be73e53e14.gripelements.com/publications/king_county_wa_opportunity_mapping_apr_2010.pdf.

9 *See* Jerry Kang, *Trojan Horses of Race*, 118 HARV. L. REV. 1489, 1498 (2005).

have toward that group. The Implicit Association Test (IAT) and other measures used to assess the prevalence of implicit bias have found bias toward racial and ethnic minorities to be high.[10] Indeed, 75 percent of whites show anti-black bias – as do 50 percent of blacks.[11]

For purposes of environmental decision-making, implicit attitudes matter only if they affect behavior, but evidence suggests that they are likely to have such an effect. Studies have shown that implicit attitudes are better predictors of certain kinds of behavior than are self-reported attitudes.[12] The behaviors affected by implicit bias range from decisions to deny allocation of scarce and important resources such as jobs and medical treatment to stigmatized groups, to an unwillingness to interact socially with members of such groups.[13]

To date, no one has studied the precise issue of whether implicit bias affects decision-making about environmental protection. However, studies of the correlation between race and environmental risk provide ample reasons to explore the issue. Scores of studies have documented that communities made up primarily by people of color suffer a disproportionate burden of various forms of pollution.[14] The vast majority of studies also conclude that race is a more powerful predictor of environmental risk than poverty. Our initial challenge is to understand the nodes of decision-making that determine which communities are being burdened by pollution. We can then hypothesize both how implicit bias may affect decision-making in the context of environmental protection and how it may be possible to ameliorate the effects of implicit bias in this critical area.

II. LANDSCAPE OF ENVIRONMENTAL PROTECTION

Environmental protection, unlike many other areas of concern to civil rights advocates, is rarely experienced individually. Rather, whether a person is adequately protected from pollutants tends to depend on the place or places in which the person spends most of his or her time, such as home, work, school, or recreational facilities. Some of those places have high degrees of air pollution, or abut contaminated water supplies, or encase contaminated land. If particular individuals – regardless of race – can leave a highly polluted place and live and work in a place

---

[10] Anthony Greenwald & Linda Hamilton Krieger, *Implicit Bias: Scientific Foundations*, 94 CAL. L. REV. 957–58 (2006).

[11] Jerry Kang & Mahzarin Banaji, *Fair Measures: A Behavioral Realist Revision of Affirmative Action*, 94 CAL. L. REV. 1063, 1073 (2006).

[12] A.G. Greenwald et al., *Understanding and Using the Implicit Association Test: III. Meta-Analysis of Predictive Validity*, 97 J. PERSONALITY & SOC. PSYCHOL. 17–41 (2009), http://faculty.washington.edu/agg/pdf/GPU&B.meta-analysis.JPSP.2009.pdf.

[13] *Id.*

[14] *See* CLIFFORD RECHSTSCHAFFEN ET AL., ENVIRONMENTAL JUSTICE LAW, POLICY, AND REGULATION 36–69 (2d ed. 2009). *See also* LUKE W. COLE & SHEILA FOSTER, FROM THE GROUND UP: ENVIRONMENTAL RACISM AND THE RISE OF THE ENVIRONMENTAL JUSTICE MOVEMENT 167–184 (2001).

with cleaner air and water, their racial status will not "follow them" in the way it does with employment, housing, criminal justice, or education, where bias is often directed at and felt on the individual level.

Therefore, in the environmental context, we focus on the racialized places that experience these disparities, recognizing that people from multiple racial groups may live or work in an area that may be thought of as a "black community" or a "Latino community."[15] However, it is also important to realize that people experience the same levels of pollution differently depending on their levels of vulnerability to various pollutants and to their exposure. These two variables – vulnerability and exposure levels – may also differ depending on race, class, and culture. A person who consumes fish from local rivers regularly, either because of economic necessity or cultural norms, will be harmed by lower levels of water pollution than will those for whom the local rivers are merely scenic.[16] Children with asthma or elderly people will experience air pollution more acutely than healthy young adults.[17]

Therefore if our goal is to protect people equally from the harms of pollution, rather than simply provide the "same" levels of environmental protection for everyone, then we must be cognizant both of who lives or works in the places that are most polluted and what baselines of vulnerability we measure when we are setting acceptable levels of pollution or exposure.

A. Who Decides?

Many environmental protection decisions are made in the first instance by private actors. For example, industries decide where to seek to locate polluting facilities. They also decide how to transport materials in and out of their buildings – with trucks or boats – and how much to spend on pollution control devices to prevent air and water pollution. Private industry officials also decide how careful to be with hazardous pollutants and whether to use particular chemicals or pesticides. Owners of apartment buildings and homes decide how much to spend to eradicate or encapsulate lead paint. Individuals decide whether to drive or use public transportation, how much energy to consume, and what types of cleansers to use. The combination of an untold number of private decisions has a critical impact both on the overall amount and distribution of pollution.

Private actors do not have free reign, however. Government actors at the federal, state, and local level establish many of the frameworks within which individual decisions are made. Broadly speaking, the federal government has established an

---

[15] *See* Elise C. Boddie, *Racial Territoriality*, 58 UCLA L. REV. 401 (2010).

[16] *See* NATIONAL ENVIRONMENTAL JUSTICE ADVISORY COUNCIL, FISH CONSUMPTION AND ENVIRONMENTAL JUSTICE 202 (November 2002), http://www.epa.gov/compliance/ej/resources/publications/nejac/fish-consump-report_1102.pdf.

[17] *See, e.g.*, G O'Connor et al. *Acute Respiratory Health Effects of Air Pollution on Asthmatic Children in US Inner Cities*, 121 J. ALLERGY & CLINICAL IMMUNOLOGY 1133 (2008).

environmental regulatory regime that sets certain limits for industry actors. Beginning in the late 1960s, Congress enacted an array of substantive environmental laws – the Clean Air Act, the Clean Water Act, the Resource Conservation Recovery Act, the Endangered Species Act – as well as two important process statutes: the National Environmental Procedure Act (NEPA) and the Toxic Release Inventory.[18]

To a significant degree the enforcement of these substantive laws has been delegated to the states, although the Environmental Protection Agency sets certain thresholds regarding levels of pollutants that may be emitted in the air and water; it has also created a National Priorities List for the sites most contaminated by hazardous wastes that were cleaned up with federal monies (the original superfund).[19] In addition to the delegation of many enforcement decisions to the states, virtually all permitting decisions for the location of particular sites are decided at the state level.[20] And states have delegated most land use regulation – zoning – to local governments.

B. *Where Bias May Come into Play*

As noted earlier, the ultimate distribution of environmental burdens and levels of environmental protection result from a complex interplay of private decisions with varying levels of governmental regulation by federal, state, and local actors. The tale of the waste-wood incinerator offers a useful illustration to explore how race may have intersected with private and government decision-making.

1. Private Actors

The first move was by Thomas Polsinelli, the owner of Atlas Bio-Energy. He first selected a primarily white area – Southampton – for his waste-wood incinerator. His decision likely was influenced by the size of the tract, its proximity to rail transport, and its distance from any residential neighborhoods. When he sought a permit from the town council, however, local residents were highly opposed despite the fact that the incinerator would not have been close to any of their homes. Their opposition was likely based on concern about increased air pollution and the stigma associated with incineration. These residents expressed their opposition by packing a town council meeting with reportedly 200 people. Polsinelli immediately withdrew his permit request. He then decided to build on his property in East New York.

---

[18] See generally RICHARD LAZARUS, THE MAKING OF ENVIRONMENTAL LAWS (2004). The major pieces of legislation include National Environmental Policy Act of 1969, 42 U.S.C. § 4321 (2000); Clean Air Act of 1963, 42 U.S.C. § 7401 (2000); Clean Water Act, 33 U.S.C. § 1251 (2000); Resource Conservation and Recovery Act of 1976, 42 U.S.C. § 6901 (2000); Comprehensive Environmental Response, Compensation, and Liability Act of 1980, 42 U.S.C. § 9601 (2000); and Toxic Substance Control Act of 1976, 15 U.S.C. § 2601 (1994).

[19] RECHSTSCHAFFEN ET AL., *supra* note 14.

[20] Rachel D. Godsil, *Remedying Environmental Racism*, 90 MICH. L. REV. 394, 402 (1991).

The fact that Polsinelli initially selected the Southampton tract is strong evidence that his primary reason for building in East New York was not active antipathy for the primarily black and Latino residents of the neighborhood. Yet his subsequent actions suggest that race may have been salient. Polsinelli withdrew his request for a permit in Southampton after the first showing of community opposition. By contrast, in East New York, he continued to proceed in the face of highly vocal and sustained community opposition. East New York residents not only packed meetings but also picketed by the hundreds in the heat of July in front of the site.

Certainly, Polsinelli's actions are consistent with John Sampson's view stated earlier – that affluent whites will prevent any sitings of unwanted land uses in their communities so the default will be poor and minority communities. This reasoning suggests that a structural account is useful: Polsinelli likely presumed that the affluent whites in Southampton were able to wield political power and had access to legal resources sufficient to prevent the location of an unwanted land use and therefore saw no reason to press on when the opposition was apparent. By contrast, he likely made the opposite set of assumptions about the residents of East New York. Structurally, East New Yorkers have fewer financial and political resources and seemed less able to exercise their will.

However, my personal experience in the case suggests that race may have been relevant more than simply as a default and that racial biases and attitudes may also have come into play. When community leaders Charles Barron and Carlos Bristol sought a meeting with Polsinelli, he was highly dismissive. Although he eventually agreed to talk with them, his attitude was condescending. Gender, age, and anti-establishment cultural mores may have also played a role: Barron and Bristol chose to have me (a young female lawyer) accompany them during the meeting rather than an older white male lawyer from another organization who sought to replace me for high-level meetings. Barron and Bristol also rejected certain dominant mores in their dress; both eschewed ties and traditional suits. It is, of course, possible that Polsinelli may have had the same response to Southampton community leaders, particularly if they appeared typical of "environmental activists" rather than professionals who own property. Yet Polsinelli's body language and attitudes during meetings with the residents of East New York were certainly consistent with studies showing that many whites have a high level of discomfort during in-person engagement with African Americans.[21]

This case could have ended with Polsinelli's decision to respect the community's opposition – as he had in Southampton – but for reasons we cannot know with certainty (a determination to make money from one of his two sites, less confidence that community opposition would prevail, less respect for community views, or

---

[21] See, e.g., Linda R. Tropp & Rebecca Bianchi, *Interpreting References to Group Membership in Context: Feelings About Intergroup Contact Depending on Who Says What to Whom*, 37 Eur. J. Soc. Psychol. 153, 154 (2006) (citing studies).

perhaps a level of condescension or even hostility for his opponents in East New York) he chose to persevere.

2. Government Regulators

The pollutants from the Atlas waste-wood incinerator were insufficient to render its construction a violation of the Clean Air Act, despite the fact that all of New York City was then (and is now) a nonattainment area for some pollutants under this act.[22] The first relevant level of government then was the federal Environmental Protection Agency (EPA) that sets air quality standards.[23] In the 1990s, many concerned with environmental justice criticized the EPA for failing to regulate air pollution adequately – the EPA did not yet monitor or regulate particulate matter below a certain size (which was later determined to be the most dangerous to those with respiratory vulnerability).[24] In addition, the EPA historically failed to consider the cumulative and synergistic effects of various pollutants on the population; instead, it evaluated the risk of each pollutant singly.[25] It was only in 2003, after much damage had already occurred, that the EPA initiated a program to consider the effects of cumulative risks.[26] These failures to regulate have affected most harshly those who are located in polluted areas who, as discussed earlier, are disproportionately people of color.

Do these failures reflect implicit bias or simply the scientific and political challenges of environmental regulation? It is difficult to answer this question with certainty, but whenever a harm is felt most acutely by a stigmatized group, we may find it fruitful to consider that implicit bias may be playing a role. Asthma rates and respiratory vulnerability are dire problems in polluted inner cities,[27] but may not be perceived as crises to the extent they would if they affected a white, affluent population to the same degree. This difference in perception is unlikely to be the result of any conscious animus on the part of regulators, but it may stem either from implicit biases that lead people to be less protective of outgroups or from a structural

---

[22] *See, e.g., Recommendations for 2008 Ozone NAAQS Nonattainment Areas Recommendations for 2008 Ozone NAAQS Nonattainment Areas*, NYS DEPT. OF ENVIRONMENTAL CONSERVATION (March 12, 2009), *available at* http://www.dec.ny.gov/chemical/52583.html.

[23] 42 U.S.C. § 7409 (2006).

[24] See RECHSTSCHAFFEN ET AL., *supra* note 14, at 218–19.

[25] See Rachel Morello-Frosch et al., *Environmental Justice and Southern California's "Riskscape": The Distribution of Air Toxics Exposures and Health Risks Among Diverse Communities*, 36 URB. AFFAIRS REV. 551 (2001).

[26] Michael A. Callahan & Ken Sexton, *Environmental Health Perspectives: If Cumulative Risk Assessment Is the Answer, What Is the Question?*, ENVIRON. HEALTH PERSPECT. (January 24, 2007), *available at* http://ehp03.niehs.nih.gov/article/fetchArticle.action?articleURI=info%3Adoi%2F10.1289%2Fehp.9330.

[27] *Respiratory Diseases – America's Children and the Environment: A First View of Available Measures, Children's Health Protection*, U.S. EPA, http://yosemite.epa.gov/ochp/ochpweb.nsf/content/respiratory_diseases.htm (last visited July 24, 2011).

account of politics that leads regulators to focus more attention on those with more political power.[28]

The federal government was not an active participant in the East New York case; instead, the permit decisions were initially the province of New York State's Department of Environmental Conservation (DEC). New York has a state version of the federal National Environmental Policy Act (NEPA), called the State Environmental Quality Review Act (SEQR), which requires an environmental impact statement whenever a proposed action "may" have a significant impact on the environment.[29] The environment is defined broadly to include human health and community character as well as traditional effects on the air and water.

Atlas submitted its permit application to the DEC and initially received a "negative declaration" stating that an environmental impact statement was unnecessary. This decision was highly questionable in light of the level of air pollutants the facility would emit and the close proximity of day care centers, residential homes, and residences for seniors. We were able to convince the DEC to change the decision and require an environmental impact statement merely by sending them a short letter – litigation was unnecessary. What explains the DEC's initial decision?

The negative declaration may have been another moment in which implicit biases influenced otherwise egalitarian actors. I think it was highly unlikely that the DEC regulators who made the initial decision held active racial animus. I met with them when we reviewed the file, and they struck me as people who would subscribe to the accepted egalitarian norms of our society. Their decision to quickly withdraw the negative declaration provides some support for this conclusion – they did not dig in and try to support their initial decision.

Yet I am equally confident that the initial decision would not have been made if the incinerator had been located in a predominantly white Brooklyn neighborhood. Like physicians who make different treatment recommendations for blacks based on a set of unrecognized preconceptions,[30] I think it is entirely possible that the DEC regulators did not view the environmental effects as salient because of an underlying, unconscious set of assumptions about East New York and its residents. What's the harm of a little pollution in the murder capital of New York? The passion that East New York residents showed in the face of the possibility of more pollution in their community was likely a surprise to many.

Was the East New York incinerator fight about race? I think so. If Polsinelli had viewed community residents of East New York in the same light as he viewed

---

[28] *See* Gary Blasi & John T. Jost, *System Justification Theory and Research: Implications for Law, Legal Advocacy, and Social Justice*, 94 CAL. L. REV. 1119 (2006).

[29] 617: *State Environmental Quality Review*, NYS DEPT. OF ENVIRONMENTAL CONSERVATION, http://www.dec.ny.gov/regs/4490.html (last visited July 24, 2011) (Statutory authority: Environmental Conservation Law Sections 3–0301(1)(b), 3–0301(2)(m) and 8–0113).

[30] Alexander R. Green et al., *Implicit Bias Among Physicians and Its Prediction of Thrombolysis Decisions for Black and White Patients*, 22 J. GEN. INTERNAL MED. 1231 (2007).

the Southampton folks who opposed his first attempt to build his incinerator, he likely would have withdrawn in the face of their opposition or perhaps recognized after the Southampton experience that an incinerator would not be welcome near any residential community. If the percentage of white children who suffered from asthma were as high as the percentage of asthmatic black and Latino children, we might have had more aggressive regulation of certain air pollutants earlier. If the permit submitted to the DEC involved a proposed incinerator in Park Slope, Brooklyn, rather than East New York, I am confident the state would not have issued a negative declaration.

Were any of the actors "racists" in the sense that they held active animus against individual black or Latino people? I do not think so. Yet this fact did not change the outcome. Even though the actors involved probably considered themselves nonracist and subscribed to the view that all people are equal, they made decisions they may well not have made had the community involved been comprised of mostly white people.

Many East New York community members argued that their civil rights were being violated, that the law was not treating them equally. During many meetings in church basements and community centers, I agreed. Yet I also explained that a civil rights lawsuit was not likely to be successful and that instead we should pursue a strategy relying on environmental laws. This strategy was frustrating to many. In the next section I explain why I recommended a legal strategy that did not emphasize race.

III. LIMITS TO CIVIL RIGHTS JURISPRUDENCE

The Fourteenth Amendment to the Constitution promises "equal protection" under the law and was enacted after the Civil War to ensure legal equality to the freed slaves.[31] The equal protection clause is also the most well-known source of legal authority for significant civil rights victories, particularly *Brown v. Board of Education*.[32] Reasonably then, when civil rights lawyers work with people who believe that they are being treated differently because of their race, the assumed lawsuit is a civil rights suit to seek equal protection and to protect the individuals' constitutional rights.

In an era in which most people consciously subscribe to egalitarian norms, however, such a lawsuit is likely to lose because of the Supreme Court's construction of the scope of the equal protection clause. Beginning in 1976, in *Washington v. Davis*,[33] the Supreme Court interpreted the equal protection clause to prohibit only actions that lawyers can prove were "intended" to discriminate on the basis

---

[31] *See, e.g.*, Strauder v. West Virginia, 100 U.S. 303 (1879).
[32] 347 U.S. 483 (1954).
[33] 426 U.S. 229 (1976).

of race. This case followed a spate of cases beginning with *Brown* in which civil rights plaintiffs successfully challenged de jure segregation in schools and many other spheres of life. *Washington v. Davis*, by contrast, did not involve an explicitly racial statute or action; rather, it challenged an examination that was a precondition for employment as a police officer in Washington, D.C., that disproportionately excluded black applicants. The Court refused to find the use of the test a violation of the equal protection clause, holding that the fact that a government action has a disparate impact on a particular racial group is not sufficient. Instead, the Court adopted the "intent" standard, which it refined in subsequent decisions to refer to a decision made "because of" not merely "in spite" of its effect on a particular group.[34]

I explained to community residents that it would be very difficult to argue that the government actors were considering the application for the waste-wood incinerator "because" the community comprised predominantly African American and Latino residents. The DEC's initial negative declaration was aberrant, but it was reversed quickly when challenged. Then the DEC began the environmental impact statement process, which was standard practice. I also explained that to date, no one had won an equal protection challenge to the siting of a noxious land use – even when the facts seemed compelling.

Several lawyers tried to bring such cases in the 1980s, but every one was unsuccessful.[35] Some involved facts that seemed to be in powerful support of a conclusion that race dictated the government's decision; for instance, a waste landfill sited 1,000 feet from a high school and a county in which all of the landfills were in black neighborhoods (the single landfill in a white neighborhood was shut down after the community protested). Yet, in each case, even when willing to concede that the decision itself seemed unreasonable (the landfill near the high school), the judge was unwilling to conclude that the government actors acted with the intention of denying equal protection of the laws based on race.

The mind sciences offer us insight into why plaintiffs have difficulty prevailing in a suit requiring proof of discriminatory intent: the standard encourages empathy with the government actor. The judge is asked to conclude that the government actor possessed a certain state of mind (discriminatory intent) that is deeply antithetical to American values. To reach this decision, the judge naturally places him- or herself in the position of the government actor, which gives rise to a fairly automatic tendency to justify the actions as a result of something other than racism unless some sort of smoking gun evidence proves otherwise.[36] In addition, in a case that involves government testimony, the government actor likely did not act with conscious racial animus and therefore is persuasive when testifying. Yet as discussed earlier in this

---

[34] Personnel Administrator v. Feeney, 442 U.S. 256 (1979).

[35] For discussion, *see* Godsil, *supra* note 20, at 410–16 (1991).

[36] *See* Rachel D. Godsil, *Expressivism, Empathy, and Equality*, 36 U. MICH. J.L. REFORM 247 (2003).

chapter and in this book in general, most of us are unaware that implicit bias may have been at play in our decision-making. Beginning with Charles Lawrence's iconic article, *The Id, the Ego, and Unconscious Racism*,[37] the intent standard has been criticized as problematic for these reasons.

In the 1990s, administrative regulations to Title VI of the Civil Rights Act of 1964 offered a possible alternative to the intent standard.[38] Although the Supreme Court considered Title VI itself to be coterminous with the equal protection clause and therefore required proof of intent, federal agencies' regulations contained a different standard. These regulations prohibited any entity that receives funding from the federal government from conducting its programs and practices in a way that has the *effect* of discriminating on the basis of race.[39]

Several suits were brought that successfully challenged government programs under Title VI's regulations. Among the most notable was a 1996 challenge to the Los Angeles Metropolitan Transit Agency's funding scheme, *Labor/Community Strategy Center v. Los Angeles County Metropolitan Transportation Authority* (MTA).[40] The MTA intended to spend billions of dollars funding light rail from predominantly white neighborhoods to downtown while it cut funding to buses that operated in predominantly communities of color. This suit would likely not have been successful under the equal protection clause – the stated justification for the funding decision was the need to address the air pollution resulting from commuters from outlying suburbs. However, the Transit Riders Union and its lawyers at the NAACP Legal Defense Fund and the Southern California ACLU presented a compelling case of the funding stream's disparate impact: buses were overcrowded, bus routes were being cut, and many of the riders had no other transportation options. In addition, the light rail was bypassing neighborhoods in which many people of color lived. In 1996, on the eve of trial, the parties agreed to, and the district court approved, a consent decree that committed MTA "to a wide array of improvements in its bus services, including instituting new bus lines to and from centers of employment, education, and health care in the county; ... enhancing security on buses; improving bus shelters; and maintaining its fares at specific levels."[41]

In *South Camden Citizens in Action v. New Jersey Department of Environmental Protection*, in 2000, a community group challenged a permit to locate a cement plant in an already highly polluted neighborhood in Camden, New Jersey.[42] The

---

[37] Charles R. Lawrence III, *The Id, the Ego, and Equal Protection: Reckoning with Unconscious Racism*, 39 Stan. L. Rev. 317 (1987).

[38] See Richard Lazarus, *Pursuing "Environmental Justice": The Distributional Effects of Environmental Protection*, 87 Nw. U. L. Rev.787 (1993).

[39] See 40 C.F.R. § 7.35(b) (1984).

[40] Labor/Community Strategy Ctr. v. L.A. Cnty. Metro. Transp. Auth., 263 F.3d 1041, 1043 (9th Cir. 2001).

[41] *Id.*

[42] *See* S. Camden Citizens in Action v. N.J. Dep't of Envtl. Prot., 145 F. Supp. 2d 446 (D.N.J. 2001).

community group contended that New Jersey's Department of Environmental Protection (NJDEP) violated Title VI's regulations in issuing permits to polluting sources located disproportionately in black and Latino neighborhoods. The NJDEP claimed that it did not consider race in its permit decisions and therefore argued that its actions were not in violation of Title VI's regulations. The federal judge issued an order enjoining the cement plant from operating and found that the plaintiffs' data showing a disparate impact from the permits granted by the NJDEP were sufficient to require NJDEP to justify its decisions and that failing to consider the racial impacts of its actions when it was receiving federal funds subject to Title VI's regulations was itself problematic. This victory lasted for five days. It was upended when the Supreme Court handed down a decision in *Alexander v. Sandoval*,[43] holding that individuals lack a private right of action to enforce the Title VI regulations. With the loss of the right to sue under Title VI's regulations, the civil rights laws no longer seemed to be a promising source for a legal challenge.

IV. OVERCOMING IMPLICIT BIAS AND STRUCTURAL RACIALIZATION IN ENVIRONMENTAL DECISION-MAKING

This part discusses actions that have been taken to address environmental disparities and considers whether they are adequate to address the potential for both implicit bias and structural obstacles to equality.

A. *Environmental Justice at the Federal Level*

In the early 1990s, as advocates organized and protested around issues of environmental justice, President Clinton issued an Executive Order on Environmental Justice. It required federal agencies to do the following:

> Conduct programs, policies, and activities that substantively affect human health or the environment, in a manner that ensures that [they] do not have the effect of excluding persons (including populations) from participating in, denying persons (including populations) the benefits of, or subjecting persons (including populations) to discrimination under, such programs, policies, and activities, because of their race, color, or national origin.[44]

The Executive Order provides some detail, requiring agency strategies to promote enforcement of health and environmental statutes, ensuring public participation, improving research and data collection, and identifying different patterns of consumption of natural resources, including fish and wildlife. It does not, however, contain a private right of action, but instead states that it is "intended only to improve

---

[43] 532 U.S. 275 (2001).
[44] Exec. Order No. 12, 898, 3 CFR 859 (1994), *reprinted in* 42 U.S.C. § 4321 (2006).

internal management of the executive branch."[45] Many advocates have argued that without a right to sue, the Executive Order is of little utility because its hortatory nature is unlikely to have any significant impact. According to a number of analyses of agency actions following the order's enactment, this concern proved true under both the Clinton and Bush administrations.[46]

Many advocates hoped that the Obama administration would prove more receptive to environmental justice concerns; in certain important respects, it has been. It created a White House Inter-Agency Working Group and has reached out to activists and community groups with requests for input and with offers of grants to address local health and environmental justice issues.[47] However, advocates remain concerned that other interests will prove too powerful and will prevent the EPA from addressing substantive concerns. For example, in February 2011, the EPA announced its plan to exempt an air permit at a California power plant in a largely Latino community from new nitrogen dioxide (NO_2), greenhouse gas (GHG), and other limits that have taken effect.[48] As troubling, the EPA has refused to install air monitors immediately adjacent to major highways. Often, it is low-income and communities of color who suffer the localized effects of the car and truck pollution, but it is impossible to accurately measure how much without appropriately located air monitors.

B. Environmental Justice at the State Level

Before the *Sandoval* case, some state governments and private actors became concerned about possible legal liability (in the case of government) or obstacles to efficient siting of facilities (in the case of large corporations) if their decisions could be shown to have a disparate impact based on race. This concern and, undoubtedly, the desire to conform to the ideal of providing equal protection prompted many states to enact Environmental Justice Statutes.[49] Indeed, by 2007, forty-one states devoted some attention and resources to addressing issues of environmental justice.[50] However, few of these statutes provide individuals with a private right of

---

[45] *Id.* at 6–609.

[46] *See, e.g.*, Denis Binder et al., *A Survey of Federal Agency Responses to President Clinton's Executive Order 12898 on Environmental Justice*, 31 ENVT. L. REP. 11,133 (2001); BRADFORD C. MANK, EXECUTIVE ORDER 12,898 in THE LAW OF ENVIRONMENTAL JUSTICE THEORIES AND PROCEDURES TO ADDRESS DISPROPORTIONATE RISKS 101, 103 (Michael B. Gerrard & Sheila R. Foster eds. 2d ed. 2008). For other reports, *see* RECHSTSCHAFFEN ET AL., *supra* note 14.

[47] *See, e.g.*, *Environmental Justice Small Grants Program*, U.S. EPA (last updated on April 20, 2011), http://www.epa.gov/environmentaljustice/grants/ej-smgrants.html.

[48] Dawn Reeves, *EPA Sets High Bar for GHG Limits in First 2011 Permit, Prompting Worries*, InsideEPA. com (February 2, 2011), https://environmentalnewsstand.com/OLD-Clean-Energy-Report-Daily-News/Daily-News/epa-sets-high-bar-for-ghg-limits-in-first-2011-permit-prompting-worries/menu-id-1. html.

[49] For a matrix of state initiatives citing a Fifty State Survey, *see* RECHSTSCHAFFEN ET AL., *supra* note 14, http://www.uchastings.edu/site_files/plri/EJ2007.pdf.

[50] *Id.*

action. Instead, most focus on a combination of community participation, funding for technical grants for community groups, and the consideration of the demographics of communities during permitting decisions.

How well these statutes fared depends on the level of expectations we bring. Like their federal counterpart, the statutes have often resulted in greater inclusion of community representatives on community advisory boards and the like. Many require consideration of the effect on environmental justice communities before decisions are made.[51] Yet advocates argue that even states considered to be on the cutting edge, such as California, still engage in practices that disproportionately harm communities of color. California's poor air quality continues to be a problem that harms communities of color most acutely – and a federal court recently found its State Implementation Plan to be inadequate after being challenged by community groups represented by the Natural Resources Defense Council.[52]

C. *Implicit Bias and Structural Racialization*

Are the inadequacies of protection at the federal and state level issues of implicit bias or a structural obstacle, such as posed by powerful economic interests, or both? Many of those working at the EPA under the Obama administration or in government in California are committed to environmental justice concerns; in fact at the federal level many were environmental justice advocates before entering the administration (and, in the interests of full disclosure, are people with whom I worked and are often my friends). So they (and I) would argue that decisions like the one described earlier may not be motivated by *their* implicit biases. Yet I would suggest that the implicit biases and ingroup preferences that many voters possess result in less concern and respect for communities of color and, in turn, make attempts by environmental justice advocates to challenge powerful economic interests vastly more difficult. It is the synergy of structure and bias that proves difficult to unseat.

We know that implicit biases can be ameliorated and, particularly, that decision-makers can self-correct.[53] However, the attitudes and preferences of decision-makers are only part of the equation. For environmental protection to be equally distributed, decision-makers need not only to correct their own potential biases but also need the political cover to challenge powerful and entrenched interests. Therefore, voters' implicit biases are also salient. The structural racialization that results in segregated communities and fewer economic opportunities for people of color challenges the sense that we are all part of the same community of interest and reifies stereotypes. Moreover, the current climate in which attempts to discuss the effects of race are

---

[51] *Id.* at 5.
[52] Association of Irritated Residents v. U.S. E.P.A., 632 F.3d 584 (9th Cir. 2011), *available at* http://www.ca9.uscourts.gov/datastore/opinions/2011/02/02/09–71383.pdf.
[53] *See e.g.*, Kang & Banaji, *supra* note 11, at 1090–93.

often deemed "playing the race card" undercuts our ability to address these issues explicitly, which is necessary to invite voters to self-correct against bias.

V. CONCLUSION

The East New York challenge ended with a resounding victory for the community, but not because we prevailed on our argument that race had infected environmental decision-making. Instead, the community organizing resulted in local knowledge that unearthed an obscure city law.[54] The story has some very hopeful elements: our community organization was multiracial at every level, and the community leader, Charles Barron, used the victory as a platform for his election to office. Other individual communities have had analogous victories against unwanted land uses, but as a country, we have quite a way to go to provide equality in environmental protection.

---

[54] To stop the many apartment building incinerators from polluting, the city passed a law in the early 1970s making waste burning illegal. It stated, "No person shall cause or permit the installation of refuse burning equipment." The law specifically mentioned "wood" as a kind of waste if discarded.

13

Federal Indian Law

Implicit Bias against Native Peoples as Sovereigns

Susan K. Serrano and Breann Swann Nuʻuhiwa

In the midst of a contentious political debate about Native Hawaiian sovereignty, former Hawaiʻi governor Linda Lingle implored the U.S. Senate to reject the "Akaka Bill," proposed legislation designed to restore a small measure of self-governance to the Native Hawaiian people. In short, the bill would facilitate the formal recognition of Native Hawaiians as a self-governing Native community, bringing their political and legal status roughly on par with that of other Native peoples in the United States.[1] Lingle based her opposition, in part, on the unfounded assumption that a Native Hawaiian government with self-governing powers similar to those possessed by Native American and Native Alaskan governments would exercise those powers "in a way that is inconsistent with State criminal statutes otherwise applicable to all citizens, and inconsistent with virtually every conceivable state law that serves to protect the public." She also maintained that restoring Native Hawaiian self-governance would require the state to develop a plan to "enforce its interests against

The authors thank Justin Levinson, Kapua Sproat, and Eric Yamamoto for their valuable comments; Nat Noda for his proofreading and citation expertise; and law students Eryn Reyes and Aitofele Sunia for their outstanding research assistance.

[1] The United States maintains government-to-government relationships with more than five hundred Native American and Alaska Native communities. See Indian Entities Recognized and Eligible to Receive Services from the United States Bureau of Indian Affairs, 75 FED. REG. 60,810, 60,814 (Oct. 1, 2010). However, the federal government has neither formally recognized Native Hawaiians as a self-governing Native community on par with federally recognized Native Americans and Alaska Natives nor confirmed a government-to-government relationship with the Native Hawaiian people. The Native Hawaiian Government Reorganization Act (colloquially referred to as the "Akaka Bill" after its chief sponsor, Senator Daniel Akaka) seeks to rectify this political and legal disparity between Native Hawaiians and federally recognized Native Americans and Alaska Natives by (1) reaffirming that the United States has a special political and legal relationship with Native Hawaiians that is generally of the same type and nature as the "relationship the United States has with the several federally recognized Indian tribes" and (2) providing a process for the reorganization of a Native Hawaiian governing entity within the framework of federal law. S.675, 112th Cong. §§ 2(20), 3(14), 4(a)(1)-(2) (2011).

unlawful or irresponsible actions by the [Native Hawaiian] governing entity or its elected leaders or employees."[2] Although the public will probably never know the extent to which Lingle's opposition stymied the bill's progress, her opposition is significant because it highlights a pernicious process that functions to dispossess Native peoples of land, resources, and governing authority.

This process began nearly two centuries ago when European Americans began using U.S. law and legal discourse to justify the appropriation of Native lands, resources, and governing authority. To legitimize the dispossession, European Americans stereotyped Native peoples as a foreign race of savages who lacked the requisite knowledge and industry to exercise full sovereignty. Reinforced by literature and media, the image of Native peoples as "nothing more than wandering hordes, held together only by ties of blood and habit, and having neither laws or government, beyond what is required in a savage state,"[3] came to dominate. Within a few generations, this negative stereotype became an unquestioned assumption that formed the basis of contemporary implicit bias against Native peoples.

Implicit bias is a pervasive phenomenon characterized by the automatic activation of stereotypes or attitudes about other social groups. Without conscious direction, the human mind draws on cognitive filters – constructed in part by accumulated knowledge, experiences, and cultural influences – to organize people into social categories such as race and to attribute characteristics to those categories. These cognitive shortcuts cause the mind to make assumptions about other people, distort judgment and memory, and trigger discriminatory behaviors, even when one consciously rejects negative stereotypes and discrimination.[4] Accordingly, although contemporary discourse openly denounces stereotyping of Native peoples, empirical studies show that modern-day implicit bias corresponds with the age-old negative stereotype.

What the studies do not explain, but we aim to demonstrate in this chapter, is that implicit bias against Native peoples advances the continuing dispossession of Native land, resources, and governing authority in much the same way that explicit bias advanced the initial dispossession. We begin by describing the dominant stereotype

---

[2] Letter from Linda Lingle, former governor of the State of Hawaiʻi, to U.S. Senator (Mar. 23, 2010) (on file with authors).

[3] Cherokee Nation v. Georgia, 30 U.S. 1 (1831).

[4] *See* Linda Hamilton Krieger, *The Content of Our Categories: A Cognitive Bias Approach to Discrimination and Equal Employment Opportunity*, 47 STAN. L. REV. 1161, 1188 (1995); Anthony G. Greenwald & Linda Hamilton Krieger, *Implicit Bias: Scientific Foundations*, 94 CAL. L. REV. 945, 951, 961 (2006); Jerry Kang, *Trojan Horses of Race*, 118 HARV. L. REV. 1489 (2005); Justin D. Levinson, *Forgotten Racial Equality: Implicit Bias, Decisionmaking, and Misremembering*, 57 DUKE L.J. 345 (2007); Jerry Kang & Mahzarin R. Banaji, *Fair Measures: A Behavioral Realist Revision of "Affirmative Action,"* 94 CAL. L. REV. 1063 (2006); Gary Blasi, *Advocacy Against the Stereotype: Lessons from Cognitive Social Psychology*, 49 UCLA L. REV. 1241 (2002); Christine Jolls & Cass R. Sunstein, *The Law of Implicit Bias*, 94 CAL. L. REV. 969 (2006); Linda Hamilton Krieger & Susan T. Fiske, *Behavioral Realism in Employment Discrimination Law: Implicit Bias and Disparate Treatment*, 94 CAL. L. REV. 997 (2006); Kristin A. Lane et al., *Implicit Social Cognition and Law*, 3 ANN. REV. L. SOC. SCI. 427, 438 (2007).

of Native peoples and how it was used to assert privilege over and aggression against Native peoples. We then consider specific assumptions underlying the dominant stereotype and explore how those assumptions, manifesting as implicit bias, undergird modern barriers to Native self-governance, such as legislation, case law, and administrative action limiting Native peoples' governing power. In conclusion, we propose that eliminating implicit bias against Native peoples as sovereigns is an integral element of a larger, ongoing project to repatriate Native land, resources, and governing authority to their rightful possessors, and we suggest potential ways to facilitate elimination of the bias.

I. CREATING THE DOMINANT STEREOTYPE OF NATIVE PEOPLES

Kevin Gover, director of the National Museum of the American Indian, described modern negative portrayals of Native peoples as "a continuation of a process that began a long time ago to define [Native peoples] in a very limited way, as less than human, in order to rationalize the dispossession."[5] In other words, contemporary portrayals perpetuate the negative stereotype of Native peoples created in the eighteenth and nineteenth centuries to justify the appropriation of Native territory and political power. That original stereotype was produced by racializing Native peoples to diminish their political identities, attributing negative characteristics to them in their group capacity, and conjuring legitimacy for the negative attributions by injecting them into law and legal discourse.

A. *Transforming Native Peoples into a Race*

At the time of its creation, the newly formed U.S. government possessed inferior claims to land, resources, and political control within its claimed territory than the Native polities that had been operating in that same territory for millennia. To justify its exercise of dominion, the burgeoning nation needed to recast the pivotal *legal-political* question – whether one sovereign may unilaterally dispossess another sovereign of its territory and political power – as a *racial* question about the competing rights of the European Americans who controlled the colonizing government and the Native peoples who controlled the preexisting Native governments.[6] The recasting of this question transformed the image of Native peoples in the collective American consciousness from "potentially equal governments burdened solely by lack of religion and civilization to barbarous natives whose differences were rooted

---

[5] Courtland Milloy, *It's Time Once Again to Tell Washington's Football Team to Ditch the 'Redskins' Racist Moniker*, WASH. POST, Jan. 4, 2011, *available at* http://www.washingtonpost.com/wp-dyn/content/article/2011/01/04/AR2011010405217.html.

[6] Bethany R. Berger, *Red: Racism and the American Indian*, 56 UCLA L. REV. 591, 599 (2009); Carole Goldberg, *Descent into Race*, 49 UCLA L. REV. 1373, 1373–74 (2002).

in nature."[7] Bethany Berger describes this act of racializing Native peoples to diminish their political identities as "the basic racist move at work in Indian law and policy."[8]

Examples of this "basic racist move" appear repeatedly in Supreme Court jurisprudence. For instance, in its 1846 decision, *U.S. v. Rogers*, the Court considered whether a "white man" treated, recognized, and adopted by the Cherokee as a tribal member entitled to all the rights and privileges of membership could be considered a Cherokee under the Intercourse Act of 1834. Denying that Mr. Rogers was a "Cherokee" under the act, the Court averred that, although adoption by the Cherokee might entitle Mr. Rogers to certain privileges in the tribe and make him amenable to their laws and usages, "he is not an Indian; and the exception is confined to those who by the usages and customs of the Indians are regarded as belonging to their race. It does not speak of members of a tribe, but of the race generally, . . . of the family of Indians."[9] Similar racializing language appears in other early Supreme Court decisions such as *U.S. v. McKee* (1875) and *Beecher v. Wetherby* (1877).[10]

Treating Native peoples as a race rather than a collection of independent political entities not only allowed the United States to recast difficult questions regarding Native rights to land, resources, and governing authority but it also enabled the fledgling nation to use classic racist discursive strategies[11] to justify its colonial domination. For example, in a 1783 letter to New York State Senator James Duane, George Washington equated Native Americans with "wild beasts" to justify the United States' westward encroachment into Indian territory:

> [P]olicy and economy point very strongly to the expediency of being upon good terms with the Indians, and the propriety of purchasing their Lands in preference to attempting to drive them by force of arms out of their Country; which as we have already experienced is like driving the *Wild Beasts of the Forest* which will return as soon as the pursuit is at an end and fall perhaps on those that are left there; when the gradual extension of our Settlements will as certainly cause the Savage as the Wolf to retire; *both being beasts of prey tho they differ in shape.*[12]

---

[7] Berger, *supra* note 6, at 600.

[8] *Id.* at 599–600.

[9] U.S. v. Rogers, 45 U.S. 567, 571, 573 (1846).

[10] U.S. v. McKee, 91 U.S. 442 (1875) (referring to "warlike tribes of that race"); Beecher v. Wetherby, 95 U.S. 517 (1877) (describing relationship between United States and Native peoples as relationship between Christian people and "ignorant and dependent race"). *But cf.* Lucas v. U.S., 163 U.S. 612 (1896) (acknowledging that race not necessarily dispositive of tribal membership).

[11] According to Albert Memmi, racism in the colonial context involves "the generalized and final assigning of values to real or imaginary differences, to the accuser's benefit and at his victim's expense, in order to justify the former's own privileges or aggression." *See* ALBERT MEMMI, DOMINATED MAN: NOTES TOWARD A PORTRAIT 194 (1968).

[12] THE WRITINGS OF GEORGE WASHINGTON 133–40 (John C. Fitzpatrick ed., 1938) (emphasis added).

More than a century later, U.S. Senator Johnson of Indiana used similar racialized rhetoric to legitimize the annexation of the Hawaiian Islands to the United States against the will of the Native Hawaiian people:

> Side by side on their islands were two civilizations, higher and a *lower civilization*. On the side of the higher civilization were ranged intelligence, the progress, the thrift, the aspirations for enlarged liberty and for the legalization of a great destiny for Hawai['ji. On the other side was ranged the monarchy with its narrow, contracted view of human rights, with its *semibarbarous* face turned toward the past, unwilling to greet the dawning sun. . . . From the very nature of things these two civilizations could not exist together forever. One was to survive and the other would have to perish.[13]

Washington contrasted negative images of Native peoples as "Wild Beasts of the Forest," wolves, and "beasts of prey" with positive images of white Americans as "enlightened" and "generous" to justify driving Native peoples out of their ancestral lands by purchase or, if necessary, by force of arms. Similarly, Johnson juxtaposed positive descriptions of white Americans as "intelligent," "progressive," and "thrifty" with a negative depiction of Native Hawaiians as "semibarbarous" to legitimize the destruction of Native Hawaiian self-determination through annexation. In other words, once Native peoples were racialized as "red," American law and politics worked to transform red into the universal symbol of Native peoples' alleged inferiority to rationalize American privilege and aggression.[14]

B. *Targeting Native Societies Rather than Native Individuals*

Importantly, early racism against Native peoples focused primarily on their alleged inferiority as societies rather than as persons. As Berger explains, to justify the assimilation of Native individuals into non-Native society and the subsequent appropriation of Native land and resources, European Americans needed to theorize Native "*societies* as fatally and racially inferior while emphasizing the ability of Indian *individuals* to leave their societies and join non-Indian ones."[15] Specifically, because the United States sought to dissolve Native societies and dispossess them of the land and resources under their stewardship, racist discourse needed to focus on the perceived racial deficiencies of the Native society as a whole and the supposed impacts of those deficiencies on the society's politics, economics, and culture.[16] Thus, although Native individuals did not completely escape the type of racism levied against members of other communities, early U.S. decision-makers focused

---

[13] 53 Cong. Rec. 1885 (1894) (emphasis added).
[14] Berger, *supra* note 6, at 611, 622–23.
[15] *Id*. at 593 (emphasis added).
[16] *Id*. at 599, 618–19; Goldberg, *supra* note 6, at 1373–74.

on Native peoples' purported racial inferiority as collective entities to assert privilege over and aggression against them in their collective capacities.

C. *Legitimizing the Negative Stereotype through Law and Legal Discourse*

Robert Williams Jr. observed that no self-regarded "civilized" society can engage in the horror of destroying another people for very long without appealing to a revered legal discourse to justify its acts.[17] For that reason, although popular media played a significant role in the initial racialization and denigration of Native peoples in the United States, law and legal discourse were the most forceful tools for forming and advancing the dominant negative stereotype. For instance, the foundational U.S. Supreme Court cases that articulated the federal government's purported right to control Native lands and peoples, described Native peoples as "fierce savages, whose occupation was war" and "remnants of a race once powerful, now weak and diminished in numbers."[18] Enshrining those depictions in hallowed Supreme Court opinions legitimated those ideas for subsequent generations of Americans, who accepted as given the notion that Native peoples comprised a weak and unsophisticated racial group, as well as the attendant belief that the United States had a right and duty to control them. In the present day, those early Supreme Court opinions and their progeny are routinely cited as the defining texts of the Native–federal relationship, with little or no attention paid to the antiquated racist notions that they contain and promote.[19]

II. THE DOMINANT STEREOTYPE AND IMPLICIT BIAS

The dominant image, enshrined in early U.S. law and legal discourse, of "[t]he mythical Indians of stereotype-land," who are "fierce," "dwell in primitive splendor," and live a way of life that is "dreadfully wrong" and "un-American," persists in modern implicit bias against Native peoples.[20] Using various measures, including the Implicit Association Test (IAT),[21] social scientists have documented the existence of implicit bias against Native Americans, Native Hawaiians, and Canadian Aboriginals. The

---

[17] Robert A. Williams, Jr., *Documents of Barbarism: The Contemporary Legacy of European Racism and Colonialism in the Narrative Traditions of Federal Indian Law*, 31 ARIZ. L. REV. 237, 247 (1989).

[18] Johnson v. McIntosh, 21 U.S. (8 Wheat.) 543 (1823); U.S. v. Kagama, 118 U.S. 375 (1886).

[19] *See* Wallace Coffey & Rebecca Tsosie, *Rethinking the Tribal Sovereignty Doctrine: Cultural Sovereignty and the Collective Future of Indian Nations*, 12 STAN. L. & POL'Y REV. 191, 196 (2001) (describing and challenging the tendency to adhere automatically to the Marshall Trilogy and its limited notion of Native sovereignty).

[20] VINE DELORIA, JR., CUSTER DIED FOR YOUR SINS: AN INDIAN MANIFESTO 2, 4, 13 (1988).

[21] The IAT requires the test taker to rapidly categorize various concepts in order to measure how strongly associated two types of concepts are. The more associated the concepts, the faster the test taker should be able to respond, and vice versa. *See FAQs*, PROJECT IMPLICIT, https://implicit.harvard.edu/implicit/demo/background/faqs.html#faq7 (last visited Sep. 3, 2011).

empirical studies collectively show that today's implicit views of Native peoples reflect at least three of the specific racist assumptions underlying the dominant stereotype – that Native peoples are foreign, savage, and ignorant. These lasting racist assumptions fuel the notion that Native peoples are unable to govern and justify continuing acts of deprivation and dispossession against them.

A. *Foreignness*

1. Foreignness in Implicit Bias Studies: Native Peoples as Less "American"

As counterintuitive as it may seem, a groundbreaking empirical study on implicit bias showed that Native Americans are viewed as less American – more foreign to the United States – than white Americans. The study, conducted by Brian Nosek and his colleagues, used IATs and measures of participants' self-reported (explicit) beliefs to examine the extent to which "American identity was implicitly and explicitly associated with Native Americans and White Americans."[22] In the IAT portion, participants were asked to quickly pair Native American and white American faces with the attribute "American," as represented either by natural scenes from the American landscape that are easily associated with Native Americans or names of cities or states that have Native American origin. Participants more quickly associated those American landmarks, cities, and states with the faces of white Americans. This was true for all ethnic groups, except Native Americans and Native Alaskans, who more easily associated Native American with "American." At the same time, participants' self-reported responses reflected the view that Native Americans were more "American" than whites. The study thus revealed a dramatic dissociation between explicit and implicit responses: non-Native Americans explicitly identify Native Americans as American, but *implicitly* identify them as *more foreign* than whites.

These striking findings suggest that the historical assertion that whites are more "American" than Native people is now a deeply ingrained implicitly held view. In addition, unlike explicit reasoning, implicit views cannot be consciously controlled: "implicit measures often document stronger biases than explicit measures because the motivation to avoid these biases . . . produces more egalitarian explicit responses, but is relatively ineffective at changing implicit responses."[23] Thus, according to the study's authors, the dissociation between explicit and implicit responses might

---

[22] Thierry Devos, Brian A. Nosek, & Mahzarin R. Banaji, *Aliens in Their Own Land? Implicit and Explicit Ascriptions of National Identity to Native Americans and White Americans* (2007) (unpublished manuscript) (on file with authors). *See also* Brian Nosek et al., *Pervasiveness and Correlates of Implicit Attitudes and Stereotypes*, 18 EUR. REV. SOC. PSYCH. 1, 2, 20 (2007) (summarizing data from more than 2.5 million IATs and self-reports and finding, among other things, that participants more easily associated European American than Native American faces with "American").

[23] Devos et al., *supra* note 22, at 11.

reflect people's "intentional reasoning" that Native Americans *should* be considered more American (or at least as American) because they are the original inhabitants of what is now America, and in light of egalitarian principles. However, the study revealed that everyday images of prominent (white) Americans and people's daily experiences reinforce strong implicit associations between America and white *that cannot be consciously altered.*[24]

2. Foreignness in Law and Legal Discourse: Casting Native Peoples as an Unentitled Other

The widely held view of America as "white" has deep historical roots. The federal government acted early and often to equate the term "Americans" with whites, thereby relegating indigenous Americans to the margins of society, along with non-white immigrant communities. In *Dred Scott v. Sandford*, the U.S. Supreme Court described the tribes comprising the "Indian race" as vastly foreign to America:

> These Indian Governments were regarded and treated as foreign Governments, as much so as if an ocean had separated the red man from the white . . . and the people who compose these Indian political communities have always been treated as foreigners not living under our Government. . . . But they may, without doubt, like the subjects of any other foreign Government, be naturalized by the authority of Congress, and become citizens of a State, and of the United States; and if an individual should leave his nation or tribe, and take up his abode among the white population, he would be entitled to all the rights and privileges which would belong to an emigrant from any other foreign people.[25]

Similarly, in *Elk v. Wilkins*, the Supreme Court opined that "[t]he Indian tribes . . . were not, strictly speaking, foreign states; but they were alien nations."[26]

By labeling Native peoples as foreign communities, the federal government established white Americans as the proper inhabitants of the United States, with all other "foreign" peoples, including Native peoples, purportedly existing within the United States at white Americans' sufferance.[27] This initial relegation of Native peoples to the periphery of U.S. life and political structure privileged the claims of white Americans, acting through the federal government, to Native land, resources, and political power. Over time, the federal government firmly entrenched this

---

[24] *Id.* at 11–12 (describing "prominent Americans" as "U.S. presidents, most political and social leaders, celebrities, and a majority of the population").

[25] Dred Scott v. Sandford, 60 U.S. (19 How.) 393, 404 (1856), *superseded by constitutional amendment*, U.S. Const. amend. XIV.

[26] Elk v. Wilkins, 112 U.S. 94, 100 (1884).

[27] This notion was articulated clearly by Thomas Jefferson, who declared that Native peoples "must see we have only to shut our hand to crush them, and that all our liberalities to them proceed from motives of pure humanity only." 10 The Writings of Thomas Jefferson 369–71 (Andrew A. Lipscomb ed., 1904).

hierarchy by developing and applying legal principles such as federal plenary power over Native peoples, the related trust responsibility of the federal government to act for and on behalf of Native peoples, and the doctrine of discovery, all of which purport to place supreme power in the hands of the federal government and legitimate the continuing wrongful deprivation of Native lands, resources, and governing authority.

The Supreme Court's *Rice v. Cayetano* decision in 2000 illustrates the detriment that can flow to a Native community when it is improperly characterized as foreign alongside immigrant communities. In *Rice*, the Court invalidated a requirement that individuals be Native Hawaiian to vote for the trustees of the Office of Hawaiian Affairs, a semi-autonomous organization created by the state constitution to manage certain funds and benefits for Native Hawaiians. In doing so, the Court asserted that, when considering the rights of Native Hawaiians, it must recount the immigration story of "many different races and cultures" to Hawai'i and how those groups faced and overcame discrimination. The Court implicitly assumed that Native Hawaiians are similarly situated to "Chinese, Portuguese, Japanese, and Filipinos," who also had their "own history in Hawai['i]," their "own struggles with societal and official discrimination," their "own successes," and their "own role in creating the present society of the islands."[28] By characterizing Native Hawaiians as simply another racial group alongside immigrant groups and by omitting white Americans from the list of immigrants to Hawai'i, the Court effectively erased the unique status of Native Hawaiians, the harms of U.S. colonization, and the present-day need to rectify those harms. Working from this incorrect characterization of Native Hawaiians, the Court deemed the Native Hawaiian voting system an illegal "racial preference" for Hawaiians and "reverse racial discrimination" against the white American, Freddy Rice.[29]

B. *Violence*

1. Violence in Implicit Bias Studies: Native "Aggressiveness" in the Criminal Law Context

A study by Justin Levinson found that it was easier for participants to correctly remember and falsely remember the aggressiveness of Native Hawaiians as compared to that of whites depending on the factual situations. College students at the University of Hawai'i read two legal stories, with the primary independent variable being the protagonist's race. The first story, *The Confrontation*, involved a fistfight,

---

[28] Rice v. Cayetano, 528 U.S. 495, 506 (2000).

[29] Eric K. Yamamoto & Catherine Corpus Betts, *Disfiguring Civil Rights to Deny Indigenous Hawaiian Self-Determination: The Story of Rice v. Cayetano*, in RACE LAW STORIES 563 (Rachel F. Moran & Devon W. Carbado eds., 2008). Harold "Freddy" Rice is a descendant of white American Christian missionaries who built a ranching empire on Hawai'i Island. *Id.* at 545.

in which the criminal defendant was either William (Caucasian), Tyronne (African American), or Kawika (Native Hawaiian).[30] After reading the stories, participants received a "distraction task" and answered questions about the stories.

Participants exhibited systematic errors in their memories of *The Confrontation* – they had an easier time correctly recalling the aggressive actions of Tyronne and Kawika, compared to William. For example, "[p]articipants who read about Tyronne or Kawika were significantly more likely to recall correctly [facts that would tend to indicate that the defendant initiated the fight] than participants who read about William." Moreover, participants who read about Tyronne or Kawika were "significantly more likely to *misremember* [certain facts] in a manner that would be detrimental to the actor in a legal proceeding."[31]

These findings are significant. They suggest that historic characterizations of Native Hawaiians as aggressive, discussed in the next section, now persist as implicit memory biases. They also show that judges' and juries' recollections of legal stories can be systematically shaped by the race of the legal actors, which has significant consequences for Native Hawaiians who are grossly overrepresented in Hawaiʻi's criminal justice system.[32]

2. Violence in Law and Legal Discourse: Rationalizing External Intrusion into Native Justice Administration

Explicit characterizations of Native peoples as groups of violent savages appear throughout early U.S. law and legal discourse. In the 1823 *Johnson v. McIntosh* decision, one of the first Supreme Court cases to address Native legal issues, Chief Justice Marshall proclaimed that "the tribes of Indians inhabiting this country were fierce savages, whose occupation was war."[33] Similarly, mid-nineteenth-century discourse in the territorial assembly of South Dakota depicted Native peoples as "revengeful and murderous" savages, "implacable enemies, hell hounds, and wild, turbulent, and hostile people."[34] Explicit characterizations of Native peoples as violent savages remained present in the law throughout the nineteenth century, with the Supreme Court in *Ex Parte Crow Dog* asserting in 1883 that Native peoples lived a "free though savage life."[35]

---

[30] *See* Levinson, *supra* note 4, at 347, 349. The second story involved an employee, with the protagonist as Brenda (Caucasian), Keisha (African American), or Kaʻolu (Hawaiian). *Id.* at 394.

[31] *Id.* at 398–99 (emphasis added). On the other hand, individuals who read about Kawika were more likely to exhibit false memories of mitigating factors compared to those who read about William or Tyronne. *Id.* at 401. This finding might relate to the "complex and unique relationship between localism in the community (among Native Hawaiian and non-Hawaiian people alike) and positive and negative stereotypes," including those involving aggression and mitigation. *Id.* at 402.

[32] *See* Office of Hawaiian Affairs, The Disparate Treatment of Native Hawaiians in the Criminal Justice System, Executive Summary (2010), *available at* http://www.oha.org/images/stories/files/pdf/reports/es_final_web.pdf.

[33] Johnson v. McIntosh, 21 U.S. (8 Wheat.) 543 (1823).

[34] Bone Shirt v. Hazeltine, 336 F. Supp. 2d 976, 1029 (D.S.D. 2004).

[35] Ex parte Kan-Gi-Shun-Ca (Crow Dog), 109 U.S. 556, 571 (1883).

The alleged savagery of Native peoples was often used to justify the United States' unilateral exercise of power over them. Elsewhere in *Johnson v. McIntosh*, Chief Justice Marshall declared that "the character and religion of [America's] inhabitants afforded an apology for considering them as a people over whom the superior genius of Europe might claim an ascendancy."[36] That claimed ascendancy provided justification for the imperial powers to deny Native peoples their rights and to freely appropriate Native land and resources. Subsequently, it legitimized the United States' relegation of Native peoples to domestic dependent nation status and the usurpation of Native sovereignty. As James Lobsenz asserts, "The 'quasi-sovereign' or 'dependent' status of the Indian tribe is inextricably linked to past concepts of the Indian as an uncivilized savage who was to be gradually elevated to the level of a civilized human being."[37]

The characterization of Native peoples as violent savages also extended to Native Hawaiians. American missionaries described Native Hawaiians as "having an appearance of half-human and half-beast...form[ing] a link in creation...connecting man with the brute" to rationalize the missionaries' aggressive proselytization of the Native community.[38] U.S. Senators, while pushing for economic control over Hawai'i, bristled at the thought of incorporating into the U.S. polity "a country of dusky ex-cannibals" and "a half-civilized people" who were "prone to insurrections" and who once "ate our missionaries."[39] Believing themselves to be from a "higher civilization" destined to bring "salvation," progress, and liberty, and labeling Native Hawaiians as savage brutes in need of direction, American missionaries and members of Congress justified the mass confiscation of Hawaiian land, the near decimation of the Hawaiian language, and the destruction of Hawaiian culture and self-governance.

Subsumed within the racist assumption that Native peoples are violent is a related notion that Native peoples are not prone to peace, rationality, or the fair resolution of disputes. From the nineteenth century to the present, this assumption has undermined Native efforts to administer justice and has supported the unwarranted intrusion of external governments into internal Native community matters. For example, in 1885, Congress passed the Major Crimes Act, which gave the federal government jurisdiction over certain serious crimes committed in Native territory. More than a century later, in 2010, the Tribal Law and Order Act reaffirmed that Native governments have limited sentencing authority and offered an opportunity to enlarge that authority only to those Native governments that are willing to adhere to certain standards and practices mandated by the federal government. Although these acts were passed more than a century apart, they are based on the same

---

[36] *McIntosh*, 21 U.S. at 543.
[37] James E. Lobsenz, *"Dependent Indian Communities": A Search for a Twentieth Century Definition,* 24 Ariz. L. Rev. 1, 2 (1982).
[38] Lilikalā Kameʻeleihiwa, Native Land and Foreign Desires: Pehea Lā E Pono Aī? 139 (1992).
[39] *See* State Historical Society of North Dakota, North Dakota History 9 (1989) (quoting Senator William Roach of North Dakota).

implicit assumption that Native peoples are not sufficiently peaceful, rational, and fair to competently administer justice without strict external constraints. Williams explains that many federal attempts to disempower Native justice systems flow from this idea that Native governments are incapable of protecting the rights of those who come under their jurisdiction. In support of his assertion, he cites congressional and judicial characterizations of Native courts as "Kangaroo Courts" that act with "no pretense of due process or judicial integrity."[40]

In the Native Hawaiian context, explicit allegations of savagery played a major role in the initial appropriation of Native Hawaiian lands, resources, and self-governing authority by American missionaries and Congress. In the present day, certain opponents of Native Hawaiian self-governance base their opposition, in part, on the related implicit notion that Native Hawaiians are unfettered by the same notions of peace, rationality, and fairness that bind non-Natives. As evidenced by former Governor Lingle's baseless prediction that Native Hawaiian self-governing powers would be exercised in an "unlawful," "irresponsible" manner "inconsistent with virtually every conceivable state law that serves to protect the public," described earlier, such implicit assumptions undergird the continuing deprivation of Native Hawaiian self-governance by the state and federal governments.

C. *Ignorance*

1. Ignorance in Implicit Bias Studies: Native Peoples as "Nonacademic" and in Need of "Benevolent" Assistance

Two empirical studies show that long-held racist assumptions about the ignorance of Native peoples manifest today as implicit bias and stereotypes. A study by Amanda Burke that linked negative implicit attitudes about Native American *mascots* with race-based social behaviors toward Native American *people* found that Native Americans are viewed as preferring stereotypical, nonacademic tasks. In the first part of the study, Caucasian college students at Oklahoma State University completed various tasks including an IAT that measured the strength of the association between Native American mascots (Redskins, Braves, Indians, Warriors, Chiefs, Fighting Sioux) and Caucasian mascots (Celtics, Vikings, Pirates, Rebels, Mountaineers, and Fighting Irish), and six positive traits (successful, responsible, smart, healthy, clean, educated) and six negative traits (worthless, lazy, dirty, fat, freeloader, poor).[41] The results showed that people hold implicit negative stereotypes of Native mascots.

---

[40] Williams, *supra* note 17, at 271, 274.

[41] Amanda L. Burke, Behavioral Correlates of Implicit Evaluation and Stereotyping of Native American Mascots 1, 7, 28–29, 35, 38–39, 41, 48 (July 2009) (unpublished Ph.D. dissertation, Oklahoma State University) (on file with authors). A companion study included a self-report questionnaire and an IAT that measured the strength of association of Native Americans (Cherokee, Navajo, Sioux, Apache, Comanche, Iroquois) and European Americans (English, Irish, German, French, Scottish, Dutch),

In the next part of the study, participants were told that they would be interacting with a Native American partner – Joe Tallchief or Joanna Tallchief – on academic (e.g., mathematics, verbal ability) and nonacademic (e.g., general cultural knowledge and environmental issues) tasks. Participants were told to choose tasks for themselves and for their partners that would give the partnership the best combined score and then rate "how well they expected themselves and their partners to perform on each of the tasks." Individuals who showed greater implicit bias on the mascot IAT were significantly more likely to perceive their Native American partner as enjoying "stereotype-consistent" nonacademic tasks. "In other words, greater implicit stereotype bias toward *symbolic representations* of Native people (i.e., Native mascots) was related to the expectation that a Native *person* would be more likely to enjoy tasks of a non-academic nature." Thus, the study concluded that "Native American mascots are not merely insignificant representations of Native Americans." Instead, they may perpetuate the stereotype that Native Americans are less interested in academics, resulting in severe consequences at school, at the workplace, and within society's institutions.[42]

In another study, Cherie Werhun and April Penner found that negative stereotypes about Aboriginal Canadians as uneducated, lazy, and incompetent can influence benevolent prejudicial behavior toward them.[43] Non-Aboriginal college students at the University of Winnipeg were told that the campus newspaper was conducting research on the qualities associated with success at the newspaper. Participants were assigned to the role of "editor" and viewed photographs representing either Aboriginal stereotype images (images associated with the negative stereotype of Aboriginal Canadians) or neutral images.[44] The stereotype images included a homeless person, a close-up shot of a guitar and tattooed hand, a metal fence through which a prison tower and yard were visible, and a prison shank and a bottle of moonshine. The neutral images included a hockey player and the northern lights over a city, a field of sunflowers, and a snowman.

---

and positive (successful, responsible, intelligent, healthy, clean, and educated) and negative (worthless, lazy, dirty, fat, freeloader, and poor) attributes. The results showed implicit bias against Native Americans. *Id.* at 36, 48.

[42] *Id.* at 28, 48–49, 55–56. *See also* Scott Freng, The Role of Chief Wahoo in Implicit Stereotype Activation (2001) (unpublished Ph.D dissertation, University of Nebraska) (on file with authors); Chu Kim-Prieto et al., *Effect of Exposure to an American Indian Mascot on the Tendency to Stereotype a Different Minority Group*, 40 J. APPLIED SOC. PSYCH. 534 (2010) (finding that participants primed with a Native American sports mascot increased their stereotyping of a different ethnic minority group).

[43] Cherie D. Werhun & April J. Penner, *The Effects of Stereotyping and Implicit Theory on Benevolent Prejudice Toward Aboriginal Canadians*, 40 J. APPLIED SOC. PSYCHOL. 899 (2010). Although this study was conducted in Canada, it is relevant to this discussion in light of Native Americans' and First Nations' shared histories and somewhat similar experiences in their respective countries.

[44] Priming refers to the effect in which exposure to a stimulus activates "knowledge structures, such as trait concepts and stereotypes" and influences the response to an unrelated task. *See* John A. Bargh et al., *Automaticity of Social Behavior: Direct Effects of Trait Construct and Stereotype Activation on Action*, 71 J. PERSONALITY. & SOC. PSYCHOL. 230, 230 (1996).

The participants then read mock newspaper articles "that were manipulated to induce either an entity or an incremental frame of mind." Entity and incremental theories "are the core assumptions people use to understand, interpret, and predict human behavior." Entity theorists believe human attributes are fixed and emphasize personal traits, whereas incremental theorists contend that human attributes are malleable and focus on "mediating factors specific to the situation."[45]

After completing these tasks, participants edited identical essays that they were told were written by either a Caucasian or an Aboriginal student writer. They were then asked about their willingness to recommend the writer to their publishing team and to help the writer beyond their duties as editor. When negative Aboriginal stereotypes (i.e., "[Aboriginals] are uneducated, lazy, and incompetent") were active by way of the images, participants who were primed with entity theory (that human attributes are fixed) were more willing "to engage in benevolent prejudicial behavior toward an Aboriginal student writer"; in other words, to provide extra help to the subordinate Aboriginal writer. At the same time, those participants were less willing to recommend the Aboriginal writer to their team, as compared with the Caucasian writer. According to the authors, the perspective of intelligence as fixed influenced the stereotypical perception that the Aboriginal writer required extra help and attention.[46] Thus, "a greater willingness to help the Aboriginal writer, compared to the Caucasian writer, within the context of negative stereotypical information about Aboriginal Canadians and despite identical performance information for both writers," suggests the "endorsement of the stereotype of Aboriginal Canadians as incompetent." For the authors, these findings are significant because benevolent prejudice may "undermine the target person's competency[,] strengthen negative stereotypes about the target's group," and have negative social ramifications in organizational contexts.[47]

2. Ignorance in Law and Legal Discourse: Justifying Federal Plenary Power

In the U.S. Supreme Court's 1831 decision in *Cherokee Nation v. Georgia*, Chief Justice Marshall famously described Native peoples as being "in a state of pupilage," and he likened the relationship between Native peoples and the United States to the relationship between a "ward" and its "guardian."[48] Following *Cherokee Nation*, this image of Native peoples as ignorant, and therefore in need of the federal government's teaching and guidance, appeared repeatedly in Supreme Court

---

[45] Werhun & Penner, *supra* note 43, at 902, 907.

[46] *Id.* at 902–10. In contrast, incremental-primed editors did not express any differences in their willingness to provide extra help or in their team recommendations for either the Aboriginal or Caucasian writers. *Id.* at 908–09. This suggests that the perspective of intelligence as malleable eliminated the Aboriginal stereotype's influence on behavioral intentions toward the writers. *Id.* at 910.

[47] *Id.* at 902–03.

[48] Cherokee Nation v. Georgia, 30 U.S. 1 (1831).

opinions, even opinions that purportedly affirmed tribal sovereignty. For example, the Court's 1883 decision in *Ex Parte Crow Dog*, which is generally lauded as an affirmation of Native sovereignty, characterized Native peoples as "a dependent community who were in a state of pupilage, advancing from the condition of a savage tribe to that of a people who, through the discipline of labor, and by education, it was hoped might become a self-supporting and self-governed society."[49] Likewise, in its 1913 *U.S. v. Sandoval* decision, the Court described the people of Santa Clara Pueblo as "essentially a simple, uninformed, and inferior people . . . regarded and treated by the United States as requiring special consideration and protection, like other Indian communities."[50]

According to the Court's 1886 *U.S. v. Kagama* decision, Native peoples' alleged state of pupilage required the United States to assume a duty to protect them and a corollary power over them.[51] Contemporary law and legal discourse commonly refer to this duty and power, respectively, as the federal government's trust responsibility and plenary power over Indian affairs.[52] Pursuant to this so-called trust responsibility and plenary power, Congress enacted legislation such as the Dawes General Allotment Act of 1887, which purported to "civilize" Native peoples through the introduction of individual private property ownership, but had the practical effect of dispossessing Native peoples of millions of acres of land. The executive branch established the Indian Police and Courts of Indian Offenses and founded "a series of boarding schools deliberately designed to remove Indian children from tribally based child rearing and socialization and thereby stamp out all tribal influences, including language."[53] This concerted effort to "educate" Native peoples and raise them out of their alleged state of pupilage had extremely deleterious effects on Native culture, political power, and landholding that continue to benefit the federal government and non-Natives to this day.

American and European elite also characterized Native Hawaiians as "babes in character and intellect" to deprive the Native community of its sovereign authority.[54] The *Daily Bulletin*, an English-language newspaper in circulation during the reign of King Kalākaua, claimed that the king and his people were still "wedded by ignorance to superstitious ideas and practices" and thus were inherently unable to govern themselves – "unable to stand side by side, on the same plane with Bulgarian or American, as a free citizen of a free country."[55] The newspaper further alleged that,

---

49 Ex parte Kan-Gi-Shun-Ca (Crow Dog), 109 U.S. 556, 571 (1883).
50 U.S. v. Sandoval, 231 U.S. 28, 40 (1913).
51 U.S. v. Kagama, 118 U.S. 375 (1886).
52 Carole E. Goldberg et al., American Indian Law: Native Nations and the Federal System 86–107, 583–618 (6th ed. 2010).
53 *Id.* at 35.
54 *See* Noenoe K. Silva, Aloha Betrayed: Native Hawaiian Resistance to American Colonialism 130 (2004).
55 *Id.* at 115.

although exposure to European mores "helped" Native Hawaiians, Native Hawaiians still had "much to learn before . . . [they were] fit to graduate [as] free citizens of a free country."[56] Similarly, American military and plantation owners, while lobbying fervently for annexation, alternatively characterized Native Hawaiians as uncivilized or childlike – in either case, in need of American control.

The implicit assumption that Native peoples are ignorant and require teaching and assistance from others continues to deprive Native communities of independent self-governing authority. As discussed earlier, Congress recently passed the Tribal Law and Order Act, which requires Native governments to mirror certain aspects of the U.S. judicial system in order to exercise expanded sentencing authority. Although the intent of the act is a positive one – to increase Native governing authority and further crime abatement in Indian country – certain incidental effects may be detrimental to Native peoples. Namely, to take advantage of the expanded sentencing authority offered by the act, many Native governments will begin to approximate non-Native justice systems more closely, which will almost certainly diminish the influence of Native values and understandings on the administration of justice in those communities. It may also reinforce the faulty assumptions underlying the act, including the notions that Native governments are more "just" if they more closely resemble western governments and that the federal government's alleged superior understanding of dispute resolution enables it to dictate the overarching terms and conditions of Native justice administration. As such, the Tribal Law and Order Act, like many other contemporary federal government actions, reinforces the implicit assumption that Native peoples are not sufficiently sophisticated and knowledgeable to govern properly without external constraints, effectively fortifying the federal government's purported plenary power over Native peoples.

For Native Hawaiians, the tacit assumption that Native governments cannot function appropriately without external constraints supports limitations on governing authority that are far more restrictive than those affirmed by the Tribal Law and Order Act. For instance, in 2007, the U.S. Department of Justice cited the possibility that a proposed Native Hawaiian governing entity might exercise "sweeping" self-governing powers as a reason to refuse to acknowledge Native Hawaiians as a sovereign, self-governing political entity on par with other Native peoples in the United States.[57] As a result, the federal government currently legislates on behalf of Native Hawaiians regarding important community issues such as education, graves

---

[56] *Id. See also* CHRISTOPHER MARK MCBRIDE, THE COLONIZER ABROAD: AMERICAN WRITERS ON FOR-EIGN SOIL, 1846–1912 63 (2004) (highlighting "a widely held imperialist belief [that] the foolish natives, all of whom share indistinguishable names, will waste their newfound political freedom on ill-conceived plans").

[57] Statement of Gregory G. Katsas, Principal Deputy Associate Attorney General, United States Department of Justice, Before the Committee on Indian Affairs, United States Senate: Hearing on S. 310, The Native Hawaiian Government Reorganization Act of 2007, 110th Cong. 2–3, 6 (May 3, 2007).

protection, indigenous language perpetuation, and culture and art development,[58] and does not acknowledge the authority of the Native Hawaiian community to develop its own legal standards to address these and other community issues. This arrangement forces Native Hawaiians into a deeper "state of pupilage" vis-à-vis the federal government than federally recognized Native polities, leaving the Native Hawaiian community vulnerable to political attacks and placing the resolution of many important community issues at the discretion of the federal and state governments.

III. STEPS FORWARD: ADDRESSING BIAS AGAINST NATIVE PEOPLES

On the eve of the 500th anniversary of European arrival in the Americas, the National Conference of Catholic Bishops on Native Americans urged its churches and followers to rethink long-held stereotypes against Native peoples: "All of us need to examine our own perceptions of Native Americans – how much they are shaped by stereotypes, distorted media portrayals or ignorance. We fear that prejudice and insensitivity toward Native peoples is deeply rooted in our culture and our local churches."[59] Although the Conference did not expressly reference implicit stereotypes or bias, it did recognize a salient point: negative perceptions of Native peoples are ubiquitous and deeply rooted in American society.

Social scientists have confirmed that these persistent "historical representations are associated with contemporary outcomes" in subtle and implicit ways.[60] As this chapter contends, the connection between historical characterizations, implicit manifestations, and modern barriers to Native self-governance is real and pervasive. Yet more must be done to empirically examine these associations.

We therefore urge researchers to investigate a broader range of stereotypes about Native peoples and the behavioral consequences of implicit bias against Native communities. Although studies addressing an array of Native stereotypes are needed, studies specifically tailored to the stereotype of Native peoples as "incapable of self-government" would be particularly valuable. In light of this stereotype's deep historical and cultural roots, it would be surprising to find that a study on Native

---

[58] Native Hawaiian Education Act, 20 U.S.C. § 7201 (2006); Native American Graves Protection and Repatriation Act, 25 U.S.C. § 3001 (2006); Native American Languages Act, 25 U.S.C. § 2901 (2006); American Indian, Alaska Native, and Native Hawaiian Culture and Art Development Act, 20 U.S.C. § 4401 (2006).

[59] CATHOLIC CHURCH, 1992: *A Time for Remembering, Reconciling, and Recommitting Ourselves as a People*, in 6 PASTORAL LETTERS OF THE UNITED STATES CATHOLIC BISHOPS: 1989–1997, AT 421 (1998). *See also* Kim Chandler Johnson & John Terrence Eck, *Eliminating Indian Stereotypes from American Society: Causes and Legal and Societal Solutions*, 20 AM. INDIAN L. REV. 65, 86–107 (1995–96) (describing educational, legal, and legislative efforts to eliminate negative Native American stereotypes represented by mascots, logos, or nicknames).

[60] Phillip Atiba Goff et al., *Not Yet Human: Implicit Knowledge, Historical Dehumanization, and Contemporary Consequences*, 94 J. PERSONALITY & SOC. PSYCH. 292, 305 (2008).

people's ability to govern would yield different results than the others described here. Nonetheless, more research must be conducted to empirically confirm this.

At the same time, other efforts are needed to help moderate or eliminate bias against Native peoples. Educating decision-makers, lawyers, and advocates – both Native and non-Native – about the existence of implicit bias is a first step. "Debiasing" strategies – interventions that can attenuate or temporarily halt the impacts of implicit biases – should also be explored. Debiasing techniques include forming new personal connections with members of outgroups and exposure to "counterstereotypes," among others.[61] Legal scholars have examined how the law can also aid in debiasing and in addressing the societal harms of implicit bias.[62]

With this in mind, we suggest some initial ways to think about or to address bias against Native peoples in a legal and cultural context. These suggestions, painted in broad strokes, are merely introductory steps toward examining the underexplored area of implicit bias and Native peoples. Of course, examining the myriad ways to address bias against Native peoples and to create lasting social change is beyond the scope of this chapter.

Studies show that greater exposure to outgroup members under certain conditions can reduce implicit attitudinal bias or prejudice.[63] In an effort to expose non-Native law students and community members to Native jurists, justice systems, and legal traditions, Native American Law Students Associations partnered with the Navajo Nation to bring sessions of the Navajo Nation Supreme Court and the Navajo Nation Peacemakers Court to law schools across the country.[64] Similarly, Chief Judge Martha Vázquez of the U.S. District Court for the District of New Mexico has been working to develop closer relationships between federal justice systems and Native governments. In December 2005, Judge Vázquez convened a federal criminal trial within the territory of the Navajo Nation, marking the first time that federal court has been held on the Navajo reservation and possibly the first time that a federal trial has ever been conducted in Indian country.[65] The experience exposed the trial participants to the Native community and provided the Native community greater access to the federal justice system, which Judge Vázquez perceived as mutually beneficial. At the 2010 meeting of the Indian Law Section of the Federal Bar Association, Judge Vázquez addressed Native leaders, attorneys, and scholars,

---

[61] Kang & Banaji, *supra* note 4, at 1105–10; Greenwald & Krieger, *supra* note 4, at 963–64; Levinson, *supra* note 4, at 411–13.

[62] *See, e.g.,* Kang & Banaji, *supra* note 4; Jolls & Sunstein, *supra* note 4; Krieger & Fiske, *supra* note 4; Kang, *supra* note 4; Levinson, *supra* note 4.

[63] Kang & Banaji, *supra* note 4, at 1101 (listing the "conditions that contribute to a debiasing environment[:] People must be: (1) exposed to disconfirming data; (2) interact with others of equal status; (3) cooperate; (4) engage in non-superficial contact; and (5) receive clear norms in favor of equality.").

[64] *See, e.g.,* Jess McNally, *Supreme Court of the Navajo Nation visits Stanford Law School,* Stanford Report, May 10, 2010, *available at* http://news.stanford.edu/news/2010/may/navajo-supreme-court-051010.html.

[65] Troy A. Eid & Carrie Covington Doyle, *Separate but Unequal: The Federal Criminal Justice System in Indian Country,* 81 U. Colo. L. Rev. 1067, 1105 (2010).

among others, and called for further relationship-building between federal and Native justice systems.

Exposure to individuals in counter-stereotypic roles also has been shown to reduce implicit bias. For example, studies found that viewing images of positively viewed African Americans and negatively viewed white Americans, or imagining a "female leader," temporarily diminished implicit biases.[66] The American Indian College Fund's recent advertising campaign "Have You Ever Seen a Real Indian?" that profiled pictures of successful Native Americans in professions like law, medicine, science, business and the arts to challenge Native American stereotypes may have had this type of debiasing effect.[67]

Importantly, repeated exposure to "countertypical exemplars in positions of authority" can have dramatic bias-reducing effects.[68] In one study, after one year at an all-women's college, female students' implicit stereotypes equating "male" with "leader" were eliminated, whereas female students at a coeducational college developed "stronger implicit stereotypes of male [and] leader." The heightened exposure to countertypical female teachers and administrators at the all-women's school was found to be the cause of the decrease in bias.[69] Thus, in the legal context, efforts to increase the numbers of Native law professors, lawyers, decision-makers, leaders, and other countertypical exemplars in authority positions may help lessen implicit bias against Native peoples.

Exposing participants to a multicultural viewpoint or learning values of diversity can also moderate implicit bias.[70] In this way, incorporating more Native American or Native Hawaiian law courses into the law school curriculum or including federal Indian law or Native Hawaiian law on bar exams in light of the diverse and multicultural values they bring could prove meaningful. At the same time, as others have maintained, such an endeavor can make Native law more visible, promote respect for Native peoples and their sovereign rights, diversify the bar, foster positive relationships and discourse among Natives and non-Natives, and increase access to justice.[71] It may also operate to increase the number of Native attorneys and legal academics, thereby creating more "counterstereotypic" agents.

---

[66] Kang & Banaji, *supra* note 4, at 1105–07.

[67] *See About Us*, American Indian College Fund, http://www.collegefund.org/content/real_indian (last visited Sept. 5, 2011). *See also generally* Stephanie A. Fryberg et al., *Of Warrior Chiefs and Indian Princesses: The Psychological Consequences of American Indian Mascots*, 30 Basic & Applied Soc. Psychol. 208, 215 (2008) (finding that exposure to the American Indian College Fund's advertising campaign did not depress Native American students' self-concept, whereas exposure to Native American mascot stereotypes did).

[68] Kang & Banaji, *supra* note 4, at 1108.

[69] Lane et al., *supra* note 4, at 428.

[70] Levinson, *supra* note 4, at 415–16.

[71] Gloria Valencia-Weber & Sherri Nicole Thomas, *When the State Bar Exam Embraces Indian Law: Teaching Experiences and Observations*, 82 N.D. L. Rev. 741, 751–52 (2006); Gabriel S. Galanda, *Bar None! The Social Impact of Testing Federal Indian Law on State Bar Exams*, Fed. Lawyer, Mar.-Apr. 2006, at 30–33; The National Congress of American Indians Resolution #MOH-04–001, at 1 (2004).

These efforts must be closely aligned with the larger, ongoing project of changing the structures that maintain these stereotypes and inhibit genuine justice for Native peoples. As Eric Yamamoto and Ashley Obrey contend, this broader project may involve "scrutiniz[ing] the history of the grievance and decod[ing] stock stories embodying cultural stereotypes that seemingly legitimize the injustice" and "examin[ing] the institutional – the ways that organizational structures can embody discriminatory policies that deny fair access to resources or promote aggression."[72] It may also require governments to recognize the harms done against Native peoples; accept responsibility for the damage and for taking action to repair that damage; work to reconstruct Native governance and new productive relationships between the federal, state, and Native governments; and take reparatory actions that promote reconciliation between the United States and its Native peoples. Although this effort can take many forms, it means the United States must support greater Native political authority, control of lands and resources, and cultural sovereignty to begin repairing the persisting damage of historic injustice.

IV. CONCLUSION

Justin Levinson maintains that "debiasing measures may be highly scientific and sometimes cognitively inaccessible." For this reason, he asserts that reducing or eliminating implicit bias requires both a de-biasing and a "cultural" solution, which "requires recognizing the link between historical and societal discrimination and the continued exhibition of implicit biases." Addressing implicit racial biases thus "requires more than a scientific effort at debiasing through cues and primes. It requires a recognition that their very existence reflects the state of American culture. And this recognition, in turn, calls for steps that will facilitate cultural change" as "part of a larger movement to achieve social equality, healing, and the overcoming of historical injustice."[73]

As such, we contend that attempts to lessen or eliminate implicit bias against Native peoples as sovereigns form an integral element of the larger, ongoing project of repatriating Native lands, resources, and sovereignty to Native peoples. This effort must take into account the deep historical, cultural, social, and psychological roots of the negative stereotypes that serve to legitimize injustices, as well as seek to change the structures (legal, cultural, political, and otherwise) that serve to maintain these stereotypes.

---

[72] Eric K. Yamamoto & Ashley Kaiao Obrey, *Reframing Redress: A "Social Healing Through Justice" Approach to United States–Native Hawaiian and Japan–Ainu Reconciliation Initiatives,* 16 ASIAN AM. L.J. 5, 33 (2009).

[73] Levinson, *supra* note 4, at 418.

14

Capital Punishment

Choosing Life or Death (Implicitly)

Robert J. Smith and G. Ben Cohen

"Even under the most sophisticated of death penalty statutes, race continues to play a major role in determining who shall live and who shall die."

– Justice Harry Blackmun[1]

A Fulton County, Georgia, jury sentenced Warren McCleskey, a black man, to death for the murder of a white police officer. McCleskey argued on appeal that his sentence should be reversed because race discrimination plagued the administration of the death penalty in Georgia. To make the claim, McCleskey presented a comprehensive statistical study that tracked more than 2,000 Georgia murder cases.[2] The raw numbers established that defendants charged with killing white persons received the death penalty in 11% of cases, whereas defendants charged with killing black persons received the death penalty 1% of the time.[3] The raw numbers also established that black defendants charged with killing white victims (as opposed to those who killed black victims) were twenty-two times more likely to be sentenced to death.[4] Once adjusted to account for more than two-hundred case-related factors, the Baldus study demonstrated that a defendant charged with killing a white victim was 4.3 times more likely to receive a death sentence than a defendant charged with killing a black victim.

In 1987 in *McCleskey v. Kemp*,[5] the U.S. Supreme Court rejected the challenge to Georgia's death penalty system despite the overwhelming statistical evidence suggesting that race (and especially race of the victim) played a significant role in whether a defendant received the death penalty. The Court accepted the race

---

[1] Callins v. Collins, 510 U.S. 1141, 1153 (1994) (Blackmun, J., dissenting from denial of certiorari).
[2] McCleskey v. Kemp, 481 U.S. 279, 286 (1987).
[3] *Id.* at 287.
[4] *Id.*
[5] 481 U.S. 279, 297–98 (1987).

disparities for the sake of argument, but observed that the studies that McCleskey presented could not prove that race bias affected *his* particular case. In dissent, Justice Brennan labeled the Court's position that such claims "would open the door to widespread challenges to all aspects of criminal sentencing" as "a fear of too much justice."[6]

Fast forward to the present. Although it is more difficult to imagine juries making explicitly race-based decisions, empirical studies continue to document the presence of race discrimination in the administration of the death penalty. For instance, in 2010, Professors Michael Radelet and Glen Pierce compared the race of the victim in roughly 15,000 homicides that occurred in North Carolina between 1980 and 2007 with the race of the victim in the 352 homicide cases that resulted in a death sentence over the same time period.[7] The researchers documented that a defendant is three times more likely to get a death sentence in North Carolina for murdering a white person than for killing a black person.[8]

A 2010 study of homicides in East Baton Rouge, Louisiana, documented the same trend. Professors Radelet and Pierce researched 1,100 potentially capital crimes committed in East Baton Rouge Parish between 1990 and 2008.[9] Their research indicated that prosecutors pursued capital cases 364% more often when the victim was white than when the victim was black. The researchers also found that black citizens represented 82% of homicide victims in East Baton Rouge Parish, yet the victim was white in more than half of the cases in which a death sentence was imposed.

With the appearance of declining explicit racism, the continued presence of race disparities, and a reluctant Supreme Court, explaining and remedying race effects in capital punishment resemble a Gordian knot. Reframing the issue through the lens of implicit bias, however, helps explain the dogged persistence of race disparities and also points us toward the steps that courts, as well as defense lawyers and egalitarian-minded prosecutors, might take to decrease the risk of race effects before a jury issues a death sentence in a particular case. It also gives rise to the view that the post-Gregg[10] death penalty schemes – where a jury's determination that a specific defendant should receive the death penalty is made with unfettered discretion in which "subtle, less consciously held racial attitudes could also influence a juror's decision"[11] – are unable to eliminate the concern that animated the Court in *Furman v. Georgia*[12] to eliminate the death penalty.

---

[6] *Id.* at 339 (Brennan, J., dissenting).
[7] Michael L. Radelet & Glenn L. Pierce, *Race and Death Sentencing in North Carolina 1980–2007*, 89 N.C. L. Rev. (Forthcoming 2011).
[8] *Id.*
[9] Glenn L. Pierce & Michael L. Radelet, *Death Sentencing in East Baton Rouge Parish, 1990–2008*, 71 La. L. Rev. 647 (2011).
[10] Gregg v. Georgia, 428 U. S. 153 (1976).
[11] Turner v. Murray, 476 U.S. 28, 42 (1986).
[12] Furman v. Georgia, 408 U.S. 238 (1972) (Stewart, J., concurring) ("These death sentences are cruel and unusual in the same way that being struck by lightning is cruel and unusual. For, of all the people

This chapter proceeds in three parts. Part I provides context by describing implicit racial bias and exploring the broad contours of its relationship to death penalty prosecutions. Part II focuses on three discrete locations in a capital trial where the operation of implicit racial bias could have the most damaging effect: (1) during consideration of aggravating evidence, (2) during consideration of mitigating evidence, and (3) during the introduction of victim impact statements. In Part III, we offer concluding thoughts and also consider how the capital trial–related phenomena we discuss throughout the chapter might also apply in the capital plea-bargaining context.

I. IMPLICIT RACE BIAS AND DEATH PENALTY PROSECUTIONS

Implicit social cognition describes the process by which the brain uses "mental associations that are so well-established as to operate without awareness, or without intention, or without control."[13] Professor Jerry Kang gives the following example:

> When we see something with a flat seat, a back, and some legs, we recognize it as a "chair." Regardless of whether it is plush or wooden, with wheels or bolted down, we know what to do with an object that fits into the category "chair." Without spending a lot of mental energy, we simply sit.[14]

The mental associations that allow us to recognize an object as a "chair" operate through the mind's use of schemas. Schemas are "templates of knowledge that help us organize specific examples into broad categories."[15] These schemas may represent actual shortcuts in the neural network. "Stereotypes" refer to the schemas that we use to categorize people. The stereotypic beliefs we hold often do not operate explicitly. Although we are increasingly unlikely to admit to harboring (or even to be consciously aware of) negative racial attitudes, a plethora of research studies show that people of all races continue to harbor negative implicit biases against black citizens and members of a variety of other groups. Indeed, implicit social cognition studies often detect bias in people who sincerely believe that they are color-blind or race neutral.

The pernicious effects of implicit racial bias are concentrated around decision points marked by a high degree of discretion. The decision to sentence someone to death is inherently subjective and depends, in part, on how jurors quantify harm: All

convicted of rapes and murders in 1967 and 1968, many just as reprehensible as these, the petitioners are among a capriciously selected random handful upon whom the sentence of death has in fact been imposed. My concurring Brothers have demonstrated that, if any basis can be discerned for the selection of these few to be sentenced to die, it is the constitutionally impermissible basis of race.").

[13] FAQ #22, PROJECT IMPLICIT, https://implicit.harvard.edu/implicit/demo/background/faqs.html#faq2 (last visited September 26, 2011).

[14] JERRY KANG, IMPLICIT BIAS: A PRIMER FOR COURTS (2009), http://wp.jerrykang.net.s110363.gridserver.com/wp-content/uploads/2010/10/kang-Implicit-Bias-Primer-for-courts-09.pdf.

[15] *Id.*

murders are horrible, but is *this* murder among the "worst of the worst"? How much suffering did the murder cause the victim's family? What are the characteristics and attributes of the person who committed the crime? This triangle of factors drives capital sentencing determinations. Each requires emotional and moral processing, which, despite our best efforts, is mediated by race. The argument we make here is that implicit bias could have an impact at multiple points from the initial decision to charge a case capitally, to the decision whether to offer (and accept) a plea to life imprisonment, to the consideration of aggravating and mitigating evidence, to the penalty phase deliberation process. We claim that these instances of bias aggregate throughout the capital case and become visible as we look at statistical disparities over a number of cases.

The bottom line is that black individuals do worse as both defendants and victims in capital trials. We propose that this might be because when decision-makers (e.g., prosecutors, judges, and jurors) think of people who deserve the ultimate punishment, they think of black defendants as more inherently violent, dangerous, and prone to criminality than white defendants. Jurors might also see black defendants as being less fully human and thus might be more likely to believe in the need to resort to physical means of control or retaliation, whereas these same jurors might believe that the possibility of change, rehabilitation, or redemption in white offenders calls for less severe punishment.

Consider the following two studies, both of which suggest that something about the capital trial itself produces discriminatory outcomes. First, a study by Professor Jennifer Eberhardt investigated whether a capital defendant's afro-centric features influenced evaluations of his death-worthiness.[16] Eberhardt used pictures of forty-four black capital defendants who had been convicted of killing white victims and whose trials reached the penalty phase. She then asked participants (who were not told that the men in the pictures had committed any crime) to rate each picture in terms of how stereotypically black the person appeared to be (e.g., thick lips, wide nose). After controlling for nonracial factors known to have an impact on capital sentencing, she found that afro-centric features correlated with being sentenced to death. Indeed, black defendants whose afro-centric features situated them among the top half of the stereotypicality distribution were more than twice as likely to receive a death sentence.

In another study, Professor Jack Glaser and his colleagues tested whether a defendant's race has an impact on the likelihood that jurors find him to be guilty of first-degree murder in a case in which the death penalty is a sentencing option.[17] Participants read materials from a fictional triple murder. Half of the participants were told that death was the maximum punishment possible, whereas the other

---

[16] *See* Jennifer L. Eberhardt et al., *Looking Deathworthy: Perceived Stereotypicality of Black Defendants Predicts Capital-Sentencing Outcomes*, 17 PSYCHOL. SCI. 383, 386 (2006).

[17] *See, e.g.*, Jack Glaser et al., *Possibility of Death Sentence Has Divergent Effect on Verdicts for Black and White Defendants*, GOLDMAN SCHOOL OF PUBLIC POLICY WORKING PAPER NO. GSPP09–002 (2009), *available at* http://ssrn.com/abstract=1428943 (last visited September 26, 2011).

half were told that life without the possibility of parole was the maximum sentence. Half of the defendants were black, and half were white. Participants told that the death penalty was the maximum possible punishment convicted black defendants 25% more often than white defendants, whereas participants told that the maximum sentence was life without the possibility of parole did not convict black defendants significantly more often than white defendants. Because defendant race appears to have a stronger impact on verdict outcomes in cases where death is a possible sentence, Professor Glaser and his colleagues suggested that "capital punishment may be more than another domain of racial disparities; it may actually be a cause."[18]

Taken together, the results of these two studies, each of which show the possibility that something in the capital trial process itself drives discriminatory results at both the guilt and penalty phases of a capital trial, warrants a careful review of the primary avenues by which implicit racial bias enters into capital cases. The remainder of this chapter explores the unique ways in which implicit racial bias can operate in trials where the government seeks the death penalty. Our thesis is that implicit race bias presents an unacceptably high risk that race will infect *all or almost all* interracial capital trials (but especially those with a black defendant and a white victim). Moreover, the comparative lack of bias against white defendants, or the diminished perception of gravity of harm with black victims, completes an ugly privilege. Ultimately, the decision to sentence a person to death is based not on a rational determination, a weighing of the evidence, or the finding that the particular defendant is indeed guilty of the worst of the worst offenses, but rather on a series of unconscious decisions, by prosecutors, judges, jurors, and even defense lawyers in which race affects the processing of the underlying evidence and tilts the scales of justice.

The remainder of the chapter proceeds with a focus on the operation of implicit racial bias at three points in capital cases where discretion is at its peak and thus arbitrary factors such as race are most likely to creep into the process. The next section focuses on how implicit race bias might color consideration of facts that aggravate a crime. We then explore how implicit bias can inhibit full consideration of factors presented by the defendant to mitigate the crime or to humanize him- or herself to the jury. Finally, we consider how the introduction of victim impact evidence might activate implicit biases that are responsible for a significant part of the often documented race-of-the-victim effect.

II. UNDERSTANDING THE ROLE OF IMPLICIT BIAS IN A CAPITAL TRIAL: AGGRAVATING EVIDENCE, MITIGATING EVIDENCE, AND VICTIM IMPACT STATEMENTS

In 1972 the U.S. Supreme Court enacted a sea change in the administration of capital punishment, holding in *Furman v. Georgia* that the Eighth Amendment requires that the death penalty be reserved for the worst offenders who commit the worst

---

[18] *Id.*

offenses. The elements introduced at trial that determine whether a particular case satisfies that criteria are known as aggravating factors (those that tend to make death the more appropriate punishment) and mitigating factors (those that tend to make life the more appropriate punishment). Balancing these aggravating and mitigating factors, which nearly all states require capital jurors to do, is the epitome of a high-stakes, hopelessly discretionary determination. Justice Kennedy described this effort as "still in search of a unifying principle" and "not all together satisfactory."[19] It requires jurors to reach a decision that "reflect[s] a reasoned moral response to the defendant's background, character, and crime."[20] It leaves plenty of room for implicit bias to operate.

Jurors are asked to distinguish among defendants who have done horrible things and to make a reasoned moral response as to which of these people who have committed murder deserve to be executed and which deserve to be sentenced to life imprisonment. Implicit racial bias colors the way that the jurors evaluate the evidence, and thus in identical cases jurors assessing the evidence against black defendants might find them to be more dangerous (or to have committed a more brutal crime) or less deserving of empathy (or mercy) than if they had been white. Research by Professor Justin Levinson and Dr. Danielle Young supports the argument that jurors need not hold explicit negative attitudes toward black defendants for implicit beliefs to have an impact on how the juror assigns weight to evidence.[21] In their study, after reading about a fictional robbery at a Mini Mart, each participant was then asked to view five pictures from the crime scene in sequence for four seconds each. The first, second, fourth, and fifth pictures were irrelevant. The third picture depicted a masked assailant reaching over the counter with a gun in his left hand. Half of the participants saw a picture with the visible forearm of a dark-skinned suspect; the others saw the visible forearm of a light-skinned suspect. The participants were told the police had apprehended a suspect and were asked to evaluate several pieces of ambiguous evidence and determine the probative value of each piece.

Participants shown the photo of the dark-skinned suspect found the ambiguous pieces of evidence to be more probative of guilt and determined the suspect to be guilty far more often than those shown the light-skinned suspect. These findings correlated with the implicit biases of participants (as measured by performance on the IAT) but not with their explicit racial attitudes. This study demonstrates that the implicit attitudes and stereotypes that a juror holds can influence how that juror evaluates otherwise neutral pieces of evidence. When the evidence being evaluated

---

[19] Kennedy v. Louisiana, 128 S. Ct. 2641, 2659 (2008).

[20] *See* Stephen B. Bright, *Counsel for the Poor: The Death Sentence Not for the Worst Crime but for the Worst Lawyer*, 103 YALE L.J. 1835, 1837 n.14 (1994) (quoting Penry v. Lynaugh, 492 U.S. 302, 319 (1989).

[21] *See* Justin D. Levinson & Danielle Young, *Different Shades of Bias: Skin Tone, Implicit Racial Bias, and Judgments of Ambiguous Evidence*, 112 W. VA. L. REV. 307 (2010).

is relevant to the evaluation of how aggravated a murder (or murderer) is, and the preconceived implicit stereotype is that black persons are violent and prone to criminality, then it is reasonable to conclude that implicit race bias introduces an arbitrary factor into the capital sentencing determination.

A. *Aggravating Evidence*

Every death penalty jurisdiction has a list of statutory aggravating factors, at least one of which the prosecution must prove to a jury beyond a reasonable doubt before a convicted murderer can be "death-eligible." Two aggravating factors in particular require subjective moral evaluations of the crime and the offender and thus are particularly subject to the influence of implicit racial bias. One of the most common aggravators is known as the Heinous, Atrocious, or Cruel (HAC) aggravator.[22] States define HAC differently. For instance, in *Maynard v. Cartwright*, the Court implicitly approved of a definition of the Oklahoma HAC aggravator as being applicable to murders with "some kind of torture or physical abuse."[23] Similarly, in *Walton v. Arizona*, the Court noted its approval of the Arizona Supreme Court's construction of the Arizona HAC aggravator as applying to a murder in which "the perpetrator inflicts mental anguish or physical abuse before the victim's death" and the "[m]ental anguish includes a victim's uncertainty as to his ultimate fate."[24] To determine whether HAC applies, jurors must make "reference to community-based standards, standards that incorporate values,"[25] and thus the decision that a murder was heinous, atrocious, or cruel is not the same as finding that an objective fact (for instance, that the defendant pulled the trigger on a gun that killed a convenience store clerk) exists.

Jurors asked to determine whether a crime was heinous, atrocious, or cruel necessarily must answer whether the defendant intended to commit a murder with the degree of depravity required to find the HAC aggravator applicable. As jurors look over to the defendant, what they see might have an impact on that finding. If they see a black person, then that visual cue might activate stereotypes about black citizens, such as the stereotypes of black persons as violent, dangerous, and prone to criminality. Recall the Eberhardt study (discussed in Chapter 3 on criminal law and procedure[26]), in which participants were able to identify an object as a "knife" or a "gun" more quickly when primed with a consciously imperceptible image of a black face. The study suggests that simply looking at a black defendant could trigger

---

[22] *See, e.g.,* Schriro v. Summerlin, 542 U.S. 348, 361 (2004) (Breyer, J., dissenting) (noting that "[t]he leading single aggravator charged in Arizona . . . requires the fact-finder to decide whether the crime was committed in an "especially heinous, cruel, or depraved manner").

[23] Maynard v. Cartwright, 486 U.S. 356, 365 (1988).

[24] Walton v. Arizona, 497 U.S. 639, 654 (1990).

[25] Schriro, 542 U.S. at 361 (Breyer, J., dissenting).

[26] *See* Chapter 3 at 48.

negative associations that color the perception that a murder is particularly heinous, atrocious, or cruel.

A second aggravating factor – statutorily defined in some states and implicitly referenced in catchall aggravators in other states – is whether a defendant is a "future danger." Like the HAC aggravator, the future dangerousness aggravator does not require that jurors simply determine that an objective fact has been proved. Instead, it requires jurors to answer subjective questions about how scary a defendant (and his or her past actions) seems to be and then to make a probabilistic determination about future conduct. Thus, the future dangerousness finding requires the type of moral processing that triggers associations between black persons and criminality and violence. As the Court wrote in *Turner v. Murray*, "a juror who believes that blacks are violence prone... might well be influenced by that belief in deciding whether petitioner's crime involved the aggravating factors specified under [the] law."[27]

The stereotype of black persons as violence prone also appears to elicit fear, which in turn amplifies the perception that a defendant is dangerous. This stereotype that black persons are fearsome appears to be so powerful as to activate a discriminatory response at the neurological level. Professor Matthew Lieberman and colleagues used functional magnetic resonance imaging (fMRI) scans to record brain activity in participants who had just been exposed to either a black face or a white face.[28] The study found that, when participants were shown black faces, brain activity spiked (for both white and black participants) in the region of the brain responsible for responding to possible threats and other hostile activity. The presence of a stereotypic belief that a black defendant is more violence prone combined with a fear-based response toward the black defendant creates an unacceptable risk that the dangerousness evaluation is influenced by the race of the defendant.

B. *Mitigating Evidence*

To be eligible for a possible death sentence a capital defendant must be convicted of murder plus an aggravating factor. However, the jury is not authorized to return a death sentence against a death-eligible offender until it has considered any mitigating evidence that the defendant proffers. In *Woodson v. North Carolina*, the Supreme Court held that the Eighth Amendment requires that the jury consider the "relevant aspects of the character and record of each convicted defendant before the imposition upon him of a sentence of death," to determine whether any "compassionate or mitigating factors stemming from the diverse frailties of humankind" warrant a sentence less than death.[29] The most common types of mitigation evidence offered

---

[27] Turner v. Murray, 476 US 28, 35 (1986).
[28] Matthew D. Lieberman et al., *An fMRI Investigation of Race-Related Amygdala Activity in African-American and Caucasian-American Individuals*, 8 NATURE NEUROSCIENCE 720 (2005).
[29] Woodson v. North Carolina, 428 US 280, 304 (1976).

by the defense include evidence of diminished intellectual functioning, of childhood abuse, and of severe mental illness. This section argues that the persuasiveness of mitigating evidence could be mediated by implicit racial bias, or as the Court wrote in *Turner*, once negative stereotypes about black persons are activated, jurors "might also be less favorably inclined towards the defendant's evidence of mitigating circumstance."[30]

There are at least three ways that implicit bias could seep into this process. First, negative stereotypes about black defendants could create active hostility, which could block an empathic response. This factor is the flip side of the dynamics discussed in the previous section. Second, the defendant might become dehumanized, which also could block an empathic response. For example, in *Darden v. Wainwright*,[31] the Court discussed a case where the prosecution referred to the defendant during closing arguments as an "animal" that "shouldn't be out of his cell unless he has a leash on him and a prison guard at the other end of that leash." In a recent Louisiana case, the prosecution referred to the black capital defendant as "[a]nimals like that (indicating)" and implored the jury to "be a voice for the people of this Parish" and to "send a message to that jungle."[32] The use of animal imagery in reference to the accused stirs up the exact type of emotional response that allows jurors to stop pondering the accused as an individual human being.[33]

Compelling empirical research suggests that referring to the accused in non-human terms dehumanizes the defendant in the eyes of the jurors and results in harsher punishment. Professor Philip Goff and colleagues asked participants to view a degraded image of an ape that came into focus over a number of frames.[34] When primed with a consciously undetectable image of a black face, participants were able to identify the ape in fewer frames; conversely, when primed with a consciously undetectable white face, participants required more frames to detect the ape than when they received no prime at all. These studies indicate that citizens implicitly associate blacks with apes, a finding that heightens the concern surrounding the use of animal imagery during prosecution.

Building on this theme, Professor Goff next explored the black-ape association in the context of capital decision-making by comparing the frequency of animalistic references to black capital defendants with that of similar references to white defendants in a dataset of 600 capital cases prosecuted in Philadelphia between 1979 and

---

[30] Turner, 476 U.S. at 35.

[31] Darden v. Wainwright, 477 U.S. 168 (1986).

[32] Louisiana v. Harris, 820 So. 2d 471 (La. 2002). *See also* Philip A. Goff et al., *Not Yet Human: Implicit Knowledge, Historical Dehumanization, and Contemporary Consequences*, 94 J. PERSONALITY & SOC. PSYCHOL. 292, 292 (2008) (noting that "[o]ne of the officers who participated in the Rodney King beating of 1991 had just come from another incident in which he referred to a domestic dispute involving a Black couple as 'something right out of *Gorillas in the Mist*'").

[33] *See id.* (quoting Caldwell v. Mississippi, 472 U. S. 320, 340 n.7 (1985) (discussing the "highly subjective, unique, individualized judgment regarding the punishment that a particular person deserves").

[34] *See* Goff et al., *supra* note 32, at 294–97.

1999.[35] The study found that coverage from the *Inquirer*, Philadelphia's major daily newspaper, of black capital defendants included, on average, nearly four times the number of dehumanizing references *per article* than articles covering white capital defendants. Furthermore, the study found a strong correlation between the number of times an animalistic reference was made and the likelihood that the defendant was sentenced to death.[36]

The government – in capital cases – is seeking nothing less than an agreement of twelve jurors to kill another human being. As cognitive scientist David Livingstone Smith recently wrote, "thinking of humans as less than human" is essential to exterminate a human being in "cold blood."[37] Implicit racial bias research teaches us that transforming defendants into a less-than-human species is easier when the defendant is black.

The third way in which implicit bias could affect evaluations of mitigating evidence relates not to a disfavoring of black defendants, but to a favoring of white defendants. The aim of mitigation evidence is to trigger an empathic response in jurors by creating a narrative that humanizes a person who has been convicted of committing what most imagine to be an unfathomable act. To be receptive to mitigation evidence jurors must be able to place themselves in the defendant's position. This is a difficult task. Neuroimaging studies reveal that members of extremely marginalized groups (e.g., the homeless) – a category in which convicted murderers likely fall – "are so dehumanized that they may not even be encoded as social beings."[38] Professor Goff explained that individuals from outgroups "who elicit disgust" and those "who are the least valued in the culture" appear not to be "deemed worthy of social consideration on a neurological level."[39] If all defendants who enter the penalty phase begin at this disadvantage of being dehumanized by virtue of their conduct, then it takes powerful mitigation evidence presented in a compelling narrative to humanize a capital client.

The task is often more difficult still when the defendant is black. Most jurors in capital cases are white. When white jurors connect the mitigation evidence presented by the defendant to their own life experiences (or to those of family or friends), the process is adulterated by the phenomenon of ingroup bias. Or, as Justice Scalia put the point in his dissent in *Powers v. Ohio*, there exists an "undeniable

---

[35] *Id.*

[36] *See id.* at 305 ("despite the fact that we controlled for a substantial number of factors that are known to influence criminal sentencing, these apelike representations were associated with the most profound outcome of intergroup dehumanization: death").

[37] DAVID LIVINGSTONE SMITH, WHY WE DEMEAN, ENSLAVE, AND EXTERMINATE OTHERS (2011). Smith traces, for instance, the manner in which Nazis explicitly referred to Jews as "subhumans" in order to render it more permissible to exterminate them.

[38] *See* Goff et al., *supra* note 32, at 294.

[39] *Id.*

reality... that all groups tend to have particular sympathies and hostilities – most notably, sympathies toward their own group members."[40]

The result is that white citizens receive the benefit of an enhanced ingroup empathic response. A recent study used transcranial magnetic stimulation (TMS) to measure corticospinal activity level in participants who were shown short video clips of a needle entering into the hand of either a light-skinned or dark-skinned target.[41] Consistent with the ingroup empathic bias explanation, researchers here found that region-specific brain activity levels are higher when a light-skinned participant views the clip of a light-skinned participant experiencing pain than when a light-skinned participant sees a clip of a dark-skinned target being subjected to pain.

According to Professor Jerry Kang this "[i]ngroup bias is so strong that people explicitly report liking 'ingroups' even when they are randomly assigned to them, and even when the groups are made up. For example, being arbitrarily placed in the category 'Quan' or 'Xanthie' – groups that do not exist, and thus should be considered equivalent – generated implicit biases within participants in favor of their assigned group."[42] Kang highlighted that the most disturbing element of ingroup bias is that the more socially privileged a group is perceived to be – for example, white over black – the stronger the biases held in favor of the group.

Of course, in the capital sentencing context, we are not talking about "Quans" or "Xanthies" but people – and when white jurors view the world through ingroup bias, then those jurors can imagine themselves in the shoes of the white defendant; for example, that defendant could remind one juror of her brother who suffers from schizophrenia, or another juror of his borderline mentally retarded cousin, or a third juror of her friend who was sexually and physically abused as a child. When jurors can imagine that defendant's experiences as something that someone they know could experience, that empathic response triggers a favorable implicit bias toward the white defendant. In contrast, if white jurors are not able to connect with the mitigation evidence because they see a black defendant, and the negative stereotypes of black people have been automatically triggered, then that lack of empathic response biases the black defendant, even though jurors might not hold any explicit racial prejudices against black persons.

Black jurors likely are more able to empathize with mitigation evidence presented by black defendants. It is very possible, however, that this ability to empathize with a black defendant's struggles and defects results in the disqualification of a disproportionate number of black jurors from jury service in the first place. Capital juries – unlike any other – are asked whether they could impose a death sentence

---

[40] Powers v. Ohio, 499 U.S. 400, 424 (1991).

[41] Alessio Avenanti, *Racial Bias Reduces Empathic Sensorimotor Resonance with Other Race Pain*, 20 Current Biology 1018, 1018–22 (2010).

[42] Jerry Kang & Kristin Lane, *Seeing Through Colorblindness: Implicit Bias and the Law*, 58 UCLA L. Rev. 465, 475 n.37 (2010).

on the defendant sitting in front of them. As such, death-qualification jury selection tests whether a juror, looking over at a defendant, can imagine imposing a death sentence. Considering imposition of a death sentence at the outset of voir dire – before the presentation of evidence that generates moral outrage – requires some ability to set aside the human condition. By this, we mean that considering a death sentence – not in the abstract but for the person sitting fifty feet away – requires potential jurors to contemplate whether they are willing to be responsible for deciding to end a particular person's life (should the facts so warrant) before they know anything about the person. If white jurors view a black defendant as inherently dangerous or as someone less human than themselves, then they might find it easier to agree to being able to consider a death sentence. In what he deemed "the death penalty priming hypothesis," Professor Justin Levinson contemplated that the process of questioning jurors about their ability to return a possible death sentence ("death-qualification") activates stereotypes about black persons, which in turn, make jurors more punitive against black defendants.[43] It might be that as these stereotypes become activated black potential jurors are eliminated from consideration because they express hesitation about the prospect of returning a death sentence and white jurors are seated because they are able to picture sentencing the dangerous, less-than-human defendant to death. If so, the operation of implicit bias interrupts consideration of mitigation evidence before the trial even begins.

C. Victim Impact Statements

The previous subsection on implicit racial bias and the evaluation of mitigating evidence demonstrated that, all things being equal, white jurors are more likely to magnify the humanity of white victims and marginalize the humanity of black perpetrators. This dynamic also negatively affects defendants who murder white victims, because the favorable implicit biases that flow toward white victims enhance the perceived harm of the crime when the victim is white. This process occurs most clearly through the introduction of victim impact evidence in capital cases. The family members of victims in capital trials are allowed to introduce evidence about how the death of their loved one has affected their own lives. Such evidence describes the physical, emotional, and financial impact and is often highly emotional. Justice Stevens described one example of extremely powerful victim impact evidence in a recent California death penalty case:

> The prosecution played a 20-minute video consisting of a montage of still photographs and video footage documenting [nineteen year-old] Weir's life from her infancy until shortly before she was killed. The video was narrated by the victim's mother with soft music playing in the background, and it showed scenes of her swimming, horseback riding, and attending school and social functions with her

---

[43] Justin Levinson, *Race, Death and the Complicitous Mind*, 58 DePaul L. Rev. 599, 631 (2009).

family and friends. The video ended with a view of her grave marker and footage of people riding horseback in Alberta, Canada – the "kind of heaven" in which her mother said she belonged.[44]

This type of heart-wrenching testimony easily can overcome the presentation of mitigating evidence regardless of the race of the victim or the defendant. The level of emotion induced by the presentation of victim impact statements encourages jurors to decide whether capital punishment is appropriate on the basis of empathy for the victim (and not on the relative severity of the crime or culpability of the offender). Intricately tied to the display of empathy toward the victim are feelings of anger and frustration toward the perpetrator. In white victim/black defendant cases, white jurors likely display both enhanced ingroup empathy toward the white victim and outgroup anger, fear, and frustration toward the black defendant.

Research suggests that jurors quantify harm to families of murdered victims by predicting the impact that the murder-death of a person will have on their friends and family members. This type of evaluation requires empathy, and white jurors – especially those who live in vastly different socioeconomic circles from many victims' family members – are likely able to empathize more with the family members of white victims. Experimental evidence indicates that the level of emotion displayed by the testifying victim moderates verdict outcomes. The point here is that jurors assess the level of emotion displayed – and the perception of a corresponding ability to cope with the loss – as predicting overall harm. As Professor Jeremy Blumenthal explained,

> When a juror observes a witness who plausibly predicts future pain and suffering above that which a juror might expect her to reasonably experience, that juror's assessment of the amount of harm caused may increase. On the other hand, seeing a witness who is apparently "coping" well with the aftermath of a crime – perhaps even more than the juror might think "appropriate" – may, conversely, lead to assessing the harm as lower than the juror may otherwise judge.[45]

When we consider the impact of predicting continued feelings of loss in the future and implicit social cognition together, especially in the context of a cross-racial homicide case, it is not difficult to see how differences in cultural displays of emotion, language use in conveying a sense of loss, or even dress can intermix with stereotypes about the offender and about the victim to result in a race-influenced assessment of victim impact evidence. For example, when a video is introduced as victim impact evidence that depicts a young girl with fair skin, blonde hair, and blue eyes running around a yard in a suburban neighborhood with other white children, white jurors are able to imagine that victim as a close relative or friend and predict how they

---

44 Kelly v. California, 129 S.Ct. 564 (2008) (Stevens, J., dissenting from denial of certiorari).
45 Jeremy A. Blumenthal, *Affective Forecasting and Capital Sentencing: Reducing the Effect of Victim Impact Statements*, 46 Am. Crim. L. Rev. 107 (2009).

would feel if that victim had been their friend or relative. Again, this empathic response triggers an inaccurate prediction about how one is going to feel after time has passed, so the juror overstates the harm. Conversely, if white jurors see a video of a little black girl, with braided rows of hair, playing in an urban neighborhood with other black children, they are less likely to be able to picture their family member or relative as the girl in the picture. The empathic reaction is dampened or nonexistent.

III. CONCLUSION

It is important to consider that aggravating, mitigating, and victim impact evidence might influence a capital case far before the trial begins. Often the best outcome in a capital case is a plea deal that avoids a death sentence, and indeed the vast majority of death penalty cases are resolved by plea agreements. Yet implicit race bias could influence these pretrial plea negotiations.

Research by Professors Sheri Lynn Johnson and Theodore Eisenberg on implicit bias by defense attorneys in capital cases demonstrates that white male capital trial and habeas attorneys display the same level of implicit racial bias (including associating white people with "good") that exists in the public at large.[46] Imagine that two defendants are charged with murder in the course of a robbery. The robberies are unrelated to each other. Both occurred in the same county. In both instances, the evidence of participation in the robbery, if not the actual murder, is beyond dispute; this leaves both defendants at the bare minimum susceptible to a life sentence. Both defendants are young and male. One is black and one is white. They have the same attorney – a committed public defender who wants what is best for his clients. The prosecution seeks the death penalty against both defendants.

With Client A, who is black, the public defender informs him of the charge and that a plea might be possible. Client A, who adamantly denies shooting anyone, becomes frustrated at the suggestion of a plea to life without the possibility of parole. Therefore no plea offer is taken to the prosecutor. The public defender takes the case to trial, presenting a defense that the client participated in the robbery but did not shoot the victim (making the defendant a principal to first-degree murder and at least susceptible to a life sentence). The attorney contacts family members in preparation for the penalty phase. They tell him that the defendant suffered from fetal alcohol syndrome. He is convicted of first-degree murder. The jury hears of the defendant's bad conduct in jail as a juvenile and sentences the defendant to death despite evidence of fetal alcohol syndrome.

Client B is white. The public defender informs him of the charge and explains that a plea deal might be possible. Client B also adamantly denies shooting anyone and becomes frustrated at the suggestion of a plea to life without the possibility of

---

[46] *See* Theodore Eisenberg & Sheri Lynn Johnson, *Implicit Racial Attitudes of Death Penalty Lawyers*, 53 DePaul L. Rev. 1539 (2004).

parole. The public defender sees something of his own son – troubled but essentially good – in Client B. He meets with him more to discuss the charges, he relates to Client B's family, and he brings family members into the jail to meet with Client B. They explain to Client B the legal theory of principals and how Client B's statement and proposed defense make him guilty of first-degree murder as a principal. After family members detail how difficult it has always been to communicate with Client B, expert assistance in communicating with him is secured. The public defender speaks to the district attorney on Client B's behalf, explaining that Client B's oxygen intake at birth was reduced, likely leading to intermittent anger disorder that is now being managed with medication. The State agrees to a life plea.

Client A was not sentenced to death because he is black, nor did Client B avoid the death penalty simply because he was white. Yet race played an integral role in the disparity in sentence. This is what implicit bias does to the administration of capital punishment. It seeps into areas where discretion is at its peak. It has the ability to tip the scales in close calls – sometimes leading to the finding of an aggravating factor or the failure to find a mitigating factor. If we could add up all the instances in the life of a capital case where it has an impact, the disparities that it drives could be detected across multiple cases. The lesson here is that, no matter how many procedural rules we invent, we will never have a death penalty reserved for the worst of the worst until we take substantive steps to deal with the role that implicit racial bias plays in capital trials.

15

Reparations Law

Redress Bias?

Eric K. Yamamoto and Michele Park Sonen

As a widow, I have nothing. I lost my house, my animals, all my possessions.... I have found no work, my mind is full of [negative] thoughts. I ask my leaders to open their eyes and see my suffering.[1]

Because of the inadequacies of the reparation process, the limitations of the reparations themselves, and the problems facing the rebuilding of South Africa, many women remain unhappy and less than fully "repaired."[2]

I. INTRODUCTION

Redress initiatives mark the global landscape. Governments faced with historic racial and gender injustice are attempting to build bridges from the past into the future by healing peoples' persisting wounds and repairing lingering damage to society. Nations worldwide – South Africa, Canada, Peru, Guatemala, Chile, El Salvador, Timor-Leste, Argentina, Cambodia, Rwanda, and Sierra Leone – embark on far-reaching reparatory initiatives in the wake of systemic violence or long-term mistreatment of racial communities or indigenous peoples.[3] Within the United States, African Americans, Native Americans, Native Hawaiians, Japanese, Latin Americans, Latino "Bracero" itinerant farm workers, Filipino U.S. World War II veterans, and indigenous Chamorus of the U.S. territory of Guam assert claims for reparatory justice.[4]

---

[1] Galuh Wandita et al., *Learning to Engender Reparations in Timor-Leste: Reaching out to Female Victims*, in WHAT HAPPENED TO THE WOMEN? GENDER AND REPARATIONS FOR HUMAN RIGHTS VIOLATIONS 284, 305 n.81 (Ruth Rubio-Marin ed., 2006).

[2] Beth Goldblatt, *Evaluating the Gender Content of Reparations: Lessons from South Africa*, in WHAT HAPPENED TO THE WOMEN?, *supra* note 1, at 48, 75.

[3] *See generally* THE HANDBOOK OF REPARATIONS (Pablo de Greif ed., 2006).

[4] *See* Eric K. Yamamoto & Ashley Kaiao Obrey, *Reframing Redress: A "Social Healing Through Justice" Approach to United States–Native Hawaiian and Japan-Ainu Reconciliation Initiatives*, 16 ASIAN AM. L.J. 5, 19 (2009).

These redress initiatives are salutary. They speak to the heart of a democracy's commitment to human rights and a fundamentally just society. Yet, as illuminated by the epigraph, something significant is often missing. Some, perhaps many, initiatives overlook key aspects of the larger injustice they ostensibly endeavor to redress – harms that are specific to women or women of color who are asking us to "open [our] eyes and see my suffering." This chapter explores – and suggests further study of – one likely reason for this at least partial absence in the redress realm: implicit biases with deep cultural roots. Many redress policymakers and frontline advocates seem to treat women's and women of color's unique harms as of lesser consequence and therefore as less worthy (or unworthy) of repair. To illustrate, despite decades of extensive sexual violence during hostilities, the United Nations Security Council only recently characterized the mass rape of women as a crime against humanity warranting redress.[5]

Experiences of injustice are multilayered. In some situations, mainly men are harmed – abused prisoners are mostly male. Sometimes men and women experience common injuries – white South Africans in power barred black men and women from voting or holding political office. Women also suffer gender-specific harms, particularly sexual violence or exclusion from male-dominated economic opportunities. And women of color at times sustain unique injuries that arise at the intersection of racism and sexism – for example, Imperial Japan racialized and sexualized Korean women as commodities at the bottom of Japanese society's hierarchy of human worthiness, enabling the World War II Japanese military to conscript 200,000 primarily Korean women into brutal sexual slavery.

Despite these multilayered harms, many who frame redress tend mainly to focus on harms to men or harms common to men and women. In light of this and related flaws in framing the damage warranting reparation, scholars and advocates are beginning to place gender harms and gender-sensitive redress on the reparatory justice table.[6] Intersectional[7] race–gender sensitive redress may soon follow.

Why have progressive redress movements themselves intent on repairing widespread damage tended to overlook the unique harms to women and women of color? Several possible answers emerge, including the lack of supportive organized political constituencies. Yet, another answer may prove significant: implicit biases even among those seeking to "do the right thing."

---

[5] Rome Statute of the International Criminal Court art. 7, *opened for signature* Jul. 17, 1998, 2187 U.N.T.S. 90 (entered into force July 1, 2002), http://untreaty.un.org/cod/icc/statute/english/rome_statute(e).pdf.

[6] *See generally* IDENTITIES IN TRANSITION: CHALLENGES FOR TRANSITIONAL JUSTICE IN DIVIDED SOCIETIES (Paige Arthur ed., 2010); Naomi Cahn et al., *Returning Home: Women in Post-Conflict Societies*, 39 U. BALT. L. REV. 339 (2010).

[7] "Intersectionality" refers to experiences arising out of multiple systems of oppression. *See infra* Section III.

Cognitive scientists, including psychologists and sociologists, have documented implicit gender bias in a variety of settings.[8] Yet implicit gender bias, moreover intersectional bias, remains largely uninvestigated in the redress realm. Empirical studies have yet to examine the extent to which implicit biases obscure or devalue particular types of harms and therefore render them less worthy of redress. Equally important, studies have yet to delineate approaches to "de-biasing" reparatory justice initiatives.

Making implicit bias explicit is likely a crucial next step on the path toward redress that comprehensively heals the wounds of injustice.

II. REDRESS FOR WOMEN

A. *An Absence of Gender-Sensitive Redress*

UN Women, the United Nations organization dedicated to gender equality and the empowerment of women, implores policymakers to acknowledge that "women bear the brunt of modern conflicts."[9] Many redress initiatives nonetheless tend to overlook women's harms. The otherwise commendable Tuskegee Syphilis Experiment reparations and the South African Truth and Reconciliation Commission, discussed later, are emblematic.

Rendering Women Invisible: The Tuskegee Syphilis Experiment

For forty years, beginning in 1932, the U.S. government used African American men as laboratory animals to study late-stage syphilis. The Public Health Service denied more than 400 black men the known cure for the fatal disease and watched them painfully deteriorate. The sexually transmitted disease predictably spread to the men's partners.

After numerous deaths and immense suffering, in the 1970s a former researcher publically exposed the Tuskegee Syphilis Experiment. The government's abuse of the men quickly became front-page news. Yet the women remained mostly "unseen and unheard, bearing in silence a legacy of anger and shame as well as damage to their health."[10]

Amid public outrage, a shamed U.S. Department of Health condemned the experiment and established a review panel. Consistent with the news reports, the

---

[8] E.g., James C. Kaufman et al., *In the Eye of the Beholder: Differences Across Ethnicity and Gender in Evaluating Creative Work*, 40 J. APPLIED SOC. PSYCHOL. 496 (2010), http://psychology.csusb.edu/facultystaff/docs/KaufmanNiuSextonCole.pdf.

[9] *Focus Areas*, U.N. WOMEN, http://www.unwomen.org/focus-areas/ (last visited February 9, 2011).

[10] Carol Kaesuk Yoon, *Families Emerge as Silent Victims of Tuskegee Syphilis Experiments*, in TUSKEGEE TRUTHS: RETHINKING THE TUSKEGEE SYPHILIS STUDY 457, 457 (Susan M. Reverby ed., 2000); *see also* SUSAN M. REVERBY, EXAMINING TUSKEGEE: THE INFAMOUS SYPHILIS STUDY AND ITS LEGACY 129 (2009).

panel focused primarily on the men – the formal subjects of the experiment. It largely ignored the suffering of women who had contracted the disease, given birth to children with syphilis, or watched their families' health disintegrate. The African American men filed a class action lawsuit against the government, which only named women as personal representatives of deceased men – not in their own capacity as those who also suffered.[11]

In 1997, then-President William Clinton publically apologized to the participants, their wives, children, and grandchildren, admitting that the experiment was "clearly racist" and promised government action on future bioethics research. The apology referred to the "lives lost, the pain suffered, the years of internal torment and anguish," but primarily addressed the men's "betrayal." It mentioned the wives mainly as adjuncts to their husbands' mistreatment – not for their own physical and emotional pain.[12]

Marginalizing Women's Suffering: South Africa

South Africa's often heralded Truth and Reconciliation Commission has a similarly mottled record. In 1995, emerging from decades of violence under apartheid, the newly elected South Africa legislature created a Truth and Reconciliation Commission (TRC) to help heal the country's deep racial wounds and rebuild the nation. The legislature mandated the TRC to investigate gross human rights violations, consider amnesty for those who confessed political crimes, and recommend reparations.

Backed by government violence, the ruling white elites had long oppressed black South Africans in nearly all aspects of societal life – denying black men and women the right to vote, subjecting them to politically motivated violence, removing them from land, and privileging whites in housing, schools, and jobs. Apartheid also damaged women through sexual violence, and it left many women with the overwhelming burden of raising children in dangerous living conditions with little money or family support.

Although commendable for its groundbreaking reconciliatory approach, the TRC appeared to marginalize the harms of black South African women. By limiting

---

[11] The government paid $10 million in reparations to the living men and the heirs of those deceased. It also provided lifetime health benefits to the living participants, widows, and children who tested positive for syphilis. Excluded from the settlement were the women's individual claims for pain and suffering. Fred Gray, *The Lawsuit*, in TUSKEGEE'S TRUTHS: RETHINKING THE TUSKEGEE SYPHILIS STUDY, *supra* note 10, at 473, 487.

[12] William J. Clinton, President of the United States, *Remarks by the President in Apology For Study Done in Tuskegee*, http://clinton4.nara.gov/New/Remarks/Fri/19970516-898.html (last visited July 16, 2011). In 2010, the U.S. government apologized for a similar syphilis experiment in Guatemala. Scott Hensley, *U.S. Apologizes for Syphilis Experiments in Guatemala*, NPR (Oct. 1, 2010), http://www.npr.org/blogs/health/2010/10/01/130266301/u-s-apologizes-for-medical-research-that-infected-guatemalans-with-syphilis.

reparations to victims of "gross" human rights abuses,[13] the TRC excluded much of the women's "ordinary" sexual violence and harsh socioeconomic suffering. The TRC succeeded only minimally in addressing South Africa's patriarchal norms that shamed many sexually violated women from coming forward.[14] According to South African scholar and activist Beth Goldblatt, "[b]ecause of the inadequacies of the reparation process, the limitations of the reparations themselves, and the problems facing the rebuilding of South Africa, many women remain unhappy and less than fully 'repaired.'"[15]

B. *The Emergence of Gender-Sensitive Redress*

Responding to redress initiatives' failure to adequately heal women's wounds, reparations advocates have increasingly called for gender-sensitive approaches. Timor-Leste embarked on a path-breaking initiative that specifically designated gender as one of its five foundational principles.

Guiding Gender-Sensitive Redress: Timor-Leste

The 2002 Timor-Leste redress initiative opened the way for gender-sensitive redress worldwide. After two decades of Indonesian occupation and military brutality – marked by mass starvation, murder, torture, rape, and sexual slavery – in 1999 Indonesia relinquished control and a newly independent Timor-Leste slowly emerged. After repeated criminal court prosecution failures, women from across the country aggressively mobilized to demand redress – including gender-specific reparations particularly for the ubiquitous sexual abuse.[16]

Timor-Leste's Commission for Reception, Truth, and Reconciliation (known by the Portuguese acronym "CAVR") integrated a gender perspective. Working with women's NGOs, it detailed specific gender harms and devoted a chapter of its final report to sexual violence. That report called for reparatory programs that specifically promoted women's recovery – for example, directing those administering reparations to allocate at least 50 percent of resources to women.

Integral to its commitment to "put[ting] victims at the heart of the commission's work," the CAVR had earlier determined that many women's injuries were severe and persisting and concluded that their healing could not await the CAVR's final

---

[13] The South African legislature defined gross human rights as politically motivated killing, abduction, or severe ill treatment. The Promotion of National Unity and Reconciliation Act 34 of 1995 (S. Afr.), http://www.justice.gov.za/legislation/acts/1995-034.pdf.

[14] The TRC attempted to make a safe space for women by creating special women's-only hearings. But few women came forward. Lyn Graybill, *The Contribution of the Truth and Reconciliation Commission Toward the Promotion of Women's Rights in South Africa*, 24 WOMEN'S STUD. INT'L F. 1, 5 (2001).

[15] Goldblatt, *supra* note 2, at 75.

[16] Women called for an international criminal tribunal, a truth commission, a special court for women, and rehabilitation programs. Wandita et al., *supra* note 1, at 284; for an in-depth discussion *see* SUSAN HARRIS RIMMER, GENDER AND TRANSITIONAL JUSTICE: THE WOMEN OF EAST TIMOR (2010).

recommendations. It therefore initiated an urgent reparations program to address the most pressing wounds of men and women, but with an emphasis on the unique wounds of women who endured sustained sexual violence.

Through a series of group therapy sessions and practical skill-building workshops, the program helped the women "view healing as a life-long journey" centered on security, health, education, and economic well-being. The CAVR prioritized women's access to its limited resources. Because later political upheaval stalled final reparations for all, the gender-sensitive urgent reparations proved especially significant.[17]

Developing Gender-Sensitive Redress Theory

Influenced by Timor-Leste's pioneering gender-sensitive work, some redress theorists began to highlight women's harms. In 2006, Colleen Duggan and Adila Abusharaf documented the general absence of gender-sensitive redress and attributed it to a "gender bias" that "undermine[s] women's ability to access reparation[s]."[18] They determined that women were twice harmed – once during the underlying atrocity and again during the redress process. Ruth Rubio-Marin, consultant for the Center for Transitional Justice, built on this initial theorizing and encouraged "conceptualizing forms of redress tailored to women."[19] In *What Happened to the Women?*, she compiled case studies of reparatory initiatives that fell short of healing women's wounds. In later work, Rubio-Marin uplifted the "increasing trend to recognize that reparations must be gender sensitive" to fully rebuild damaged polities.[20]

Gender-sensitive reparations are gaining traction globally. In October 2010 the United Nations called for financial assistance, health care, and education for victims of systemic sexual violence in the conflict-ridden Democratic Republic of Congo – a country labeled the "rape capital of the world." Amnesty International recently called for repairing the damage of gender violence committed during the recent Bosnian and Herzegovinian wars.[21]

---

[17] *See Timor-Leste: Missed Opportunity to Provide Justice*, Aliran (Mar. 3, 2011), http://aliran.com/4650. html.

[18] Colleen Duggan & Adila Abusharaf, *Reparations of Sexual Violence in Democratic Transitions: The Search for Gender Justice*, in The Handbook of Reparations, *supra* note 3, at 623, 626.

[19] Ruth Rubio-Marin, *The Gender of Reparations: Setting the Agenda*, Introduction to What Happened to the Women, *supra* note 1, at 20, 32.

[20] Ruth Rubio-Marin, *Gender and Collective Reparations in the Aftermath of Conflicts and Political Repression*, in The Politics of Reconciliation in Multicultural Societies 192, 195 (Will Kymlicka & Bashir Bashir eds., 2008).

[21] *DR Congo: UN Rights Panel Calls for Support for Sexual Violence Victims*, UN News Centre (Oct. 13, 2010), http://www.un.org/apps/news/story.asp?NewsID=36424&Cr=&Cr1=; *Authorities Must Ensure Access to Reparation for Survivors of War Rapes in Bosnia and Herzegovina*, Amnesty International (Nov. 25, 2010), http://www.amnesty.org/fr/node/19726; *see also* Medical Foundation for the Care of Victims of Torture, Justice Denied: The Experiences of 100 Torture Surviving Women of Seeking Justice and Rehabilitation (2009), *available at* http://justice-denied.torturecare.org.uk/.

Indeed, recognizing gender-specific harms is key to reframing redress into a broader project of repair that engenders comprehensive social healing; that is, ameliorative actions that both heal the wounds of individuals and repair the damage to society.[22] Why then, until recently, have even progressive redress movements tended to marginalize women by overlooking their significant and often unique wounds? Reparations scholar Professor Alfred Brophy suggested that "people generally do not take gender into account because of an implicit male bias reflected in the history of . . . legislation."[23] Starting with Professor Brophy's observation, we examine several theories that offer glimpses into why the harms to women have been overlooked. Although undeveloped in the context of redress, those implicit bias theories suggest a promising path for more targeted research.

C. Implicit Gender Bias in Redress?

As detailed in other chapters, implicit bias theories reveal that hidden biases influence how we receive and interpret information. These biases are real and pervasive. They infect our decisions. Despite our good intentions, they operate beyond conscious awareness.[24] Rather than revisit these theories in-depth, this section highlights rudimentary cognitive psychological and sociological insights that may partially explain the substantial absence of gender-sensitive redress.

1. Ingroup Favoritism

Generalizing broadly, all individuals are members of various social groups that are defined by common characteristics, particularly race and gender. Those with whom we share group membership become our ingroup; everyone else belongs to the outgroup.

Psychology studies show that people with decision-making power are inclined to bestow rewards to ingroup members and to withhold rewards from outgroup members even if both are equally deserving. A study by Henri Tajfel and colleagues determined that "the clearest effect on the distribution of rewards was due to the subjects' attempt to achieve a maximum difference between the ingroup and the

---

[22] *See generally* Eric K. Yamamoto & Brian Mackintosh, *Redress and Salience of Economic Justice*, 10 OXFORD F. PUB. POL'Y (2010).

[23] Interview with Alfred L. Brophy, Professor of Law, Univ. of Ala., in Honolulu, Haw. (Mar. 1, 2006).

[24] *See generally* Linda Hamilton Krieger, *The Content of Our Categories: A Cognitive Bias Approach to Discrimination and Equal Opportunity Employment*, 47 STAN. L. REV. 1161 (1995); Jerry Kang, *Trojan Horses of Race*, HARV. L. REV. 1489 (2005); Charles R. Lawrence III, *The Id, The Ego, and Equal Protection: Reckoning with Unconscious Racism*, 39 STAN. L. REV. 317 (1987); *contra* Gregory Mitchell & Philip E. Tetlock, *Antidiscrimination Law and the Perils of Misunderstanding*, 67 OHIO ST. L.J. 1032 (2006) (asserting that research on implicit bias does not satisfy validity tests and thus courts and legislatures should not rely on that research).

outgroup."[25] This reward selection bias is unconscious. The ingroup members "do not [mean to] punish or derogate the outgroup, but simply fail to share positive outcomes."[26]

Extended to the redress realm, ingroup favoritism insights shed preliminary light onto why a redress initiative might disfavor women. Reparations are rewards in the redress context, particularly where resources are limited. Where the policymakers and advocates designing and implementing the initiative are predominantly men, men constitute the ingroup. Unaware of their ingroup favoritism, the men fail to fairly allocate reparations resources (rewards). One basis for withholding or limiting reparations may be that the male ingroup is more likely to implicitly view women's harms as less redress worthy.

Implicit ingroup favoritism appears to at least partially illuminate why the South African Truth and Reconciliation Commission and the Tuskegee Syphilis Experiment reparations appeared to marginalize women's distinct harms. Men – the dominant social majority – largely controlled the redress initiatives.[27] From one perspective, focusing on men makes sense because they suffered the most visible abuse. Women, however, also sustained significant, if less publicized, physical and emotional injuries. Ingroup theorizing suggests that, in shaping redress, the men bestowing rewards tended to devalue women's unique harms.

2. Internalized Sexism

Members of a subordinated group often unconsciously perceive their own group as less valued than the dominant group. They often accept or internalize societal perceptions of comparative group worthiness and through that lens make judgments about group members.[28] Specifically, some women internalize sexism by "incorporat[ing] sexist practices"[29] and reproducing them in dealings with others, "bolstering

[25] Henri Tajfel et al., *Social Categorization and Intergroup Behaviour*, 1 Eur. J. Soc. Psychol. 149, 149 (1971); *see also* Henri Tajfel, *Experiments in Intergroup Discrimination*, 223 Sci. Am. 96 (1970) (finding that participants allocated more money to ingroup members than outgroup members).

[26] Susan T. Fiske, *What's in a Category? Responsibility, Intent, and the Avoidability of Bias against Outgroups*, in The Social Psychology of Good and Evil 127, 129 (Arthur G. Miller ed., 2004).

[27] Seven out of seventeen TRC commissioners were women. Two of the nine Tuskegee Experiment study panel members were women. Goldblatt, *supra* note 2, at 55; Reverby, *supra* note 10, at 91.

[28] John T. Jost & Mahzarin R. Banaji, *The Role of Stereotyping in System Justification and the Production of False Consciousness*, 33 Brit. J. Soc. Psychol. 1 (1994) (noting that members of oppressed groups hold negative stereotypes of themselves); *but see* Dawn M. Szymanski & Destin N. Stewart, *Racism and Sexism as Correlates of African American Women's Psychological Distress*, 63 Sex Roles 226, 234 (2010) (finding that internalized racism and sexism were not significantly correlated with African American women's psychological distress).

[29] Steve Bearman et al., *The Fabric of Internalized Sexism*, 1 J. Integrated Soc. Sci. 10, 11 (2009) (analyzing conversations between female friends to assess internalized sexism).

ideologies and practices that support male privilege, androcentric norms [and] patriarchal structures."[30]

Other research similarly suggests that group members of "lower cultural status"
often experience "automatic ingroup devaluation." Although they explicitly "reject
social ordering of preferred groups, [minority group members] may possess implicit
motivation to maintain social and cultural hierarchies, even when it means disfavoring their own group."[31]

With this in mind, internalized sexism provides a possible explanation for why,
despite women's participation (although limited) in South Africa's TRC and the
Tuskegee Experiment reparations, both initiatives largely overlooked women's
unique harms. Although counterintuitive, internalized sexism suggests that the
women participants tended to underplay harms to women – their own ingroup.

According to Beth Goldblatt, while contemplating redress for the damage of
racial apartheid, "gender never really informed the ... approaches" of the women
commissioners on South Africa's TRC.[32] Consistent with internalized sexism, "the
existence of women in powerful positions does not necessarily mean that they are
gender aware or that they will be active in asserting these issues." From another
perspective, without a mature public consciousness about women's circumstances
during apartheid, the women commissioners were politically unable to place specific
gender harms on the redress table. Under either scenario, "[t]he lack of adequate
representation of women and women's organizations in the peace negotiations and
the creation of the TRC meant that gender justice, as an issue, was not considered."

South Africa's TRC and the Tuskegee Experiment reparations stand in contrast to
the path-breaking gender-sensitive Timor-Leste redress initiative. There, prominent
women – including women's rights advocates, some of whom were victims – played
significant roles as commissioners, staff members, and commentators in advocating
for, designing, and implementing redress.

A Women's Congress of more than 400 Timorese women explicitly called for a
tribunal to address the women's harms. Respected East Timorese women advocates
sat on the steering committee that designed the CAVR and eventually served as commissioners (although only two of the seven were women). The CAVR also partnered
with women's organizations to select members for its women's research team, conduct workshops and interviews, and facilitate reparations proposals. Without these
multiple gender-targeting and de-biasing strategies, "the CAVR would [likely] have
failed to hear the distinct voices of both men and women."[33] Timor-Leste's pervasive gender sensitivity from the outset of the redress process may have enabled the

---

[30] Elizabeth A. Sharp et al., *Reflections from the Trenches: Our Development as Feminist Teachers*, 28
      J. Fam. Issues 529, 535 (2007).
[31] Justin D. Levinson, *Forgotten Racial Equality: Implicit Bias, Decisionmaking, and Misremembering*,
      57 Duke L.J. 345, 363 (2007) (discussing System Justification Theory).
[32] Goldblatt, *supra* note 2, at 77.
[33] Wandita et al., *supra* note 1, at 296.

participating women to overcome men's ingroup bias and mitigate women's internalized sexism.

Although insightful, ingroup favoritism and internalized sexism do not fully explain *why* well-meaning redress proponents – men and women – might implicitly devalue women's harms. Social cognition theory sheds important light on this question.

3. Social Cognition Theory and the Content of Stereotypes

Social cognition studies reveal that culturally informed stereotypes sometimes manifest in biased actions. To make sense of the world, people automatically categorize individuals based on salient traits (race and gender, for example) and attribute certain characteristics to those categories (such as dull or lazy). The characteristics are based on cultural perceptions relayed en masse through various sources, including parents, friends, teachers, stories, music, television, books, and the Internet. Once attributed to members of a category, those characteristics guide our interactions.

This cognitive process creates and perpetuates stereotypes. Negative stereotypes in turn impel discrimination by implicitly biasing the decision-making process – for instance, how an employer determines who is best qualified. Because stereotypes arise from culture, they permeate our psyche from an early age and often remain even as we commit to egalitarian principles.[34]

Peter Glick and Susan Fiske have suggested that women's subordinate position in gender hierarchies implicitly contributes to a common stereotype of women as incompetent.[35] Because of past male dominance and elevated social status, men are respected as competent and thus tend to be perceived as more valuable, whereas women, positioned at the other end of the social value spectrum, are perceived as the opposite: incompetent and less worthy.

From this perspective, the patriarchal structure of relationships implicitly generates stereotypes about the role of women during war or conflict – as mere housewives (while men engage in the more "valuable" work of warfare or political resistance) or as sexual objects that serve men's needs. These stereotypes likely influence the framing of women's harms when fashioning redress. Because women are devalued as socially inferior, their harms tend to be regarded as less worthy of recognition

---

[34] *See* Laurie A. Rudman et al., *Minority Members' Implicit Attitudes: Automatic Ingroup Bias as a Function of Group Status*, 20 Soc. Cognition 294, 294 (2002); Anthony G. Greenwald & Shelly D. Farnham, *Using the Implicit Association Test to Measure Self-Esteem and Self-Concept*, 79 J. Personality & Soc. Psychol. 1022 (2000).

[35] Peter Glick & Susan T. Fiske, *Sexism and Other "Isms": Interdependence, Status, and the Ambivalent Content of Stereotypes*, in Sexism and Stereotypes in Modern Society: The Gender Science of Janet Taylor Spence 193, 200 (William B. Swann Jr. et al. ed. 1999); Peter Glick & Susan T. Fiske, *The Ambivalent Sexism Inventory: Differentiating Hostile and Benevolent Sexism*, 70 J. Personality and Soc. Psychol. 491 (1996) (suggesting that the perception of women as incompetent arises out of "ambivalent" sexism – a combination of "hostile" and "benevolent" sexism).

and repair. Characterizing women as sexual objects, society may implicitly perceive them as fulfilling their social role, even if harsh, when subjected to unwanted sex, believing women suffer little or no harm as a result.

In South Africa and Tuskegee, stereotypes of women as housewives and sexual objects may have implicitly triggered the public's and policymakers' devaluation of women's harms. By comparison, in Timor-Leste, women's rights activists who raised public awareness about gender stereotypes likely mitigated a similar devaluation by continuously highlighting women's harms and playing key roles in the redress process.

These are only suppositions. Although extrapolated studies lend insight into the absence of gender-sensitive redress, none of the theories are derived from studies about reparatory initiatives. Empirical research is needed to provide a deeper understanding of why even progressive advocates and policymakers appear to have at least partially devalued gender harms in fashioning initiatives. Research is also needed to shape de-biasing approaches to future reparatory efforts.

III. REDRESS FOR WOMEN OF COLOR

The slavery . . . we women and you men shared . . . [brought] many sorrows . . . back breaking work . . . not having a say in where we laid our heads or who could have our bodies . . . the heartbreak of having to say goodbye to too many babies. . . . But brothers, I am also for a woman's right in this matter of reparations because there are some parts of slavery that we women bore alone. . . . [F]or what we been forced to do we ain't never been seen as no woman. . . . All I ever been is a woman slave which is worst than a woman and worst than a slave. . . . So, brothers, when you think about [racial] reparations, I ask you, Ain't I A Slave?[36]

Gender- and race-sensitive redress initiatives are salutary. Yet, some tend to overlook harms that arise at the intersection of racism and sexism. Despite good intentions these initiatives tend to miss the opportunity to identify and heal women of color's unique wounds of injustice, as highlighted in this section's epigraph. This missed opportunity calls for empirical inquiry into a potential implicit intersectional bias in redress.

A. *Intersectionality and Women of Color*

In the early 1990s, critical race scholars revealed how even progressive law and scholarship advocating for equality fell short for women of color. Both feminist theory and civil rights laws tended to overlook how women of color often face

---

[36] Pamela D. Bridgewater, *Recent Developments: Ain't I a Slave: Slavery, Reproductive Abuse, and Reparations*, 14 UCLA WOMEN'S L.J. 89, 89–90 (2005) (imagining Sojourner Truth's critique of the current slavery reparations discourse).

multiple systems of oppression that interact to create nuanced experiences of subordination.

According to Professor Angela Harris, some feminist scholars' initial theorizing tended to render women of color's experiences invisible through a "gender essentialism" – the "notion that a unitary, 'essential' women's experience can be isolated and described independently of race, class, sexual orientation, and other realities of experience."[37] Calling for retooling law and policy, Professor Mari Matsuda urged justice advocates to embrace as a jurisprudential method a "consciousness of the experience of life under patriarchy and racial hierarchy."[38]

Professor Kimberle Crenshaw demonstrated that antidiscrimination law is ill equipped to handle intersectional discrimination[39] because it grounds discrimination claims on *either* race or gender – not on the complex interaction of *both* race *and* gender. Crenshaw highlighted *DeGraffenreid v. General Motors*, which dismissed five African American women's suit against their employer for discriminating against them as black women. In 1974, General Motors laid off all but one of its 155 black women employees, but retained some white women and black men. The court refused to consider the black women's intersecting race–gender claims.[40] For Crenshaw, "the court apparently concluded that Congress either did not contemplate that Black women could be discriminated against as 'Black women' or did not intend to protect them when such discrimination occurred."

B. *Intersectional Race–Gender Redress: A Missing Piece*

Although scholars have employed intersectionality analysis to interrogate many areas of law and policy,[41] that analysis remains largely missing from the redress realm. Racial redress at times underplays women of color's harms. Gender-sensitive redress is a major advance, but it too has yet to fully address how women of color often suffer unique harms because of their perceived combined gender and racial inferiority. The Guatemalan redress experience is illustrative.

Guatemala's redress initiative, although in part gender sensitive, largely failed to consider Maya women's unique intersecting harms. From the 1960s until 1996, the

---

[37] Angela Harris, *Race and Essentialism in Feminist Legal Theory*, 42 STAN. L. REV. 581, 585 (1990).

[38] Mari J. Matsuda, *When the First Quail Calls: Multiple Consciousness as Jurisprudential Method*, 14 WOMEN'S RTS. L. REP. 297, 289–99 (1992).

[39] Kimberle Crenshaw, *Demarginalizing the Intersection of Race and Sex: A Black Feminist Critique of Antidiscrimination Doctrine, Feminist Theory and Antiracist Politics*, 1989 U. CHI. LEGAL F. 139, 142 (1989).

[40] DeGraffenreid v. Gen. Motors Assembly Div., 413 F.Supp. 142 (E.D. Mo. 1976) (dismissing black women's race and sex discrimination claims); *but see* Lam v. Univ. of Haw., 40 F.3d 1551 (9th Cir. 1994) (recognizing intersectionality theory under Title VII).

[41] Celina Romany, *Themes for a Conversation on Race and Gender in International Human Rights Law*, in GLOBAL CRITICAL RACE FEMINISM: AN INTERNATIONAL READER 53 (Adrien Katherine Wing ed., 2000); Darren Lenard Hutchinson, *Identity Crisis: "Intersectionality," "Multidimensionality," and the Development of an Adequate Theory of Subordination*, 6 MICH J. RACE & L. 285, 309 (2001).

Guatemalan civil war killed or "disappeared" 250,000 people and displaced another million. Eighty-three percent were indigenous Maya.[42]

According to observers, the Guatemalan army sought to eradicate Maya culture. Implementing a scorched earth policy, the soldiers razed more than 400 Maya villages – raping and killing women and children and burying them in mass graves. They conscripted some Maya girls into sexual slavery and publicly raped women as a method of social control. The Guatemalan army subjected Maya women to complete degradation with complete impunity because they were Maya women.

Maya women sat at the bottom of Guatemala's hierarchy of human worthiness – not only as women but also as women of an inferior race. Both the white elites and the non-indigenous Guatemalans (Landinos) characterized themselves as superior and racialized Mayas as stupid and dirty. The Guatemalan government systematically denied Maya, particularly Maya women, rights afforded most Guatemalans – including citizenship, the right to vote, and land ownership.

Situated at the intersection of race and gender, Maya women were characterized and treated as Guatemala's most inferior and stigmatized group. Cultural norms required that women (but not men) retain the markers of Maya identity by wearing distinctive, traditional dress and speaking only local Maya dialects. Both Maya men and all Landino regarded Maya women who asserted themselves as whores and unmarriageable. Many Maya women faced abject poverty and isolation not common to Landino women or Maya men.

When fashioning redress, policymakers in Guatemala addressed race and gender harms, yet did so separately. In its report, the Commission for Historical Clarification specifically recognized the severe racism directed at Maya people. It also acknowledged sexual violence, including the commonplace rape of Maya women and the resulting collective shame. The report, however, did not address or recommend tailored redress for the unique ways that the war brutalized Maya women physically, economically, and culturally because of their place at the bottom of the social hierarchy.[43]

The Guatemalan initiative raises the question anew: Why do redress initiatives often overlook certain kinds of harms, particularly suffered by those at the bottom of a social hierarchy determined by race and gender? Why do some progressive redress scholars, policymakers, and advocates – given the task of repairing the deep

---

[42] For an in-depth discussion *see* Linda Green, Fear as a Way of Life: Mayan Widows in Rural Guatemala (1999); Claudia Paz y Paz Bailey, *Guatemala: Gender and Reparations for Human Rights Violations, in* What Happened to the Women?, *supra* note 1, at 92; Carol A. Smith, *Race-Class-Gender Ideology in Guatemala: Modern and Anti-Modern Forms,* 37 Comp. Stud. Soc'y & Hist. 723 (1995).

[43] Report for the Commission for Historical Clarification, *Guatemala: Memory of Silence,* pt. I, at 31–33, 85 (racism), pt. II, at 91 (rape) (Feb. 1999) (summarized translation), *available at* http://shr. aaas.org/guatemala/ceh/report/english/toc.html. Indigenous organizations unsuccessfully called for psychosocial reparations incorporating Maya spirituality and the experiences of Maya elders, midwives, and other community leaders. Bailey, *supra* note 42, at 112.

wounds of perceived racial or gender inferiority – tend to overlook intersecting harms, particularly of women of color?

One answer may be political. Those most severely stigmatized are unlikely to possess enough political capital to advance their interests through realpolitik negotiations. Yet even when women of color are acknowledged, their unique harms often fail to resonate. Something more seems to be at play. Implicit bias theories offer another possible answer.

C. An Implicit Intersectional Bias?

Category dominance and social cognition theories suggest preliminary explanations for why even gender- and race-sensitive redress proponents sometimes elide the intersection of race and gender.

1. Category Dominance

Overlapping identity categories mark all individuals. With these multiple categories, "we form simplified impressions on the basis of one single dominant category" – known as category dominance.[44] Although people often recognize multiple dimensions in others, they typically perceive one dimension as dominant. Various factors determine which category becomes dominant, including the category's salience, the perceiver's objectives, and prevailing cultural stereotypes.

Extended to the redress context, category dominance insights suggest that sometimes redress policymakers and advocates unknowingly design and implement redress initiatives from the perspective of the dominant category. In doing so, they tend to ignore intersecting harms that arise from overlapping categories. For instance, the Guatemala redress initiative recognized harms to women generally, but did not meaningfully address the unique intersecting sexualized and cultural harms of Maya women. Although gender was rightly moved to the forefront, it may have become a dominant category, rendering intersecting harms less visible and therefore less redress worthy. Social cognition theory, again, illuminates how this possible implicit intersectional bias might operate.

2. Social Cognition Theory and Stereotypes of Women of Color

Double salient categories often create distinct stereotypes for women of color. In the United States black women are sometimes portrayed as "promiscuous and sexually

---

[44] C. Neil McCrae et al., *The Dissection of Selection in Perception: Inhibitory Processes in Social Stereotyping*, 69 J. Personality & Soc. Psychol. 397, 398 (1995); *see also* Charles Stagnor et al., *Categorization of Individuals on the Basis of Multiple Social Features*, 62 J. Personality & Soc. Psychol. 207, 216 (1992) (finding participants characterized individuals based on sex more than race); Lynn M. Urban & Norman Miller, *A Theoretical Analysis of Crossed-Categorization Effects: A Meta-Analysis*, 74 J. Personality & Soc. Psychol. 894, 894 (1998) (describing the "category dominance pattern").

aggressive 'Jezebels,'" while Asian women are "docile, servile and heterosexually submissive."[45] Stereotyped in these ways, black and Asian women are relegated to the lower rungs on the hierarchy of human worthiness – below women generally and below black and Asian men. In other countries, similar stereotypes based on perceived combined racial and gender inferiority also devalue women of color.[46]

The distinct stereotypes that arise at the intersection of race and gender "come to function much like singular, dominant superordinate categories"[47] and subject women of color to the harshest treatment during periods of distress. Insights from social cognition theory, discussed earlier, suggest that, when later fashioning redress, these bottom-rung devaluations tend to render women of color's unique harms less visible. They impede women of color's path toward repair.

Consider again the Tuskegee Syphilis Experiment. Stereotypes of perceived racial and gender inferiority possibly enabled the U.S. government to largely overlook black women's suffering throughout the experiment and during much of the litigation and reparations process. Missing from news reports, lawsuit filings, and the reparations discourse, the black women who suffered physically and emotionally never gained a foothold in public consciousness.

3. Subsuming Sexual Violence: African American Slavery Reparations

The extensive salutary discourse on racial reparations for the harms of slavery also generally looks beyond intersectional injuries. Black women often served as "slave breeders" and were forced to reproduce to replenish their white slave masters' labor supply – an experience historians liken to "animal husbandry."[48] African American slaves were harshly characterized as chattel. Many black women additionally were seen as lascivious and immoral. Deemed property by slave law and subordinate to men by patriarchal notions, these black women resided at the bottom of the hierarchy of human worthiness, as suggested by the section's epigraph.

To date only Pamela D. Bridgewater, in *Ain't I a Slave: Slavery, Reproductive Abuse, and Reparations*, has expressly framed enslaved black women's harms as worthy of redress in and of themselves, rather than as subsumed within the generalized harms of slavery.[49] African American redress proponents have advocated compensation for lost wages and property, loss of freedom, and physical brutality – all common to men and women (although men mostly experienced beatings and

---

[45] Darren Lenard Hutchinson, *Ignoring the Sexualization of Race: Heteronormativity, Critical Race Theory and Anti-Racist Politics*, 47 Buff. L. Rev. 1, 79–96 (1999).

[46] *See, e.g.*, Global Critical Race Feminism, *supra* note 41, at 129, 141, 160 (three chapters discussing Chinese women in New Zealand, African women in France, and Gypsy women in Serbia).

[47] McCrae et al., *supra* note 44, at 404.

[48] Bridgewater, *supra* note 36, at 120; *see also* Patricia J. Williams, The Alchemy of Race and Rights 18 (1991).

[49] Bridgewater, *supra* note 36.

whippings).[50] But, as Bridgewater has highlighted, proponents have yet to fashion significant reparatory claims based on "the parts of slavery we women bore alone" – sexual violence and reproductive oppression.

Social cognition theory provides one possible explanation. American culture still tends to perceive black women through "negative sexualized racial constructs" that materialized during slavery. Professor Darren Hutchinson has pointed to jurors' implicit bias against black women's credibility in rape trials and the significantly shorter sentences imposed on men convicted of raping black women than on men convicted of raping white women.[51]

A similar devaluation of African American women's harms may have influenced the Tuskegee Syphilis Experiment reparations. Like most jurors, redress proponents are well meaning; indeed, they are justice driven. Yet implicit bias operates beyond the realm of consciousness – and it is pervasive. Stereotypes inhabit the subconscious of even those dedicated to achieving equality. Civil rights leader Jesse Jackson once admitted that "there is nothing more painful to me . . . at this stage in my life than to walk down the street and hear footsteps and start thinking about robbery – then look around and see somebody white and feel relieved."[52]

4. Devaluing Korean Women as Sexual Commodities: The Korean Comfort Women

Implicit bias also likely afflicts the Korean comfort women's reparatory justice struggle – the only prominent redress movement based solely on women of color's claims. During World War II, the Japanese military conscripted 200,000 women into slave-like military brothels throughout Asia; 80 percent were Korean. Existence at the "comfort stations" was horrific. Japanese soldiers forced the women to sexually "service" up to forty men a day. Escape was impossible. Soldiers brutally beat and tortured the women – holding a match to a woman's private parts until she oozed blood.[53] Thousands died.[54]

---

[50] Two prominent reparations lawsuits that might have asserted specific gender-related claims but did not are Cato v. U.S, 70 F.3d 1103 (9th Cir. 2005) (seeking damages for loss of freedom, uncompensated labor, and suffering) and In re African American Descendants' Litig., 471 F.3d 754 (7th Cir. 2006) (seeking compensation from businesses that profited from the slave trade and creation of a fact-finding commission).

[51] Hutchinson, *supra* note 45, at 84–85.

[52] Siri Carpenter, *Buried Prejudice: The Bigot in Your Brain*, SCI. AM., April-May 2008, at 33, *available at* http://www.scientificamerican.com/article.cfm?id=buried-prejudice-the-bigot-in-your-brain.

[53] U.N. Econ. & Soc. Council, Commission on Human Rights, *Report of the Special Rapporteur on Violence Against Women, its Causes and Consequences (Coormaraswamy Report)* pt. IV, ¶ 54 (January 4, 1996), *available at* http://www.unhchr.ch/Huridocda/Huridoca.nsf/0/b6ad5f3990967f3e 802566d600575fcb?Opendocument.

[54] Women from China, the Philippines, Guam, Taiwan, Malaysia, Indonesia and the Netherlands also served as comfort women. For an in-depth discussion *see* Michele Park Sonen, *Healing Multidimensional Wounds of Injustice: Intersectionality and the Korean "Comfort Women"* (forthcoming) (on file

For fifty years the Japanese government denied any role at all in the sexual servitude system. Finally, in 1993, after revelatory litigation, the Japanese government confessed to forcibly conscripting the women. Some government officials (as individuals, not on behalf of the government) offered modest apologies. In 2007, however, then-Prime Minister of Japan, Shinzo Abe, retracted the apologies and maintained that the Japanese military did not forcibly conscript the women – contradicting the 1993 confession. Why the redress impasse?

For decades before the war, Imperial Japan had racialized and dehumanized Koreans as an inferior race – as dirty, of low moral character, lazy, aggressive, and ignorant – to justify subjecting Korea to brutal and humiliating colonial rule. During World War II, this racialized identity intersected with systemic Japanese (and Korean) patriarchy that devalued women to render Korean women expendable sexual commodities for the Japanese military.[55] Yet the initial redress framing appeared to miss the Korean women's unique harms that arose out of their intersecting identities. Narrowly construing their harms, women's groups tended to emphasize sexual violence against women, while Korean nationals generally focused on the damage to Koreans (and Korea).

International postwar justice efforts ignored the Korean women, indeed *all* the comfort women – except for one small group: white Dutch women. In 1948, the Dutch Batavia Military Tribunal convicted several Japanese officers and comfort station operators for war crimes against thirty-five white Dutch women forced into sexual slavery. The tribunal, however, rejected charges of war crimes against Asian women. The postwar American-shepherded Tokyo Tribunal similarly excluded the Korean women's sexual servitude claims.[56] Five decades later U.S. courts, too, rejected their claims.[57]

It is noteworthy that the Japanese government and populace have been willing to confer reparations for wartime injustice – particularly when pressured by litigation and international disapproval. Japan recently provided reparations to conscripted World War II foreign factory laborers. However, it has starkly refused to confer meaningful reparations to the Korean women despite publicized litigation and widespread international condemnation.[58]

---

with authors); Shellie K. Park, *Broken Silence: Redressing the Mass Rape and Sexual Enslavement of Asian Women by the Japanese Government in an Appropriate Forum*, 3 ASIAN-PAC. L. & POL'Y 2, 26 (2002).

[55] By contrast, Japanese comfort women were few in number, not forcibly conscripted (according to most accounts), and reserved for high-ranking military officials far from battle.

[56] Dianne Luping, *Investigation and Prosecution of Sexual and Gender-Based Crimes Before International Criminal Courts*, 17 AM. U. J. GENDER SOC. POL'Y & L. 431, 439 (2009).

[57] Hwang Geum Joo v. Japan, 332 F.3d 679 (D.C. Cir. 2003) (dismissing the comfort women's claim against the Japanese government in part because the United States waived its wartime claims against Japan in the Treaty of Paris), *vacated*, 524 U.S. 901 (2004), *remanded*, 413 F.3d 45, 53 (D.C. Cir. 2005).

[58] The Japanese government established a privately funded Asian Women's Fund in 1995 to provide limited monetary compensation to the survivors – but refused to contribute. Many perceived the fund

Commonly embraced race–gender stereotypes of Asian women may begin to explain the glaring redress void for the Korean women. According to L. H. M. Ling, western media have tended to portray Asian women as sexual objects "perpetuat[ing] a colonial 'group fantasy,' in which the Asian woman embodies 'service,' especially for the white man."[59] The Asian sex industry exacerbates these stereotypes. Ling suggested that some among western society even deploy the "sexualized racialized Asian woman to censure other, less subordinate women."

Many in Japan likely hold similar stereotypes because of Korean women's prominence in Japan's sex industry. Postwar prostitution became heavily commercialized. Japanese men in the 1970s increasingly traveled to Korea for sex. By the 1980s, Japanese entrepreneurs began trafficking women to serve in Japan's burgeoning prostitution markets, and Korean women were among the most heavily trafficked.[60] This longstanding sexual commodification of Korean women likely informs some Japanese policymakers' implicit perceptions of Korean women and their redress worthiness.

These assessments, again, are suppositions. They are broadly grounded in theory and supported generally by empirical studies, but they are suppositions nonetheless. Targeted inquiry is needed to reveal the extent to which implicit intersectional bias has hindered comprehensive redress for the Maya, Tuskegee, and Korean women – for women of color everywhere.

IV. CONCLUSION: SUGGESTIONS FOR FURTHER STUDY

Nations worldwide endeavor to repair damage in the wake of historic injustice, of persisting wounds to both individuals and societies. But redress initiatives too often prove inadequate to heal the wounds of women and women of color. Traditional racial redress initiatives tend to overlook uniquely gendered injuries. Redress policymakers, frontline advocates, and scholars mainly recognize injuries to men or common to both men and women – but not harms specific to women. Although emerging gender-sensitive redress commendably brings gender to the forefront, it (along with racial redress) appears to miss some and perhaps many of women of color's intersecting harms.

Drawing from rudimentary psychological and sociological insights into ingroup favoritism, internalized sexism, social cognition, and category dominance, this chapter offers a preliminary explanation. Like most people, those who frame redress initiatives likely hold implicit gender and intersectional biases with deep cultural roots.

---

as insincere. ERIC K. YAMAMOTO ET AL., RACE, RIGHTS AND REPARATION: LAW AND THE JAPANESE INTERNMENT 433 (2d ed., forthcoming 2012).

[59] L. H. M. Ling, *Sex Machine: Global Hypermasculinity and Images of the Asian Woman in Modernity*, 7 POSITIONS: EAST ASIA CRITIQUE 277, 288 (1999).

[60] Seiko Hanochi, *Japan and the Global Sex Industry, in* GENDER, GLOBALIZATION, AND DEMOCRATIZATION 137, 141 (Rita Mar Kelly et al. eds., 2001).

Some justice advocates, political leaders, and members of the public likely tend to implicitly characterize women's and women of color's harms as less significant and therefore less worthy of repair.

As illustrated by the South Africa Truth and Reconciliation Commission and the Tuskegee Syphilis Experiment reparations, ingroup favoritism and internalized sexism theories suggest that when men – the dominant social majority – largely control the redress process, the initiatives tend to downplay women's distinct wounds. Consistent with ingroup favoritism, the men inadvertently acknowledge male more than female suffering (or as worth more). Internalized sexism suggests that some women involved in the redress process implicitly adopt the men's approach, underplaying injuries to their own ingroup. Stereotypes about women's role during conflict also likely inform both male and female redress policymakers' apparent implicit devaluation of women's suffering. Characterizing women as housewives or sexual objects, societal norms devalue women and frame their injuries as less worthy, or even unworthy, of recognition and repair.

For women of color – Maya women in Guatemala – category dominance research sheds light on how even gender-sensitive redress initiatives might obscure intersecting harms. Category dominance suggests that gender-sensitive policymakers risk fashioning redress from the perspective of the dominant category by which they identify victims (gender), while ignoring distinct experiences at the intersection of overlapping categories (race *and* gender). Social cognition theory points to buried stereotypes that seemingly enable the public and decision-makers to at least partially devalue black, Maya, and Korean women's harms and to render them less redress worthy. Yet there may be other explanations.

Implicit bias research points generally toward gaps in framing redress. Empirical studies are now needed to assess how people implicitly perceive the redress worthiness of harms suffered by women and women of color and, if appropriate, to generate counteractive de-biasing procedures.

We propose three types of studies. Far from definitive, they suggest beginning research and illuminate prospects for future studies. Together they embrace the larger goal of comprehensive social healing through justice.[61]

The first type of study looks at specific initiatives and assesses the extent to which implicit bias influences the assessment of harms and the fashioning of redress. As a starting point, researchers might assess the extent to which African American, Korean comfort women, and Guatemalan redress proponents and policymakers have implicitly devalued black, Korean, and Maya women's unique harms.

The second investigates more generalized redress perceptions and actions. Studies might ascertain how people identify harms they consider redress worthy. Do men tend to recognize only harms specific to men or those common to both men and

---

[61] *See generally* Yamamoto & Obrey, *supra* note 4.

women? Do women tend to overlook harms that are specific to women? Do these tendencies change when an equal number of men and women are involved in redress decision-making or when public awareness is heightened?

Researchers might also study whether gender-sensitive or race-sensitive redress policymakers perceive gender or race as dominant and, if so, whether that perception obscures intersecting race–gender harms. Studies might also measure the correlation (if any) of bottom-rung redress devaluations of women of color's harms with commonly disseminated stereotypes.

The third type of study examines methods for de-biasing redress initiatives. Gender studies indicate that when women see other women in leadership positions it undermines their negative stereotypes and reduces their ingroup bias.[62] Women in leadership positions are "counter-stereopytic" – they depart from women's perceived role as passive and incompetent and trigger de-biasing.

Professors Jerry Kang and Mahzarin Banaji therefore encourage hiring more counter-stereotypic employees as de-biasing agents to mitigate implicit bias in employment.[63] Similarly, Professor Justin Levinson suggests increasing the number of counter-stereotypic law students, lawyers, and judges to produce environmental conditions that temper implicit bias in the legal profession.

We suggest studies that examine methods for de-biasing redress initiatives during their inception, operation, and implementation. The studies might address whether de-biasing involves deploying counter-stereotypic agents, producing altered environmental conditions, organizing multifaceted grassroots political campaigns (like Timor-Leste), elevating women and women of color to key roles in the redress process, or something else.

For Levinson, de-biasing actions alone only scratch the surface. Complete elimination of bias – an important step toward reparatory justice – entails "remov[ing] the socially disfavored status of a subordinated group"[64] through cultural change. Because implicit bias arises out of cultural perceptions, combating implicit bias calls for targeting the "socializing forces of culture" through public education and governmental policy. For instance, the United Nations, through its Convention on the Elimination of All Forms of Discrimination against Women, now takes seriously the predicate task of reversing negative gender stereotypes through cultural education.[65]

---

[62] Nilanjana Dasgupta & Shakti Asgari, *Seeing Is Believing: Exposure to Counterstereotypic Women Leaders and Its Effect on the Malleability of Automatic Gender Stereotyping*, 40 J. EXPERIMENTAL SOC. PSYCHOL. 642, 645 (2004).

[63] Jerry Kang & Mahzarin R. Banaji, *Fair Measures: A Behavioral Realist Revision of "Affirmative Action,"* 94 CAL. L. REV. 1063, 1110 (2006).

[64] Levinson, *supra* note 31, at 418.

[65] REBECCA J. COOK & SIMONE CUSACK, GENDER STEREOTYPING: TRANSNATIONAL LEGAL PERSPECTIVES (2011) (prioritizing eliminating stereotypes to eradicate gender discrimination).

Indeed, cultural education starts with acknowledging that culture informs implicit bias – it "is not simply a cognitive glitch, but a meaningful cultural statement that reflects the way people unknowingly carry society's weaknesses with them at all times."[66] As reparatory initiatives mark the global landscape, de-biasing redress through making implicit bias explicit is a critical step toward comprehensive social healing through justice.

---

[66] Levinson, *supra* note 31, at 420.

Index